TRANSFORMATION IN HIGHER EDUCATION

HIGHER EDUCATION DYNAMICS

VOLUME 10

SCOPE OF THE SERIES

.

Higher Education Dynamics is a bookseries intending to study adaptation processes and their outcomes in higher education at all relevant levels. In addition it wants to examine the way interactions between these levels affect adaptation processes. It aims at applying general social science concepts and theories as well as testing theories in the field of higher education research. It wants to do so in a manner that is of relevance to all those professionally involved in higher education, be it as ministers, policy-makers, politicians, institutional leaders or administrators, higher education researchers, members of the academic staff of universities and colleges, or students. It will include both mature and developing systems of higher education, covering public as well as private institutions.

The titles published in this series are listed at the end of this volume.

TRANSFORMATION IN HIGHER EDUCATION

Global Pressures and Local Realities

Edited by

NICO CLOETE

Center for Higher Education Transformation,
Cape Town, South Africa

PETER MAASSEN

University of Oslo, Norway

RICHARD FEHNEL

Consultant, Seattle, U.S.A.

TEBOHO MOJA

Department of Education, Pretoria, South Africa

TRISH GIBBON

Consultant, Durban, South Africa

and

HELENE PEROLD

Consultant, Johannesburg, South Africa

 Springer

A C.I.P. Catalogue record for this book is available from the Library of Congress.

ISBN-13 978-1-4020-6179-0 (PB)
ISBN-13 978-1-4020-4005-4 (HB)
ISBN-13 978-1-4020-4006-1 (e-book)

Published by Springer,
P.O. Box 17, 3300 AA Dordrecht, The Netherlands.

www.springer.com

Printed on acid-free paper

CONTENTS

PREFACE

At the beginning of the 1990s the world was watching with anxiety at South Africa. Would the country be able to get rid of the despicable apartheid regime without bloodshed? Could a civil war be avoided? And would it be possible to develop a democratic society without having to build up a whole new set of social institutions? The latter concern certainly referred to the educational sector that was steered at each level by a number of separate Ministries of Education, i.e. one for each identified race group.

Given the developments in other countries in the region as well as elsewhere in the world the prospects were not too hopeful. In addition, many especially white South Africans left the country the weeks before the first elections, and the stories of violence and contradictions between the various political groups in the country dominated for a while the international press' coverage of the pre-94-election situation. However, ten years after the first democratic elections in 1994 it is fair to say that South Africa has gone through a far-reaching transformation that is characterised by a remarkably low level of political violence. The general impression of the transformation suggests that the country has managed to change rather smoothly most of its social institutions, without dramatically affecting the continuity in the operations and performance of these institutions. This also refers to higher education. Most of the post-1994 conflicts on campus were related to governance issues and not to racial tensions. Further, change in higher education has taken place within the institutions, for example, in the composition of the student body, not in the institutional landscape per se. Only recently merger processes have been initiated by the national Ministry of Education; but after 1994 no major new public universities or technikons have been set up, nor has any of the pre-1994 institutions been closed down.

When trying to find out what the 'real story' is behind this positive façade, it is of importance to use the knowledge produced by scholars from South Africa. The huge interest in the transformation of the South African society also included scholarly interests. Consequently, many international publications on the social transformation of South Africa after 1994, including the changes in the higher education sector, have been produced by non-South African scholars. However, a valid examination of the developments in a sector such as higher education has to include national expertise and knowledge; not in an isolated way, but conducted within internationally recognisable and applicable conceptual frames. Only through such examinations knowledge can be produced on South African higher education that is of relevance within the South African as well as international context.

The HEDY book series aims at contributing to the strengthening of the field of higher education studies internationally, by publishing and distributing high quality, research-based manuscripts on higher education. It is for that reason that this book on the transformation of South African higher education since 1994 forms such a welcome contribution to the HEDY series. It is based on a multi-year study in which many prominent South African, and a few international scholars form the field of higher education studies were involved. It uses the expertise and experience of those involved in a way that is of relevance to a South African and an international audience.

The first edition of the book was published in South Africa in 2002 and was rapidly sold out. This new edition is meant for a South African as well as an international market. It contains a new final chapter, as well as a re-written introduction. Also a number of editorial changes have been introduced. The thematic chapters cover most of the intra-institutional aspects of South African higher education ranging from funding, leadership, and research, to students, staff and curriculum. In addition, a number of chapters are addressing the institutional developments, starting with a reflection on the impact of global change trends on higher education in South Africa. These are complemented by chapters in which the developments in the South African institutional landscape are discussed, including the rise of the private higher education sector. The final chapter discusses and interprets the developments in the governance and policy context with respect to South African higher education, applying a conceptual framework derived from more general social science literature.

The book represents a collective effort that is aimed at a large international audience. The transformation of South African higher education after 1994 deserves the interest of such an audience. As such this book represents a major contribution to the national and international understanding of what really happened in South African higher education after 1994.

As the editor of the HEDY series I want to express my gratitude to the Centre for Higher Education Transformation (CHET) in Cape Town that not only coordinated the original study, but also took care of the production of the manuscript underlying this book. In addition, I want to thank the people at Juta, the South African publishing company responsible for the first edition of this book. Without their help and cooperation this new edition would not have been possible.

Peter Maassen
Oslo

December, 2004

ACKNOWLEDGEMENTS

The past decade represents a remarkable period in South Africa generally, and in higher education in particular. This book is the product of a collective effort tracing and examining the twists and turns taken by processes of change in the South African higher education system in a context of profound societal and global transformation.

The endeavour was made possible through the generous support of the Ford Foundation, especially of Alison Bernstein and Jorge Ballan, and the encouragement of the board of directors of the Centre for Higher Education Transformation (CHET), of Colin Bundy (formerly of the University of the Witwatersrand), and Nasima Badsha (Department of Education). We hope that the results justify their support and encouragement. None of these supporters, however, are in any way responsible for the opinions expressed in this book. Nor should it be inferred that the book necessarily reflects their views on higher education policies in South Africa or elsewhere.

The development of this book would also not have been possible without the hard work of many individuals who contributed in different ways. Foremost among these was our key group of writers – Ahmed Bawa, Ian Bunting, Paula Ensor, Jane Kabaki, Tembile Kulati and Johann Mouton.

The following wrote commissioned background papers (see Appendix 1) that deepened our understanding of the local context, provided important information and helped shape the thinking of the primary writers: André du Toit, Trevor Sehoole, Adam Habib, Kallie Strydom, Bernadette Johnson, Rolf Stumpf, Andre Kraak, George Subotzky, Johan Muller, Sam Thobakgale, Nthabiseng Ogude, Edward Webster, Nic Olivier, Sarah Mosoetsa and Edward Pratt.

A number of international scholars produced case studies (see Appendix 1) of their own national systems, that provided important comparative reference points for understanding change in a global context. These were Alberto Amaral, Akira Arimoto, David Dill, K.K. George, Reji Raman, Lynn Meek, Terfot Augustine Ngwana, Lazar Vlasceanu, Jan Sadlak and Peter Scott.

A fourth group, all central players in the process of change in South Africa, willingly subjected themselves to lengthy interviews (see Appendix 2) and provided invaluable insight through critical reflection on their own personal experience. For this, thanks are due to: Marcus Balintulo, Fred Hayward, Sibusiso Bengu, Mandla ka-Mabuza, Peter Bezuidenhoudt, Chabani Manganyi, Theunis R. Botha, Roy Marcus, Margie Cairns, Njabulo Ndebele, Stef Coetzee, Carools Reinecke, Trevor Coombe, Flip Smit, Brian Figaji, Kallie Strydom, Brenda Gourley and Dénis van Rensburg.

Special conceptual assistance was provided by Johan Muller, Stephen Gelb and Rolf Stumpf, and by all those who served on reference groups and contributed to workshop discussions of draft chapters (see Appendix 3).

The development of the website, a vehicle for publishing insights, reflections, historical documents, case studies and the like, would not have been possible without the expertise of Bridget Nichols. The hundreds of documents, drafts, revisions and transcripts would have been a chaotic deluge without the diligent tracking and co-ordination done by Bharati Parekh, who completed the project when Shireen Badat, one of the original editors, left the project. Special thanks are due to Fathima Dada for interfacing with the publishers, Michelle Nadison for managing payments, and Linda Benwell who ensured that everybody arrived at their destinations.

The Editors
Nico Cloete, Peter Maassen, Richard Fehnel,
Teboho Moja, Helene Perold and Trish Gibbon

ACRONYMS

ANC	African National Congress
AUT	Advisory Council for Universities and Technikons
CEE	Central and Eastern European
CEPD	Centre for Education Policy Development
CHE	Council on Higher Education
CHET	Centre for Higher Education Transformation
Cosatu	Congress of South African Trade Unions
CSIR	Council for Scientific and Industrial Research
CTP	Committee of Technikon Principals
DACST	Department of Arts, Culture, Science and Technology
DET	Department of Education and Training
EPU	Education Policy Unit
FRD	Foundation for Research Development
FTE	Full-time equivalent
Gear	Growth, Employment and Redistribution
GNU	Government of National Unity
HBT(s)	Historically black technikon(s)
HBU(s)	Historically black university/universities
HSRC	Human Sciences Research Council
HWT(s)	Historically white technikon(s)
HWU(s)	Historically white university/universities
HWU (Afrik)	Historically white Afrikaans-medium university
HWU (Eng)	Historically white English-medium university
ICT	Information and communications technology
IDRC	International Development Research Centre
ISI	Institute for Scientific Information
IT	Information technology
Medunsa	Medical University of South Africa
NACI	National Advisory Council on Innovation
NCHE	National Commission on Higher Education
NECC	National Education Co-ordinating Committee
NECSA	Nuclear Energy Corporation of South Africa Ltd
Nedlac	National Economic, Development and Labour Council
Nehawu	National Union of Health and Allied workers
Nepad	New partnerships for Africa's Development
Nepi	National Education Policy Investigation
NGO	Non-governmental organisation

NIF	National Innovation Fund
NPHE	National Plan for Higher Education
NQF	National Qualifications Framework
NPWE	National Plan for Higher Education
NRF	National Research Foundation
NRTA	National Research and Technology Audit
NSFAS	National Student Financial Aid Scheme
NSI	National System of Innovation
NTSI	National Training Strategy Initiative
Nusas	National Union of South African Students
OECD	Organisation for Economic Co-operation and Development
RAU	Rand Afrikaans University
RDP	Reconstruction and Development Programme
RSA	Republic of South Africa. Prior to 1994 the term 'RSA' was used to refer to the parts of South Africa not included in the TBVC 'republics' (see below)
Sached	South African Committee for Higher Education
SACP	South African Communist Party
Sansco	South African National Student Congress
SAPSE	South African Post-Secondary Education
SAQA	South African Qualifications Authority
Sasco	South African Students Congress
SASM	South African Students Movement
Saso	South African Students Organisation
Sauvca	South African Universities Vice-Chancellors Association
SET	Science, Engineering and Technology
SPII	Support Programme for Industrial Innovation
TBVC	Transkei, Bophuthatswana, Venda and Ciskei. The acronym refers to these four 'republics' set up by the apartheid government.
Thrip	Technology and Human Resources for Industry Project
TSA	Technikon South Africa (the dedicated distance education technikon)
UCT	University of Cape Town
UDF	United Democratic Front
Udusa	Union of Democratic University Staff Associations
UDW	University of Durban Westville
UFH	University of Fort Hare
Unesco	United Nations Education, Science and Culture Organisation
Unin	University of the North
Unitra	University of Transkei
Unisa	University of South Africa (the dedicated distance education university)
Unizul	University of Zululand
UPE	University of Port Elizabeth
UWC	University of the Western Cape
Wits	University of the Witwatersrand

INTRODUCTION

After South Africa's first democratic election in 1994, higher education was confronted with social, political and economic demands of a kind not encountered during the apartheid era. It was initially assumed that the main driver of change would be government policy, informed by a participatory policy formulation process and implemented by a new, progressive bureaucracy. But change in higher education institutions followed a variety of routes that resulted in certain apartheid differences being accentuated and new differences emerging in the institutional landscape. This book examines the extent to which the changes were in line with policy intentions, particularly with regard to equity, democratisation, responsivity and efficiency, and how a new institutional landscape started emerging. Central to the new landscape were the different ways in which institutions responded, or adapted, to the new environment. An argument is presented for understanding reform not only as a centralised, government driven, policy-implementation-change paradigm, but also as a process affected by differences in institutional behaviour and the limits of policy driven change.

While most of the content of this book is based on the South African reform process, it also attempts to situate South Africa in an international perspective, thus contributing to the international debate on higher education transformation.

1. THE PRODUCTION PROCESS

This book is the product of a project in which six editors interacted with one another, key writers and the reference group participants over a period of 18 months to develop and explore the analytic framework that the project sought to explore, viz. how complex interactions between state, society (including the market) and the institutions shape change in higher education systems. The editors commissioned the six writers to produce empirical analyses of various aspects of the South African higher education experience post-1994, using the analytic triangle as a framework.

Fifteen researchers drafted commissioned background papers, eight international scholars wrote national-system case studies, and 18 influential vice-chancellors and senior bureaucrats shared their reflections on the policy-making and transformation process with the editors who interviewed them.

As was the case during the national policy implementation process, certain trade-offs had to be made as more material was produced than could be accommodated between the covers of a single book. The dilemma was resolved, not always to the satisfaction of all the knowledge producers, by creating a companion website (www.chet.org.za/highed1.asp) where the commissioned papers, the reflections and the case studies are published.

1

N. Cloete et al. (eds.), Transformation in Higher Education, 1-4.
© 2007 *Springer.*

In terms of objectives, there are two sets of objectives: one aimed at providing an analytic record of policy proposals developed after 1994 and at assessing outcomes; the second attempting to add to the knowledge base and develop a framework for understanding higher education reform.

Methodologically, there were also two different approaches: one privileged a quantitative, statistical record of change; while the other favoured understanding change as a more historical, interpretative narrative. The more attentive reader will be sensitive to the tension, never completely resolved, between trying to 'assert' overall coherence through a consistent editorial line versus producing an edited volume with relatively independent chapters.

Chapters 1, 11, 12 and 13 flow from a strong editorial framework, and display a powerful international influence. The chapters on the South African experience (mainly in Section 2) are, by their very focus, more local. They present a wealth of new information, both qualitative and quantitative, based on empirical findings, statistics and interpretation of trends that represent the first comprehensive attempt to document and understand the changes in higher education in South Africa's new democracy.

2. DEVELOPING THE ANALYTIC FRAMEWORK

Two threads to the narrative emerged. One grand theme was the familiar South African problematic equity and democracy. Here the aim was to assess whether progressive policy intentions had been realised, to examine how certain aspects of the racial/ethnic heritage continued to affect higher education, and to establish how this apartheid mould was breaking. It leads to the conclusion that the new emerging landscape cannot be attributed to racial/ethnic effects alone.

The second thread of the narrative involved rethinking a model of change that assumed a causal trajectory from progressive policy to implementation and realisation in transformation. This meant trying to understand why so many policy proposals did not follow the expected path. In taking this route, a whole 'new' literature about reform processes was encountered by the South Africans, enabling them to develop, as a framework, an *analytic triangle* called a 'network of co-ordination'. This analytic triangle locates change within a complex interaction between the state, society and institutions, within the context of globalisation. The overarching intention of this approach is not to attribute culpability to individual agents or agencies, but to develop a structural understanding of how systems change in the course of complex interactions between state, institutions and society.

3. DATA COLLECTION AND INTERPRETATION

In addition to trying to develop new ways of analysing and understanding higher education, a feature of the book is that it pulls together an enormous amount of data collated by different authors with access to different data sources. These include the official government South African Post-Secondary Education (SAPSE) system and certain special investigations undertaken by the Department of Education, the SAKnowledge base at the University of Stellenbosch, and the Centre for the Study of Higher Education (CSHE) at the University of the Western Cape. The project did not have resources for mining new data, but questions raised during the process of analysis often led to the re-interpretation and re-framing of existing data. However, despite having a wide range of expertise with access to very different types of information, a perennial problem faced by policy analysts and policy makers universally is inaccurate and dated information. This problem not only hampers scholarship, it also has a negative effect on policy implementation, as the National Plan for Higher Education (2001) laments.

Apart from data problems, there are also a number of areas in which higher education scholarship is highly underdeveloped. For instance, the editorial team could find no illuminating writings on campus environments where there is a remarkable lack of racial tension but also a lack of integration, as many racial and ethnic groups live apart from each other. Another area is HIV/AIDS. The country is awash with widely varying horror statistics, but no coherent, defensible picture has emerged for higher education. Quality assessment and quality promotion are other areas where, despite a number of overviews, it was impossible to obtain an incisive assessment of the current situation. In all these important areas the editors commissioned short pieces which are captured in extract boxes in the relevant chapters.

4. STRUCTURE OF THE BOOK

This book is divided into three sections. Section 1, The Transformation Context, identifies certain key global reform trends and develops an analytic framework to understand some of the reforms that occurred in the eight commissioned case studies. It identifies certain key strands for the rest of the book – the tensions between local and global reform demands, the fact that globalisation is not monolithic, that governments and institutions can and do respond very differently, and that reforms always have unintended consequences. Chapters 2 and 3 sketch the apartheid higher education landscape that confronted the government in 1994 and the policy framework that was developed, in the words of Nelson Mandela, to 'preserve what is valuable and to address what is defective and requires transformation' (NCHE, 1996:1).

Section 2, The South African Experience, consists of four parts. In Part 1, the chapters on funding and students are linked because the two components are interdependent. Funding instruments provide the means through which government can exercise considerable influence through subsidies dependent on student enrolments. The adaptive strategies of institutions, with their consequent differentiation effects, are integrally linked to the funding–student nexus. These chapters demonstrate that institutions developed very different strategies regarding students and funding, and these strategies have had marked effects on how institutions have fared in the new South Africa.

The central themes of Part 2, Staff and Leadership, are equity (changing the composition of staff) and democracy (coming to grips with the lofty aims of greater participation as part of the new co-operative governance policy). This part of the book shows that equity gains with regard to staff were much more difficult to achieve than with students, and that with increased pressures for more efficiency and workplace changes that started following global trends, different forms of managerialism emerged that put severe strains on the ideals of collegial co-governance.

Part 3 focuses on research and curriculum, and grapples with different and competing notions of responsivity. It describes government and institutional strategies to make curricula and research more responsive to national needs and markets, and explores how certain institutions responded to this with great enthusiasm, while others either resisted or could not respond.

Part 4, The New Terrain, starts with an analysis, published for the first time in a book, that examines the burgeoning private higher education sector that developed after South Africa opened up to the rest of the world. Chapter 11, The Emergent Landscape, describes a new typology of four types or categories of institutions that are developing in the post-apartheid era and shows a continuing policy oscillation between differentiation and isomorphism.

Section 3, Policy, Institutions, Society and Globalisation, consists of two concluding chapters. Chapter 12, South African Realities, shows that many positive and unanticipated changes occurred in the new policy environment. Crucially, it suggests that most of the changes occurred not as a result of centrally-driven government policies, but through complex interactions among policy, societal and market forces and, above all, through a wide range of unexpected institutional responses. It also demonstrates that global reform trends played a much more important role in driving institutional transformation than was anticipated in the initial policy emphasis on equity and democracy.

Chapter 13, Modes of Governance and the Limits of Policy unravels different understandings of policy and describes how the initial focus on symbolic and grand policy could not be implemented, even with adequate capacity. It shows that certain trade-off choices were made, with consequences that were often not commensurate with earlier policy intentions. In conclusion, it is argued that, instead of trying to apply 'grand policy', there should be a stronger recognition of the role of institutions in the transformation process within a framework of differentiated policies in which there is much greater interaction and mutual responsivity between government and institutions. More nuanced policy is needed to steer institutions with different missions and capacity towards mutually agreed-upon goals that serve regional and national needs.

SECTION 1

THE TRANSFORMATION CONTEXT

CHAPTER 1

PETER MAASSEN & NICO CLOETE

GLOBAL REFORM TRENDS
IN HIGHER EDUCATION

Towards the end of the 1980s the contours of a 'new world order' became more and more visible. Its rise was marked by the collapse of communist regimes and the increasing political hegemony of neo-liberal market ideologies. These established an environment for socio-economic and political change during the 1990s that would assert considerable reform pressures on all sectors of society, higher education included.

South Africa's negotiated settlement (Kraak, 2001) or 'implicit bargain' (Gelb, 1998, 2001) in 1994 must not only be seen as an isolated moment of a 'miracle transition' at the southern tip of Africa. It was also part of a political and economic transition process on a planetary scale that a large number of analysts have tried to capture as globalisation (Castells, 2001; Held et al., 1999). Even though globalisation is a far from uncontroversial concept, there is general agreement that most nation states are going through a transformation process that is strongly affected by global trends and pressures.[1] These trends and pressures form, for example, an important basis for national public sector reforms with respect to higher education.[2]

Globalisation impulses stem from financial markets that started operating on a global scale and from the explosion that occurred in international 'connectedness' – both virtual and real – mainly through the internet, mobile telephony and intensifying travel patterns. Simultaneously global and regional free trade agreements proliferated and expanded. The most important examples of these are the World Trade Organisation (WTO), the European Union (EU), the North American Free Trade Agreement (NAFTA), the Common Market of the Southern Cone (Mercosur in Latin America), the Southern Africa Development Community (SADC), and the Asia-Pacific Economic Co-operation Forum (APEC). These trends are also promoted through international agencies such as the United Nations and its organisations, the Organisation for Economic Co-operation and Development (OECD), the International Monetary Fund (IMF), and the World Bank.

All these 'planetary' changes created environments within which nation states had to consider a reorientation and repositioning of their still predominantly public higher education systems. This did not mean that governments were looking for alternatives to higher education. Instead the higher education institutions became a part of the national development policies in countries all over the world, with Finland, Ireland, and the East Asian Tigers as the prime examples. In South Africa a senior official in the new

7

democracy's first education department, Trevor Coombe (1991), summed up their role
as follows:

> Universities remain great national storehouses of trained, informed, inquiring and critical
> intellects, and the indispensable means of replenishing national talent. They have
> considerable 4 reserves of leadership and commitment on which to draw. Impoverished,
> frustrated, dilapidated and overcrowded as they may be, they have no substitutes.

It was within this rapidly changing global context, that six months after South Africa's
watershed first democratic election, Nelson Mandela issued a proclamation appointing a
National Commission on Higher Education (NCHE) to 'preserve what is valuable and to
address what is defective and requires transformation' (NCHE, 1996:1). This
Commission had two central tasks: to rid higher education of the aberrations of apartheid
and to modernise it by infusing it with international experiences and best practices.

With hindsight it is clear to see that few in South Africa realised at the time that these
international 'best' practices, which like little streams had slowly gathered momentum in
most other parts of the world, would overrun the national reform agenda for higher
education like a flood through a hole in the wall. The 'wall' had up till that time isolated
South Africa and other countries, such as those in communist Central and Eastern
Europe, from global changes and had been a bulwark against a pent-up demand for
internal change.

What were the global change trends that faced South Africa? A number of scholars
have shed light on these developments and the underlying starting points. The
Norwegian political scientist Johan Olsen (2000) has produced, for example, an
interesting contribution to the policy debate on the modernisation of higher education
in his country that is relevant to the South African debate.

Olsen claims that the traditional pact between society and higher education has
become problematic. The signs of this are, first, that public support for higher education
is decreasing, both politically and financially. In addition there are widespread
accusations of insufficient quality, responsiveness, effectiveness, and efficiency in higher
education. And finally there are many complaints about the lack of intellectual capacity
in higher education at a time when there seems to be a growing need for it. As a
consequence of the deterioration of the relationship between higher education and
society, the re-interpretation of higher education as a service-company with society as its
marketplace, is becoming the dominant one taking over from the traditional emphasis on
academic freedom and collegial self-steering of academics.

According to Olsen (2000) academic self-steering was part of a large democratic-
constitutional social order, with partly autonomous institutions. Constitutional
regulations defined these institutions and their roles, competence, social and political
relationships, and responsibilities. From this perspective institutional autonomy is a
condition for legitimate governmental steering of higher education and peaceful
co-existence with other institutions.

National debates about institutions are not new. They have regularly taken place and
have led to many challenges concerning institutional autonomy. What is new, however,
are the effects of international reform ideologies that fundamentally challenge the notion
of institutional self-steering in higher education. According to the underlying ideas and

assumptions of reform thinking, universities and colleges should be externally controlled, their activities should be formally evaluated, they should be held accountable for their performance, they should be steered by market forces and not by governmental or state mechanisms, they should be run by professional leaders and managers instead of by academic *primus-inter-pares* ('first among equals'), and they should be included as service industries in regional and global trade agreements.

Among the consequences of the acceptance and application of these reform ideas and assumptions at the national level are the decreasing importance of specific national and institutional characteristics, cultures, histories and interests. In the policy goals of efficiency, effectiveness, responsiveness and competition embodied in many higher education reform programmes, national authorities transform their public higher education systems from national organisations with multiple social roles into global players mainly operating on the basis of economic considerations. The role of the state is to act as a 'watchdog' and to make sure that external audits and evaluations of higher education institutions take place regularly.[3]

Another author contributing to the discussion on higher education reform and its consequences is Stanford's Patricia Gumport (2000). Her starting point is that there is a growing tension between two dominant perspectives on higher education: the first interprets higher education as a social institution while the second sees higher education mainly as a part of the national economy, in other words as an industry. The 'social institution' position states that higher education must attain goals related to its core activities, retain institutional legacies and carry out important functions for the wider society such as the cultivation of citizenship, the reservation of cultural heritage, and the formation of skills and the characters of students. The 'higher education as an industry' approach emphasises that higher education institutions sell goods and services, that they train an important part of the workforce and that they foster economic development. It argues that the exposure of universities and colleges to market forces and competition will result in improved management, programmatic adaptation, maximum flexibility, improved efficiency and customer satisfaction.[4]

These two perspectives differ fundamentally concerning the most important societal functions of higher education, the main problems confronting higher education, and the best solutions and approaches for dealing with these problems. According to Gumport (2000) the perspective of public higher education as an industry has become the dominant one, at least in the USA. The mechanisms through which this development has taken place are, first, the rise of academic institutional managers and professional administrators; second, the idea of the sovereignty of the consumer, especially students; and third, the re-stratification of academic subjects and academic staff on the basis of their use-value. These three mechanisms have led to an institutional eagerness to embrace effectiveness and efficiency as policy priorities. The vicious circle in which higher education seems to be trapped as a result of all of this, is that the leaders of higher education institutions feel forced to use more and more market discourse and managerial approaches to restructure their institutions. Yet the more they move away from the traditional basic characteristics, legacy and functions of higher education, the more they seem to face formidable legitimacy challenges as public institutions.

One of the most influential publications in recent debates on higher education reform is Burton Clark's book on entrepreneurial universities based on five case studies in four European countries: Finland, the Netherlands, Sweden, and the United Kingdom (Clark, 1998). He argues that all universities should adapt and become more entrepreneurial because societal demands with respect to higher education are growing while governmental support (financially, legally and politically) is decreasing. As a consequence of local and global changes in the context of higher education and changes in expectations with respect to higher education, the imbalance between societal demand and institutional capacity has become a global phenomenon. The success or failure of institutional strategies for dealing with this imbalance will determine whether an institution will belong to tomorrow's winners or losers.

Whether one agrees with the arguments and conclusions of the authors cited above is not the issue here. The issue is that these (and other) analysts have identified important changes in the USA and Europe in the relationship between the state, the higher education institutions and society. In addition they have pointed to the important influence of globalisation on these changing relationships. The changes in European and US higher education have paved the way for the introduction of the underlying reform ideas and assumptions in other parts of the world too. They are crucial variables in any attempt to analyse and understand the nature and effects of higher education reforms. In this book the triangular relationships between state, institutions and society and the effects of globalisation on these relationships are used as the framework for analysis. In the next sections we will discuss the way in which the three actors – state, society and institutions respectively – as well as the concept of globalisation are interpreted within this analytic triangle which is used throughout this book.

1. THE STATE

What is the role of the state in the new patterns of steering and policy arrangements emerging with respect to higher education? Since the early 19th century (Neave, 1988) the continental European nation states have taken upon themselves the regulatory and funding responsibilities with respect to higher education. This state control model was also introduced in the colonies and remained the dominant model after these countries became independent. The model implied that the state took care of the public interest in higher education. It designed and regularly adapted the regulatory frameworks for higher education, and it was the main, if not sole, funder of higher education. Social expectations with respect to higher education were not addressed in direct links between social actors and higher education, but were taken up by the state. Consequently in most countries, including South Africa, until recently the society/higher education institutions dimension was the weakest side of the triangle presented alongside.

Major exceptions with respect to governmental steering of higher education were the USA and the United Kingdom. Their steering approaches have been characterised as state-supervision (Maassen & Van Vught, 1994) or arm's length (Scott, 1996) models.

In the USA individual states are traditionally responsible for higher education. In many states a governance model has been used that promotes a market-type of interaction between higher education and society. Even though the US state governments also have funding and regulatory responsibility with respect to public higher education, in most states the financial and regulatory instruments are not very restrictive and provide a lot of autonomy to the institutions. However, this does not mean that the USA overall has a market-driven higher education system. There is considerable diversity in state governance models and in a number of US states higher education is steered in a 'state-controlled' way, with line-item budgeting comparable to the traditional European government's way of steering higher education.

In the United Kingdom the academic oligarchy has for many years played an important role in the funding and regulatory decisions concerning higher education. An important body in this respect was the University Grants Committee (UGC). After the abolition of the UGC in the 1980s the British government's 'arm's length' approach to the steering of higher education changed and became more restrictive. The successive Conservative British governments which succeeded the first Thatcher government of the early 1980s developed policy approaches that promoted the abandonment of tight government control; with respect to higher education, however, they actually tightened budgetary controls and introduced more elaborate regulatory instruments (Scott, 1996:123). Given that South African higher education has its roots in both Continental European and British traditions, an interesting mixture of traditional state control and arm's length government steering approaches can be observed in the system.

The differences in governmental steering models did not imply that the general assumptions concerning the role of the government remained constant throughout the last few decades. For example, from the late 1950s through the 1960s and early 1970s there was a worldwide belief in the political 'makeability' of society. It was assumed that society could be 'moulded' into specific forms and patterns by designing appropriate policies and implementing them with the use of the right instruments. Examples of such instruments were the Planning-Programming-Budgeting-System (PPBS; see, for example, Lyden & Miller, 1968; and Schick, 1973) and other forms of planning.

Studies of policy implementation showed convincingly that policy outcomes were hardly ever the same as the policy intentions (see, for example, Pressman & Wildavsky, 1973; and Cerych & Sabatier, 1986). This brought back a sense of reality into policy-making. Interestingly enough, while many actors directly involved in policy-making have become more modest and realistic in their policy-making efforts, many politicians in different political regimes still seem to cling to the 'societal makeability' assumption. Consequently there is a wide, and in many respects widening, gap between politics and political programmes on the one side, and the dynamics of public sectors such as higher education on the other. Policies are expected to fill this gap, sometimes being directly derived from a political programme, sometimes reflecting societal reality, sometimes a combination of both. It is obvious that the wider the gap, the more unlikely it will be that policy outcomes will be in line with the original policy objectives.

The state corner of the analytic triangle reflects this tension between high political expectations and differentiated societal and institutional realities. Part of the aim of this book is to show how this tension has worked itself out in South Africa and what its effects were on the practice of South African higher education.

Another piece of the puzzle that is needed to understand the relationship between policy intentions and policy outcomes with respect to South African higher education, concerns the relationship between educational and economic reform agendas. In South Africa there is a tension between the higher education reform agenda which emphasises national topics such as redress, democratisation and equity, and the global reform agenda which promotes issues such as efficiency, effectiveness, competition and responsiveness. The former is developed and driven by the Ministry of Education; the latter falls under the responsibility of other ministries, such as Finance, and Trade and Industry. As is the case in most other countries, in South Africa the national higher education agenda has been made subservient to the global reform agenda.

This tension can be illustrated, for example, by the way in which various ministries deal with the issues of quality and diversity (Meek et al., 1996). Ministries of Education have interpreted, and made operational, quality and diversity issues in policy-making processes from an academic point of view. However, the concepts of quality and diversity are also regularly used in the reform programmes of other ministries. In these programmes quality and diversity are not launched from an academic point of view, but mainly from an economic and accountability perspective. In practice this means, for example, that a Ministry of Education may attempt to introduce a quality assessment approach based on peer review, implying that it is improvement-oriented and mainly driven by academic values. Ministries of Economic Affairs, Labour, or Trade and Industry, on the other hand, tend to be more interested, for example, in the quality of higher education from the perspective of labour market demands, or from the perspective of using quality to increase institutional efficiency through competition between public and private providers of higher education.

Finally it is relevant to reflect upon the role of the state in the promotion of the public interest. As indicated above, until recently, the state in many countries, including South Africa, took care of the translation of social expectations with respect to higher education. It decided which social expectations and needs to include in the higher education policy agenda and how to include them. As a result of disappointments with the outcomes of state actions, however, and the growing complexity of higher education, it was generally recognised by all actors involved, including Ministries of Education, that this near monopolistic position could not be maintained. The new governmental steering approaches with respect to higher education introduced in the late 1980s and early 1990s in Europe (Gornitzka & Maassen, 2000) and other parts of the world (Neave & Van Vught, 1994) reflected this recognition. In the white papers and other policy documents in which the rationale behind the new steering approaches were explained, governments emphasised that they aimed at a more direct relationship between higher education and society. They indicated that the state should act as one of the stakeholders with an interest in higher education, instead of as the only stakeholder – again an indication of the growing prominence of the society/higher education dimension in the triangular relation between state, society and higher education.

2. SOCIETY

Over the last ten to fifteen years the social demands with respect to higher education have clearly intensified. In respect of the second corner of the analytic triangle it has been argued, for example, that higher education has to take into account, more and more, the interests of a variety of external and internal social stakeholders (Clark, 1998; Maassen, 2000). As having a higher education degree increasingly became a necessary condition for entering, not only the professions, but also the rapidly expanding service and technology-orientated jobs, the demand for access increased dramatically. This was accompanied by the need for 'retooling', or lifelong education in order to keep abreast of rapidly changing job requirements.

Increasing participation in higher education has become a global orthodoxy, promoted by national governments as well as agencies such as Unesco, the OECD and the World Bank. Several countries, for example the USA, Finland and South Korea, already have participation rates of more than 60%, implying that two out of three students leaving secondary education will enter higher education, either directly or after a certain time lag. In many developing countries with high population growth, such as Brazil and Indonesia, the participation rates may not be increasing, but the actual student numbers in higher education are growing as a result of the demographic structure of these countries.

But it is not only a matter of increased access and participation; it is also a question of access for whom. Higher education came to be regarded as a key (re-) distributor of opportunity and an interesting paradox can be observed in relation to this process. While social needs and expectations were leading to higher numbers of students enrolling in higher education worldwide, the public investments in higher education decreased, at least in real terms. This implies that compared to 1980, for example, universities and colleges now receive far less public funding per student, relatively speaking. As a consequence, higher education has been forced to move out of its ivory tower. Referring to the authors above (Clark & Maassen) one might wonder whether higher education, in coming out of its 'ivory closet' has gone to the other extreme in its relationship with society.

This would imply that instead of isolating itself from social needs, higher education is now trying to respond to all social and economic demands unloaded on it despite the growing imbalance between demands and the institutional capacity for responding to them (Clark, 1998). For example, higher education institutions are expected to address societal contestations around race, ethnicity, gender and diversity – the intensified human rights struggles of the latter part of the century – in their institutional policies. In some circles higher education is even expected to find the solutions to these social problems.

Discussing this development from a conceptual angle, we can again refer here to Olsen (1988) who set up four models to represent the relationship between higher education and society: the sovereign, institutional, corporate-pluralist, and classical liberal (or supermarket) state models.[5] The sovereign and classical liberal models are comparable to the state control and arm's length models referred to above. However, in order to understand the growing importance of society in the analytic triangle, it is useful to discuss one of Olsen's models, the corporate-pluralist model, in more detail since it can also be said to apply to the post-1994 situation in South Africa to some extent.

According to this model the state is no longer a unitary actor with a monopoly over power and control. Rather there are several competing and legitimate centres of authority and control with respect to higher education. The role of higher education reflects the constellation of interests voiced by different organised interest groups in the sector, such as student unions, staff unions, professional associations, industry and business, and regional authorities. A Ministry of Education is just one of the many stakeholders in higher education. These stakeholders all have a claim on the role and direction of development of higher education. The main arena of policy-making consists of a corporate network of public boards, councils and commissions. Parliamentary power is reduced – policy-making goes on in conference rooms and closed halls outside of parliament. Players in policy-making act strategically to further the special interests of their own organisation or interest group.

Decision-making is segmented and dominated by clusters of interest groups (government being one of them) with recognised rights to participate. The dominant mode of decision-making is one of negotiation and consultation, with an extensive use of 'sounding out'. Societal participation takes place through organised interest groups (according to Olsen, the 'corporate channel'). There is little co-ordination across policy sub-systems and the domain of government interference is dependent upon power relationships. The structured negotiations favoured by this model interfere with market forces and hierarchical decisions. The autonomy of universities and colleges is negotiated and the result of a distribution of interests and power. Changes in higher education are influenced by changes in power, interests and alliances.

In applying this model to South Africa one has to keep in mind that it was developed within a Northern European welfare state context. Therefore it will not reflect all the details and nuances of the current South African state model, nor of the institutional governance models promoted by the 1997 White Paper (Department of Education, 1997; see also Cloete & Bunting, 2000). Nonetheless, the network relations incorporated in this model seem to do more justice to the practice of the relationships between society and higher education in South Africa than the way in which the other models represent this relationship. Elements of the other models, i.e. a strong state, academic elitism, and market interactions, can be observed in the steering of South African higher education, but not as prominently as the corporate-pluralistic network connections. This will also become clear when we discuss the third corner of the triangle in which the institutions are located.

3. HIGHER EDUCATION INSTITUTIONS

Higher education institutions interact with many different actors in external and internal policy processes. In order to understand the nature of these interactions it is important, first of all, to make a distinction between academic and administrative governance structures. Higher education institutions, especially universities, have traditionally been run by academics, i.e. the professoriate. Institutional administration was seen as an 'unavoidable evil' necessary to create the optimal circumstances for the professors to operate autonomously. As such, higher education institutions were professional organisations with one dominant profession, the academic profession.

A core characteristic of professional occupations is that they want not only control over the conditions of their work, but also over the definition of work itself. Scott (1995) has distinguished three kinds of work-related control which professionals are seeking. The first is regulative control: professionals want to determine what actions are to be prohibited and permitted, and what sanctions are to be used. The second is normative control, implying that professionals want to determine who has the right to exercise authority over what decisions and actors in what situations. The third is cognitive control: the drive to determine what types of problems fall under the professionals' responsibility and how these problems are to be categorised and processed.

In addition to these general characteristics of professional occupations, some specific characteristics of universities and colleges are worth mentioning here. First and foremost, it is knowledge that provides the organisational building blocks of these institutions. Secondly, this knowledge-based structure leads to a high level of organisational fragmentation. Thirdly, these institutions have loosely articulated decision-making structures. Finally, change generally takes place in an incremental, grassroots way.

These characteristics are unique. They make universities and colleges different from other types of organisations. What we are referring to here are differences such as higher education institutions lacking a single, clearly definable production function, and demonstrating low levels of internal integration. Another important difference is that the commitment of the academic staff to their discipline and profession is higher than the commitment to their institution. With respect to the nature of institutional management important differences can be mentioned such as the low ability of institutional managers to hire and fire staff, or the fact that institutional managers are more accountable to stakeholders than to their counterparts in business.

All in all it can be argued that the traditional characteristics of universities and colleges make it difficult to initiate and steer organisational changes in them from the outside. This doesn't mean that these institutions are not influenced by external factors, but that the exact effects of these factors are impossible to control and very difficult to predict.

Over the last ten to fifteen years in Europe and Australia, and at least a decade longer in North America, this traditional set of characteristics and the academic control of administration and governance in higher education institutions have been challenged by a number of developments. With the massification and subsequent growth of higher education, this sector became more and more complex. Furthermore, the need to find alternative, non-public, sources of income to make up for reduced government funding, has added to the complexity of the institution. In many countries this complexity has led to the professionalisation of the administration, although this does not necessarily mean a growth of the administrative staff; there are indications that traditional administrative support functions (secretaries and clerks) are being replaced by professional administrators (Gornitzka et al., 1998; Gornitzka & Larsen, 2001).

Increasingly, a more professionalised management is seen as a necessary condition for the institutions' attempts to deal more adequately with both external and internal pressures and demands. External demands range from new policy initiatives and new government legislation to opportunities for the formation of industry or community partnerships. Internally, greater planning and more efficient allocation of resources are required, as well as providing incentives to academics to respond to opportunities or markets. The rising administrative profession is, implicitly and explicitly, challenging the traditional dominance of the academics in institutional affairs. This development might actually lead to the university becoming a bi-professional instead of mono-professional organisation.

The strengthening and expansion of institutional management aims at achieving a number of functions. Amongst other things, it aims to enable institutions to become more strategic and responsive in order to compete nationally and internationally, to introduce efficiency measures, and to help drive the implementation of national policy agendas. Globally it is recognised that as part of the above-mentioned complexity of higher education institutions, these institutions will have to be managed more and more as hybrid organisations, i.e. organisations containing public and private elements. In terms of the analytic triangle this can be illustrated by stating that the society/institution dimension will become the private dimension in universities and colleges, while the state/institution dimension will remain in the public domain.

A last institutional aspect to be mentioned here is that higher education institutions are increasingly attempting to present themselves as cultural sites, hoping to profit in a number of ways (including financially) from their cultural activities and their cultural image. One positive result could be that well-educated knowledge workers will expect to live within easy access distance from institutions where both new technological and cultural knowledge is produced and is available. The educated network society thus expects more interaction with higher education institutions (Carnoy, 2001:32).

This book reflects on how the three dimensions of the analytic triangle – state to society, society to institutions, and institutions to state – have affected the way in which the ambitious policy intentions of the early 1990s have been handled in the complex reality of the new institutional landscape of South African higher education. Obviously these three national dimensions have been affected in many ways by global forces from outside the country.

4. ASPECTS OF GLOBALISATION

Globalisation encompasses global financial markets, growing global interconnectedness, global and regional trade agreements, media, information systems, labour markets, telecommunication, etc. By some it is seen as a process leading to reduced poverty and a better distribution of wealth among countries and individuals, while others regard it as 'the source of all evil'. According to Held and his colleagues (1999:1) the lack of a precise definition creates the danger of globalisation becoming 'the cliché of our times: the big idea which encompasses everything [...] but which delivers little substantial insight into the contemporary human condition'.

Despite the danger of becoming a cliché, globalisation does capture the notion of rapid worldwide social and economic transformation. This notion includes many aspects of our societies, too many to capture in this book.[6] However, in order to underline the relevance of global processes, ideas, and forces for higher education reform, we will discuss some of the aspects of globalisation of relevance for higher education in more detail. These include, amongst other things, trade liberalisation and its effects on higher education. In addition we will point to some of the globalisation tensions that have arisen in higher education systems around the globe.

A tension that globalisation poses, particularly for developing countries, is that on the one hand, the nation state is expected to create the conditions for economic and social development within the framework of trade liberalisation, predominantly through producing more and better educated citizens and increasing knowledge production, which is a prized commodity in the global economy. On the other hand, globalisation introduces pressures to reduce the role and contribution of central government in education (Carnoy, 1999). The double-edged challenge is to produce more graduates with high-level knowledge skills, but with less direct government support per graduate.

Another effect is that globalisation increases the pay-off to high-level skills relative to lower level skills, thus reducing the complementarity between equity and competitiveness-driven reforms (Carnoy, 1999). The fact that the national government's capacity to steer from the top may be restricted, combined with increasing inequality, affects the government's ability to address redress. Contradictorily, while globalisation can weaken the state, it also expects, and demands, efficient state apparatuses with well-developed civil societies that provide growing markets, stable political conditions and steady public investment in human capital (Carnoy, 1999). However, not all states are weakened by globalisation; some are thriving under it, which contributes to the expanding global digital divide (Castells, 2001a).

In order for higher education institutions to be able to respond successfully to this challenge, globalisation 'encouraged' higher education to become more business like. For example, higher education is increasingly expected to interpret international student recruitment from an economic perspective. During an earlier era attracting foreign students was either part of ideological competition between east and west, or part of the development of former colonies. Thus countries such as the USA, Russia, the United Kingdom, France, the Netherlands and Germany sponsored students from third world countries to study in their advanced higher education systems. But during the late 1980s and particularly the 1990s, higher education institutions gradually started seeing fee-paying students as a source of revenue and this led to the development of an international market for higher education students.

In this market the strategy of some institutions is to attract foreign students to enrol in one of their regular programmes against far higher tuition fees than regular national students have to pay. This is especially the case in English language countries such as Australia, the United Kingdom and the USA. Another example is of institutions in non-English language countries, such as the Netherlands and Germany, that are offering English language programmes to foreign students against high tuition fees. A third example consists of institutions that are establishing branches in other countries, such as

Australian universities entering South Africa, or US institutions establishing campuses in Central and Eastern European countries, or entering partnerships with institutions in these countries to develop joint programmes for fee-paying students.

Of further interest for understanding the working of globalisation in the South African context is that, in general, politics is 'running behind the facts of global developments'. The global economic developments that gained momentum in the 1980s, amongst other things in the slipstream of the new trade liberalisation agreements, were not regulated by individual nation states, even though the legal authority for regulating these developments was and is to be found at the level of the nation states.

General examples of these developments are the lack of regulations concerning the boundary-crossing flows of capital, and the regulatory demands of the internationalisation of labour markets. In the area of higher education one can think of quality control demands rising from the growing export and import of higher education services. The only regulations coming from national governments were in the area of developing conditions that were investment-friendly, such as the lifting of trade barriers, sound management of fiscal policy and internal stability (Carnoy, 2001; Gelb, 2001).

Finally a number of institutions are using information and communication technology (ICT) in different and new types of education delivery for foreign students – thus blurring the traditional distinction between contact and distance education. In tandem with competition from public institutions in advantaged countries came the expansion of private higher education at the national level, supported vigorously by international agencies such as the World Bank and by international and local business who suddenly saw higher education as an investment opportunity.

All in all these developments covered by the heading of globalisation have created a very specific global context for national reform in higher education. It is radically different from the contexts of previous decades. This does not imply that we want to suggest that globalisation is a deterministic concept, in the sense that national governments can only act in ways allowed for by globalisation.[7] What we do assume, however, is that the global context, shaped by globalisation, influences national policy-makers in such a way that they emphasise in national policy processes and reforms issues that 'fit' the globalisation discourse, such as efficiency, effectiveness, and competition. Specific national issues, such as institutional and individual redress in South African higher education, are in the practice of national policy more often than not marginalised in favour of the global issues. Chapter 13 explores this further.

5. COUNTRY CASE STUDIES

As part of the broader project around this book a number of higher education scholars were asked to discuss recent higher education reforms in their countries: Lazar Vlasceanu and Jan Sadlak (Central and Eastern Europe), Alberto Amaral (Brazil), K.K. George and Reji Raman (India), Terfot Ngwana (Cameroon), Akira Arimoto (Japan), David Dill (USA), and Lynn Meek (Australia). They produced short case studies that are accessible on the CHET website at www.chet.org.za/papers.asp. The following reflections on the experience of higher education reforms in these countries are based on the original reports and use the analytic triangle as a framework.

5.1. Central and Eastern Europe – changing the changes

The transformations in Central and Eastern European (CEE) countries form an obvious frame of reference for South Africa. Like the South African apartheid regime the former CEE regimes were excessively ideological and repressive. Nonetheless, the state was expected to be a core actor in the reform of public sector components such as higher education after the fall of the repressive CEE regimes. As was the case in South Africa, the market and the higher education institutions significantly affected the outcomes of the state-initiated reforms.

The reforms of CEE higher education started in 1990, and the changes correlated strongly with other major transformations in the political, economic, social and cultural sectors. In interpreting these transformations through the analytic triangle, the first observation is that in reshaping the *state/higher education relationship*, the post-revolutionary CEE governments relied heavily on legislative policy instruments. The creation of new legal frameworks was considered to be the key to introducing and consolidating major changes. However, due to the lack of a strong and direct relationship between the formal rules put in place by higher education legislation and the informal rules and values of the academic ethos, no new law has been able to survive for more than two to three years. Successive laws have been adopted, giving the impression that it was inappropriate to use the law as a national institution for the purpose of generating stability in the system, at least in the way it was used by the government. Instead of creating stability, the legal framework created a situation of flux, and 'changing the changes' thus became the rule.

The national higher education policy debates were initially dominated by national topics, mostly related to the need to diversify the rigid, centralised and monolithic structural and institutional contexts of higher education. This included, for example, de-ideologising the curricula. The new CEE governments had to demonstrate a break with the past. Global policy issues, however, such as efficiency and effectiveness, were also gradually entering the policy debates in the CEE countries. What we can see in the CEE *state/higher education relationship* is a state that is trying to diversify the national higher education system and the structural and legal conditions under which higher education is expected to operate. At the same time the policies of each state are being influenced more and more by global trends. These trends give a clear message: increase the autonomy of the universities and colleges with the expectation that they will become more efficient, effective, competitive and responsive. Furthermore, because the state's treasury cannot afford to fund higher education at an appropriate level, the market is introduced as an arena in which the higher education institutions should seek new resources, while it is also assumed that the global expectations (of efficiency, responsiveness, etc.) will be addressed. In the CEE countries, however, the market entered the equation without much regulation, thus accounting for 'disorganised complexity' in *the higher education/society relationship*. As a consequence the higher education system is today characterised by constant change: changes in institutional forms, in funding mechanisms, in curricula, and in governance and management. While initially the change-emphasis was on the system and the structural functioning of its institutions, it has now become obvious that what is going on inside the structures, in terms of research, teaching and learning, is just as important if not more so.

The frequency of changes and changing issues have had two major effects. First, the changes have left traces in the structure of the system that will have long-lasting effects. Secondly, many academics have become sceptical of the constant flow of change and have returned to the tradition of operating within the system. Thus, they continue to do 'business as usual' while trying to avoid the external demands for change as much as possible.

This book will show some remarkable similarities between the South African and the Central and Eastern European reforms, particularly in terms of themes, the types and sequence of change, the shift from an initial emphasis on the national to the global, and the discussions now taking place on the perceived failure of policy implementation.

5.2. Brazil – testing institutions rather than students

Another country that is often regarded as having similarities with South Africa is Brazil. Not only do the two countries vie for position at the top of the Gini-coefficient league table (measuring social inequality), but Henriques Cardoso, a world renowned left-wing sociologist and activist, became president of Brazil in 1994, the same year Nelson Mandela became president of South Africa.

For Cardoso higher education was also high on the reform agenda, but instead of trying to reform the entire system, the focus was on three broad areas: higher education evaluation, full institutional autonomy and increasing access. Unlike in Central and Eastern Europe, the Brazilian academics vigorously opposed autonomy because they saw it as a move towards privatisation. Another difference is that by the beginning of the 1990s Brazil already had a strongly developed private higher education sector. The market was thus a well-established factor in higher education.

In order to understand the nature and outcomes of the Brazilian higher education reform programme, the structure of the higher education system has to be taken into account. The largest concentration of public and private institutions, students and staff can be found in the state of Sao Paolo. The state authorities are responsible for all public institutions in this state. The other states also have state-steered public higher education institutions. In addition to the state system there is a federal university system which is one of the best-funded public higher education systems in the world. None of the federal universities is located in Sao Paolo.

The major and most controversial reform that has been implemented is the establishment of a national quality assessment agency that runs national examinations across public and private institutions. The evaluations are undertaken not so much to test and influence individual students, but to assess the institutions. If students do not perform satisfactorily, institutions can be downgraded from universities to university centres, meaning that they mainly have a teaching function. Inspectors are sent to the worst performing institutions and if they do not improve within two years, the institutions lose their accreditation.

In terms of governance, a surprise for the institutions was that under Cardoso, who has well-known links to left-wing movements 'the universities were faced, against all expectations, with a more authoritarian educational policy, with less dialogue and participation, with the possible foundations of a new culture of compliance. Indeed the government has in several cases presented or approved new legislation without previous discussion with anyone' (Amaral, 2001:6).

In the *state/higher education relationship* Cardoso adhered strongly to a global agenda, i.e. income diversification for institutions, quality as an external labour market concern, and increasing participation. The role of the (federal) state authority shifted from providing the resources for public higher education, to being both provider and evaluator – an example of Neave's evaluative state (Neave, 1988). The market was also encouraged to become more powerful in the *higher education/society relationship*. While enrolment increased by only 12.4% in the public system between 1994 and 1998, in the private sector it increased in the same period by 36.1%.

As a left theorist of globalisation, Cardoso focussed immediately on changes in both the *state/society* and *state/higher education relationship* that were expected in the first place to strengthen the Brazilian economy. The Brazilian higher education reform initiative was therefore much more targeted than the South African one, and the main reform, national testing, was actually implemented. Initial reform moves in South Africa were focussed on a local agenda of equity and democratisation of governance, but can now be seen to have shifted to incorporate global trends. Another similarity related to this is that, more recently, the South African government also seems to be moving towards a less consultative and more directive approach.

5.3. India – a Niagara Falls of policy reports and a Sahara of action

Given its history, size, social structure and democratic tradition, India is a unique and fascinating country. When looking at recent higher education reforms, these characteristics are relevant and should be taken into account in assessing the outcomes of the reform attempts.

For a long time India followed a central planning model for its economy. Only in the 1980s could a gradual shift to a reliance on market forces be noticed. Since 1991 in particular, when India borrowed heavily from the IMF and the World Bank, the country's policies have been marked by a growing emphasis on liberalisation, privatisation and globalisation. This is clearly visible, for example, in the current programme for economic reforms called the Structural Adjustment Programme (SAP).

The governmental policy initiatives for changing the nation's education system reflect this shift in economic ideology. Many national committees were established from the mid-1980s and produced a great number of reports. Despite the almost continuous flow of suggestions, ideas, recommendations and policy proposals coming from these committees, however, in practice hardly any deliberate changes took place in the higher education system. The main problem in the Indian system is a lack of policy implementation – a problem which, according to George and Raman, 'lies in the failure of the committees and successive governments to appreciate the trade-offs involved in following multiple objectives. They did not take into account the strength of resistance to institutional changes from well-entrenched interest groups. They also did not suggest concrete methods for mobilising resources. The lack of political will is clearly evident from the present status of education in the country'. Consequently the Indian education policy framework has been characterised as a clear case of 'a Niagara Falls of reports on educational policy issues and a Sahara of action' (George & Raman, 2001:1).

The main challenge facing higher education in India is a continuous 'public under-funding' that is getting worse and worse through the gradual decrease in the relative share of the gross national product (GNP) invested in education, and the decrease in expenditure on higher education as part of the education budget. This has led to growing pressures on the higher education institutions to privatise and raise funds. The financial situation for Indian higher education is deteriorating further on account of two factors: first, rich students are increasingly taking advantage of the liberalisation of foreign exchange control to migrate to countries such as the USA, UK, Australia and Russia; secondly, India features a market segmentation where a few world-class institutions co-exist alongside a vast number of mediocre institutions. In this sense higher education reflects the duality of the economy and the society.

All stakeholders involved in higher education argue publicly for restructuring and reforming the higher education system. The reality is different from the rhetoric, however, because restructuring and reform would potentially affect the vested interests of all sectional interests which include highly politicised unions of students, teachers and administrative personnel, and the political leadership.

In terms of the analytic triangle what we can observe in India is a relatively weak state that is incapable of effectively implementing higher education reforms against powerful societal and institutional interests. Rather than challenging the powerful vested interest groups head-on, the state has favoured the 'softer' option of bypassing the existing system by facilitating the establishment of a new breed of institutions to respond to the demands of the different market segments of the economy and society. This option is made possible partly because the need for changing the system as a whole has not been felt by the vocal and influential sections of the society, namely the rising middle class. Their requirements for quality education are being met by institutions of excellence, funded lavishly by the federal government, corporate interests and educational entrepreneurs of a new breed. In addition, the most affluent and influential sections of society are already voting with their feet against India's higher education system by opting for educational and career possibilities abroad.

The privileges of the middle classes (in terms of numbers India has the largest middle class in the world) are served by a regular exercise of 'compensatory legitimisation' where the state engages in commissions and investigations that count as action, rather than implementing the recommendations. Consequently the dynamics between *society (and the market) and the higher education institutions* shape the system in a rather haphazard manner that may in the long term not serve the interests of the stakeholders involved, not to mention the 'aspirations of the voiceless majority' (George & Raman, 2001:8).

India set great store by policy commissions – even more than South Africa. However, not unlike the 1997–2001 period in South Africa, policy implementation has been regarded as very disappointing by most stakeholders involved. Another similarity is that making trade-offs between interest groups in countries with deep social inequalities seems very difficult to achieve.

5.4. Cameroon – an inability to adapt the policy infrastructure

During the period from independence in 1960 to the 1990s, the Cameroonian higher education system, like those of many other developing countries, was unable to adapt adequately to the changing needs of its socio-economic and political environments. The main problems confronting higher education at the start of the 1990s were a language imbalance through the dominance of French, a dramatic growth in student enrolment without a corresponding increase in infrastructure and staff appointments, high drop-out rates, outdated curricula, high unemployment rates among university graduates, and insufficient public funds. Drastic measures were needed and in 1992/93 the government initiated a number of far-reaching innovations in the higher education system.

The main measure taken was the creation in 1993 of five new universities in a system that until then had only one university. This was intended to increase the overall participation rate and it was hoped that the enlargement of the system would provide for higher levels of non-governmental funding through introducing tuition fees, amongst other things.

The government had several intentions with respect to the new university system: first, to provide the universities with more academic and management autonomy; second, to give all Cameroonians who were qualified, the opportunity to obtain university education; third, to make university programmes more professional and more responsive to market forces; fourth, to make universities more accessible to local, regional, national and international communities; fifth to decongest the overcrowded University of Yaounde; sixth to make better use of higher education infrastructure, facilities and services; and finally, to revive and maximise inter-university and international co-operation (Ngwana, 2001). Furthermore, one of the five new universities was an English language institution and in this way the government hoped to deal with the problem of language imbalance.

According to an evaluation carried out in 1999 (ADEA/WGHE, 1999) the reforms were initially successful. Student enrolments increased rapidly in all universities leading to a more balanced regional distribution of, and participation in, higher education. The overall teacher/student ratio improved from 1:54 in 1992/93 to 1:34 in 1995/96 and the drop-out rate decreased. The universities were accorded greater administrative autonomy, while the newly introduced student tuition fees covered around 30% of the institutions' budgets.

Looking more closely at the developments after 1993, however, a number of weaknesses can be observed. Firstly, the English language university did not receive the amount of funding required to enrol all eligible English language students, with the result that many applicants were rejected. Their only options were to enrol in one of the French language institutions or to stay out of higher education. Secondly, there were still not enough places in the new university system to enrol all eligible students. As a result, Cameroon saw the rapid growth of a private higher education sector which the government has not been able to regulate, to ensure, for example, that quality and equity prevail.

Thirdly, the growth of the system was accompanied by mismanagement, a lack of adequate management capacity at all levels, and inadequate academic staff capacity. Public funding of higher education remained a problem with insufficient and irregular allocations, and international donors were reluctant to provide financial support because of the lack of transparency, amongst other things, of the higher education system. Finally, the instruments to be used both by the government and the individual institutions in the new steering relationship were either absent or totally inadequate.

An examination of the Cameroon experience through the lens of the analytic triangle suggests that Cameroon is a state that is being influenced, amongst other things, by global forces (such as the World Bank and Unesco) and is attempting to change its steering approach with respect to higher education. As was shown above, it is aiming at greater institutional autonomy, more non-governmental income for the institutions, and greater awareness of the need for academic quality. The Cameroonian state is stepping back, hoping that a more direct *interaction between institutions and society* will result in a better functioning, more responsive, and better funded university system. Although some positive quantitative effects of the reforms can be discerned, Cameroonian realities have caused major problems in the introduction of the new steering approach and the implementation of the reforms. As was shown above, these include inadequate government funding levels, management capacity problems, academic staff shortages, insufficient student places in the public institutions, and a lack of appropriate policy instruments. These implementation problems in turn led to a number of social pressures in the *society/institutions relationship*, resulting in the rise of a private higher education sector that is not regulated by government.

An interesting comparison emerges with the Indian and South African higher education reform experiences. In India and in South Africa, as will be argued in this book, the role of vested institutional interests played a major role in the failure of the respective governments to implement their proposed policies. In Cameroon the failure seems more a case of a lack of appropriate institutional infrastructure such as policy instruments, management and academic staff capacity, and adequate and stable funding. Major efforts on the side of the government and the institutions in Cameroon are needed in order to prevent the higher education system from sliding back to a pre-1993 situation.

5.5. Japan – a tension between quantity and quality in the post-massification period

Japanese higher education is characterised by, amongst other things, a high participation rate (>50%), a large private sector, and a strong national (that is, public) sector that forms the top of the status hierarchy. It is a mature system that is confronted with issues and reform challenges quite different from those in the four systems discussed above.

The Japanese system of higher education has grown dramatically since the 1960s. The massification of Japanese higher education consisted of quantitative growth without an accompanying focus on the necessary qualitative adaptations. The public sector aimed to sustain the quality of academic work by limiting its expansion, while the private sector expanded rapidly. As a result, by the end of the 1990s about 25% of all students were enrolled in public institutions and 75% with private providers. (However, in 1999 almost 70% of the graduate students were enrolled in public institutions.)

The rapid quantitative expansion of Japanese higher education implied a convergence towards homogeneity, uniformity and standardisation which, in turn, led to all kinds of qualitative problems. Now that the quantitative growth of higher education has more or less stabilised, the government has introduced qualitative reforms to solve the problems created by the massification of the system. It is now using a combination of market mechanisms and governmental instruments and actions to strengthen the qualitative side of the system.

Consequently the main policy challenge for the Japanese government is to stimulate Japanese higher education to become more diversified in the 'post-massification' era. The challenge has become more urgent as a consequence of the Japanese economic crisis and the assumed role of higher education in economic development. It is complicated, however, by the historical development of Japanese higher education institutions which has led to a situation in which, today, research is being prioritised over teaching.

Japanese higher education is dominated by a research paradigm stemming from a 'German university model' introduced at the beginning of the 20th century in the public university system. Although the further development of the higher education system after 1945 was based on a US university model, the research paradigm remained one of its pillars. This explains why there is a strong research orientation among the staff in all the institutions in the massified higher education system – whether they be high-status imperial research universities or two-year junior colleges.

One consequence of this emphasis on research has been the neglect of teaching by most staff members in the higher education institutions. The Ministry of Education tried to address this issue on the basis of recommendations made by the University Council, set up in 1987. The first set of initiatives sought to reform undergraduate education by integrating general and professional education curricula, and by moving away from the traditional homogeneous teaching model so as to bring teaching practice more in line with the diversified needs of the mass higher education system. Neither strategy has been successfully implemented to date, mainly for intra-institutional reasons.

The second set of reform initiatives was concerned with the increasing reliance on market mechanisms in higher education co-ordination and steering, as well as the introduction of formal evaluation mechanisms. Through the lens of the analytic triangle, these reforms can be regarded as Japanese responses to the pressures stemming from global reform trends and ideas. They suggest that in Japan the emphasis in higher education steering and policy-making is shifting from *the state/higher education institutions* relationship to a stronger emphasis on the relationship between *the society and higher education institutions.*

An example of this shift can be observed in the developments concerning the evaluation of the quality of teaching and research. In the early 1990s, the evaluation consisted of a self-evaluation followed by a peer review; at the end of the 1990s the University Council criticised this approach and recommended the establishment of an independent national evaluation agency. Such an agency, called the National Institute for Evaluation, was indeed set up in 2000. It is presently focusing on public institutions and not on private institutions because the government wants to align the allocation of public funds for higher education more closely with the socio-economic needs of the main Japanese stakeholders. The re-allocation of funds on the basis of institutional performance is also intended to strengthen the global competitiveness of Japanese universities. In practice this means that the former imperial universities as 'key institutions of graduate schools' have received up to 25% more funding each year, while the other public institutions have received no extra funding.

In addition, from 2002 onwards, the public universities have to transform into 'independent management agencies', a legal structure which has features of both a public and a private institution. This can be interpreted as the Japanese version of the privatisation of public higher education institutions, a development which is all the more remarkable given that 80% of the institutions are already private (comprising some 75% of the student enrolment by the late 1990s, as was mentioned above). One explanation might be found in demographic projections. The size of the 18-year age cohort will drop dramatically until 2010 and it appears that the government intends reducing the total number of institutions on the basis of competition instead of through direct government action (Arimoto, 2001).

What is interesting is that initially both the national and global reform efforts showed implementation problems. As in India and South Africa, vested academic and institutional interests seemed to resist the initiated reforms successfully. Now, however, a clear interaction between national and global reform agendas can be observed in the Japanese higher education system. Nationally and academically oriented curricular and teaching reforms go hand in hand with the introduction of performance evaluation linked to funding, and the strengthening of inter-institutional competition.

5.6. USA – market competition may not have increased efficiency and effectiveness

According to Clark's (1983) triangle of co-ordination, the co-ordination of US higher education is dominated by the market. In terms of the analytic triangle presented in this book, it is the interplay between the society, higher education institutions and government that is of relevance for understanding recent changes in US higher education, as Dill (2001) demonstrates. Dill indicates that during the post-1994 period the US higher education system confronted many of the same forces for change as did other systems in the world. These included enrolment growth, which was very uneven across states, declining units of resources in public higher education, new forms of quality assurance, and innovations in Internet-based higher education.

For Dill there are three distinguishing features of the current US system. Firstly, there is the influence of an emerging national higher education market on the diversity and the size of the system; secondly, the decentralised nature of government policy-making; and thirdly, the large private sector in higher education. In terms of the student market, many institutions found that changes in national testing, financial aid, transportation and communication resulted in their recruitment market getting much bigger. Instead of being limited to a regional market, the institutions started recruiting more and more students from a national and, in some cases, even international higher education market. This resulted in many regional higher education monopolies coming under competitive pressure for students, resources and prestige – competition which has altered the programme structure and the management of institutions.

In terms of the analytic triangle which this book seeks to explore, it was expected that in the relationship between US *society and the higher education institutions*, it would be market-related interactions which would ensure efficiency and effectiveness. An example that undermines this assumption concerns the worries in the post-1994 period over the fact that in both public and private sectors, the increase in tuition fees consistently exceeded inflation. In addition to numerous state level attempts to curb this trend, a federal congressional panel was appointed and the 'jawboning' contributed to slowing down tuition increases. By the end of the decade, however, tuition fees were still rising and exceeding inflation.

Another example concerns the decision of the Clinton administration in 1992 to establish State Post-Secondary Review Entities that would provide greater rationalisation and monitor institutional effectiveness through consumer-based accountability measures. The higher education community responded by forming a National Policy Board on Higher Education Institutional Accreditation to support and develop public understanding for voluntary self-regulation and the accreditation of a myriad of existing agencies. These proposals for reforming academic accountability fell apart in 1994 when the Republican Party gained control over Congress. By the end of the 1990s a 'number of objective observers had concluded that while there had been a great deal of discussion about student assessment in the US system and several interesting institutional experiments, the assessment movement had generally failed to have any systematic influence on improving student learning' (Dill, 2001:6).

Based on these examples, Dill concludes that in terms of efficiency and effectiveness, 'the lack of national benchmarks for student learning as well as processes for aligning local standards contributes substantially to the "academic arms race" in pursuit of prestige based upon entering student test scores and research rankings. This imperfection in the US market for higher education, along with the weaknesses in student finance, help to explain the conclusion that market competition in the US system appears not to have produced the expected social benefits of increased efficiency and effectiveness' (Dill, 2001:7).

While the US higher education system does not seem comparable to the South African system, it can be argued that in the USA attempts at federal steering produced more unintended consequences than actual planned change, that institutions will seek to counter state initiatives, and that societal electoral changes can have more effect, even if negative, than state plans and policies. It also shows that the market is by no means a perfect mechanism for improving efficiency and effectiveness.

5.7. Australia – the interplay between management capacity and political will

Australia can be regarded as one of the prime examples of how the interaction between government intervention, institutional responsiveness and the active stimulation of market forces brings about major reforms, the outcomes of which differ in many respects from the original intentions of the reformers.

Meek comments that in the last decade, and particularly during the period 1994 to 1999, it was the federal government's political intention to shift the funding of higher education from the state to the consumer, and to treat higher education more as a private than a public good. Little of this could have been accomplished had it not been for the capacity of the institutional managers to become much more corporate-like and entrepreneurial in the running of individual institutions. However, things have moved so far in the direction of privatising public higher education that government policy and management's complicity with it are in danger of creating an era of higher education mediocrity from which the system may never recover (Meek, 2001:2).

Australian reform started through strong government intervention in the late 1980s when the new Labour government embarked on a set of dramatic reforms that abolished the binary divide and created a unified national system with a much smaller number of significantly larger institutions. Underpinning this were the following long-term trends: a shift in costs from the state to the individual; enhanced national and international competition for students and research funds; more accountability (with some performance-based funding); greater deregulation; and an increased reliance on diversified income sources.

The new federal government of 1996 introduced much stronger market steering mechanisms by reducing operating grants, putting an end to the practice of the commonwealth supplementing salaries, and demanding the return of funds for enrolment targets not met. The privatisation of public higher education and the introduction of market-like relationships to achieve both greater institutional efficiency and adaptability became national policy goals.

In summary, the changes can be described as having been driven by reduced public expenditure, increased emphasis on efficiency and resource utilisation, performance assessment, institutions having to make a demonstrable contribution to the economy, and the strengthening of institutional management.

In assessing these efforts, Meek points out that institutional management has been very successful in finding additional resources. For example, the introduction of a market approach led to the enrolment of 157.000 foreign students contributing $3-billion in 1999, making the education of overseas students one of the countries largest export earners. In Meek's view, these reforms have had three major effects. The first is the corporatisation of higher education institutions which is resulting in the decline of traditional methods of collegial decision-making. Secondly, although market competition was supposed to stimulate diversity, there are increasing concerns that instead of a diversified range of institutions creating their own, different, forms of excellence, many of the weaker institutions are becoming pale imitations of their more powerful and prestigious brethren. According to Meek it would seem that formally regulated and separate policy environments are better suited to encouraging differentiation than market competition.

The third and the most serious negative effect, is the reduction of investment in research and infrastructure. Although the government recently produced a research and development plan which depends on state and business investment, the concern is that it will not be enough to address the backlog.

The Australian higher education reform process has been one of the few in the world in which all three actors represented in the corners of the analytic triangle have been actively involved. Government reform in higher education was driven mainly by a global reform agenda, bringing into play both the market and the institutions. Although the aim of institutional restructuring was to develop bigger, more comprehensive institutions, the institutions were not instructed with whom to merge; rather, a set of financial levers were put in place to stimulate mergers and incorporation. The state also stimulated expansion by providing incentives for increasing student numbers and attracting foreign students. And in the latest election, higher education became a significant issue in the election campaign.

Not surprisingly, the reforms had unanticipated outcomes, such as a weakening of the research and infrastructure base, and the development, perhaps, of less, rather than more diversity.

6. CONCLUSION

The policies and reform experiences in each of the seven countries discussed above reflect the complex realities of higher education policy processes that are also visible in post-1994 South Africa. Such policies and reforms have been initiated in a period characterised as an age of transformation. Our societies, with economies that have for a long time been based on manufacturing, are transforming into knowledge societies. In addition there are many manifestations of the growing impact of global forces, structures and connections on national economies. As a consequence, the effects of higher education policies initiated and implemented at a national level can no longer be understood solely by examining the policy process in a national context. It was widely assumed until recently, both in policy practice and the scholarly field of policy analysis, that a policy process is a causal, linear process consisting of a number of phases that could each be examined separately, i.e. initiation, decision, implementation, evaluation, and feedback. Practical and theoretical disappointments have gradually led to the recognition that a policy process might be more interactive in nature than causal and linear.

This book tries to address these complex realities of the higher education policy process in the 'network of co-ordination' triangle. The interactions of state, society and higher education institutions have changed rapidly and dramatically in many countries, including South Africa, as the remainder of this book illustrates. We have also included in our triangular figure the growing influence of global trends and ideas on these national interactions. This inclusion, however, does not imply a deterministic influence. The main regulatory and funding responsibilities with respect to higher education remain in the domain of the nation state. While there is the undeniable impact of global reform trends such as competitiveness, responsiveness, efficiency and effectiveness on national higher education debates, it is still up to the national political structures to make decisions about the level of public investment in higher education and the way in which these investments are going to be allocated. In addition, the regulatory frameworks within which higher education has to operate are determined by national politicians, even though supra-national decisions are having a growing influence on national regulations as, for example, in the EU member states.

The interactive nature of the policy process, the number of actors involved in policy-making and policy-implementation, and the growing but uncontrollable effects of the reform modes of thought offered by globalisation provide some of the explanatory frames necessary when trying to account for the differences between policy intentions and policy outcomes. In South Africa, as in other countries, these differences have been interpreted as implementation failure, but in our view this explanation is too superficial. While the policy implementation process can be improved generally, for example by a more effective use of policy instruments, even an improved policy implementation process would never guarantee an optimal outcome. We live in an 'age of side-effects' (Beck, 1994:175), implying that we are regularly confronted with the unintended effects of our human interventions. The biggest challenge presented to us by these unintended effects is to learn from them. There is room for improvement in the policy process. We need to and can learn much more about what works and what does not work. From that perspective the notion of responsiveness is highly relevant – not just for the higher education institutions in their relationships with the state and society, but also for state authorities. They should be responsive to the unintended effects of their interventions, not by blaming the higher education institutions, globalisation or capacity problems for any implementation failures, but by trying to understand the how, what and why of the unintended effects, and use this understanding in future policy processes.

This also applies to South Africa. This book is an attempt to analyse the post-1994 higher education reforms and policies from the perspective of original policy intentions and actual outcomes. The policy processes analysed in the chapters which follow provide clear examples of policy intentions and unintended effects and outcomes. These examples are uniquely South African, but they fit the global higher education reform trends which have been discussed in this chapter. We hope that positioning the post-1994 South African higher education reform experience in its global context will help to bring home the fact that policy implementation problems are unavoidable and attempts at reform inevitably have unintended effects. In Chapter 13 we return to these problems and unintended effects, and provide some analytical tools that will contribute to understanding the underlying reasons for their manifestation.

NOTES

1   Some scholars (e.g. Olsen, 2000) interpret these global reform trends as ideologies. Since we realise that the term ideology is somewhat controversial in the South African context we will use in general the term 'trends'. However, the Concise Oxford Dictionary interprets ideology as 'a system of ideas and ideals forming the basis of an economic or political theory' (2001) and is in line with our interpretation of these global trends. We do not see the ideas and assumptions underlying the global reform ideologies with respect to higher education as part of a 'globalisation conspiracy', but we do assume that they assert consistent pressure on the way in which higher education is reformed throughout the world.

2   Slaughter and Leslie (1997:31) also refer to these societal transformation processes in their discussion of the link between globalisation theories and higher education for four English speaking countries (Australia, Canada, United Kingdom, and the USA). They state, for example, that at first glance, globalisation theories do not seem to speak directly to higher education. However, they do outline the magnitude of the political economic changes occurring across the four countries. 'These changes are putting pressure on national higher education policy makers to change the way tertiary education does business.'

3   It is from this perspective that Neave (1988) discusses 'the rise of the evaluative state' and Power (1997) the notion of 'the audit society'. See also Henkel (1991).

4   For a concise and informative synthesis of these trends from a South African perspective, see Singh (2001).

5   For an application of Olsen's models in the European context, see Gornitzka and Maassen (2000).

6   The authors referred to earlier in this book can be recommended as excellent introductions to the many attempts to conceptualise globalisation, i.e. Castells (1996), Held and his colleagues (1999), and in the context of South Africa, the book edited by Muller, Cloete and Badat (2001).

7   This point is also made by Slaughter and Leslie (1997:12) who indicate that 'movement toward academic capitalism is far from uniform; indeed it is characterised by unevenness. Even within the English-speaking countries, there exists a continuum on this dimension, with Canadian academics probably least involved with the market and US academics perhaps most involved.'

REFERENCES

ADEA/WGHE. (1999). Reforming a National System of Higher Education: The Case of Cameroon. Washington DC: ADEA/World Bank. This report is also available at www.unesco.org/education/educprog/wche/index.html.

Amaral, A. (2001). Reflections on Brazilian Higher Education: 1994–1999. Case study. www.chet.org.za/papers.asp.

Arimoto, A. (2001). Trends of Higher Education and Academic Reforms from 1994 onwards in Japan. Case study. www.chet.org.za/papers.asp.

Beck, U. (1994). The Reinvention of Politics: Towards a Theory of Reflexive Modernisation. In: U. Beck, A. Giddens & S. Lash (eds), *Aesthetics in the Modern Social Order*. Cambridge: Polity Press.

Carnoy, M. (2001). The Role of the State in the New Global Economy. In: J. Muller, N. Cloete & S. Badat (eds), *Challenges of Globalisation: South African Debates with Manuel Castells*. Cape Town: Maskew Miller Longman.

Carnoy, M. (2000). *Sustaining the New Economy: Work, Family and Community in the Information Age*. New York: Russell Sage; Cambridge: Harvard University Press.

Carnoy, M. (1999). *Globalisation and Educational Reform: What Planners Need to Know*. Paris: UNESCO International Institute for Educational Planning.

Castells, M. (1996). *The Rise of the Network Society*. Oxford: Blackwell Publishers.

Castells, M. (2001). The New Global Economy. In: J. Muller, N. Cloete & S. Badat (eds), *Challenges of Globalisation: South African Debates with Manuel Castells*. Cape Town: Maskew Miller Longman.

Castells, M. (2001a). *The Internet Galaxy: Reflections on the Internet, Business and Society*. Oxford: Oxford University Press.

Cerych, L. & Sabatier, P. (eds) (1986). *Great Expectations and Mixed Performances.* Stoke: Trendham Books.

Clark, B. (1983). *The Higher Education System: Academic Organisation in Cross-National Perspective.* Berkeley: UCLA Press.

Clark, B. (1998). *Creating Entrepreneurial Universities: Organisational Pathways of Transformation.* Oxford: Pergamon Press.

Cloete, N. & Bunting, I. (2000). *Higher Education Transformation. Assessing Performance in South Africa.* Pretoria: CHET.

Coombe, T. (1991). *A Consultation on Higher Education in Africa: A Report to the Ford Foundation and the Rockefeller Foundation.* London: Institute of Education.

Department of Education (1997). Education White Paper 3: A Programme for the Transformation of Higher Education. General Notice 1196 of 1997, Pretoria.

Dill, D. (2001). Reflections on US Higher Education: 1994–1999. Case study. www.chet.org.za/papers.asp.

Gelb, S. (1998). The Politics of Macroeconomic Reform in South Africa. Conference on Democracy and the Political Economy of Reform, Cape Town.

Gelb, S. (2001). Globalisation, the State and Macroeconomics. In: J. Muller, N. Cloete & S. Badat (eds), *Challenges of Globalisation: South African Debates with Manuel Castells.* Cape Town: Maskew Miller Longman.

George, K.K. & Raman, R. (2001). Changes in Indian Higher Education – An Insider's View. Case study. www.chet.org.za/papers.asp.

Gornitzka, Å. & Maassen, P. (2000). Hybrid Steering Approaches with Respect to European Higher Education. *Higher Education Policy,* 13, 267–285.

Gornitzka, Å., Kyvik, S. & Larsen, I.M. (1998). The Bureaucratisation of Universities. *Minerva,* 36, 21–47.

Gornitzka, Å. & Larsen, I.M. (2001). Restructuring of Administrative Workforce in Universities. Paper presented at the CHER conference 2–5 September, Dijon, France.

Gumport, P. (2000). Academic Restructuring: Organisational Change and Institutional Imperatives. *Higher Education,* 39, 67–91.

Held, D., McGrew, A., Goldblatt, D. & Perraton, J. (1999). *Global Transformations. Politics, Economics and Culture.* Stanford: Stanford University Press.

Henkel, M. (1991). *Government, Evaluation and Change.* London: Jessica Kingsley.

Kraak, A. (2001). Policy Ambiguity and Slippage: Higher Education Under the New State, 1994–2001. Commissioned paper. www.chet.org.za/papers.asp.

Lyden, F.J. & Miller, E.G. (1968). *Planning, Programming, Budgeting: A Systems Approach to Management.* First edition. Chicago: Markham.

Maassen, P. (ed.) (2000). Higher Education and the Stakeholder Society. *European Journal of Education,* (Special Number) 35(4), 377–497.

Maassen, P. & Van Vught, F. (1994). Alternative Models of Governmental Steering in Higher Education. In: L. Goedegebuure & F. van Vught (eds), *Comparative Policy Studies in Higher Education.* Utrecht: Lemma.

Meek, L. (2001). Reflections on Australian Higher Education: 1994–1999. Case study. www.chet.org.za/papers.asp.

Meek, V.L., Goedegebuure, L., Kivinen, O. & Rinne, R. (eds) (1996). *The Mockers and Mocked: Comparative Perspectives on Diversity, Differentiation and Convergence in Higher Education.* Oxford: Pergamon.

Muller, J., Cloete, N. & Badat, S. (eds). (2001). *Challenges of Globalisation: South African Debates with Manuel Castells.* Cape Town: Maskew Miller Longman.

National Commission on Higher Education (1996). *A Framework for Transformation.* Pretoria: NCHE.

Neave, G. (1988). On the Cultivation of Quality, Efficiency and Enterprise: An Overview of Recent Trends in Higher Education in Western Europe, 1986–1988. *European Journal of Education,* 23, 7–23.

Neave, G. & Van Vught, F. (eds) (1994). *Government and Higher Education Relationships Across Three Continents: The Winds of Change.* Oxford: Pergamon Press.

Ngwana, T.A. (2001). The Implementation of the 1993 Higher Education Reforms in Cameroon: Issues and Promises. Case study. www.chet.org.za/papers.asp.

Olsen, J. (2000). Organisering og Styring av Universiteter. En kommentar til Mjøsutvalgets Reformforslag. Oslo: ARENA Working Paper WP 00/20. www.arena.uio.no/nor_publications/wp00_20.htm.

Olsen, J. (1988). Administrative Reform and Theories of Organisation. In: C. Campbell & B.G. Peters (eds), *Organising Governance; Governing Organisations*. Pittsburgh: University of Pittsburgh Press.

Power, M. (1997). *The Audit Society*. Oxford: Oxford University Press.

Pressman, J. & Wildavsky, A. (1971). *Implementation*. Berkeley: University of California Press.

Scott, P. (1996). University Governance and Management. An Analysis of the System and Institutional Level Changes in Western Europe. In: P. Maassen & F. van Vught (eds), *Inside Academia. New challenges for the academic profession*. Utrecht: De Tijdstroom.

Scott, P. (2001). Leadership and Management – Some Thoughts for the UK. Case study. www.chet.org.za/papers.asp.

Scott, W.R. (1995). *Institutions and Organisations*. Thousand Oaks: Sage.

Shick, A. (1973). A Death in the Bureaucracy: The Demise of Federal PPB. *Public Administration Review*, 33, March/April.

Singh, M. (2001). Re-inserting the "Public Good" into Higher Education. *Kagisano*, Issue 1. Pretoria: CHE.

Slaughter, S. & Leslie L.L. (1997). *Academic Capitalism. Politics, Policies and the Entrepreneurial University*. Baltimore: The Johns Hopkins University Press.

Vlasceanu, L. & Sadlak, J. (2001). Changes in the Higher Education System and Institutions of the Central and Eastern European Countries: 1994–1999. Case study. www.chet.org.za/papers.asp.

CHAPTER 2

IAN BUNTING

THE HIGHER EDUCATION LANDSCAPE UNDER APARTHEID

This chapter lays out the South African higher education landscape as it was shaped by the apartheid policies of the National Party government prior to 1994. It describes how the disenfranchisement of the African majority culminated in the establishment of five separate legislative and geographic entities (the Republic of South Africa and four 'independent republics') and traces the process by which this policy led to the establishment of 36 higher education institutions controlled by eight different government departments. The chapter also describes the apartheid thinking which led to the differentiation of higher education in South Africa into two distinct types – universities and technikons – and shows how sharp racial divisions, as well as language and culture, skewed the profiles of the institutions in each category.

1. POLICIES OF THE APARTHEID GOVERNMENT

1.1. Racial divisions in South Africa

At the beginning of 1994, South Africa's higher education system was fragmented and unco-ordinated. This was primarily the result of the white apartheid government's conception of race and the politics of race, which had shaped the higher education policy framework that it laid down during the 1980s.

The apartheid government, under the influence of the ruling National Party, had, by the beginning of the 1980s, divided South Africa into five entities:

- The Republic of Transkei (formed from part of the old Cape Province).
- The Republic of Bophuthatswana (formed from part of the old Transvaal Province).
- The Republic of Venda (also formed from part of the old Transvaal Province).
- The Republic of Ciskei (formed from another part of the old Cape Province).
- The Republic of South Africa (which consisted of the vast majority of the land holdings of the old South Africa).

The first four entities became known as the 'TBVC countries' (using the first letter of each in the acronym) and the fifth as the 'RSA'.

N. Cloete et al. (eds.). Transformation in Higher Education, 35-52.
© 2007 Springer.

The South African government at the time considered the first four entities to be legally independent countries, but they never received international recognition of their 'statehood'. The international community regarded these four 'republics' as apartheid creatures, the only purpose of which was that of disenfranchising the majority of the citizens of South Africa. In terms of the National Party's ideology, Africans (who constituted close to 80% of the population of the old South Africa) were supposed to be citizens of one of these and other potentially 'independent' republics (e.g. one for Zulus in the old Natal Province). They were presumed to be 'aliens' in the Republic of South Africa and therefore not entitled to representation in the national parliament.

The apartheid government extended the disenfranchisement of its African citizens by introducing, in 1984, a new constitution for the Republic of South Africa (RSA). This constitution divided the national parliament into three chambers (the 'tricameral' parliament): one house for representatives of white voters (the House of Assembly), one for representatives of coloured voters (the House of Representatives) and one for representatives of Indian voters (the House of Delegates). No provision was made in the 1984 constitution for any representation of Africans in the RSA parliament, even though this group constituted at least 75% of the population living in the RSA, outside the TBVC countries.

A key element in the creation of the three separate parliamentary houses in the RSA in 1984 was a distinction drawn between 'own affairs' and 'general affairs'. What were described as 'own affairs' were matters specific to the 'cultural and value frameworks' of the coloured or Indian or white communities. 'General affairs' were those which had an impact across all racial communities. Education was considered by the 1984 constitution to be an 'own affair' as far as whites, coloureds and Indians were concerned. This implied that all education for whites (primary, secondary and higher) was the responsibility of the House of Assembly, for coloureds that of the House of Representatives, and for Indians that of the House of Delegates. This constitution considered education for Africans in the RSA to be a 'general affair'. Responsibility for the education of Africans was therefore vested in a 'general affairs' government department which was termed the 'Department of Education and Training' (DET).

2. THE CONCEPTUAL FRAMEWORK FOR HIGHER EDUCATION UNDER APARTHEID

The introduction of the 1984 constitution in the RSA, with its distinction between 'general' and 'own affairs', entrenched the apartheid divisions in education in South Africa. A direct consequence was that higher education institutions had to be designated as being for the exclusive use of one of the four race groups: African, coloured, Indian and white. By the beginning of 1985, a total of 19 higher education institutions had been designated as being 'for the exclusive use of whites', two as being 'for the exclusive use of coloureds', two 'for the exclusive use of Indians', and six as being 'for the exclusive use of Africans'. The six institutions for Africans did not include the seven institutions in the TBVC countries, even though it was expected that the latter would be used almost entirely by the African citizens of the four 'independent republics'.

The National Party government put in place legal constraints to prevent institutions designated for the use of one race group from enrolling students from another race group. For example, an institution designated for coloureds could register a student from one of the other three race groups only if that institution obtained a permit from the education department to which it was accountable. Permits were supposed to be granted only if it could be shown that the applicant's proposed programme of study was not available at any institution designated for the race group to which she/he belonged.

This dispensation was shaped in line with that government's view on the status of public higher education institutions. The government maintained that any public higher education institution in the RSA was essentially a legal entity, a 'creature of the state'. It was brought into existence by an action of the state, and its existence could be terminated by another action of the state. This made legitimate, the government believed, any decision to restrict institutions to serving the interests of one and only one race group.

In line with its belief that higher education institutions are creatures of the state, the government further fragmented the racially divided higher education system: higher education institutions were divided into rigid groups in terms of the functions they were and were not permitted to perform. By the beginning of the 1980s the National Party government had in fact drawn such a rigid distinction between institutions it termed 'universities' and a new set of institutions to which it gave the new and unique term 'technikons'.

The foundations of the distinction between universities and technikons lay in the important philosophical underpinning of much of the National Party ideology, including that concerned with higher education, viz. a naïve belief in the existence of 'essences'. It viewed the notion of 'essence' as a unique property, characteristic, or feature which distinguished objects (or institutions, or race groups[1]) from all others. The National Party government believed that it had been able to identify the essence of each of the two types of institutions into which it divided the South African higher education system: the essence of a university was *science* and the essence of a technikon was *technology*. It used the term 'science' to designate all scholarly activities in which knowledge for the sake of knowledge is studied, and the term 'technology' to designate activities concerned with the applications of knowledge. It followed from its philosophy of 'essences' that the government at that time believed that universities *could not* become involved in technology (in the sense of the application of knowledge) and that technikons *could not* become involved in scholarly activities involving the generation of new knowledge.

As a consequence of drawing this divide between universities and technikons in terms of a distinction between science and technology, the government built specific policies about the functions of each type of institution into its higher education framework. Some of the features of its policy framework were these:

- The policy statements argued that drawing rigid distinctions between science (in the sense of any systematic or scholarly approach to the development of knowledge) and technology (in the sense of the application of knowledge), and assigning science to universities and technology to technikons, did not imply that technikons were inferior to universities. The policies stressed that high-level and separate studies could be undertaken in science and in technology. This view was implemented by giving universities and technikons separate but equal qualification structures, which looked like this:

University qualification	Equivalent technikon qualification
Doctorate	Laureatus in technology
Masters degree	National diploma in technology
Honours degree	National higher diploma
Postgraduate diploma	Postdiploma diploma
Professional first bachelors degree	First national diploma (4 years)
General first bachelors degree	First national diploma (3 years)

- The notion of separate, but equal, qualification structures was taken to imply that technikon students could begin with a three-year diploma (equivalent to a three-year bachelors degree in a university), could eventually achieve a national diploma in technology (equivalent to a masters degree), and finally a national laureatus in technology (equivalent to a doctoral degree).
- As a consequence of these distinctions, the policies stressed that the primary function of technikons had to be that of training students who would be able to apply scientific (or scholarly) principles within the context of a specific career or vocation. The courses at technikons therefore had to concentrate on *applications* of knowledge rather than on knowledge itself, and technikon students had to be less concerned than university students with abstract thinking and scientific or scholarly approaches to knowledge.
- The policies stressed that the main function of universities had to be that of educating students in a range of fundamental scientific or scholarly disciplines to enable them to enter high-level professions. Universities were supposed to train basic scientists and basic researchers, and therefore had to be concerned with the development rather than with the application of knowledge.

3. THE INSTITUTIONAL LANDSCAPE PRIOR TO 1994

There were two major consequences which flowed from these conceptions of race and the nature of knowledge:

- Firstly, the South African higher education system was divided into two mutually exclusive types of institutions: universities and technikons.
- Secondly, eight different government departments controlled the institutions in these categories.

If responsible government authority is taken to be the key element, then the higher education landscape, at the beginning of 1994, could be described as follows:

Table 1. *Numbers of public higher education institutions in South Africa: 1990–1994*

Responsible authority	Universities	Technikons	Total institutions
House of Assembly (for whites)	11	8	19
House of Representatives (for coloureds)	1	1	2
House of Delegates (for Indians)	1	1	2
Department of Education and Training (for Africans)	4	2	6
Republic of Transkei	1	1	2
Republic of Bophuthatswana	1	1	2
Republic of Venda	1	0	1
Republic of Ciskei	1	1	2
Totals	21	15	36

The classifications contained in this table do not, however, bring out sharply enough the racial divisions which existed in the South African higher education system in the years up to 1994. A better way of classifying higher education institutions in South Africa prior to 1994 would be to use the broad categories 'historically white/historically black' and 'university/technikon' within a framework of their pre-1994 government authority (RSA or TBVC).

The remaining sections deal with certain key features of the pre-1994 groupings, generated by this way of classifying institutions. An overview of the classification of individual institutions is contained in Table 2 on page 49.

3.1. Historically white universities in the RSA

In terms of South African law, historically white universities remained part of the Republic of South Africa (RSA) throughout all the years of apartheid. The group has to be divided into two distinct sub-groupings: those in which the main medium of communication and instruction was Afrikaans (which was the home language of most people in government) and those in which the main medium of communication and instruction was English.

Nevertheless, it was not the question of language that was the primary basis for the divide. The key element in making the distinction between the two sub-groupings is that some universities in the group supported the National Party government, including its apartheid higher education policies, and others did not.

3.1.1. Historically white Afrikaans-medium universities
The first sub-group comprised six universities, five of which used Afrikaans as the official medium of communication and instruction: the University of the Orange Free State, Potchefstroom University, the University of Pretoria, the Rand Afrikaans University and

the University of Stellenbosch. The sixth member was the dual-medium University of Port Elizabeth, which had been set up in the early 1960s as a way of bringing conservative white English-speaking students into the government fold. This university, despite being officially both Afrikaans and English, was dominated by Afrikaans-speaking executives and governing bodies.

These six universities were run by executives and councils which gave strong support to the apartheid government. They accepted the government's ideology of universities being 'creatures of the state' and therefore took their chief function to be that of acting in the service of government. They believed that this obliged them to support the higher education policies of the apartheid government. Their implementation of the government's race-based policies is shown by the fact that the combined student enrolment of the six universities was 96% white in 1990 and 89% white in 1993. They made few attempts to use the permit system to bring black students on to their campuses. As was discussed earlier, the permit system was one which allowed a white institution to apply for government permission to enrol black students in programmes not offered by a black institution. The few black students enrolled by these institutions tended to be postgraduates who did not have to attend classes on campus.

The support given by the six historically white Afrikaans-medium universities to the government was a major aspect of their adaptive strategies. They saw their support of the apartheid government as being essential to their survival as institutions, at least up until 1990 when the national liberation movements were unbanned. Their student recruitment depended on being seen primarily as institutions involved in the training of staff required for the apartheid civil service and for various professions. But most importantly, their financial strength depended on them having good relations with the apartheid government as well as the business sectors with which it had close ties.

The high level of support which these universities gave to government had a major impact on their academic and governance cultures: by the 1990s they could be described as instrumentalist institutions which were governed in strongly authoritarian ways. An instrumentalist higher education institution can be defined, for these purposes, as one which takes its core business to be the dissemination and generation of knowledge for a purpose defined or determined by a socio-political agenda. Knowledge is not regarded as something which is good in itself and hence worth pursuing for its own sake. It follows that knowledge which could be used for a specific social, economic or political purpose would be the primary form pursued in an instrumentalist institution.

The effect which instrumentalism had on the educational culture of these universities in the years up to 1994 is summed up well by Jansen (2001). Even though he was commenting on his experiences in the period 2000–2001 in one of the larger historically white Afrikaans-medium institutions, what he said was true of all six universities in the years leading up to the ending of apartheid in South Africa:

> [There is at this institution a] lack of critical discourse in the disciplines as well as in more public spheres with respect to pressing social and human problems. There is a pervasive and narrow problem-solving, applications-based pedagogy and research, but not much of a standing back and posing of critical questions in an attempt to understand, probe, disrupt official policy or standard practice. (p4)

There were two main reasons why this comment was true of the six historically white Afrikaans universities in the years before 1994. The first was that the international academic boycott against South Africa resulted in these institutions being disconnected from the international academic community. By the 1980s they had lost their close links with universities in Europe, particularly in Holland. Consequently they made few attempts to build relations with international donors, for example, and this limited the flow of private or non-governmental funding. Their only secure sources of private funds were their contracts with organisations serving the apartheid regime, and their fee-paying students, most of whom came from government-supporting white families.

The second reason was that the intellectual agendas of the six institutions were by and large determined by the perception that they had a duty to preserve the apartheid status quo. They did engage in research activities, but much of this had a local South African focus. A great deal of their research involved policy work for the government and government agencies, and technological work undertaken on contract for defence-related industries.

Their instrumentalist commitments to the agenda of the apartheid government led to these six universities being run in strongly authoritarian ways. Open protests by students or staff over government policies and actions were not countenanced, and were swiftly crushed on these campuses. Objections to institutional policies and actions, especially from those not entrenched in the central power structures, were also not accepted. Jansen (2001), in the same paper referred to earlier, gives this account of the current governance culture of an historically white Afrikaans university – an account which would have been true of all six in the years up to 1994:

> The first thing that hits an outsider … is the powerful role of centralised authority within the institution. I was thoroughly shocked when I discovered how meetings are managed on the campus. The chairperson was not a facilitator who generated the best ideas on a problem … from the collective minds of the attendees, before seeking an appropriate set of resolutions … No: the chairperson, in most cases, already had the solutions and, it often appeared, had decided in advance what solution would be proposed (imposed?) and accepted. Now this has two dampening effects on institutional cultures and the individuals within them: it reduces the participants to powerless observers of a centralised process, and it reinforces the notion that intellectual authority vests in seniority rather than in the mix of personal talent in attendance …
>
> The second thing that I observed was the relationship between staff, and especially between senior and junior academics. I observed, with some intrigue, the all-powerful role of senior academics (heads of department, deans, vice-principals, principal etc … [There are many institutional] messages, layered on each other, that tell the junior person over and over again, that she is simply another body in the area, devoid of authority to act, inspire, lead, differ, contradict, change, initiate. She is simply a void whose intellectual and emotional life needs 'filling' by the promoter, the professor, the higher authority. (p2)

An important feature of the governance of these six institutions is that they always had the crucial mid-level management capacity to control the institution and to implement change. They had tight administrative and financial systems in place throughout these years, had adequate numbers of posts in the management tiers below the institutional executive (the principal and vice-principals); most importantly, they were able to fill these posts with competent and efficient staff.

A concluding comment which must be offered is this: by 1994, many of these historically white Afrikaans-medium universities faced serious internal concerns about their future viability as institutions. Many of those involved in their governing bodies and executives believed that a change in government, from the National Party to the African National Congress, would place at risk their flows of government subsidy funds. They believed that their financial reserves could possibly be 'confiscated' by the new government for use for redress purposes, and that the flow of private funds would diminish as the wider society was transformed in post-apartheid South Africa. These concerns set the stage for a range of developments which are described in Section 2 of this book.

3.1.2. Historically white English universities

The second sub-group consists of the four historically white English-medium universities: the University of Cape Town, the University of Natal, Rhodes University and the University of the Witwatersrand. Institutions in this group referred to themselves as the 'liberal universities' and did so partly as a way of signalling their refusal to adopt the apartheid government's view that universities are simply 'creatures of the state'. As a result, the four universities developed highly ambiguous relationships with the government during the apartheid years.

The ambiguity can be summed up in this way: the four universities accepted that they were public institutions and that they were, as a consequence, entitled to government funding. However, they argued that by their very nature as universities, they were not servants of the state and thus that they would not accept that their functions could be limited to those of serving the needs and implementing the policies of the government of the day. Indeed they believed that their commitment to the universal values of academic freedom made it impossible for them to act as the servants of the apartheid state. From time to time, therefore, they objected strongly to the policies and actions of the apartheid government, even while accepting substantial subsidy funding from that government.

The four institutions took academic freedom to imply that universities could teach whatever they deemed to be important, that they could admit all who qualified for admission to any of their programmes, and that they could select any suitable candidate as an academic teacher. Prior to the 1990s they had declared publicly that 'academic freedom in South Africa was dead' because of apartheid restrictions on teaching materials, student admissions and the selection of academics. Being, by law, institutions for whites only, these universities were not permitted to admit black students, nor to employ black academic staff members. They were also not permitted to teach any courses or to use any materials which the apartheid government deemed to be of a 'subversive nature designed to further the aims of communism'. The Communist Party was one of the organisations which was banned during the apartheid years; this implied that support for that party or for any of its aims was construed to be a criminal offence.

During the years after the introduction of the 1984 tricameral parliament, these four universities attempted to bring larger numbers of black students on to their campuses. Some exploited the ministerial permit system as fully as they could: wherever possible they interpreted applications from black students as being for programmes not offered by black institutions, and they specifically guided black applicants towards such programmes. Some also deliberately admitted black students into formal student housing even though it was illegal in the 1980s to have blacks and whites sharing the same residential space. The effect of these efforts was that by 1990, 28% and by 1993, 38% of the students registered at these four universities were either African or coloured or Indian. Most of these black students were registered for classes offered on the main campuses of the four universities.

One reason why these four historically white English-medium universities took a strong anti-government stand during the 1980s was this: they did not believe that their existence was dependent on the patronage of the apartheid government. Their view was that any university in any country, by its very nature, had to maintain a 'distance' from government. They regarded themselves as being part of an international community of scholars which was dedicated to the advancement and propagation of all human knowledge. They therefore believed it to be essential that their academic staff maintain close relations with international disciplinary bodies as well as with major overseas universities. Their anti-apartheid stance during these years helped the four universities raise considerable funds from international donors. During the 1980s this enabled them to diversify their income flows and so to lessen their reliance on government subsidy funds.

The governance systems in these institutions were a mix of the collegial and the authoritarian. In the general management of the institution, they were collegial in levels down to those of full professor. The professoriate, the principal and the registrar, and his/her senior staff constituted a collegium of the traditional English kind. This collegium in effect ran the institution, particularly as far as its academic and political affairs were concerned. But below this level, the institutions tended to be as authoritarian as the historically white Afrikaans-medium universities. Junior staff and students had few, if any, rights as far as the management of the institution was concerned.

The four institutions shared another important governance feature with the six historically white Afrikaans-medium universities. During these years they had the mid-level management capacity necessary for controlling the institution and implementing change: tight administrative and financial systems, and sufficient numbers of posts in the tiers of management below the principal and vice-principals which, most importantly, they were able to fill with competent and efficient staff.

The intellectual agendas of the four historically white English-medium universities were set by their perception that they were international institutions engaged in the same kinds of knowledge production as universities in, for example, Britain or the USA. This knowledge was not limited to instrumental knowledge. The four universities believed that knowledge was a good in itself and hence that the pursuit of knowledge for its own sake was a major responsibility for any university. Nevertheless, all four played major roles in educating students for the professions. They were thus instrumentalists in the narrow sense of producing graduates who could move readily into a profession.

Because they believed both that 'blue-skies' research was fundamental to the nature of a university and that they had to distance themselves from the apartheid status quo, very little of the research undertaken by these institutions had direct links with government. None of the four permitted their academic staff members to become involved in any kind of policy work for the government and government agencies. Specific bans were put in place forbidding staff to become involved in any contract work for defence-related industries, because of the significant role these played in apartheid conflict and oppression.

The four historically white English-medium universities faced the transition in 1994 with a great deal of confidence. They saw the demise of the apartheid government as a victory for the ideals for which they had fought throughout the 1980s. They also believed that the new government would recognise that they were 'national assets' and would therefore permit them, in a spirit of 'business as usual', to continue pursuing their academic teaching and research agendas.

It could be argued that this confidence was misplaced. Mamdani (1998) has commented that the historically white English-medium universities were never major agents for social and political change in South Africa, despite the anti-apartheid stance they had adopted. He maintains that their systems of governance and their intellectual agendas made these four institutions islands of white social privilege during the years of apartheid oppression, and maintains further that they displayed little sense of social accountability to the broader South African community during this period. Jakes Gerwel (1987), former Vice-chancellor of the University of the Western Cape, described the contradictions in this way:

> In spite of our genuine commitment to free scholarly discourse and research every South African university has a dominant ideological orientation which describes the context of its operations. ... This is demonstrably true of both the subsets of historically white Afrikaans-language and English-language universities. The Afrikaans universities have always stood and still firmly stand within the operative context of Afrikaner nationalism. Networking in a complex way into its various correlative institutions ... Equally the English-language universities operate within the context of Anglophile liberalism, primarily linking and responding to its institutional expressions as in the English schools, cultural organisations and importantly big business. The one ideological formation under-represented or not at all represented in a similar way within the South African university community is that of the more radical Left. (p2–3)

3.2. Historically black universities in the RSA

The historically black universities in the Republic of South Africa (RSA) were a heterogeneous grouping which after 1984 consisted of two sub-groups:

- First, a sub-grouping of four universities 'for Africans' controlled by the RSA's Department of Education and Training. These were Medunsa University, the University of the North, Vista University and the University of Zululand.
- Second, a sub-grouping of two universities: one 'for Indians' (the University of Durban-Westville) and one 'for coloureds' (the University of the Western Cape). Both were controlled by houses in the tricameral parliament.

The establishment of these universities was overtly political and instrumental; they were not established because of an academic need for institutions of the kind they became. They were instrumental institutions in the sense of having been set up to train black people who would be useful to the apartheid state, and political in the sense that their existence played a role in the maintenance of the overall apartheid socio-political agenda. Their 'useful graduates' were primarily the black teachers required by the black school systems and the black civil servants required by the racially divided civil service of the RSA.

The apartheid notion that the universities controlled by the Department of Education and Training must be for African students only, was maintained through the 1980s and into the 1990s. Their student enrolment was close to 100% African in 1990 and 98% African in 1993.

The University of the Western Cape and the University of Durban-Westville were different. In their early years they were, like the 'universities for Africans', institutions that supported the basic ideology of the National Party government. By 1990, however, the tight government control of these two universities had begun to slip. During the 1980s, both had rejected their founding apartheid principles with the effect that Durban-Westville (which was supposed to be an Indian 'own affairs' university) had an Indian enrolment of 59% in 1990 and only 53% in 1993, while Western Cape (which was supposed to be a coloured 'own affairs' university) had a coloured enrolment of 68% in 1990 and only 55% in 1993.

Throughout the 1980s the governance systems in these institutions tended to be highly authoritarian. The apartheid government made every effort to ensure that the councils and the executive managers of these institutions supported the basic ideology of the National Party government. In the early years of the 1980s it did this by ensuring that the leadership and most of the academic staff of these universities were white Afrikaners who had been trained at one of the six historically white Afrikaans-medium universities. Later in that decade, black vice-chancellors were appointed in all these institutions, but government control continued to be exercised through the appointment of members of council. The authoritarian structures were retained through mechanisms designed to ensure that the main administrative departments as well as the senate of each institution (i.e. the chief academic body) continued to be dominated by white Afrikaner heads of department.

The intellectual agendas of the RSA's six historically black universities were set by their apartheid origins. In their early years their academic staff members tended to come primarily from the historically white Afrikaans-medium universities which, as was said earlier, functioned with instrumentalist notions of knowledge. These academics therefore accepted readily an academic agenda with a strong training focus and, in particular, a focus which placed little emphasis on the production of new knowledge. As a consequence, few of the academics employed by the historically black universities believed it necessary to introduce research and postgraduate programmes in these universities. The intellectual agenda of the institutions often became no more than that of reproducing material taught in previous years at historically white Afrikaans-medium universities.

The turmoil of the late 1980s and early 1990s overtook even this limited intellectual agenda. The historically black universities in the RSA became sites of struggle against the apartheid regime. Political agendas came to the fore and many months of teaching and learning were lost at these institutions as a result of students boycotting classes and authorities responding by closing institutions.

This same turmoil affected the authoritarian governance structures of these universities. New structures such as transformation forums were introduced in the early 1990s which gave substantial political powers to students and to administrative and service staff. These new powers dislodged the old governance structures and their associated administrative systems, but the levels of contestation in these institutions were so high that no new governance models and no new administrative systems were put in place. By 1994 many experienced managers and administrators had left these institutions, a development which contributed to continued battles around governance in subsequent years.

3.3. Historically black universities in the TBVC countries

A further grouping of four historically black universities was linked to the 'independent republics' of the Transkei, Bophuthatswana, Venda and Ciskei (the TBVC countries): the University of Transkei, North West University, the University of Venda and the University of Fort Hare. Because each of these 'republics' had been established in a 'homeland for Africans' their universities enrolled mostly African students, many of whom came from the urban areas of the RSA, i.e. 'white South Africa'. In 1990, their combined enrolment was 14.000 and in 1993 it was about 20.000.

The governments of these 'republics' treated the universities as an extension of the civil service and so held them under tight control at all times. The universities were regarded by these governments primarily as the training grounds for the civil servants and school teachers whom they required. They were, as a consequence, as explicitly authoritarian and instrumental as the historically black universities in the RSA.

In a background paper written for this book, Habib (2001) describes the context of the University of Transkei (Unitra) as follows:

> This institutional structural location of Unitra as a lower grade bantustan[2] university situated in the capital of the homeland had two significant implications for the institution in the era of apartheid. First, it had a captive student market. Apartheid restricted the educational mobility of students on the basis of racial and tribal ancestry. Moreover, with no other university in the Transkei, the homeland's middle classes, many of whom were located in Umtata, were restricted to Unitra as their only avenue to higher education. This meant that a significant proportion of Unitra students had the financial resources and were academically relatively well prepared for tertiary education. Second, as a bantustan university, Unitra was not a financially autonomous institution. In fact, it was treated as any other department within the homeland civil service, and had its finances taken care of by whichever regime was in power in the Transkei. In a very real sense, Unitra was simply another line item in the budget of the Transkei's Department of Finance. A culture of financial accountability and modern systems of financial control were thus almost non-existent in the institution even as late as the 1990s. (p9)

The turmoil of the early 1990s affected these institutions as seriously as the RSA's historically black universities. They became sites of struggle against their governments which were viewed as being no more than pawns of the apartheid regime. As was the case with the other historically black universities, major challenges were launched against the authoritarian, undemocratic ways in which these universities operated. As a consequence, many months of teaching and learning were lost at these institutions as a result of student boycotts of classes, of staff strikes and of governments closing down institutions.

3.4. Historically white technikons

Seven institutions are clustered in this grouping: Cape Technikon, Free State Technikon, Natal Technikon, Port Elizabeth Technikon, Pretoria Technikon, Vaal Triangle Technikon and Technikon Witwatersrand.

These seven institutions could not be divided into Afrikaans and English sub-groupings. All tended to be conservative institutions which, like the Afrikaans-medium universities, aligned themselves with the National Party government and its higher education policies.

In terms of governance structures they were authoritarian institutions. They made little effort to 'play the permit system' and by 1990 a very high proportion of their students, 89%, remained white. By 1993, however, their proportion of white students had dropped to 75%.

The historically white technikons were highly instrumentalist as far as knowledge was concerned. These institutions had no intellectual agenda other than that of offering vocational training programmes to young white South Africans. They took themselves to be training the future 'middle managers' and 'technologists' for business and industry. They undertook little research and offered little by way of postgraduate training.

3.5. Historically black technikons in the RSA and TBVC

These institutions fell into groupings consistent with those of the historically black universities:

- Two technikons were controlled by the national Department of Education and Training: Mangosuthu Technikon and Technikon Northern Transvaal. They were small, conservative institutions which had, in 1990, a 100% African student enrolment which totalled about 4.000. By 1993 their combined enrolment had increased to 8.000 students.
- Three technikons had been established in the TBVC countries towards the end of the 1980s: Border Technikon, Eastern Cape Technikon and North West Technikon. They had a combined, 100% African student enrolment of less than 2.000 by 1990 and of 3.500 by 1993.
- Two technikons were controlled by departments in the tricameral parliament, but before 1990, as was also the case with the universities controlled by these departments, they had rejected their founding apartheid principles: ML Sultan

Technikon (which was supposed to be an Indian 'own affairs' technikon) had an Indian enrolment of 73% in 1990 and 63% in 1993, and Peninsula Technikon (which was supposed to be a coloured 'own affairs' technikon) had a coloured enrolment of 73% in 1990 and only 58% in 1993.

The intellectual agendas of these groupings of historically black technikons was similar to those of the historically white technikons. They took their primary function to be that of offering vocational training programmes to young black South Africans. They undertook no research and offered little by way of postgraduate training.

3.6. Dedicated distance education institutions

During the 1980s South Africa had two dedicated distance education institutions, one of which was described as a university (the University of South Africa, also known as Unisa) and one as a technikon (Technikon South Africa, also known as TSA). Both were controlled during the 1980s by the House of Assembly in the tricameral parliament, and so were in effect historically white institutions. However, since their students studied entirely off-campus, these institutions were not affected by the permit system and could enrol any black applicant who qualified for admission to one of their programmes.

Both institutions were governed during the period up to 1994 by councils and executives that were supportive of the apartheid government. Consequently, the University of South Africa was more akin to historically white Afrikaans-medium than historically white English-medium universities. When conflicts arose within the university system, it tended to support the Afrikaans rather than the English universities and so became the seventh member of this Afrikaans bloc. Its intellectual agenda was also typical of that of an historically white Afrikaans-medium university. It had a very large, well-qualified academic staff complement, but engaged in little or no research and maintained few international linkages.

Technikon South Africa was typical of an historically white technikon in terms of the extent of its support for the apartheid government and in the composition of its governing council and executive. A major part of its effort went into offering vocational training and upgrading programmes for the civil service. This technikon had, for example, responsibility for police training in South Africa.

4. OVERVIEW OF THE PUBLIC
INSTITUTIONAL LANDSCAPE PRE-1994

Table 2 offers an overview of the state of the South African higher educational landscape in 1994, which was the year in which the African National Congress came to power through the government of national unity. It also places institutions into the categories which are used in many of the discussions which follow in the book.

Table 2. Classification of public universities and technikons by racial origin and by historical advantage/disadvantage: 1994

Categories	Institutions included	Key characteristics up to 1994	Historically advantaged/ disadvantaged
(1) Historically black universities: RSA	University of Durban-Westville, Medunsa University, University of the North, Vista University, University of the Western Cape, University of Zululand	• Top management originally supportive of apartheid government • Originally authoritarian institutions, which became sites of anti-apartheid struggle during the course of the 1980s • Intellectual agenda determined by instrumentalist notion of knowledge and function being that of training 'useful black graduates'.	Historically disadvantaged
(2) Historically black universities: TBVC	University of Fort Hare, North West University, University of Transkei, Venda University	• Perceived in 1980s as extensions of civil service of 'independent republics' • Authoritarian institutions which became sites of anti-apartheid struggle at the beginning of the 1990s • Intellectual agenda determined by instrumentalist notion of knowledge and function being that of training 'useful graduates' for 'independent republics'.	Historically disadvantaged
(3) Historically black technikons: RSA	ML Sultan Technikon, Mangosuthu Technikon, Technikon Northern Transvaal, Peninsula Technikon	• Top management originally supportive of apartheid government • Authoritarian institutions, which became sites of anti-apartheid struggle in the early 1990s • Intellectual agendas determined by instrumentalist commitment to vocational training	Historically disadvantaged

Table 2. *(cont.)*

Categories	Institutions included	Key characteristics up to 1994	Historically advantaged/disadvantaged
(4) Historically black technikons: TBVC	Border Technikon, Eastern Cape Technikon, North West Technikon	• Perceived as extensions of civil service of 'independent republics' • Small institutions with primary focus on vocational training	Historically disadvantaged
(5) Historically white (Afrikaans) universities: RSA	University of the Orange Free State, University of Port Elizabeth, University of Pretoria, Potchefstroom University, Rand Afrikaans University, University of Stellenbosch	• Authoritarian institutions which supported the apartheid government • Good management and administrative systems in place • Intellectual agenda affected by instrumentalist commitments and by the severing of contacts with international academics during the academic boycott in the 1980s.	Historically advantaged
(6) Historically white (English) universities: RSA	University of Cape Town, University of Natal, Rhodes University, University of the Witwatersrand	• Did not support apartheid government • Collegial institutions at top levels of senate and heads of academic departments, but authoritarian at lower levels • Good management and administrative systems in place • Intellectual agendas set by commitments to knowledge as a good in itself, and strong international disciplinary teaching and research links.	Historically advantaged

Table 2. (cont.)

Categories	Institutions included	Key characteristics up to 1994	Historically advantaged/ disadvantaged
(6) Historically white technikons: RSA	Cape Technikon, Free State Technikon, Natal Technikon, Port Elizabeth Technikon, Pretoria Technikon, Vaal Triangle Technikon, Technikon Witwatersrand	• Authoritarian institutions which supported the apartheid government • Intellectual agendas determined by instrumentalist commitments to vocational training.	Historically advantaged
(7) Distance education universities and technikons	University of South Africa (Unisa), Technikon South Africa (TSA)	• Authoritarian institutions which supported the apartheid government • Unisa: instrumentalist intellectual agenda with little outward or international focus on teaching and research • TSA: primary focus on vocational education.	Historically advantaged

5. CONCLUSION

Under apartheid, higher education in South Africa was skewed in ways designed to entrench the power and privilege of the ruling white minority. Higher education institutions established in the early part of the century (Fort Hare, UCT, Wits) were incorporated into a system which was subsequently shaped, enlarged and fragmented with a view to serving the goals and strategies of successive apartheid governments.

By 1994, the landscape of 36 higher education institutions included ten historically disadvantaged universities and seven historically disadvantaged technikons designated for the use of black (African, coloured and Indian) South Africans, while ten historically advantaged universities and seven historically advantaged technikons were designated for the exclusive development of white South Africans. Two distance institutions catered for all races.

By 1994 there had been considerable resistance to the apartheid regime in the historically black and in some of the historically white institutions and, as was demonstrated in this chapter, the racial profile of student enrolments in some of the institutions had departed considerably from apartheid's intentions.

It was in this context that the new higher education policies of South Africa's first and second democratic governments sought to reshape the system into one that met the goals of equity, democratisation, responsiveness and efficiency. Working off the landscape described in this chapter, the chapters in Section 2 capture the developments since 1990 in respect of funding, students, staff, leadership, curriculum and research.

NOTES

[1] The notion of 'essential' difference informed not only the National Party's approach to knowledge, but also to race. This thinking underpinned its whole approach to apartheid with the assumption that things could be 'separate but equal'.

[2] The word 'bantustan' was used by opponents of the apartheid government to refer to the supposedly independent republics of Transkei, Bophuthatswana, Venda and Ciskei. In a sense it was a term of derision which had its origins in the tendency of the apartheid government to use the word 'bantu' as a generic term to refer to Africans. Its use by the apartheid government made 'bantu' an ideologically tainted term. So the use of the term 'bantustan' to refer to a TBVC 'state' would indicate that the speaker regards it as little more than a creature of the apartheid government.

REFERENCES

Gerwel, J. (1987). Inaugural address given by Professor Jakes Gerwel at his installation on 5 June 1987 as sixth Vice-Chancellor and Rector of the University of the Western Cape.

Habib, A. (2001). Structural Disadvantage, Leadership Ineptitude and Stakeholder Complicity: A study of the Institutional Crisis of the University of the Transkei. Commissioned paper. www.chet.org.za/papers.asp.

Jansen, J.D. (2001). Why Tukkies Cannot Develop Intellectuals (and what to do about it). Innovation Lecture Series, 11 May, Pretoria.

Mamdani, M. (1998). Is African Studies to be Turned into a New Home for Bantu Education at UCT? Centre for African Studies, University of Cape Town.

CHAPTER 3

NICO CLOETE

POLICY EXPECTATIONS

Higher education in South Africa in the post-1994 period is woven into the bargain struck by President De Klerk and prisoner Mandela – both in terms of the baggage it carried and the promises it offered. The 'miracle' transition put enormous pressure on supporters of the new government, in all sectors, not to fail Mandela, arguably the last saint of the 20th century.

The post-1994 period saw unprecedented changes in South African higher education. The first two years were dominated by a massive, participatory drive towards policy formulation that culminated in a report from the National Commission on Higher Education (NCHE) in 1996. The next phase converted the Commission's report into a White Paper (Department of Education, 1997) and a new Higher Education Act, promulgated in 1997. During 1997 the newly constituted higher education division within the new unified Department of Education started the implementation process. In 2000 Kader Asmal, the second education minister to be appointed under the democratic dispensation, started a process of reassessing whether the system was putting South Africa 'on the road to the 21st century'.[1] While the phase from 1994 to 1999 was mainly about putting a new policy and legislative framework in place, the post-1999 phase was declared to be a period of implementation (Department of Education, 2000).

This chapter describes some of the assumptions, the policy processes and the main recommendations of the government-driven approach to transformation.

1. THE APPROACH TO TRANSFORMATION[2]

When the new government came to power in 1994 on the basis of an 'implicit bargain' (Gelb, 2001) reached between the National Party and the liberation movement led by the African National Congress (ANC), there was agreement in the government of national unity that higher education was in need of transformation.

The concept of 'transformation' was a compromise between 'revolution' and 'reform' – 'revolution' being a victory that only the most ardent liberation movement supporters claimed for 1994, and 'reform' being the outcome which many people suspected was most likely to occur, but dared not admit in public. Apartheid had been driven through one of the most formidable social engineering exercises ever undertaken by a government anywhere in the world, and the common sense view amongst activists and academics was that the new government would have to undo what the previous government had done.

N. Cloete et al. (eds.), Transformation in Higher Education, 53-65.
© 2007 Springer.

The only question was how direct state steering would be. A paper written in 1994 by three participants in the NCHE process (published in 1996), argued that all over the world new relations between the state and civil society were emerging which rendered old conceptions of the dichotomy between self- regulation and state intervention obsolete (Moja, Muller & Cloete, 1996). The authors noted the emergence, worldwide, of more co-operative, interactive and functionally interdependent forms of state/civil society regulation. In their discussion on state/higher education relationships, they introduced three ideal types of state regulation:

- *Model one: State control.* This is premised on effective and systematic state administration of higher education and training, executed by a professional and competent civil service – the 'continental model' characteristic of Western Europe in the 20th century.
- *Model two: State supervision.* This model is founded on less centrist forms of control in higher education and sees the locus of power shifting from 'centralised control' to 'steering'. In this model, governments provide the broad regulatory framework within which the administrations of higher education institutions are expected to produce the results which governments desire. It is a 'leaner' state because fewer civil servants are required in the central state apparatuses. It is also 'smarter' because state action is less focussed on actual administration and concentrates more on defining the parameters of 'steering'.
- *Model three: State interference.* This is based on control in higher education that is neither systematic (model one) nor 'regulation through steering' (model two), but which involves arbitrary forms of crisis intervention. These interventions are 'either sporadic, or they become an attempt to control through a fairly narrow and rather crude set of measures aimed at establishing quiescence' (Moja, Muller & Cloete, 1996). Key characteristics here would include a weak education ministry and education department, and a poorly trained bureaucracy unable to implement higher education policy. Also characteristic, unlike the first model cited above, is the conflation of the political (managing institutional crises) with the professional (an independent civil service, freed from political interference, able to implement policy). The bureaucracy is politicised to the detriment of effective administration. The authors refer here to the experiences of higher education and training in certain post-independent African countries in the 1980s and 1990s (Moja, Muller & Cloete, 1996).

According to Kraak (2001) it is clear that the state supervision model was highly influential within the National Commission for Higher Education and underpinned the 1997 White Paper. The Commission adopted the concept of 'co-operative governance' between the state and civil society, where the two players clearly 'find themselves in a relationship of functional interdependence'. A relationship of this kind 'signals the necessity of a shift away from the traditional opposition between state and civil society to negotiated co-operation arrangements' (NCHE, 1996:57–60). In developing a co-operative governance relationship, however, the Commission warned that the 'state' must occupy the leadership role in this partnership:

A shift in the overall direction of society requires leadership by the government, the only actor with powers of political co-ordination in society. This means there is always a possible tension between central government trying to assert authority directly to implement change, and the more indirect regulation and steering that is the trademark of co-operative governance. ... Having said that, it should at the same time be emphasised that the shift to co-operative governance arrangements is not unique to South Africa. It is an international trend that the relationship between government and civil society is being redefined. Government is increasingly becoming a partner, albeit a very powerful one, which, through regulation arrangements, involves a range of other institutions, bodies and agencies in governing. This shift, from government from the centre to government becoming a powerful partner in a multitude of governing arrangements, is part of a movement from government to governance, a process of redefining and reconfiguring the state. (NCHE, 1996:57–60)

Co-operative governance has implications for relations between the state and higher education institutions. It seeks to mediate the apparent opposition between state intervention and institutional autonomy. The directive role of the state is reconceived as a steering and co-ordinating role. Institutional autonomy is to be exercised within the limits of accountability. A co-operative relationship between the state and higher education institutions should reconcile the self-regulation of institutions with the decision-making of central authorities. The viability of such a reconciliation depends to a significant degree upon the success of a proposed intermediary body with delegated powers, and of proposed structures for consultation and negotiation. The state uses financial incentives and other steering mechanisms as opposed to commandist measures of control and top-down prescriptions (Kraak, 2001).

Co-operation also has implications for relations between higher education and the organs of civil society. It requires the establishment of new linkages and partnerships between higher education institutions and commercial enterprises, parastatals, research bodies and non-governmental organisations, nationally as well as regionally. In the process, local stakeholders acquire a greater interest in participating in the governance of higher education institutions (Kraak, 2001).

The White Paper for higher education transformation (Department of Education, 1997) embraced the notion of co-operative governance at the heart of which was the idea of a single nationally co-ordinated system of higher education that would be achieved through state co-ordination. The government would strategically 'steer' the system via a regulatory framework of financial incentives, reporting and monitoring requirements (particularly with regard to key performance indicators) and a system of programme approval. In line with the constitutional notion of co-operative governance, the central state's role would be to manage the system in co-operation with other role players and not through prescriptive fiat or other interventionist mechanisms. The state would govern through a 'softer' regulatory framework, which sought to 'steer' the system in three important ways:

• *Planning* would be used to encourage institutions to outline a distinctive mission, mix of programmes, enrolment targets and overall institutional plan. The process would involve institutions developing three-year rolling plans, while the government would develop a national plan for higher education.

- *Financial incentives* would encourage institutions to reorientate provision to address national, regional and local education and training needs and priorities.
- *Reporting requirements* would be developed, using performance indicators dedicated to measure, in the spirit of greater institutional accountability, the extent to which the institutional plan and national priorities were being met. In so doing, these performance indicators would be highly influential in shaping the allocation of the next cycle of financial awards.

Despite the model of co-operative governance which assumes a certain 'dialogical' notion of change, the assumption in the policy documents was quite uni-directional: from centre to periphery, or from top to bottom.

2. POLICY DEVELOPMENT

2.1. From protest to policy proposals

In the political turmoil following the 1948 assumption of power by the apartheid regime and its introduction of separate systems of education, higher education experienced sporadic disruptions and protests. Some 40 years later, from the middle of the 1980s to 1993, higher education protests and disturbances were virtually a weekly occurrence as campuses became 'sites of struggle' for the various anti-apartheid organisations. In certain cases the resistance was spontaneous, but mostly it was organised by one of the many anti-apartheid education organisations active on the campuses. The most prominent ones were the National Education Co-ordinating Committee (NECC), the Union of Democratic University Staff Associations (Udusa), and the National Union of Health and Allied workers (Nehawu). Most of the opposition was initiated by the national student organisations such as the National Union of South African Students (Nusas – the second oldest student body in the world), the South African Student Organisation (Saso), the South African National Student Congress (Sansco) and the South African Students Congress (Sasco).

The manifestation of campus protests was not uniform across the system. The Afrikaans-medium institutions, with their student bodies being almost exclusively white, experienced no serious disruptions while the University of Cape Town experienced only one violent protest and the institution was never closed. At the University of Witwatersrand in Johannesburg, with many black students living close by, in Soweto, students and a minority of staff regularly fought battles with the police; one academic, Professor David Webster, was assassinated off-campus by the security police. A number of academics and large numbers of students from the historically white English-medium institutions were detained without trial or charged, mainly under the Suppression of Communism Act.

The real sites of struggle, however, were the historically black universities. At many of these institutions police and even the army fought pitched battles with students and some staff. Hardly a year went by without at least a few of these institutions being closed for months at a time. Thousands of students never completed their studies, either dropping out because study conditions were impossible, or going into political exile, or joining the underground within South Africa. Although no students were killed on campus, thousands still bear the physical and emotional scars of beatings and teargassing, and a number paid the ultimate penalty for political struggles that started on the campuses. Steve Biko and Onkgopotse Tiro (Nkondo, 1976) are perhaps the best known amongst those for whom a university education led to sacrificing their lives for their beliefs. Whilst the black universities had been established mainly to provide separate training for black teachers and homeland bureaucrats (Habib, 2001), these institutions became major sites for opposition to the government. This was perhaps the first major instance in South Africa of a higher education policy having serious unintended consequences.

Following the 1994 election, President Mandela promulgated the National Commission on Higher Education to 'preserve what is valuable and to address what is defective and requires transformation' (1996:1). The appointment of a commission was not unexpected; it was a continuation of a policy formulation process that started in the late 1980s. During 1989 progressive academics who were involved in critiques of apartheid education and in endless street demonstrations, were informed by leaders of the United Democratic Front (UDF) – the internal mass movement – and the National Education Co-ordinating Committee that secret talks between the National Party and the ANC leadership had started. For intellectuals this meant a shift from critique to policy deliberation, while continuing to march against apartheid in the streets. The shift from a role in the struggle as critics of apartheid education to developing policy for the new government, meaning a change from opposition to governing, has been described in number of publications (Muller & Cloete, 1987). (For a much more detailed history of higher education policy development, see www.chet.org.za/papers.asp.)

The first major policy document that formed the basis for the development of much higher education policy during the 1990s was the Post-Secondary Education report of the National Education Policy Investigation (Nepi, 1992). This 'peoples education' project put together education activists and trainee policy experts in a participatory, consultative and argumentative process. The project understood that this was just the first stab at policy-making and therefore focussed more on frameworks and options than actual policy proposals. (For a review of the National Education Policy Investigation see Muller, 2000.)

Following the Nepi exercise, the Union of Democratic University Staff Associations (Udusa) established a policy forum to enable the organisation and its member institutions to participate in the debates about restructuring higher education. This group produced a document that was widely discussed in higher education institutions and was often called the 'red book' – both a reference to the colour of the cover and to what many saw as its leftist leanings. It was based on five principles: non-racialism, non-sexism, democracy, redress and a unitary system. The new framework for higher education embodied all these in 'four pillars' which are still the central frames for higher education policy: equity, democracy, effectiveness and development (Udusa, 1994).

Referring to the Nepi Report and the work of the late Harold Wolpe, the Udusa document argued that policy formulation had to locate itself within sets of tensions or contradictions, particularly between equity and development. For example, it argued that a higher education system could be established that would be more democratic than the past system (through representative government and councils) and more equitable with large numbers of black students in cheap courses (biblical studies and languages). Because increases in enrolments, however, could lead to massive increases in student-to-staff ratios, such a system could lead to a drastic reduction in quality and might contribute little to economic development. Another strategy would be to maintain high entry requirements and to put disproportionate amounts of resources into science, engineering and other forms of technology. This might increase effectiveness and directly contribute to development, but would not satisfy the demands of the majority for greater access (equity) and would be difficult for a democratic government to defend.

In anticipation of winning the first democratic elections in April 1994, the ANC's education department-in-waiting, located at the newly-established Centre for Education Policy Development (CEPD), produced a Policy Framework for Education and Training (ANC 1994). As the product of a political movement about to accede to power, the ANC education policy framework promised all that the pre-election policy deliberations recommended, but contained no warnings about the possible trade-offs between equity and development, or between individual and institutional redress, that might be required. Chapters 12 and 13 deal extensively with how this tension played itself out.

The pre-election period of policy formulation could be characterised as having a strong emphasis on redress for individuals and for the historically disadvantaged institutions. The debate slowly shifted from institutional equality (Nepi) to 'reducing institutional differences in status', but with the assurance that high quality education would be offered by all institutions (ANC). Another feature of this pre-governance period was that the emphasis on redress was not accompanied by concrete implementation strategies.

2.1.1. National commission on higher education

The National Commission on Higher Education started operating in January 1995 and submitted its report to the Minister in September 1996. The Commission consisted of 13 members (nine blacks, four women), comprising a fair balance between people with policy expertise (mostly the policy trainees from Nepi who by now had four years of experience) and people representing certain powerful constituencies, such as university and technikon principals, labour and business. At this stage, operating under a government of 'national unity', the Commission's membership also included people who had served in senior positions in the previous government. The Commission mobilised more than a hundred local and international academics and policy experts who made contributions in five working groups. This largely voluntary group produced more than a hundred papers and reports in less than a year.

From the outset the NCHE decided that part of its role must be to break out of the academic isolation of the apartheid years. The commissioners visited several industrialised and developing countries to draw on their experiences in reforming the South African system and to re-establish contact with the international higher education community. The countries consulted included ten in Europe, seven in Africa, two in

Latin America, as well as the USA, India, Malaysia, Japan and Australia. Policy experts from some of the world's best-known agencies such the Centre for Higher Policy Studies (CHEPS, Netherlands), Commonwealth Higher Education Management Services (CHEMS, UK), the American Council on Education (ACE, Washington) and the World Bank were invited to contribute to working groups. The five working groups also held seminars to which prominent academics from developed and developing countries were invited. There was great interest in the transformation of South African higher education and there was a certain amount of competition amongst funders and exchange agencies to sponsor policy work.

The central proposal of the NCHE was that South African higher education should be massified. Massification was the first policy proposal that attempted to resolve the equity-development tension since increased participation was supposed to provide greater opportunity for access (equity) while also producing more high-level skills that were necessary for economic growth. This was not a simple-minded 'more for all' proposal because the NCHE was quite aware that massification is a driver for both differentiation and efficiency. There is no 'equal' massified system anywhere in the world since massified systems are by definition differentiated systems. For example, as the US, UK and Australian systems massified, differentiation increased dramatically.

Efficiency would be driving expansion of the system without increasing funding levels, thus doing more with the same. The NCHE acknowledged that the government could not increase the proportion of its education budget to higher education, and that handling more students would have to occur through innovative delivery systems and co-operation in course delivery. To ensure that increased numbers of students would not lead to a serious decline in standards, the establishment of a national Higher Education Quality Committee was proposed. Massification was to be the key policy and implementation driver.

The second and third pillars of the NCHE report, namely increased responsiveness and co-operation, were intended to deal mainly with development needs. Greater responsiveness would require new forms of management and assessment of knowledge production, dissemination and curricula. It was hoped that this would result in a more dynamic interaction between higher education and society, which in turn would promote development and accountability. The third pillar, increased co-operation, was intended to improve co-operation amongst a broad range of constituencies, leading to greater participation and accountability.

Apart from a small group of black intellectuals who complained that the report did not sufficiently locate higher education within an African context, the proposals of the NCHE were received with great acclaim. In an interview recently conducted, Trevor Coombe, formerly education department Deputy-Director General, had this to say (2001:5):

> The [NCHE] Report was a superb piece of work. What it did for the country was ensure, through its members and its chairperson, that it delivered something of high authority, of unquestionable authority, which had been painstakingly negotiated, not just consulted upon, and which would have international recognition. International recognition was consciously worked on right up to the last minute. In all of those respects, I think the National Commission Report is an ornament to our post 1994 dispensation.

> But the Commission was an extremely difficult thing for the Department to manage, right
> from the beginning. For reasons that were never very clear to the leadership of the
> Department, it used its autonomous status as a National Commission to take a very
> independent, bureaucratic organisational course of its own.

As will be shown later, implementation did become a major problem and the key proposal of the NCHE, namely a massified system, was not accepted. The 'independence' of the Commission, and the tensions alluded to by Coombe, could be one of the reasons why the capacity mobilised by the Commission was not fully utilised by the new higher education branch.

2.2. From policy to implementation

After another period of consultation the Department of Education, drawing heavily on the NCHE report, published the new higher education policy in the form of Education White Paper 3: A Programme for the Transformation of Higher Education (Department of Education, 1997). The White Paper started by stating that despite acknowledged achievements and strengths, the present system of higher education was limited in its ability to meet the moral, political, social and economic demands of the new South Africa. It was characterised by the following deficiencies:

- An inequitable distribution of access and opportunity for students and staff along lines of race, gender, class and geography. In particular, there was a shortage of highly trained graduates in fields such as science, engineering, technology and commerce (largely as a result of discriminatory practices that limited the access of black and women students), which had been detrimental to social and economic development.
- While parts of the South African higher education system could claim academic achievement of international renown, too many parts of the system observed teaching and research policies which favoured academic insularity and closed-system disciplinary programmes.
- The governance of higher education at a system-level was characterised by fragmentation, inefficiency and ineffectiveness, with too little co-ordination, few common goals and negligible systemic planning. At the institutional level, democratic participation and the effective representation of staff and students in governance structures was still contested on many campuses (pp4–5).

The new policy of the government was, and continues to be, underpinned by the following principles: equity and redress; democratisation, effectiveness and efficiency; development; quality; academic freedom; institutional autonomy and public accountability (pp8–10). According to the White Paper:

> The transformation of the higher education system and its institutions requires:
>
> - Increased and broadened participation. Successful policy must overcome an historically
>   determined pattern of fragmentation, inequality and inefficiency. It must increase access

for black, women, disabled and mature students, and generate new curricula and flexible models of learning and teaching, including modes of delivery, to accommodate a larger and more diverse student population.

- Responsiveness to societal interests and needs. Successful policy must restructure the higher education system and its institutions to meet the needs of an increasingly technologically-oriented economy. It must also deliver the requisite research, the highly trained people and the knowledge to equip a developing society with the capacity to address national needs and to participate in a rapidly changing and competitive global context.
- Co-operation and partnerships in governance. Successful policy must reconceptualise the relationship between higher education and the state, civil society, and stakeholders, and among institutions. It must also create an enabling institutional environment and culture that is sensitive to and affirms diversity, promotes reconciliation and respect for human life, protects the dignity of individuals from racial and sexual harassment, and rejects all other forms of violent behaviour. (p7)

In order to give effect to the above, the government promised to put into place measures that would:

- Provide for expanded access (with a focus on equity and redress) through the planned expansion of the system over the next decade (but not massification).
- Develop a single co-ordinated system of higher education encompassing universities, technikons, colleges and private providers.
- Incorporate the colleges of education, nursing and agriculture into universities and technikons, and develop a new further education sector spanning general, further and higher education.
- Expand the role of distance education and high quality 'resource-based' learning.
- Institute a system of rolling three-year institutional plans and develop a national higher education plan.
- Develop a new goal-orientated performance related funding system that combines block grants with earmarked funds.
- Include higher education programmes in the National Qualifications Framework (NQF), and in a new quality assurance system to be developed within the broad ambit of the new South African Qualifications Authority (SAQA).
- Expand the national student loan scheme (Tertiary Education Fund of South Africa) and funding for programmes to bridge the gap between further and higher education.
- Promote the importance of research within higher education and its contribution to a National System of Innovation.
- Establish programmes for capacity development. (White Paper 3, 1997)

In not accepting massification as a driver both for redress and efficiency (having to do more with the same), the White Paper implied that efficiency gains would have to be achieved through the implementation of a number of policy instruments such as a planning dialogue with institutions, a new funding formula, a reliable information system and a national plan that would provide benchmarks for planning and funding. In many respects, the White Paper was similar to the NCHE report because it was also a policy framework and did not go beyond the NCHE by being more specific about policy instruments and the trade-offs that would be necessary. Chapter 13 explores further the problems which arise with this type of policy formulation.

The ambitious implementation agenda outlined in the White Paper would have been daunting for a well-established education department in a first world country. For a department still in the process of being established, it was always going to be many steps too far. Some of the implementation problems that occurred during the post-1994 period are discussed in chapters 4 to 11.

2.3. New implementation priorities?

It was in the context of a perceived lack of implementation that the education minister appointed after the second democratic election in 1999, asked the Council on Higher Education (1998/99) to review the institutional landscape of higher education as a matter of urgency. 'This landscape was largely dictated by the geo-political imagination of apartheid planners. As our policy documents make clear, it is vital that the mission and location of higher education institutions be re-examined with reference to both the strategic plan for the sector, and the educational needs of local communities and the nation at large in the 21st century.' (p5)

In June 2000, almost exactly three years after the publication of the White Paper and four years after the government announced its new macro-economic policy (Gear, 1996), the Council on Higher Education (CHE), established in May 1998, produced a report called 'Towards a New Higher Education Landscape'. According to the CHE (2000), the key perceived problems in the system were the continued and increasing fragmentation of the system, the geographic location of some institutions, major inefficiencies related to throughput and graduation rates, skewed patterns of student distribution between science, commerce, the humanities and education, low research outputs, and poor equity with regard to academic and administrative staff.

From this analysis, the CHE (2000) identified three key challenges:

- Effectiveness, relating mainly to the relevance of higher education to the labour market.
- Efficiency, concerned mainly with quality and throughputs.
- Equity, concerned mainly with setting equity targets for the distribution of students and staff by race, gender and social class in different fields of learning and teaching.

For the first time in a post-1994 South African national policy document, effectiveness and efficiency were listed before equity. The remedies that the CHE prescribed were to establish a differentiated system with hard boundaries between three types of institutions:

- Bedrock institutions whose sole mission would be to provide undergraduate programmes of high quality to the majority of learners.
- Extensive masters and selective doctoral institutions whose main orientation would be to provide quality undergraduate programmes, an extensive range of masters

level programmes, a limited number of doctoral programmes, and selected areas of research.
- Comprehensive postgraduate and research institutions which would offer undergraduate programmes, comprehensive course-work doctoral programmes and extensive research across a broad range of areas.

In addition, the CHE (2000) recommended, without offering any selection criteria, a list of 'examples' of institutions that should be considered for 'combination' (more commonly understood as merger) with other institutions.

Whilst the NCHE report and the White Paper had been received by the higher education community with a fair degree of consensus, at least in relation to their principles if not all the details, the CHE proposals caused a heated debate and were opposed not only by the university principals (Kotecha, 2000), but by the government.

In February 2001, the Ministry of Education published a National Plan for Higher Education which, in the words of the Minister 'outlines the framework and mechanisms for implementing and realising the policy goals of the White Paper' (Foreword). The plan was also a response to, and had been prompted by, the report of the CHE (2000).

The Minister of Education rejected the three-level differentiation between institutions because 'the danger with structural differentiation is that it introduces an element of rigidity, which will preclude institutions from building on their strengths and responding to social and economic needs, including labour market needs, in a rapidly changing regional, national and global context.' (Department of Education, 2001:54)

The NPHE quite unambiguously started by saying that the 'main focus over the next five years will therefore be on improving the efficiency of the higher education system through increasing graduate outputs.' (p1) The central tenets of the plan were to use the interaction between institutional and national planning to make the system more efficient and effective. It proposed, through a National Working Group, a 'more rational arrangement for the consolidation of higher education provision through reducing, where appropriate, the number of institutions, but not the number of delivery sites.' (p3) The intention was thus to transform the system through a combination of steering (using planning and funding) and legislative intervention in identified cases. Amendments to the Higher Education Act (1997) were subsequently made in 1999 and 2000 (Olivier, 2001).

The NPHE acknowledged major policy implementation shortfalls by using the term 'implementation vacuum'. The NPHE stated that 'it is arguable whether a more robust and timely implementation of key policy instruments would have been possible, given the capacity constraints at both the national and institutional levels. However, it is clear that the *implementation vacuum* (my emphasis) has given rise to a number of significant developments, including unintended and unanticipated consequences which, if left unchecked, threaten the development of a single, national, co-ordinated, but diverse higher education system.' (p8) As Chapter 1 intimates and later chapters in this volume will show, the manifestation of unanticipated consequences has to be understood as arising from a much more complex set of factors than a lack of capacity or an implementation vacuum.

3. CONCLUSION

The post-1994 period can be summarised as having started with a huge, participatory policy effort within a context of optimism for both the expansion of the system and redress for past inequities. This was followed by an 'implementation vacuum' in relation to the new policies, a shift in emphasis after 1997 to efficiency, and finally a reassessment of priorities and a more interventionist approach by government in 2001.

Chapter 1 on global reform trends alerts us, in hindsight, to the reality that whilst the South African transformation process invested heavily in a state-driven, linear, overly rationalistic notion of progressive policy formulation, policy implementation and change, other countries had not found this form of change very successful. The NCHE and the White Paper were silent on the role of institutions and the market as drivers of change, while co-operative governance created unrealistic expectations about direct societal participation. The policy was indeed a basket of 'best practices' culled from different parts of the world, but it did not adequately take into consideration the global pressure for increasing efficiency, nor that the two pillars of transformation (policy and implementation) were inadequately theorised. The remaining chapters in this book show that both these factors had considerable implications for what followed.

While Nelson Mandela's famous walk to freedom resulted in a definable moment of triumph with South Africa's first democratic election in 1994, the new South Africa is a complex mixture of remarkable achievements and unexpected disappointments. Similarly, the progressive road of higher education transformation, based on a grand policy narrative and driven, 'co-operatively', from the centre by the new government, can claim many achievements. However, the path also led to consequences and effects not remotely anticipated in 1994. The rest of the chapters in this book tell the story.

NOTES

1   Education Minister Kader Asmal in the Foreword to the National Plan for Higher Education, 2001.
2   This section draws on a paper written for this project by Kraak (2001).

REFERENCES

African National Congress (ANC) (1994). *A Policy Framework for Education and Training*. Braamfontein: ANC.
Bunting, I. (ed.) (1994). Reconstructing Higher Education in South Africa. Selected Papers. The Udusa Policy Forum.
Cloete, N. & Muller, J. (1998). South African Higher Education Reform: What Comes After Post-colonialism? *European Review*, 6(4), 525–542.
Coombe, T. (2001). Interview. www.chet.org.za/reflections.asp.
Council on Higher Education (2000). *Towards a New Higher Education Landscape: Meeting the Equity, Quality and Social Development Imperatives of South Africa in the 21st Century*. Pretoria: CHE.
Department of Education (1997). Education White Paper 3. A Programme for the Transformation of Higher Education. General Notice 1196 of 1997. Pretoria.

Department of Education (2001). *Education in South Africa. Achievements since 1994.* Pretoria.

Department of Education (2001). *National Plan for Higher Education.* Pretoria.

Department of Education (2001). Implementation plan for Tirisano (2001–2002). www.education.pwv.gov.za/Tirisano_Folder.

Department of Trade and Industry (1996). Growth, Equity and Redistribution: A Macroeconomic Strategy (GEAR). Pretoria. www.gov.za/reports/1996/macroeco.htm.

Habib, A. (2001). Structural Disadvantage, Leadership Ineptitude and Stakeholder Complicity: A Study of the Institutional Crisis of the University of the Transkei. Commissioned paper. www.chet.org.za/papers.asp.

Higher Education Act 101 of 1997. Pretoria: Department of Education.

Kotecha, P. (2000). *Towards a New Higher Education Landscape: Meeting the Equity, Quality and Social Development Imperatives of South Africa in the 21st Century. South African Vice-Chancellors Association's Response to the Council on Higher Education.* Pretoria: SAUVCA.

Kraak, A. (2001). Policy Ambiguity and Slippage: Higher Education Under the New State, 1994–2001. Commissioned paper. www.chet.org.za/papers.asp.

Moja, T., Muller, J. & Cloete, N. (1996). Towards New Forms of Regulation in Higher Education: The Case of South Africa. *Higher Education*, 32, 2.

Muller, J. & Cloete, N. (1987). The White Hands: Academic Social Scientists, Knowledge and Struggle in South Africa. *Social Epistemology*, 1, 141–154.

Muller, J. (2000). *Reclaiming Knowledge: Social Theory, Curriculum and Education Policy.* London: Routledge/Falmer.

Nkondo, G. (1976). *Turfloop Testimony.* Johannesburg: Ravan Press.

Olivier, N. (2001). The Relationship between the State and Higher Education Institutions with Reference to Higher Education Policy Documentation and the Legislative Framework. Commissioned paper. www.chet.org.za/papers.asp.

Udusa Policy Forum (1994). Reconstructing Higher Education in South Africa. Selected Papers. Braamfontein: Udusa.

SECTION 2

THE SOUTH AFRICAN EXPERIENCE

PART 1

FUNDING AND STUDENTS

INTRODUCTION

Higher education is about students – about educating and socialising students, about preparing them for the world of work, and about training students to become critical citizens as well as responsive professionals. Consequently, any government taking its responsibilities with respect to higher education seriously should develop policies and use instruments for creating the right circumstances so that its higher education institutions can achieve their student-related ambitions. Important instruments for a democratic government in this regard are, for example, the law and funding. The law provides a regulatory framework for the day-to-day operations as well as for the longer-term strategies of the higher education institutions. In simple terms government funding is used to provide all higher education institutions with a basic income. This can also be used by government to steer institutions and students in certain directions through the use of incentives.

This section on the South African experience of transforming higher education after 1994 starts with a discussion of the changes with respect to government funding and students. Funding is potentially the most powerful instrument at a government's disposal. It is appropriate, therefore, to start the empirical examination of the dynamics of the South African higher education system by reflecting on the way in which the funding instrument was used in higher education by the political regime before 1994, as well as by the governments in power since 1994.

Obviously the funding of higher education is a matter of ongoing concern for any government. The concern can be understood within a framework of five overarching themes (Johnstone, 1998) which manifest themselves in higher education institutions:

- The funding consequences of the expansion and diversification of higher education with respect to enrolments, participation rates, and number and types of institutions.
- Fiscal pressure as measured in low and declining per-student public expenditures and as seen in the overcrowding of higher education facilities, in low-paid faculty, lack of innovation in and maintenance of the academic infrastructure (including libraries), and deteriorating physical plant.
- The rise of market orientations and solutions, and the search for non-governmental income.
- The demand for greater accountability of the institutions and the academic staff by students, employers, and those who pay the costs of higher education (especially taxpayers).

N. Cloete et al. (eds.), Transformation in Higher Education, 69-71.
© 2007 *Springer.*

- The demand for greater quality and efficiency, implying demands for more rigour, greater relevance, and better learning.

In the two chapters which follow, these themes are clearly recognisable. Chapter 4 (on funding) and Chapter 5 (on students) show how South Africa has tried to incorporate these global themes into its own national higher education policies.

In order to understand fully how the South African government is using the instrument of funding, a broader analysis is required than can be provided in this book. We lack, for instance, the necessary information on and insight into government fiscal policy. Nonetheless, the funding issues addressed in Chapter 4 reflect core aspects of South African higher education policies. Central here is the question of whether, and if so how, the funding instrument contributed to moving student enrolment patterns towards the equity goals articulated in the education department's 1997 White Paper. Of further interest is the impact of two different political regimes using the same funding instrument when they had clearly different policy goals with regard to student enrolment.

The chapter on students shows that in South Africa's public higher education system, overall greater race and gender equity was achieved in the 1990s. Even though important inequities continue to exist, the improved race and gender balance is a major achievement. The dramatic change in the composition of the student body had far-reaching effects on student life and student culture on the campuses throughout the country. The impact of these changes is not discussed in the chapter, mainly because little valid knowledge is available about them. Nevertheless, some of the interviews conducted during the project (see www.chet.org.za/reflections.asp) refer to the ways in which more equitable and demographically representative student enrolments changed campus life. The interviewees pointed to examples of racial integration especially in sports and cultural activities. Another remarkable feature is that, since 1994, there have been no group-based racial incidents on any of the South African campuses. In this respect South Africa can be argued to have moved beyond other countries, such as the United Kingdom and the USA, where such incidents have recently been reported.

In addition to providing a concise overview of the funding mechanisms and funding allocations applied during the 1990s, the two chapters demonstrate that within a similar government funding environment, marked institutional differences emerged. These differences, which are explained in Section 3 of the book, were the result of a variety of factors – historical development, geographical location, societal and market changes, and institutional strategies. The chapters on funding and students shed some light on the factors which, in some cases, exacerbated differences that were already in the system, and in others allowed innovative institutional responses to emerge.

After going through the two chapters, the reader might wonder where to go from here. How can the instrument of funding be used more effectively, amongst other things, to deal with the remaining inequalities in the system, as well as from the perspective of limited public funds? This basic question generates further questions (Jongbloed, 2000:12–19) such as:

- How much higher education can South Africa afford? How much of its productive capacity should be invested in higher education? How does the level of public resources for higher education compare with the levels available for primary and secondary education? (Salmi, 1991:8) What proportion of South Africa's youth should study some form of higher education? How many universities and other higher education institutions should there be, and what should their target enrolments be?

- How much should be spent per student, per graduate or per unit of new knowledge? What are appropriate faculty salaries, teaching loads, class sizes, equipment and library investments, etc? How can the government make sure that everything possible is done to produce the maximum output with the available resources, i.e. maximum efficiency?

- How much should be paid by public sources, how much by private? How should institutional costs and students' living expenses be shared among parents, students and taxpayers? What is the appropriate balance in the policy instruments to be used to achieve the conflicting goals of access, efficiency and equity?

- How should public sources for higher education be made available to institutions and students? Which of the four basic types of resource allocation – negotiated funding, input-based funding, output-based funding, or student-based funding – is most appropriate for South Africa? (Albrecht & Ziderman, 1992)

Answering these questions adequately and in a way that is acceptable to all involved, is a huge task. As is shown in the following two chapters, the South African government has been successful in addressing some of these questions, but most of them still remain to be answered. In this respect South Africa is not alone, as the examples in Chapter 1 and the country case studies included on the book's web page show (see www.chet.org.za/papers.asp).

REFERENCES

Albrecht, D. & Ziderman, A. (1992). *Funding Mechanisms for Higher Education: Financing for Stability, Efficiency and Responsibility*. Washington: The World Bank.

Johnstone, B. (1998). *The Financing and Management of Higher Education: A Status Report on Worldwide Reforms*. Washington: The World Bank.

Jongbloed, B. (2000). The Funding of Higher Education in Developing Countries. In: B. Jongbloed & H. Teekens (eds), *The Financing of Higher Education in Sub-Saharan Africa*. Utrecht: Uitgeverij LEMMA.

CHAPTER 4

IAN BUNTING

FUNDING

In the period before 1994, the South African government's funding policies mirrored apartheid's divisions and the different governance models which it imposed on the higher education system. As shown in Chapter 2, before 1994 control of South Africa's 36 universities and technikons was divided amongst four government departments in the 'independent republics' (the TBVC countries: Transkei, Bophuthatswana, Venda and Ciskei) and four government departments in the Republic of South Africa (RSA). Different funding policies and practices applied within these government departments.

This chapter begins by offering a broad outline of the different funding policies and of the relationship between these policies and the apartheid governance structures in the years before 1994. It also describes the effects which apartheid policies had on the funding of higher education institutions before 1994.

The main body of the chapter discusses the changes to government funding policies and mechanisms which were proposed by the National Commission on Higher Education and accepted by the 1997 White Paper on higher education transformation. In particular, it focuses on a crucial issue which influenced the institutions' responses to the new policy framework, viz. that by 2001 the proposed changes to government funding policies and mechanisms had not yet been implemented in the higher education system. This resulted in a discredited apartheid-era funding system remaining in place throughout a key phase in the transformation of higher education in South Africa.

1. FUNDING UNDER THE APARTHEID GOVERNMENT

Two broad types of government funding were in place in South Africa (RSA and the TBVC) during the years up to 1994. The first type was that of negotiated budgets and was associated with the historically black universities and technikons. The second was that of formula funding which was associated initially with the historically white universities. The two funding systems were instruments used in the implementation of the government's so-called 'separate-but-equal' policy.

The historically white universities, within the apartheid constraint of being required to serve the 'white community' only, were given considerable administrative and financial powers. They could decide, for example, how their funding grants from government were to be spent, how many staff members they should employ, what their tuition fees should be, and how any surplus funds should be invested.

N. Cloete et al. (eds.). Transformation in Higher Education. 73-94.
© 2007 Springer.

The other higher education institutions in the RSA were not given similar administrative and financial powers. Their tuition fees and the details of their expenditure budgets had to be approved by their controlling government department. For example, they had to apply for approval from this government department before employing new members of staff, even down to the level of clerical and service staff. They could not take decisions on what the maintenance programmes should be for the buildings they occupied or on what major items of equipment they should purchase. Aspirations for the same levels of autonomy as the historically white universities played a major role, throughout the early 1980s, in the relationship between these 18 universities and technikons and their controlling RSA government departments. They saw the main vehicle for the achievement of that autonomy to be the adoption by their departments of the funding framework of the historically white universities.

By 1988 the 18 institutions had achieved their ambition to be placed on the same funding basis as the historically white universities. The discussion which follows will show that this was an adaptive strategy which had unintended, but serious, consequences for all historically black higher education institutions in South Africa – not just during the years 1988–1994, but also during the years following 1994.

1.1. Negotiated budgets and formula funding

The system of negotiated budgets involved the university or technikon concerned submitting a budget for expenditure and partial income to its controlling government department. The income side would have been primarily the amount the institution expected to collect from student fees. The final amount which the institution was permitted to spend in that financial year would have been a nett amount of approved expenditure less student fees. This nett amount would have appeared as a line item in the overall budget of the controlling government department.

Two key features of this budgetary mechanism were the following:

- As would be the case with all government expenditure, any unspent balances on a negotiated budget would have to be returned to the national treasury. Institutions were not permitted to transfer these amounts to reserves under their control. This had two consequences: a spending spree at the end of every year to discharge accumulated funds and no build-up of a reserve fund.
- The expenditure budgets finally approved were not determined by the student enrolments of the institutions concerned. They were based on assessments of current needs in the context of historical expenditure patterns. In many cases this amounted to adding a percentage to the allocation for the previous year, and did not overcome disparities with the more advantaged institutions or ensure adequate library, laboratory and computer facilities.

In 1982 the government developed a formula funding framework for the historically white universities (Department of National Education, 1982). The framework was based on a set of underlying principles (see Bunting, 1994:137–138). The first three rested on the distinction between the private and public benefits of higher education. These principles stated that costs must be shared between government as the recipient of public benefits and students as the recipients of private benefits, and that government must subsidise only those higher education activities which generate substantial public benefits. The final three principles dealt with issues of efficiency, institutional autonomy and government intervention in the higher education market. They stated that institutions operate most efficiently when granted high levels of autonomy by government, and that government should intervene directly in the higher education system only when the need existed for market failures to be corrected.

Known as the South African Post-Secondary Education (SAPSE) formula, the funding framework was a highly complex one (Department of National Education, 1982). A few of its main features are these (taken from Bunting, 1994:129–137):

- *Subsidy students.* The student input variables in the formula were composites consisting of 50% full-time equivalent *enrolled* and 50% full-time equivalent *successful* students.
- *Subject groupings.* Subsidy students were placed in two groupings for the purposes of the formula: a *natural sciences* grouping which included the life, physical and mathematical sciences, health sciences, engineering, computer science, agriculture, architecture and building sciences, and a *humanities* grouping which included all other disciplines.
- *Course levels.* Subsidy students were also placed into one of four course levels which carried weightings ranging from one to four. Subsidy students at a doctoral level were multiplied by four, at a masters level by three, and at fourth year (or honours) level by two. All other subsidy students had a weighting of one.
- *Cost units.* The formula contained a total of ten cost units which were based on calculations made of the actual costs of the historically white universities in 1981. These cost units covered three categories of staff, supplies and services, and building renewals, and four categories of library books and periodicals. The rand value of these cost units increased each year in line with inflation in the higher education sector.
- *Gross formula totals.* The formula contained tables of ratios between the ten cost units on the one hand, and humanities and natural sciences subsidy students on the other. These tables permitted a calculation to be made of the gross formula total of individual higher education institutions.
- *Nett subsidy total.* A key principle of this funding framework was that costs had to be shared by government and by the consumer of higher education. The nett subsidy payment by government to an institution was therefore determined by its gross formula income total less the amount which had to be raised from students and/or their families as well as from other private sources. The amount to be raised from private sources was dependent on the size of the institution, and in the early years ranged from 18% to 22% of the gross formula totals of the historically white universities.

- *a-factors.* Soon after introducing this funding framework, the government found that the total of nett subsidies exceeded its budget for these historically white universities. It therefore introduced a final adjustment factor, called the a-factor, to bring the subsidies paid to the universities in line with the national budget. The a-factor for the historically white universities was initially close to 1, but dropped during the 1980s. It was, for example, 0.83 in 1986, and approximately 0.75 in 1988 and 1989.

1.2. Application of formula funding to all RSA institutions: 1988 to 1994

By the mid-1980s the arguments for the greater autonomy which the SAPSE formula gave to higher education institutions had been accepted by the RSA government. All four of the RSA government departments involved in the controlling of universities and technikons began to apply versions of the formula to their institutions, but did so within the overall constraints of apartheid ideology. The subsidy per student that these institutions received was very similar, and in some cases even higher than that which the historically white institutions were receiving. The problem was that the universities were small, mainly located in rural areas where it was expensive to run an institution. They were relatively new institutions without book collections that had been built up over a period of time, and staff costs were very high. This meant that 'academic infrastructure' such as the library and science and computer laboratories, was chronically under-equipped. But the biggest disadvantage was the limited academic capacity of the expensive staff.

By the end of the 1980s, a funding framework which had been explicitly designed for the historically white universities was applied to the six historically black universities in the RSA. These institutions accepted this funding framework together with its underlying apartheid assumptions and principles because they believed, firstly, that the formula would give them greater administrative and financial autonomy and, secondly, that they would receive substantial financial benefits from the growth in student enrolments which they were experiencing at this time. The growth was due to larger numbers of students coming through the school system, despite the school boycotts. By 1988 an adapted version of the formula was also applied to the twelve historically white and historically black technikons in the RSA. The adaptations made to the formula for technikons did not affect its underlying assumptions and principles. They mainly involved changes which were supposed to reflect the different cost structures of technikons. A lower rand value than that applicable to universities was set for the technikon cost unit for academic staff, and lower ratios between cost units and subsidy students than those for universities were set for technikons. This was because it was assumed that universities with a research mission and postgraduate students would be more expensive to run than vocationally orientated institutions.

One main effect of the extension of the SAPSE formula to all universities and technikons was that the RSA government, by 1988, had adopted a 'hands-off' approach to the funding and steering of the higher education system. It believed that, provided its overall ideological framework of separate institutions for separate race groups remained intact, all universities and technikons should be given high levels of administrative and financial autonomy. The government held the view that the size of the higher education system and its shape by course enrolment should, within the constraints of the apartheid ideology, be determined solely by the higher education market.

The role which government funding was supposed to play in this market-driven environment by 1988 can be summed up in the following way:

- Students and/or their families were assumed to be rational agents. As rational agents they would be able to read the labour market, and thus choose those courses and directions of study likely to generate the maximum possible benefit for them, and ultimately for the country.
- The actual size of the higher education system and its shape in terms of courses or programmes of study selected was determined by these student choices. Government intervention would be necessary only to correct failures in the student-choice-driven market.
- Since the SAPSE funding formula generated an ideal cost of the higher education system shaped by student choice, and since it determined what share of this ideal cost should be carried by government and what share by individual institutions, a national budget for higher education could be settled relatively easily.
- This national budget for higher education was allocated in a mechanical way to universities and technikons. The allocation method was mechanical in the sense that it eliminated the possibility of political interference in the shaping of the higher education system.
- Competition between institutions for available students was essential. Higher education institutions had to read the labour market and try to predict what student choices were likely to be.

2. GOVERNMENT APPROPRIATIONS AND INSTITUTIONAL INCOME: 1986–1994

As outlined above, by 1988 all 29 universities and technikons in the RSA were operating within the same government funding framework. This switch of funding frameworks, when linked to the rapid growth in student enrolments in the RSA, led both to government funding requirements increasing rapidly and to an increased diversification in the income flows of higher education institutions in the RSA. But it also sowed the seeds of the serious financial problems which South Africa's historically black institutions were to experience in the late 1990s.

Government appropriations for higher education in the RSA increased nearly three-fold between 1986 and 1994: from R1.161-million in 1986 to R3.227-million in 1994, which was the last budget year of the apartheid government. Details of the changes which occurred by higher education sector can be seen in Figure 1.

This graph hides a serious problem which the RSA government had begun to experience by the early 1990s: it could not meet the level of formula funding which

Figure 1. *Government appropriations for universities and technikons*
in RSA (rands millions): 1986–1994

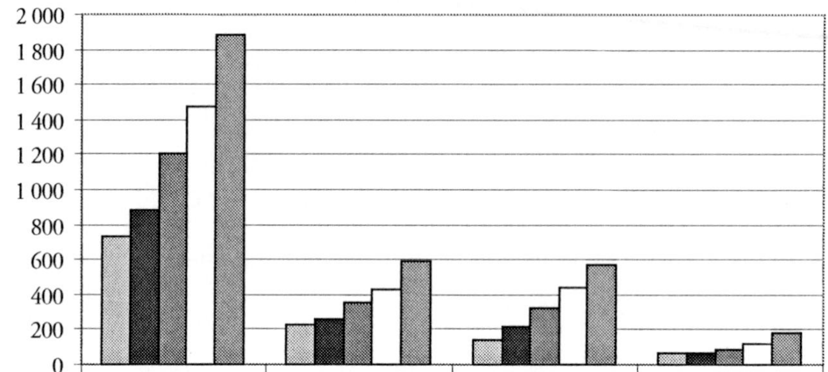

	HWUs	HBUs	HWTs	HBTs
☐ 1986	729	222	144	66
■ 1988	886	260	211	64
▨ 1990	1 205	350	321	91
☐ 1992	1 474	432	441	122
▦ 1994	1 883	595	570	179

Source: Department of Education, 2001

student growth in the system had generated. Between 1986 and 1994, government appropriations for the 29 universities and technikons grew in nominal rands by 178%. Because of South Africa's high inflation rate at the time, however, the growth in real rands (i.e. in rands deflated by the consumer price index) was only 3% in 1994 compared with 1986.

This increase in the real total of government appropriations was considerably lower than the growth which occurred in student enrolments in the RSA's universities and technikons. In 1986, about 300.000 students were enrolled in universities and technikons in the RSA, and in 1994 more than 520.000. This represented a total growth of 220.000 (or 73%) over this period. So the unit value of government funding per student fell sharply in real terms between 1986 and 1994. Further details of these growth rates in student enrolments between 1986 and 1994 can be seen in the chapter on students which follows.

The South African government used the mechanism of the a-factor to reduce the share it was supposed to meet, in terms of the provisions of the SAPSE formula, of the 'ideal costs' of the higher education system. The functioning of these a-factors was described earlier in this chapter. Figure 2 sets out the a-factors which were applied in the RSA between 1986 and 1994. The falling value of the a-factors over this time period is an

Figure 2. *a-factors applied to universities and technikons: 1986–1994*[1]

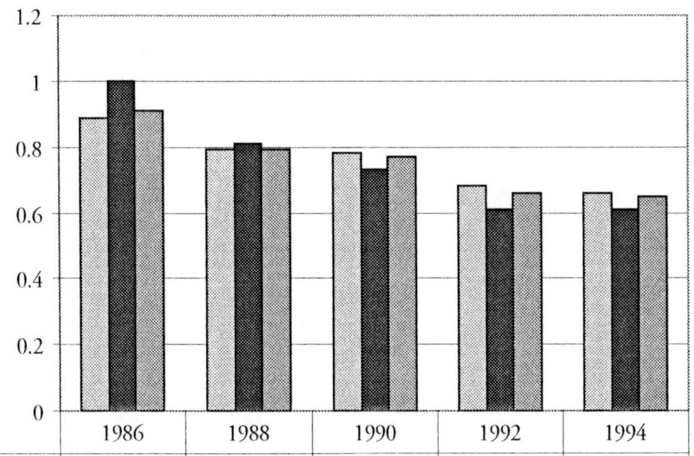

	1986	1988	1990	1992	1994
▢ Univ Average	0.89	0.79	0.78	0.68	0.66
▮ Tech Average	1	0.81	0.73	0.61	0.61
▦ Overall Average	0.91	0.79	0.77	0.66	0.65

Source: Department of Education, 2001

indication that the national RSA budget was not able to cope with the financial demands generated by rapid increases in student enrolments. It shows that in 1986 the RSA government was able to meet 90% and in 1994 only 65% of the commitment generated by the SAPSE formula.

The shortfalls in government subsidy funding reflected in Figure 2 had to be found by universities and technikons from private funding sources. Over this period, government subsidy appropriations had a steadily declining share of the total income of all universities in the RSA and of the historically white technikons. The proportion which government appropriations constituted of the income of the historically white universities fell from 54% in 1986 to 47% in 1994, and the proportion for the historically black universities in the RSA fell from 73% in 1986 to 49% in 1994. In the case of the historically white technikons, the share which government appropriations had of their total income fell from 64% in 1988 (1986 information is not available) to 54% in 1994. The share government appropriations had of the income of historically black technikons in the RSA remained constant at 63%–64% throughout this period.

A major effect of this need for institutions to diversify their funds away from government to private sources between 1988 and 1994, was that student tuition fees increased rapidly. Student tuition fee increases were seen by most institutions to be the easiest way to overcome the problems caused by the a-factor cuts imposed by government. This can be seen in Figure 3.

Figure 3. Student tuition fees as a percentage of total income: 1988–1993

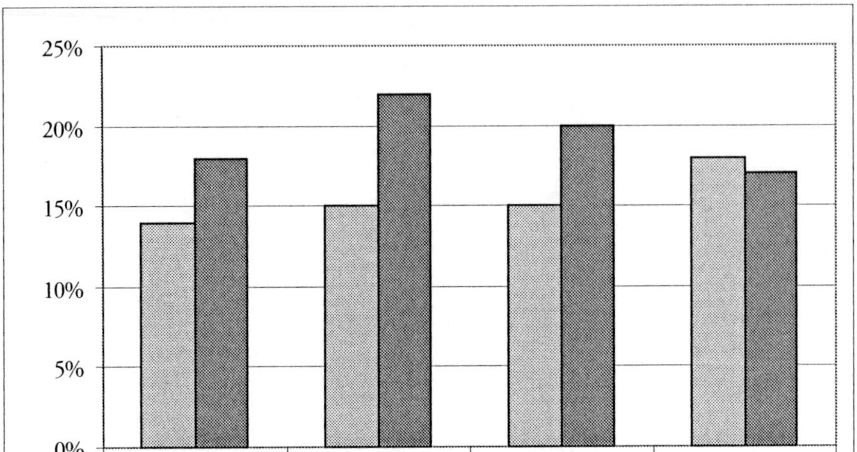

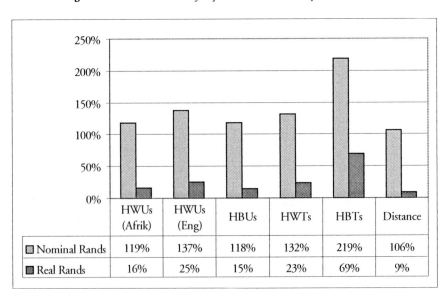

	HWUs	HBUs	HWTs	HBTs
▨ 1988	14%	15%	15%	18%
▧ 1993	18%	22%	20%	17%

Sources: Hendry & Bunting, 1993(a) and 1993(b); Bunting & Bunting, 1998; Bunting & Smith, 1998

Figure 4. Increases in tuition fees per student: 1993 compared with 1988

	HWUs (Afrik)	HWUs (Eng)	HBUs	HWTs	HBTs	Distance
▨ Nominal Rands	119%	137%	118%	132%	219%	106%
▧ Real Rands	16%	25%	15%	23%	69%	9%

Sources: Hendry & Bunting, 1993(a) and 1993(b); Bunting & Bunting, 1998; Bunting & Smith, 1998

Figure 3 shows that student tuition fees as a share of total institutional income increased in all parts of the higher education system in 1993 compared with 1988. This reliance by institutions on student tuition fees as a way of balancing their budgets placed severe financial burdens on individual students because in nominal as well as in real terms fees per student increased rapidly in the period up to 1994. Examples of these increases can be seen in Figure 4. The increases in nominal rands are indications of the high levels of consumer price inflation which South Africa experienced during the late 1980s and early 1990s.

The discussion in later sections of this chapter will show that tuition fee increases of this scale did not occur in the period after 1994.

3. CHANGES TO FUNDING POLICIES: 1994–1997

3.1. The SAPSE formula and the historically black institutions

By 1994 it was clear that a strategy adopted during the 1980s by the RSA's historically black universities had had serious implications for their financial well-being. This was the strategy of using the extension of the funding formula for white universities to all sectors as a way of increasing their levels of institutional autonomy. Three aspects of their financial performance in the years between 1986 and 1994 had generated severe financial strains on the RSA's historically black university sector:

- Because government appropriation totals in real terms remained flat over this period even though student enrolments had grown rapidly, the real government income per student at the historically black universities had fallen sharply by 1994 compared with 1988.
- The RSA's historically black universities had been forced to rely to an increasing extent on student tuition fee collections to build up their required income. This had placed a heavy burden both on students and on these institutions. Many of their students came from economically disadvantaged sectors of South African society, and were not able to meet large increases in their tuition fees and cost of living expenses. The historically black institutions were forced to project their expenditure budgets on the assumption that they would be able to collect 100% of their student fee billings, even when there was evidence that they knew that at least 33% of all fees charged would remain uncollected.
- The problems which this funding framework generated for historically black institutions emerged even more clearly when the universities and technikons of the TBVC countries were incorporated into the South African higher education system after the 1994 elections. These seven universities and technikons had not been placed on the SAPSE formula in 1988. Unlike black universities and technikons in the RSA, they remained, until 1994, on a negotiated budget system within regimes of tight state control. When they became the responsibility of a new unified national Department of Education after June 1994, they were informed

that from 1995 they would be subject to the same funding framework as all other universities and technikons in South Africa. However, because their funding under the TBVC regimes had been generous in comparison with that of black as well as white institutions in the old RSA, they were given a limited time frame of about five years to adapt to lower levels of government funding.

3.2. First objections to the SAPSE formula

In the early 1990s various non-governmental investigations were launched into future higher education policies for a post-apartheid South Africa. During these debates the SAPSE funding formula was taken to be a flawed document, and strong objections were expressed to its underlying assumptions and principles (see Bunting, 1994:141–149).

These pre-1994 objections to the SAPSE funding formula were taken up by the National Commission on Higher Education (NCHE). For example, its finance task team drew this conclusion about the SAPSE formula in its March 1996 report to the NCHE:

> ... most of the mechanisms used by the South African government for distributing its higher education funding should not be employed in a new, transformed system. The fundamental problems are that current mechanisms are based on assumptions which clash with certain of the values and principles which flow from the 1995 Education White Paper, and that the present formulae have contained incentives which have distorted the higher education system. (NCHE finance task team, 1996:38)

The key problems which the NCHE finance task team highlighted in this 1996 report were these:

- *Access equity*
  Because the SAPSE formula was originally formulated for the historically white universities only, it assumed that access to higher education in South Africa was fair, and hence that no provision should be made by government for the improvement of equity through, for example, the provision of funds for financial aid and for preparatory or remedial instruction. The task team stressed that in a transformed higher education system in South Africa, government should make financial provision for the improvement of equity of access in the higher education system (NCHE finance task team, 1996:35).
- *Efficiency and autonomy*
  The 'hands-off' aspects of the formula flowed from an assumption that institutions would function most efficiently in the long-term national interest when given as much control as possible of their own planning and finances. The task team reached these conclusions on the basis of detailed analyses of the financial state in 1993 of universities and technikons in the old RSA (ie. not including TBVC institutions):
  - Major financial inequalities existed between the historically white and historically black institutions which were on the SAPSE formula. Black institutions in the years up to 1993 had had to raise student fees rapidly and were consequently faced with serious problems in collecting fees from impoverished students.

° The physical infrastructure of the higher education system was running down rapidly, primarily due to declining proportions of institutional expenditure being devoted to building and equipment maintenance, to building renewals and to the purchase of new fixed assets.

° Some institutions had excess facilities, in the sense that the facilities were seriously under-utilised by students, while others were carrying student loads far above capacity. The physical facilities of the higher education system were not being put to optimal use (NCHE finance task team, 1996:30).

- *Unintended consequences*

The NCHE finance task team argued that the formula and its application to institutions other than the historically white universities had resulted in a number of unintended consequences. Some of these were created by incentives which had by 1995 severely distorted the South African higher education system. These were clearly not the intended consequences of these incentives. The task team highlighted these specific problems in the formula for universities as well as that for technikons:

- The higher education system has grown rapidly at rates which have not been sustainable in financial terms (hence the introduction of a-factors which in effect place upper limits on the numbers of students which the government will subsidise). This growth has been encouraged by elements in the formulae which generate substantial benefits for institutions which grow and substantial penalties for institutions with declining student numbers.
- The formulae further encourage institutions to increase enrolments in the cheaper humanities fields and not in the more expensive science and technology fields.
- The formulae contain powerful incentives for all higher education institutions to engage in distance learning activities, and to use the funds generated from this source as a way of cross-subsidising their contact education activities.
- The formulae encourage institutions to grow at cheaper undergraduate levels rather than at more expensive postgraduate levels despite the apparently higher weightings given to postgraduate students. (NCHE finance task team, 1996:37)

In its final report of March 1996 the task team recommended to the NCHE that the SAPSE higher education funding framework should be dropped and replaced by a fundamentally different one.

3.3. A planning/steering model of higher education funding

The proposals formulated by the finance task team of the NCHE (1996) were consistent with at least some international accounts of the role which government funding should play in the implementation of national higher education policies (see for example Albrecht & Ziderman, 1992; Williams, 1992). The literature and the consultants appointed to advise the task team had at that time placed particular stress on the steering role of government funding mechanisms.

These emphases were adopted by the NCHE when it accepted the arguments of its finance task team that the SAPSE funding framework should be replaced by a fundamentally different one. The NCHE formulated this proposal in its final report:

A new funding framework for higher education in South Africa should be developed which is consistent with the principles of equity (including redress), development, democratisation, efficiency, effectiveness, financial sustainability and shared costs. (1996:216)

On the NCHE's proposal, the key principles which government funding of a transformed higher education system would have to satisfy are these:

- *Principles of equity and redress.* Government funding of higher education must be employed to ensure that the South African higher education system becomes an equitable one.
- *Principle of development.* The higher education system must be responsive to the needs of a developing economy which is aspiring to become internationally competitive. Government funding of the system has to encourage responsive programmes in institutions which will help satisfy the vocational and employment needs of the economy.
- *Principles of effectiveness, efficiency, and sustainability.* Government funding of the higher education system must be directed at ensuring that the system achieves its pre-determined goals at the lowest possible cost. The system must be an affordable one.
- *Principle of shared costs.* The costs of higher education must be shared by both the government and students or their families, because of the public and private benefits generated.

The government funding framework of the 1980s and early 1990s (the SAPSE funding framework) satisfied in an explicit way only the last of the principles set out above. This framework explicitly rejected the principles of equity and redress, holding that it was not the business of the higher education system to deal with social inequalities which affected either individuals or institutions. Its built-in assumptions about institutional autonomy and the efficacy of the free market implied, as has been noted above, that the SAPSE funding framework could not satisfy the principles of development or those concerned with efficiency and effectiveness. It satisfied the principle of financial sustainability only through its use of the a-factors which were in effect *post hoc* cuts imposed on the subsidisable student enrolments of institutions.

The new South African government accepted the proposals of the NCHE regarding funding of the higher education system. In its August 1997 White Paper on higher education transformation it states that a goal-oriented, performance-related framework of public funding would be introduced in South Africa. The new framework would be implemented as follows:

- *Step 1.* The Ministry of Education would interact regularly with individual higher education institutions. These high level interactions would involve discussion concerning institutional missions, institutional programme offerings, and institutional planning proposals.
- *Step 2.* The Ministry of Education would, at the end of the consultative process, publish a national plan for the size and shape of the South African higher education system.

- *Step 3.* Within the framework of this national plan for higher education, and after examining key aspects of institutional performance, the Ministry would, approve rolling three- to five-year plans for programmes and student enrolment for each individual higher education institution.
- *Step 4.* At the same time as it is considering and approving institutional plans, the Ministry would negotiate a budgetary allocation for higher education with the national Department of Finance.
- *Step 5.* The amounts allocated in the national higher education budget would, together with the national plan and with the approved plans of individual institutions, determine how the government allocation would be divided between institutions in a given funding year.

3.3.1. Anticipated consequences

Most universities and technikons accepted that the implementation of the new funding-planning system would have a number of crucial effects on the South African higher education system. Three of these can be summed up in these ways:

- *End of the apartheid higher education market.* During the years of apartheid, higher education in South Africa operated in a set of 'compartmentalised' markets. The limits of each market were set by the various racial categories and policies described in Chapter 2. The size and shape of each racially defined higher education sub-system was determined by student and institutional readings of the labour market relevant to that sub-system (labour markets in South Africa were also racially defined in the years before 1994), and by competition between institutions within these racial categories. In a sense, within each racial category, a 'free' higher education market had been functioning, characterised by government exercising no control over student enrolments within institutions and within overall academic programmes.
- *Future reliance on student markets in higher education.* The apartheid government's version of higher education markets ended after 1994. The funding-planning model set out in the 1997 White Paper stressed that the size and shape of the higher education system in South Africa would not in future be determined by student and institutional readings of the labour market, nor by students exercising programme choice in a context of strong inter-institutional competitiveness. The size and shape of the system would be determined by government in the context of national policies related to equity and to development, and in accordance with its readings of labour market requirements.
- *Institutional autonomy and institutional competitiveness.* An important consequence of the implementation of the funding-planning model laid out in the 1997 White Paper would be a dampening down of institutional competitiveness. Competition between institutions would still be possible, but only within the constraints of nationally approved plans for higher education. This implied further that a key premise of the state supervision model of the 1980s, viz. that institutions function

most efficiently and effectively when given close to total administrative and financial autonomy, would be abandoned. Under the 1997 model, institutions would have to function within the framework of a national plan for higher education and an individual institutional plan approved by the Minister of Education.

A major problem for the higher education system has been the delay in the implementation of this 1997 planning/steering model. It had not been implemented by the 2001/2002 financial year, and is unlikely to be fully in place before the 2003/2004 financial year. As we shall see in the section which follows, this implementation delay has had positive effects on some higher education institutions and negative effects on others.

4. CHANGES IN INSTITUTIONAL FUNDING PATTERNS: 1994–2001

By the beginning of 1998, public universities and technikons in South Africa were clearly faced with strong indications that radical changes would be made to the funding framework under which they had operated for some years. At the same time it was clear that some years would pass before the radical new framework and its accompanying mechanisms would be put in place.

This section offers a brief account of changes that occurred in the funding patterns of institutions in the period while the SAPSE formula was under detailed scrutiny, but was still functioning as the sole government funding mechanism. The conclusion to Part 1 (p113) offers an analysis of the strategies adopted by institutions in the face of these impending changes.

4.1. Government appropriations: 1995–2001

In the 1995 financial year all 36 universities and technikons in South Africa were brought on to the SAPSE funding formula. This total included the 29 institutions in the former RSA and the seven incorporated from the TBVC countries.

As can be seen from Table 1, the new government's funding of this enlarged higher education system increased in both real and nominal terms throughout the period 1995–2001.

Details of total government allocations to the system in nominal rands can be seen in Figure 5. The growth in real rands which occurred in government appropriations for the system between 1995 and 2001 was matched by the growth which occurred in student enrolments. In other words, the government was not able to increase in real terms its appropriations per higher education student. The overall government units of funding nevertheless remained constant over the period, as can be seen in Figure 6. This shows that in real rands, government appropriations per subsidy student unit remained constant over the five-year period from 1997 to 2001. As the earlier discussion showed, this did not occur between 1988 and 1994, the last years of the apartheid government.

During those years subsidies per student fell in real terms. The refrain so often heard in South African higher education, namely that the system is 'suffering' from a decrease in government funding, is empirically incorrect. An argument could be made that the level of funding is not high enough, but not that funding has decreased since 1994.

Table 1. *Average annual increases in government appropriations: 1995–2001*

	Nominal rands	*Real rands on base of 1995 = 100*
Universities	10%	2%
Technikons	13%	4%
Total	11%	2%

Source: Department of Education, 2001

Figures 6 and 7, however, hide important shifts which occurred within the various groupings of institutions. Figure 7 shows clearly that the flows of government funds to institutions were uneven during this period, primarily because of the changing patterns of student enrolment within different groups of institutions (details of these enrolment shifts are offered in Chapter 5).

Figure 7 shows that government appropriations to the historically white Afrikaans-medium universities increased in real terms over the period 1995 to 2001, and increased

Figure 5. *Total government appropriations in nominal rands (rands millions): 1995–2001*

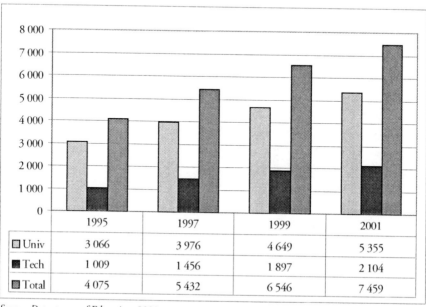

	1995	1997	1999	2001
☐ Univ	3 066	3 976	4 649	5 355
■ Tech	1 009	1 456	1 897	2 104
☐ Total	4 075	5 432	6 546	7 459

Source: Department of Education, 2001

Figure 6. *Government appropriations per subsidy student unit in real rands² of 1997*

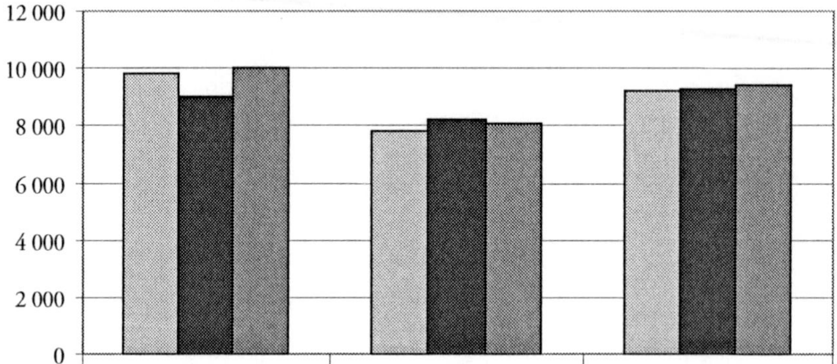

	Univs	Techs	Average
1997	9 800	7 800	9 200
1999	9 000	8 200	9 300
2001	10 000	8 100	9 400

Sources: Department of Education, 2001; SA Reserve Bank at www.resbank.co.za

Figure 7. *Government appropriations by institutional grouping in 1995 real rands (millions)*

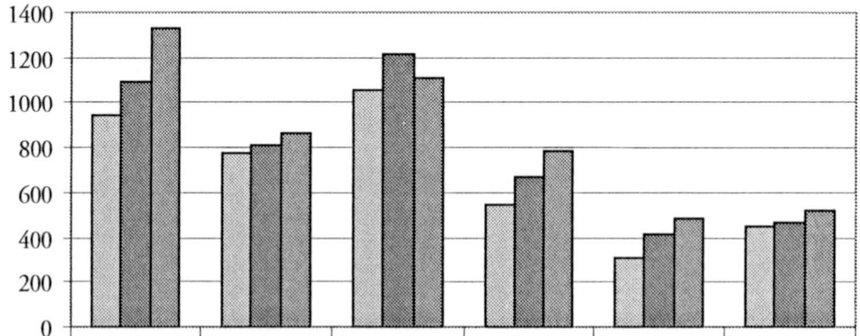

	HWUs (Afrik)	HWUs (Eng)	HBUs	HWTs	HBTs	Distance
1995	945	771	1059	546	308	446
1999	1089	813	1214	668	412	464
2001	1328	867	1112	780	488	519

Source: Calculations based on information contained in Department of Education, 2001

particularly sharply between 1999 and 2001. In terms of real rands, the government appropriations of the historically white Afrikaans-medium universities increased by R239-million (or 22%) between 1999 and 2001. Those of the historically white English-medium universities increased in real rands by R54-million (or 7%) between 1999 and 2001. In marked contrast, the government appropriation total of the historically black universities fell in real rands by R102-million (or 8%) between 1999 and 2001. The key reasons for these marked differences in growth in government appropriations totals can be found in the different adaptive strategies which institutions employed during the years 1995 to 1997, particularly those related to government funding of the higher education system. A discussion of these different strategies is offered in the conclusion which follows Chapter 5.

5. TOTAL INCOME AND LONG-TERM INVESTMENTS 1993–1999

Figures 8 and 9 compare government appropriations and private income as proportions of total institutional income for the years 1993 and 1999. The institutions which appear in these categories are those which formed part of the old RSA – those parts of South Africa which were not included in the four TBVC states prior to 1994. The data thus apply to 29 of the current 36 universities and technikons in South Africa.

Figure 8 shows that, other than for the group of six historically white Afrikaans-medium universities, government appropriations as a proportion of total income remained stable in the remaining 23 institutions in 1999 compared with 1993. The government appropriation proportion of the historically white Afrikaans-medium universities fell to a level comparable with that of the historically white English-medium universities, not because of declines in the government appropriations but because of sharp increases in their levels of private funding. This private funding would have been income which the Afrikaans institutions generated from non-government contracts, but most importantly income derived from long- and short-term investments.

Figure 9 compares, for 1999 only, the extent to which the different groups of institutions were dependent on student tuition fees as the major source of their private or non-government income. By international standards, the proportion of government funding in relation to the overall budget is low. For example, Albrecht and Ziderman (1992) placed various countries in three bands as far as their dependency on government funding was concerned: high, medium and low. In 1995 South Africa was placed in the low dependency band, along with countries such as the USA and Japan. The medium dependency band included countries such as Britain and India, and the high dependency band a wide range of European, African and other countries such as the Netherlands, Norway, Kenya, Nigeria, Brazil and China.

Figures 10 and 11 show what effect the 1993–1999 changes in income patterns had on the long-term investment holdings of 27 of the 29 universities and technikons in the old RSA (information for Unisa and Technikon SA was not available at the time of writing). Figure 10 shows somewhat starkly that the total market value of the long-term investments of the six historically white Afrikaans-medium and the four historically

Figure 8. *Government appropriations as percentage of total income: 1993 and 1999*

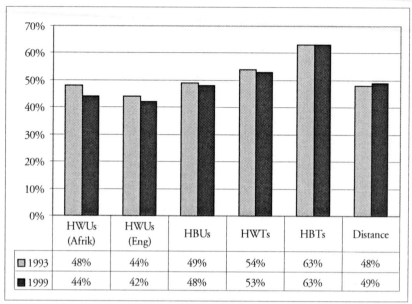

	HWUs (Afrik)	HWUs (Eng)	HBUs	HWTs	HBTs	Distance
1993	48%	44%	49%	54%	63%	48%
1999	44%	42%	48%	53%	63%	49%

Source: Bunting, M., 2001

Figure 9. *Private income as a percentage of total income in 1999*

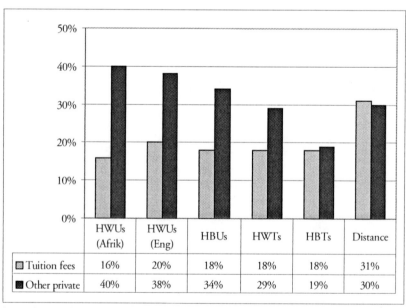

	HWUs (Afrik)	HWUs (Eng)	HBUs	HWTs	HBTs	Distance
Tuition fees	16%	20%	18%	18%	18%	31%
Other private	40%	38%	34%	29%	19%	30%

Source: Bunting, M., 2001

white English-medium universities nearly doubled between 1993 and 1999. In 1993, these ten universities held long-term investments with a market value of R2.078-million; in 1999 their long-term investments had a market value of R4.008-million. In 1993 as well as in 1999 these historically white universities held 82% of the total of long-term investments of the 27 contact universities and technikons of the old RSA. This suggests clearly that no redistribution of funds between historically white and historically black institutions occurred in the years after 1994.

The most significant increase which occurred in the long-term investments of the 27 institutions reflected in Figure 10, was that of the historically black technikons. Two of these technikons had by 1999 accumulated substantial long-term investments off very low bases in 1993.

The problems faced by the historically black universities emerge clearly from Figures 10 and 11. The market value of their total long-term investments dropped slightly in 1999 compared with 1993. When calculated in terms of the days of operating income which these investments represented, a much sharper decline occurred. By 1999, the market value of the long-term investments of the historically black universities was equivalent to only 84 days of operating income, compared with an already low figure of 116 in 1993.

The sharp growth that occurred in the long-term investment holdings of the historically black technikons is reflected in Figure 11 in a sharp increase in the income-days-equivalent of these holdings. The graph shows also that the figure for the historically white technikons remained as low in 1999 as it was in 1993.

These last graphs show that South African higher education institutions had by the end of the 1990s diversified their income to an extent not achieved in many developed countries. For example, by the mid-1990s more than 10% of the income of universities in South Africa came from grants and contracts from industry and commerce. This was a proportion matched at the time only by private universities in the USA (Ziderman & Albrecht, 1995). A further proportion of 10% of the income of universities in South Africa is generated by their investment holdings. When these proportions are added to the more than 20% generated by tuition and residence fees, it is clear that the government cannot realistically expect the proportion of its contribution to decrease in future years.

The inability of certain institutions to successfully attract non-governmental funding is a key contributor to some of the institutional crises presently being faced, and this raises the crucial issue of whether higher education in South Africa has in fact been under-funded by government throughout the 1990s. In international comparative terms, however, the proportion that South Africa spends on education (22% of total state budget) and on higher education (15% of the education budget and 0.8% of GDP) compares favourably with middle- and even some high-income countries (Task Force on Higher Education and Society, 2000).

It was argued earlier that claims that government subsidies have been cut in the years after 1994 are in fact wrong. The total amount appropriated by government, particularly in the years between 1997 and 2001, increased in real terms, and the subsidy amount per student remained constant. These arguments do not affect the critical issue of whether

Figure 10. Market value of long-term investments (rands millions): 1993 and 1999

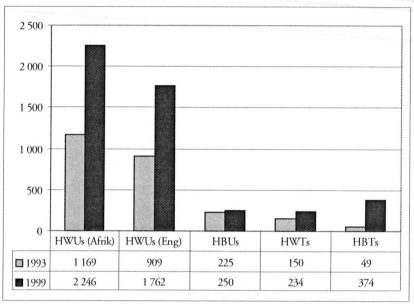

	HWUs (Afrik)	HWUs (Eng)	HBUs	HWTs	HBTs
1993	1 169	909	225	150	49
1999	2 246	1 762	250	234	374

Source: Bunting, M., 2001

Figure 11. Long-term investments as days of operating income: 1993 and 1999

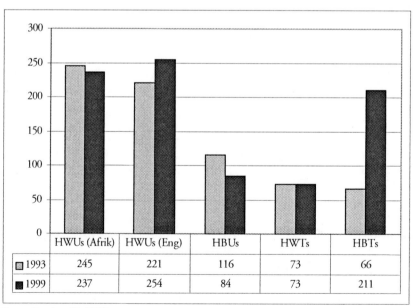

	HWUs (Afrik)	HWUs (Eng)	HBUs	HWTs	HBTs
1993	245	221	116	73	66
1999	237	254	84	73	211

Source: Bunting, M., 2001

government appropriations should not have been higher during this period, given in particular the financial aid crises faced by many institutions. The South African government's contribution to institutional budgets has consistently been at a level seen only in highly developed countries. Should it not have been at the levels seen in less developed countries than the USA?

6. INSTITUTIONAL ADAPTIVE STRATEGIES: 1997–2001

By 1997 most public universities and technikons in South Africa had accepted that they would in future have to adapt to two crucial changes:

- *Mission and values.* They would have to ensure that their institutional missions and values were consistent with those of the 1997 White Paper on higher education transformation. For some, this involved changing in major ways their 'institutional ideologies'.
- *SAPSE framework.* The SAPSE funding framework which had been established in 1982 for the historically white universities, and which had been applied throughout the late 1980s and early 1990s to all other universities and to all technikons, would be abolished. It became generally accepted that this was essentially an apartheid funding framework and could not be used in a transformed higher education system committed to equity and to strong linkages with national development needs. It was also accepted that the abolition of the SAPSE funding framework would result in major benefits for some groups of institutions and major costs for others.

It was also generally accepted by the institutions that it would take some years after the publication of the 1997 White Paper for the Ministry of Education to develop, to implement, and to phase in a new funding framework. This was a reasonable expectation. If work on the development of a new framework had begun in 1998, soon after the establishment of the higher education branch in the Ministry of Education, then even on a fast-track implementation process, it would have taken at least five years (ie. up to about 2002) before government funds could have been distributed to institutions under the provisions of a new funding framework.

Consequently it was assumed that, as far as higher education funding was concerned, the primary emphasis of government in the first few years after 1998 would be that of changing 'higher educational 'institutional ideologies' in South Africa. This assumption was reinforced to a certain extent by the emphasis placed on equity in the requirements circulated to institutions (in 1998) for the submission of the first set of three-year rolling plans for the years 1999–2001.

As is shown in the conclusion on page 113, the strategies adopted by institutions in the years after the publication of the NCHE report in 1996 and the White Paper in 1997 were to a large extent determined by perceptions – perceptions about the extent to which they would have to recast institutional missions and values, and the extent to which they would lose or benefit from the dropping of the SAPSE funding framework. Because of the close links between funding strategies and student enrolment strategies, these are discussed in the conclusion which follows Chapter 5.

NOTES

1 These a-factors represent the actual proportion which the government paid of its share of the ideal institutional cost generated by the subsidy formula.
2 Real rands were determined by deflating nominal rand totals by the consumer price index supplied by the South African Reserve Bank.

REFERENCES

Albrecht, D. & Ziderman, A. (1992). *Funding Mechanisms for Higher Education: Financing for Stability, Efficiency and Responsibility.* Washington: World Bank.

Bunting, I. (1994). *A Legacy of Inequality.* Cape Town: University of Cape Town Press.

Bunting, I. & Bunting, L. (1998). Research Reports 9, 10, 11, 12, 13, 14. Cape Town: Educational Policy Unit, University of the Western Cape.

Bunting, I. & Smith, M. (1998). Research Report 15. Cape Town: Educational Policy Unit, University of the Western Cape.

Bunting, M. (2001). Analyses of the Financial Statements of Universities and Technikons. Unpublished research papers. Grahamstown: Rhodes University.

Department of National Education (1982). *An Investigation of Government Funding of Universities.* Pretoria.

Department of Education (2001). *Information on the State Budget for Higher Education.* Pretoria.

Hendry, J. & Bunting, I. (1993a). SA Universities: 1985–1990. Research Report. Cape Town: University of Cape Town.

Hendry, J. & Bunting, I. (1993b). SA Technikons: 1988–1990. Research Report. Cape Town: University of Cape Town.

National Commission on Higher Education (1996). *A Framework for Transformation.* Pretoria: NCHE.

National Commission on Higher Education (1996). *Finance Task Team.* Pretoria: NCHE.

Salmi, J. (1994). *Higher Education: The Lessons of Experience.* Washington: The World Bank.

Task Force on Higher Education and Society (2000). *Higher Education in Developing Countries: Peril and Promise.* Washington: The World Bank.

Williams, G. (1992). *Changing Patterns of Finance in Higher Education.* Buckingham: Society for Research into Higher Education and Open University Press.

Ziderman, A. & Albrecht, D. (1995). *Financing Universities in Developing Countries.* Washington: Falmer Press.

CHAPTER 5

IAN BUNTING

STUDENTS

The student profile of the South African higher education system in 1994 was characterised by a number of imbalances: white and male South Africans were over-represented throughout the system while students were concentrated in the humanities and under-represented in the fields of science, technology and commerce.

This chapter describes these imbalances, but also shows that by 1994 there were other major problems in the system. A low participation rate overall (17%), low throughput levels and small graduate outputs resulted in a severe shortage of high-level skills in the country. The challenge for the new South Africa was to transform the higher education system from one that satisfied none of the imperatives of equity, efficiency and development, to one that would meet all three of these national goals.

The recommendations made by the National Commission on Higher Education (NCHE, 1996) and the policies subsequently adopted by the Department of Education ranged from prescribing the massification of the system (NCHE, 1996), to planning for growth (Department of Education, 1997) and improving throughput rates, to increasing postgraduate enrolments (Department of Education, 2001). (See Chapter 3 for a full analysis of these policy changes post-1994.) Not anticipated by these new policies was the development of a higher education market in the post-1994 period that stimulated unprecedented competition for students among institutions: public higher education institutions competed with one another to increase their student intake while at the same time they faced increasing competition from the emerging private (and international) higher education sector.

Institutional competitiveness was fuelled by the fact that government funding of higher education institutions was, and still is, based largely on student numbers and that the institutional landscape was thus influenced by the size and shape of student enrolments. In the context of the new policy environment created by the 1997 White Paper, this competitiveness resulted in new types of differentiation amongst the institutions.

This chapter begins to tell the story of how new institutional differences started to emerge, many of which were not anticipated by government policies, nor by the market, and in many cases, not by many of the institutions themselves. It examines the higher education student body during the period under review and looks at three aspects in particular: changes in student enrolment during the 1990s, how these changes measured up to the policy goals set after 1994, and how changing patterns of student enrolment and graduation contributed to the development of a new typology of higher education institutions by 2000.

95

N. Cloete et al. (eds.), Transformation in Higher Education, 95-111.
© 2007 *Springer.*

1. CHANGES IN STUDENT ENROLMENTS DURING THE 1990s[1]

1.1. Growth, inequities and early optimism

Pressures for change in the higher education system began in February 1990 when it became clear from the unbanning of the national liberation movements that the apartheid era would soon be ending. Higher education policy debates started among a variety of groupings, including the National Education Policy Investigation (Nepi), the Union of Democratic University Staff Associations (Udusa) and the education desk of the African National Congress (ANC). The common conclusion was that all higher education institutions in South Africa would have to give priority to democratising their governance structures, to achieving equity and to becoming responsive to national and regional social and economic development needs.

Unrelated to these policy debates, and prior to the attainment of the new democratic order in 1994, three significant changes in institutional enrolment patterns occurred between 1990 and 1994:

- Institutions which under apartheid had been designated for one race only, opened their doors to all South Africans (see Chapter 2) and enrolments in all universities and technikons grew between 1990 and 1994. Overall, university plus technikon enrolments increased by more than 130.000 (or 33%) in 1994 compared with 1990. This rate of growth contributed strongly to the high-growth scenarios which were developed by policy-makers in the years after 1994.
- The historically black universities grew by 28.000 (or 37%) and the historically white universities by a combined total of 10.000 (or 8%) between 1990 and 1994.
- High rates of growth occurred in all technikons. The major growth, in terms of numbers, occurred in the distance education institution, Technikon South Africa (TSA): its enrolment grew by 38.000 (or 126%) between 1990 and 1994. Overall, historically black technikon enrolments grew by 11.000 (or 60%) and historically white technikon enrolments by 19.000 (or 41%).

Figure 1 provides a summary of changes in headcount student enrolments in the different sectors between 1990 and 1994. These student enrolment patterns and the rapid growth rates which occurred between 1990 and 1994 shaped the context in which the first major higher education policy interventions were attempted between 1994 and 1997.

By 1994 two major systemic problems were confronting policy-makers: firstly, the prevalence of racial and gender inequities in the higher education system and, secondly, the fact that the system was not configured to contribute to national social and economic reconstruction in a post-apartheid South Africa. Figure 2 shows that in 1993 there were unjustifiable inequalities in the participation rates[2] of the various population groups. These proportions must be seen in the context that at this time whites had a share of about 13% of the total population and Africans a share of more than 75%.

The actual shape of student enrolments and outputs in the public higher education system can be seen in Figure 3. It was information of this kind that provided a clear

Figure 1. *Headcount enrolments by sector (thousands): 1990–1994*

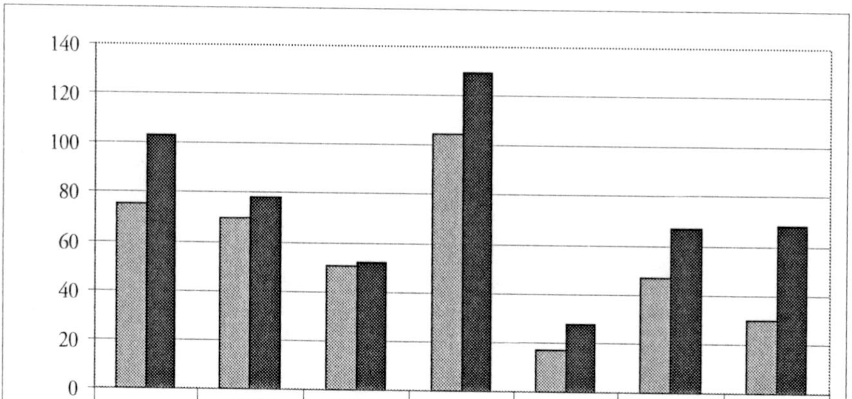

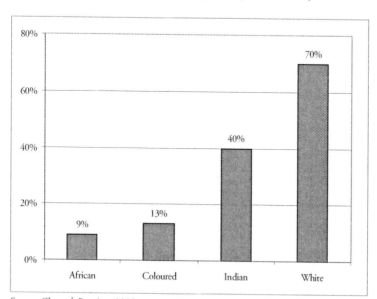

	HBUs	HWUs (Afrik)	HWUs (Eng)	Unisa	HBTs	HWTs	TSA
1990	75.6	69.8	50.4	104.3	17.4	47.1	30.1
1994	103.3	78.3	51.7	129.2	28.0	66.5	68.0

Sources: Hendry & Bunting, 1993(a) and 1993 (b); Department of Education, 1994

Figure 2. *Gross participation rate[4] in the public higher education system: 1993*

Source: Cloete & Bunting, 2000

Figure 3. Shape of student enrolments by sector and by major field of study: 1994

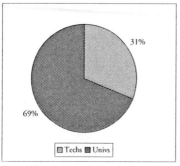

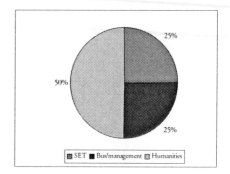

Source: Department of Education, 1994–1998

indication that the public higher education system was overly dominated by universities, and particularly by programmes in the humanities.

In the changing political context, a view developed among policy-makers that the development needs of the South African economy would be best served by graduates in science, engineering and technology, and by diplomates obtaining vocational qualifications from technikons. A system which had 69% of its enrolments and 79% of its in graduates in the university sector was regarded as 'development-unfriendly' particularly because the major fields of study of more than 50% of these university enrolments and graduates were in the humanities.

1.2. Policy interventions: 1994–1997

The changing nature of student enrolments constitutes one aspect of the context in which policy intervention in higher education started in 1995 with the appointment of the National Commission on Higher Education (NCHE, 1996). As is outlined in Chapter 1, the central proposal of the NCHE was that the higher education system should be massified. Increased participation was intended to provide greater opportunity for access while also producing the high-level skills necessary for economic growth.

On the basis of the commission's report in 1996, the second policy intervention came with the publication of the White Paper which accepted much of what the NCHE had recommended in its final report. In particular, it accepted two conditions which the NCHE had set for the transformation of the South African higher education system: firstly, increasing participation in higher education so as to overcome the legacy of fragmentation, inequality and inefficiency; and secondly, improving the responsiveness of the higher education system to deliver the research, knowledge and highly trained people required for South Africa to compete in a rapidly changing international context.

However, the government did not accept the view of the NCHE that the realisation of these two conditions required a formal commitment to the massification of the system.

The NCHE had argued that the demands of equity and responsiveness could be met if a participation rate of 30% was set as a national target and if this became the major policy driver for higher education in South Africa. The view expressed by government in the 1997 White Paper was that future growth in the system was essential if equity goals were to be achieved, but that a commitment to massification prior to eliminating inefficiencies in the higher education system would place its financial sustainability at serious risk.

The White Paper nevertheless set clear goals for equity and responsiveness and outlined performance measures for student enrolments and outputs as follows:

- Total student enrolments in the higher education sector must grow.
- The composition of the student body must begin to reflect the demographic reality of the broader South African society and the participation rates of black and of women students must increase.
- Private higher education institutions must play a role in achieving growth, particularly in expanding access to higher education.
- Career-oriented programmes must be expanded, particularly in science and technology.
- The throughput and output rates of students in the public higher education system must improve.

The period 1994–1997 was characterised by a high level of optimism among policy-makers and institutions which flowed from expectations that the pressure for access to the higher education system would continue in a post-apartheid South Africa. It was taken as given that student enrolments in universities as well as technikons would increase rapidly throughout the rest of the decade.

The evidence available at the time supported the belief that student enrolments in South Africa were on a steep upward trajectory. Figure 4 shows that by 1997 the headcount enrolment for the university plus technikon sectors had reached a total of more than 600.000 – an increase of nearly 206.000 (or 52%) over the total for 1990. The increase in 1997 compared with the enrolment figure in 1993 was 127.000 (or 27%). The average annual increase in headcount enrolments between 1990 and 1997 was 4%.

The increases in headcount enrolments also generated expectations in the higher education system that government funding would grow in future years, particularly because government funds had been allocated to institutions on the basis of formulae which were driven primarily by student enrolments (one formula for universities and another for technikons). Figure 4 shows that the rate of growth in all sub-sectors (other than in the historically white English-medium universities) was high in the period between 1993 and 1997. On the basis of the subsidy formulae all the sub-sectors predicted with a high degree of confidence that their government subsidy payments would grow throughout the 1990s. What transpired, however, was somewhat different.

Figure 4. Headcount student enrolments by sub-sector (thousands): 1990–1997

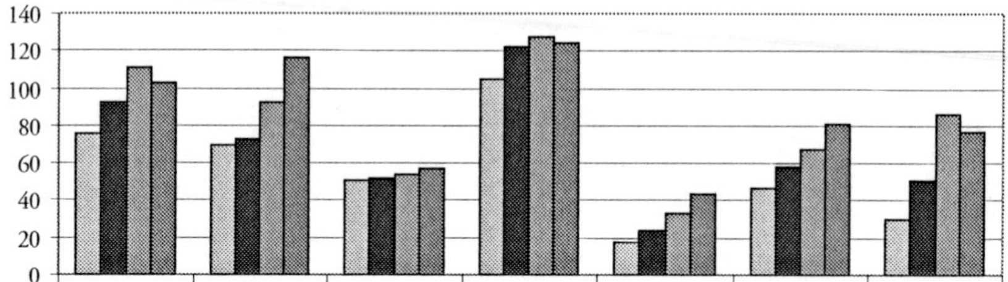

	HBUs	HWUs (Afrik)	HWUs (Eng)	Unisa	HBTs	HWTs	TSA
1990	75.6	69.8	50.4	104.3	17.4	47.1	30.1
1993	92.6	73.0	52.3	122.5	24.3	58.0	50.5
1995	110.6	92.2	53.9	128	32.7	67.8	85.7
1997	102.2	115.8	56.8	124.2	43.6	81.4	76.8

Sources: Hendry & Bunting, 1993(a) and 1993(b); Department of Education, 1994–1998

1.3. Public system enrolments decline: 1998–2000

By 1998 it had become clear that the public higher education sector would not be able to satisfy the White Paper goal of expanded student enrolments which had been based primarily on the NCHE's growth predictions. By 1999, and certainly by 2000, it was clear that the NCHE's projections were seriously over-optimistic. Figure 5 illustrates this point.

The graph shows clearly that actual enrolments began to deviate from the NCHE's predictions as early as 1997. In that year 21.000 (or 3%) fewer students actually enrolled in the higher education system than the total predicted by the NCHE. A more serious problem was that in 1998 and 1999, nearly 140.000 fewer students than had been predicted by the NCHE entered the university and technikon sectors. The effect was that, contrary to all expectations, enrolments in the higher education system in fact reached their peak in 1998, and then fell by 23.000 (or 4%) between 1998 and 1999. In 2000 enrolments increased by 15.000 (or nearly 3%), primarily due to sharp increases in distance education student enrolments at some of the historically white Afrikaans-medium universities.

The unexpected failure of the NCHE's growth model was caused by a number of factors. Among them were the productivity levels of the school system. Between 1995 and 2000 the school system did not produce the numbers of qualified school-leavers that had been expected at the time the NCHE was doing its work. South African universities, and to a large extent technikons, expect new entrants to have what is described as 'matriculation exemption' which is gained when school-leavers obtain a minimum set of marks in sets of prescribed subjects. The NCHE had expected one consequence of the ending of apartheid in the education sector to be a rapid growth in the numbers of

Figure 5. *Headcount enrolments in public universities and technikons.*
NCHE projections compared with actual enrolments (thousands): 1995–2000

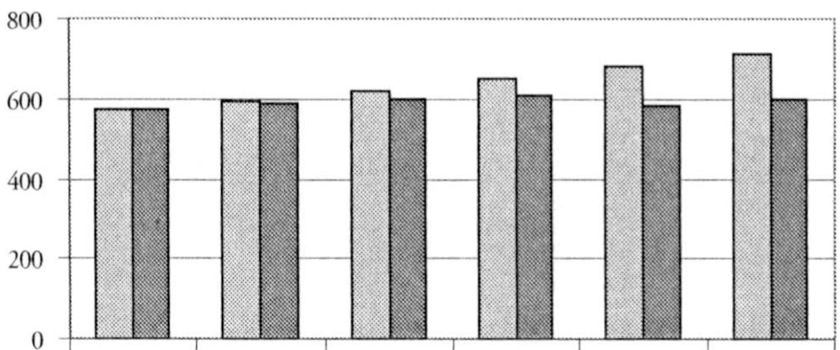

	1995	1996	1997	1998	1999	2000
NCHE	571	595	620	650	680	710
Actual	571	590	599	608	585	600

Sources: Cloete & Bunting, 2000; Department of Education, 1999–2000

school-leavers obtaining matriculation exemption. This did not occur, as can be seen in Figure 6 which compares the NCHE predictions with actual totals of school-leavers obtaining matriculation exemption.

The data rows in the graph show that over the six-year period from 1995 to 2000, 320.000 fewer matriculants were produced by the school system than the NCHE had predicted. One consequence of these low totals was that annual inflow of first-time entering undergraduates (undergraduates who had not previously been registered at any higher education institution) into the university and technikon sectors remained under 120.000 between 1997 and 2000. Since these first-time entering undergraduates normally constitute about 20% of the enrolment of the system, an intake of around 120.000 could not have supported a headcount enrolment total of the size predicted for 1999 and 2000 by the NCHE.

The 1997 White Paper's goal of expanded student enrolments had clearly not been met by 2000. Furthermore, given the current flows of students into the public higher education system, the goal is unlikely to be realised by the public higher education system over the next few years.

Figure 7 compares changes in headcount enrolments by sector over the period 1995 to 2000: The graph clearly depicts the sharp declines which have occurred in the historically black universities and in the dedicated distance education institutions in the period up to 2000. It also shows the sharp increases which occurred in the headcount enrolments of the historically white (Afrikaans-medium) universities and in the historically white technikon sectors.

Figure 6. *Predicted and actual totals of matriculation exemptions (thousands): 1995–2000*

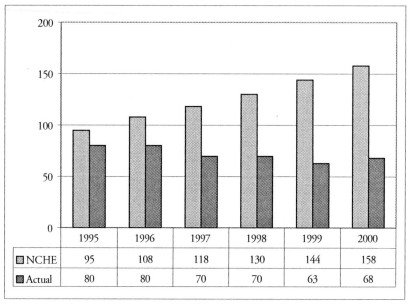

	1995	1996	1997	1998	1999	2000
NCHE	95	108	118	130	144	158
Actual	80	80	70	70	63	68

Sources: Cloete & Bunting, 2000; Department of Education, 1999–2000

Figure 7. *Headcount enrolment totals by sector (thousands): 1995–2000*

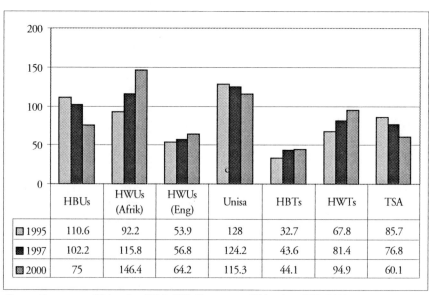

	HBUs	HWUs (Afrik)	HWUs (Eng)	Unisa	HBTs	HWTs	TSA
1995	110.6	92.2	53.9	128	32.7	67.8	85.7
1997	102.2	115.8	56.8	124.2	43.6	81.4	76.8
2000	75	146.4	64.2	115.3	44.1	94.9	60.1

Sources: Department of Education, 1994–1998; Department of Education, 1999–2000

1.4. Enrolments in the new private sector

During the 'period of optimism' between 1994 and 1997, a commonly held view was that a burgeoning private higher education sector would be needed to deal with levels of access-demand which the public sector would not be able to satisfy. The experiences of other developing countries were often cited in this regard: where the capacity of the public higher education sector is limited, the development of a new higher education sector funded by private capital should be encouraged by government.

The 1997 White Paper offered that encouragement to private capital in South Africa and after 1998 the private sector made major efforts to launch various higher education enterprises. These developments included attempts by South African companies to launch new private higher education institutions, as well as attempts by overseas institutions to establish satellite operations in South Africa. However, most of the effort seems to have gone into the formation of partnerships between South African companies and a small group of public universities and technikons.

These partnerships typically involved a public university or technikon permitting a private institution to offer one or more of the public institution's formal qualifications. The public institution provided the teaching materials used by the private institution, and provided general oversight of the teaching and examination processes at the private institution. Because the students concerned were registered for a public institution's formal qualifications, they appeared on its database as registered students, even though they received no direct instruction from that public institution. When public institution submissions were made for government subsidies, the students registered by the private institution were nevertheless included in the public institution's claim.

A question which arises regularly in South African higher education debates is just how many students are enrolled in the private higher education sector and in the absence of more research, the figures are strongly contested. One difficulty is that all students who appear on a public institution's government subsidy claim are automatically counted as public sector students, even though their primary registration is with a private provider. According to the Department of Education, a major portion of the enrolments claimed by the private higher education system in South Africa are students who they have registered for a qualification offered by a public university or technikon, in terms of a formal partnership agreement.

The student data tables of six public institutions (five historically white Afrikaans-medium universities and one historically white technikon) involved with private higher education providers show that in the 2000 academic year they claimed a total of 24.000 full-time equivalent (FTE) students whose primary registration would have been with a private provider. This FTE student total was generated in 2000 by a headcount student total of 65.000. So according to the Department of Education, in 2000 about 11% of the public higher education system's student enrolment was being carried by private providers. The tuition fees of students would normally have gone to the private provider, and government subsidies to the public institutions.

As is shown in Chapter 10, however, other research suggests that there are many more public/private partnerships than those considered above. Figures analysed by the

Education Policy Unit of the University of the Western Cape suggest that in 1998 there were as many as 108.700 FTE students, among whom were some 15.000 individuals enrolled with private providers in first-degree programmes. These data are however open to considerable doubt as they have been derived from the application forms submitted to the Department of Education by private providers applying for formal registration. Examination of the application forms of some private providers suggests firstly, that they did not understand basic notions such as those of 'full-time equivalent student' and that they were as a consequence claiming far more students than they should have; and secondly that most of those recorded by the researchers as private students were being included by their public partner in government subsidy claims and so were being recorded in the public higher education student total.

The task of establishing how many 'private-only' higher education students there were in South Africa is complicated by the reluctance of private providers to share information which constitutes 'business advantage'. Since the passage of the Higher Education Amendment Act of 1999, the Minister of Education has been able to require private providers to register and to make available details of student numbers and curricula. In future it will thus be possible to get more accurate statistics on this sector which emerged in South Africa after 1997.

2. MEASURING CHANGES AGAINST THE POLICY GOALS

2.1. Enrolments by race group and gender

The enrolment data available suggests that the public higher education system has moved, in broad overall terms, towards the equity goals set by the 1997 White Paper. This can be seen in Figures 8 and 9 which show the percentage of black students and women in the headcount enrolment totals. The averages show that by 2000, 73% of students in the public higher education system were black and 53% female. This shows that the public higher education sector made substantial moves during the 1990s towards the achievement of race and gender equity. In 1993, 52% of students were black and 43% female.

But taken overall, this achievement hides major inequities which persist in the public higher education system. Black and female students remain under-represented in postgraduate programmes, as well as in all programmes in business and management, and in science, engineering and technology. Another factor hidden by the data is the extent to which black and female students are enrolled in distance education rather than contact programmes. In 2000, for example, 78% of distance education students and 68% of contact students were black. The proportions for female students were 53% for contact students and 55% for distance education students.

A further equity problem which remains hidden in the changing racial patterns is that of a decline in participation rates in South Africa's higher education system. Changes in the racial distribution of student enrolments are not the result of a major increase in the rate of participation among those who were previously excluded from the higher education system. They stem primarily from a sharp decline in the enrolment of white

Figure 8. *Percentage of black* students in headcount enrolment totals: 1997 and 2000

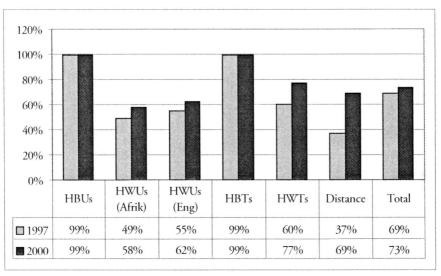

	HBUs	HWUs (Afrik)	HWUs (Eng)	HBTs	HWTs	Distance	Total
1997	99%	49%	55%	99%	60%	37%	69%
2000	99%	58%	62%	99%	77%	69%	73%

Sources: Department of Education, 1994–1998; Department of Education, 1999–2000

Figure 9. *Percentage of female students in headcount enrolment totals: 1997 and 2000*

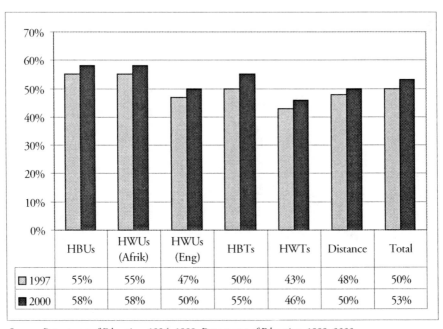

	HBUs	HWUs (Afrik)	HWUs (Eng)	HBTs	HWTs	Distance	Total
1997	55%	55%	47%	50%	43%	48%	50%
2000	58%	58%	50%	55%	46%	50%	53%

Sources: Department of Education, 1994–1998; Department of Education, 1999–2000

Figure 10. *Gross participation rates in public higher education in 1993 and 2000*

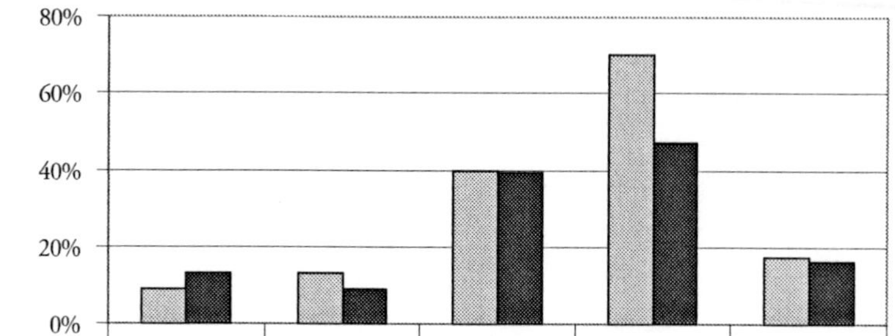

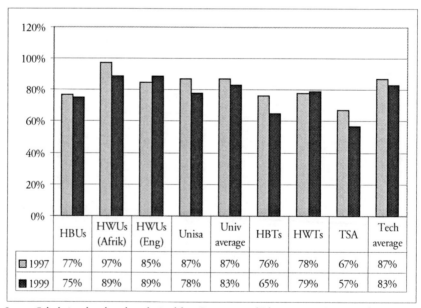

	African	Coloured	Indian	White	Average
▢ 1993	9%	13%	40%	70%	17%
■ 2000	13%	9%	39%	47%	16%

Sources: Cloete & Bunting, 2000; calculations based on headcount enrolment totals and on census data derived from Statistics South Africa at www.statssa.gov.za

Figure 11. *Retention rates in the public higher education system: 1997 and 1999*

	HBUs	HWUs (Afrik)	HWUs (Eng)	Unisa	Univ average	HBTs	HWTs	TSA	Tech average
▢ 1997	77%	97%	85%	87%	87%	76%	78%	67%	87%
■ 1999	75%	89%	89%	78%	83%	65%	79%	57%	83%

Source: Calculations based on data obtained from Department of Education, 1994–1998 and 1999–2000

students in the public higher education system. White enrolments fell from a total of 215.000 in 1995 to 164.000 in 2000, a decline of 41.000 (or 19%) over this period. Nevertheless it must be stressed that the growth in African student enrolments did have a positive effect on this group's overall participation rate.

The gross participation rates for the higher education sector in 1993 and 2000 are reflected in Figure 10. The graph shows that while there was an increase in the participation rate of Africans in the public higher education system, the loss of white student enrolments from the public sector had the effect of lowering the average participation rate from 17% in 1993 to 16% in 2000.

2.2. Responsiveness to development needs

The 1997 White Paper's goal of achieving higher levels of responsiveness to development needs by changing the shape of the public higher education system had not been achieved by 1999 and 2000. The public higher education system remained a university-dominated one, even though changes had occurred between 1994 and 2000. In 1994, 69% and in 2000, 65% of all headcount student enrolments were in universities.

By 2000 the proportion of the public sector's enrolments by major field of study had also not changed in the way envisaged by the White Paper. The system remained dominated by students following majors in the humanities (49%), with only 24% following majors in science, engineering and technology and 26% majoring in business and management.

2.3. Retention rates

A major problem which began to emerge in 1998, and which ran counter to key goals of the White Paper, was a drop in the retention rates of students in the public higher education system. Figure 11 offers a summary of retention rates by sector for 1997 and 1999. The following should be noted:

- The proportions contained in the graph were calculated in this simple way: retention rate equals (headcount enrolment total in year n less first-time entering undergraduate total in year n) divided by (headcount enrolment total in year n-1). The percentages derived can serve at best as proxies for a retention rate because they do no more than express the non-first-time-entering undergraduate enrolment of an institution as a percentage of the total enrolment of the previous year. But it is clear that if an institution has a high percentage of (say) 85% or higher, then that institution has reasonably low drop-out rates and is able to retain large numbers of its graduating students for further higher level studies. It is also clear that if an institution has a retention rate of 75% or lower, then it does have high drop-out rates and is not able to retain in its postgraduate programmes large numbers of those completing first degrees or diplomas.

Figure 12. Masters and doctoral graduates by sector in 2000

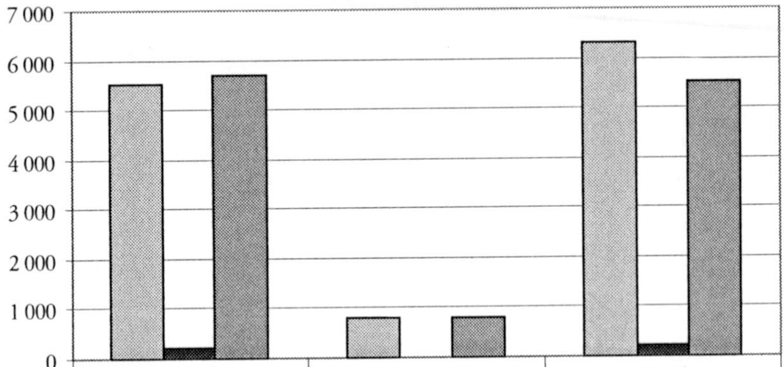

	Masters	Doctors	Total
Univs	5 510	790	6 300
Techs	200	10	210
Total	5 710	800	5 510

Source: Department of Education, 1999–2000

The graph shows clearly the extent to which retention rates in the university plus technikon sectors dropped after having reached a peak in 1997. The effect which the drop in retention rates had on the system after 1997 can be demonstrated in this way: if the system's average retention rate had remained at the 83% level of 1997, then even if the average annual flow of new students into the system had stayed at 120.000, the system would have continued to grow. The headcount total in 1998 on a retention rate of 83% and an intake of 120.000 first-time entering undergraduates would have been 620.000 (or 14.000 higher than the actual total). The headcount total in 1999, on this same set of assumptions, would have been 630.000 rather than the actual total of 586.000. In other words, the decline in retention rates cost the higher education system an aggregate of 60.000 students in 1998 and 1999.

The historically white universities had considerably higher retention percentages than the historically black universities throughout the period 1996 to 1999. This indicates that they had lower drop-out rates and had higher proportions of first-degree or first-diploma completers than the historically black universities. The university sector as a whole had better throughput rate percentages than the technikon sector, which suggests that technikons tend to have higher drop-out rates than universities.

The large numbers of 'financial exclusions' which occurred in the system in 1998 and 1999 were probably a major cause of the fall in retention rates described above. The term 'financial exclusion' is generally used in South Africa to refer to students who are refused permission to register at a university or technikon either because they have debit balances on their fee accounts from the previous year or because they are not able to pay in advance a proportion of their fees for the current year.

Large-scale financial exclusions began in 1998 when a number of historically black institutions were forced by commercial banks to produce cash-flow plans showing both their government subsidy income and their private income before extensions could be given to their overdraft facilities. Because most of the private income of the institutions affected came from the tuition fees paid by students, the cash-flow plans had to assume that students with fee debts would settle these before registering. They also had to assume that substantial up-front fee payments would be made by other students before they registered. In most cases these assumptions about cash flows turned out to be false. Far fewer students than expected were able to pay outstanding fees or make the required advance payments. Those not able to satisfy these financial requirements were refused permission to register, and enrolment totals at the historically black institutions dropped sharply as a consequence.

The majority of students affected by financial exclusions were black students from economically disadvantaged backgrounds. The national student financial aid scheme was intended to help these students register at and remain registered at higher education institutions, but the exclusion of many from university or technikon studies was a clear signal that the national financial aid scheme was being funded at inadequate levels.

2.4. Graduates and graduation rates

The 1997 White Paper's goal of a public higher education system displaying high levels of efficiency had not been realised by the end of the 1990s. For example, the system's output of graduates remained low in relation to its headcount enrolment totals: in 1993 only 17% of students registered at a university completed their degrees or diplomas and only 10% of students registered at a technikon completed theirs. The data available for the 2000 academic year suggest that these proportions have remained at the low levels of 1993. The proportion of graduates to enrolments in the university sector in 2000 was only 16% and in the technikon sector only 9%. To satisfy the efficiency requirements set out in the White Paper, the system's average should have reached at least 20% by 2000. This implies that the system produced nearly 30.000 fewer graduates than it should have in 2000.

In the three-year period from 1998 to 2000, South Africa's universities and technikons produced a total of less than 2.500 doctoral graduates. Details of the production of masters and doctoral graduates by sector in 2000 can be seen in Figure 12. Figure 13 compares the system's total production of masters and doctoral students in 2000 with the total achieved in 1989. As will be seen, the most significant change has been in the output of masters graduates. This total doubled by 2000 compared with 1989, while the doctoral graduate total in 2000 was only 22% higher than that of 1989.

A final issue to note is that by the end of the 1990s the public higher education system had not produced the increased numbers and proportions of science, engineering and technology graduates which the White Paper stated were necessary for national development needs. The graduate outputs of the higher education system continued to be dominated by the fields of education and the broad humanities. This can be seen in Figure 14 which shows the major fields of study in which graduates were produced in the 2000 academic year.

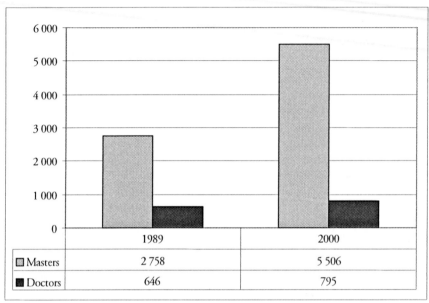

Figure 13. *Total masters and doctoral graduates in 1989 and 2000*

Source: Hendry & Bunting, 1993a and 1993b; Department of Education, 1999 and 2000

Figure 14. *Graduates by major field of study: 2000*

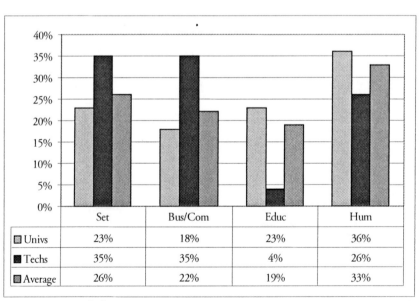

Source: Department of Education, 1999–2000

NOTES

[1] Unless otherwise specified, student data referred to in this chapter are for the public sector institutions.

[2] These rates are adjusted versions of those reported by the NCHE. The adjustments take account of under-counts in the 1991 census. They remain gross rates which have been derived by dividing the total numbers of students in the public higher education system by the numbers of the population in the age group 20–24 years.

[3] These calculations are based on the Unesco method which uses the totals of 20–24 year olds in the population as the base.

[4] For the purposes of the graph 'black' comprises African, coloured and Indian South Africans.

REFERENCES

Albrecht, D. & Ziderman, A. (1992). *Funding Mechanisms for Higher Education: Financing for Stability, Efficiency and Responsibility.* Washington: The World Bank.

Cloete, N. & Bunting, I. (2000). *Higher Education Transformation: Assessing Performance in South Africa.* Pretoria: CHET.

Department of Education (1994–1998). Student Statistics Tables, South African Post-Secondary Information System. Pretoria.

Department of Education (1999). Higher Education Amendment Act No.55 of 1999. Pretoria.

Department of Education (1999–2000). Student Statistics Tables, Higher Education Management Information System. Pretoria.

Department of Education (2001). *National Plan for Higher Education.* Pretoria.

Hendry, J. & Bunting, I. (1993a). SA Universities: 1985–1990. Research Report. Cape Town: University of Cape Town.

Hendry, J. & Bunting, I. (1993b). SA Technikons: 1988–1990. Research Report. Cape Town: University of Cape Town.

National Commission on Higher Education (1996). *A Framework for Transformation.* Pretoria: NCHE.

FUNDING AND STUDENTS

CONCLUSION

The discussion on funding in Chapter 4 emphasised that for the past 20 years close links have existed between the government funding received by universities and technikons and their student enrolments. This funding framework was initially one which had been designed specifically for the historically white universities, and which was eventually extended to all 36 public universities and technikons.

By the end of 2000 the historically black universities and many of the technikons were experiencing severe financial strains. The major problems they faced were firstly, that the SAPSE funding framework, with all its apartheid assumptions, had remained in place throughout the 1990s; secondly, even by the beginning of 2001, the revised framework spelled out in the 1997 White Paper was not yet implemented.

Chapter 4 also showed that the delay in the implementation of a new post-SAPSE framework has permitted some historically white institutions to adopt strategies which generated considerable financial benefits for them. In this context other institutions also adopted a range of strategies, evidence of which can be seen in their changing student enrolment patterns.

Chapter 5 shows that student enrolment patterns changed dramatically, and shows further that these changing patterns of enrolment can be attributed to a number of factors. First, South Africa's new political dispensation provided black students with many more choices in terms of where to study. Secondly, vocational qualifications lost their stigma and many students started seeing them as being more valuable as a basis for employment than university degrees. Third is the question of cost: technikons offered study programmes at a fraction of the cost of university programmes. Even where universities were able to offer students financial support, the resource base of the different institutions meant that more financial aid was available in some universities than in others. For example, the historically white English-medium universities were able to provide students with financial aid to cover both residential costs and fees. The historically black universities, on the other hand, spread student financial aid across the entire student body in an effort to provide support to many more students, with the result that each student got fewer rands to cover the costs of their studies at these institutions

A conclusion which can be drawn from Chapter 5 is that by 2000 three different clusters of institutions had emerged in South Africa's public higher education system: high-growth institutions, medium-growth institutions, and low-growth institutions. Student enrolments grew fastest in all technikons and the historically white Afrikaans-medium universities. Only the historically white Afrikaans-medium universities, however, seem to have employed clear adaptive strategies to achieve high rates of growth (opening up their

N. Cloete et al. (eds.), Transformation in Higher Education, 113-117.
© 2007 *Springer.*

main campuses to black students and moving vigorously into distance education provision). The technikons opened all their programmes to all students, but appear not to have employed any other adaptive strategies as far as enrolments were concerned. Medium-growth institutions (the historically black universities and the historically white English-medium universities) were those which experienced some growth between 1993 and 2000, but not as much as the institutions in the high-growth cluster. Finally, by 2000, Unisa and Technikon SA were the only low-growth institutions in the country.

The adaptive strategies adopted by institutions in dealing with financial and student enrolment issues can be summed up in the ways suggested below.

- *The 'window-of-opportunity' strategy*

  The delays in the implementation of a new funding framework created opportunities for institutions which would last for five years at most. During this period the strategy involved institutions redefining their missions and values in compliance with the requirements of the 1997 White Paper, but using the financial and administrative autonomy they had under the SAPSE funding framework to accumulate funds as rapidly as possible – primarily by boosting their student enrolments.

  This group includes five of the six historically white Afrikaans-medium universities and one of the historically white technikons, and corresponds with the institutions which by 1997 had demonstrated high growth. Up to 2000 these institutions were successful in implementing the growth strategies which they adopted during the years 1995–1997, largely because they were not challenged by government regulators or by competitors. The strategy adopted by these institutions was a simple one: they retained their traditional white student enrolments on their main campuses, formed partnerships with private providers to enrol large numbers of African students in distance programmes, and set up satellite campuses in areas where the majority of students enrolling could be expected to be African.

- *The 'increase-the-product-range' strategy*

  The strategy was based on an assumption that if an institution was able to offer a wider range of programmes, then it would attract more students, and hence more government subsidy and tuition fee income. It came to be used by institutions which took advantage of a gap that had occurred in government regulatory mechanisms. A key feature of this gap was the abolition in 1997 of the buffer body known as the Advisory Council for Universities and Technikons (AUT). This body had played a major bureaucratic role in placing limits on the expansion of the programme offerings of universities and technikons. The 1997 White Paper had, however, indicated clearly that a buffer body of that kind would no longer have a role to play in the national governance of the higher education system, and that it would be replaced by a new advisory body called the Council on Higher Education (CHE). Among the advisory responsibilities given to the CHE by the Higher Education Act of 1997 was the responsibility for programme approval and limitation previously exercised by the AUT. The CHE was established in 1998 with a staff which included few if any of the members of the staff of the AUT. The CHE experienced problems in setting up new regulatory mechanisms and during this time, up to the end of 1999, universities and technikons found that they were able to increase the range of their programme offerings relatively easily. This strategy, however, was not as successful as these institutions expected: their student enrolments did not always grow as anticipated, and their financial standing tended to remain weak.

- *The 'wait-for-redress' strategy*
  The 1997 White Paper recognised that the SAPSE funding framework had been detrimental to black higher education institutions. It therefore emphasised that funds for institutional redress would flow to these institutions under the provisions of a new funding framework. In addition to institutional redress funds, institutions would receive funds for individual redress in the form of student financial aid payments which would be paid directly to them rather than to individual students.

  Since the historically black institutions were registering the majority of disadvantaged students in South Africa, they believed that they would receive the major share of financial aid funds, and that they would consequently be relieved of the close to impossible task of collecting substantial amounts in fees from impoverished students. The strategy was thus one of waiting for government to deliver on the White Paper commitment to institutional and individual redress funds. This strategy failed in the case of the historically black universities because they did not receive government redress funds and because they lost many thousands of actual and potential students to those historically white institutions which had adopted aggressive expansion strategies.

- *The 'internal-consolidation-first' strategy*
  Some institutions believed that they were not likely to be affected in any major way, either positively or negatively, by the adoption of a new funding framework. This strategy involved institutions in internal consolidation and adaptation activities, designed primarily to change and/or strengthen institutional missions in line with the requirements of the 1997 White Paper, and to improve internal efficiencies. This group consisted primarily of the historically white English-medium universities, one historically white Afrikaans-medium university, and a few historically white and black technikons. Their strategies were focused not on ways of expanding their student enrolments and academic programmes, but rather on improving what they had been doing. Largely inward-looking, this strategy focused on changing curricula and teaching methods, improving administrative and financial efficiency, and meeting government requirements in regard to student and staff equity. In the years which followed 1997, this group of institutions had stable, low-growth student enrolments.

- *The 'go-with-the-flow-of-change' strategy*
  Some institutions accepted that they would not be able to control their student enrolments. They expected the only government intervention to be that of

directing increased amounts of redress funding. Their student enrolments grew rapidly up to 1997 and continued to grow between 1997 and 2000, even though overall enrolments in the higher education system were falling.

These five strategies are of course not mutually exclusive. There were some cases in which institutions followed the window-of-opportunity strategy whilst simultaneously increasing the range of their programme/product offerings. It is nevertheless possible to place institutions into categories related to these five strategies. The division of the system into categories related to these strategies can be seen in the table below. It suggests that 21 of South Africa's 36 universities and technikons in effect adopted passive strategies in the period 1997–2001. Thirteen were in the wait-for-redress category and eight in the go-with-the-flow-of-change strategy. Only 15 of the 36 higher education institutions actively devised adaptive strategies in the face of the major policy changes which occurred in the years after 1997.

Table 1. Public institutions and funding adaptive strategies: 1997–2001

Strategy	Institutions in category	Total
1. Window-of-opportunity	5 HWU (Afrikaans), 1 HWT	6
2. Increase-product-range	2 HBU, 2 HWT	4
3. Wait-for-redress	7 HBU, 6 HBT	13
4. Internal-consolidation-first	1 HWU (Afrikaans), 3 HWU (English), 1 HBT	5
5. Go-with-flow-of-change	1 HWU (English), 5 HWT, 2 distance	8
Total		36

The analysis above reveals both a pessimistic and an optimistic picture. On the negative side it shows that many institutions that were supposed to improve their position in the new dispensation could not do so. However, it also shows that some of the historically disadvantaged institutions did manage to grow in the new South Africa. The combined student/funding results indicate that, as in many other parts of the world, South Africa has a set of robust institutions that adapted and improved their financial situation in a radically changing environment. Most positive in the South African context, is the fact that the institutional adaptive strategies cannot be read stereotypically off the old racial and ethnic classifications.

The post-1994 period started with great expectations of funding being used as an instrument of transformation, particularly to bring about greater equity in the system. On the individual level previously excluded groups gained greater access than ever before, and unprecedented freedom of choice regarding institutions and programmes. The global reform agenda, with an emphasis on differentiation, tight fiscal controls and the stimulation of market competition amongst institutions was adopted, and steadfastly held to by the new government.

The funding policy of steering through a linked planning-funding system is in line with policies in many other countries. So is the mix of private/public benefits and the high level of income diversification – but higher education receives a smaller proportion of income from government subsidy than in many developed countries. Expenditure on education is 6% of GDP, which is comparable to that of middle income countries, and the 15% of the education budget allocated to higher education compares favourably internationally, but a difference is that in many developed countries massification meant that institutions had to do more with the same. Also, what is not in line with global trends are the following features of the South African system: a decrease in participation rates, meaning a growing shortage of high level skills, a very high level of students who drop out, and a substantial proportion (about 25%) of institutions that are not functioning well enough to provide a minimum level higher education. It could be argued that in 2001, the system, as a system, was more differentiated, and more unequal than in 1994.

While some of the 'big' questions raised in the introduction, such as how much higher education South Africa can afford, and how much should be spent per student, have not yet been answered, it could be argued that the post-apartheid South African government certainly took a much more active role in the financial affairs of the institutions than the previous government and demonstrated a much greater concern for efficiency, even if the appropriate policy instruments have not yet been put in place.

PART 2

STAFF AND LEADERSHIP

INTRODUCTION

Chapters 6 and 7 trace the changes and challenges that have confronted all those who work within higher education institutions – from institutional leaders and managers through administrators and academic staff, to technical assistants and service workers. Predictably, it is South Africa's massive social and political transformation that has prescribed the most overt of these challenges – the translation of the great principles of democracy, equity and social justice into the structures, practices, cultures and identities of higher education institutions.

At a national level, the process of entrenching the hegemonic position of social democracy in South Africa has moved its values and principles from manifestations in slogans and struggle to substantial embodiment in constitutional provision, policy intention and legal statute. The chapters on staff and leadership demonstrate a corresponding ideological shift on the terrain of higher education that produced an intense focus on issues of governance and equity in reallocating decision-making power and employment opportunity.

In relation to staff, the key policy thrust was for equity (strengthened later by the provisions of the Employment Equity Act of 1998) in order to change the demographics of all sectors of staff in line with national profiles. Transforming governance structures and practices to become more inclusive and participatory, in line with co-operative governance policy, has been a priority energised by the same political animus that won national liberation for a disenfranchised populace, but the evidence presented in the following two chapters suggests that this process has been experienced differently in different institutional contexts, with a range of consequences and effects. More importantly, the story that is told by these chapters suggests that other processes – associated with state fiscal policy and the operations of the market – may have had even more profound effects on the system and its institutions than the higher education policies formulated post-1994.

A recurring theme in both chapters is the complexity and contradictory nature of the challenges facing higher education: South Africa's internal transition corresponded with a moment in world history broadly captured in the term 'globalisation'. As higher education attempted to deal with the internal pressure for greater democratisation, it was subjected at the same time to global pressures from which it had been artificially cushioned – market competition, the commodifying of higher education products, and public accountability – particularly in the form of increased demands from the state for efficiency and effectiveness. In some instances, particular institutional histories led to such an intense pre-occupation with governance issues that the significance of these other

N. Cloete et al. (eds.), Transformation in Higher Education, 119-121.
© 2007 Springer.

pressures was obscured, leaving institutions exposed and vulnerable to their most negative effects. In other instances, traditions (or institutional culture) and capacity enabled institutions to manage and resolve conflicts around the transformation of governance structures in ways that gave them space to respond effectively and strategically to new social and economic conditions. It is here that the analysis of leadership strategies situates itself.

That leadership is addressed as a topic in and of itself in the pages of this publication is noteworthy and suggests a certain 'coming of age' in South African educational discourse. Kulati and Moja reflect on the fact that leadership is not specifically addressed in the policy documents of the transition. Perhaps this is because policy itself is seen as providing the values, direction and guidance – the vision – denoted by leadership. But as they correctly point out, the interpretation and implementation of policy in widely differing institutional contexts require another kind of leadership, the parameters of which are clearly set by history, context, material resource-levels and human resource capacity. Another explanation for this hiatus in the policy documents (and elsewhere) is the tension that lies at the heart of democratic philosophy and practice between the principles of egalitarian participation and empowerment, and the implications of hierarchy and authority associated with leadership.

This tension is marked in the text of the chapter on leadership in what is perhaps a less than conscious slippage of meaning between leadership as the practice of providing vision, devising strategies, offering guidance and direction, and leadership as the person or group of persons providing the vision. Leadership is used as a substitute term for 'leader', or 'leaders' (terms that are very rarely used in the text). This has the effect of stripping the concept of any connection with individual personality or identity. Instead, the broader, more inclusive, participatory pole of meaning is emphasised. Anyone can contribute to leadership.

A fully conscious, and very telling, articulation of this tension occurs in the dominant leadership types presented in the argument. Transformative leadership, characterised precisely by its inclusive, consultative and participatory practices, is contrasted with managerial leadership which seeks the benefits of rapid response to competitive market conditions through the decision-making authority of a sharply defined group of executive managers. The former can be seen as responding primarily to the equity and co-operative governance demands of policy, while the latter form of leadership focuses powerfully on the efficiency demands of policy. There are too many variables involved to accurately assert that current conditions favour the latter rather than the former, but a number of factors (explored in the chapter on staff) suggest that divisions amongst different sectors of staff are growing, particularly between senior managers (including academic managers) and the broad body of academic staff.

One of these factors is the relatively new phenomenon of sharply differentiated salaries. Another lies in the provisions of new labour legislation now governing academic staff. Designed to protect worker rights and interests, and promote participation in workplace decision-making, these regulations, when applied on the academic terrain, have had the contradictory effect of emphasising contractual employment relationships above collegial community. The reader is left in no doubt that higher education workplaces are changing rapidly, becoming more demanding and less secure, as more flexible forms of employment, in line with global trends, are finding favour.

Nonetheless, as Manuel Castells (2001) reminds us, higher education institutions, while taking on new roles and functions, retain many of their traditional functions. Successfully managing this complex and contradictory array of roles will be the critical test of the ability of institutions to perform within the demanding conditions of the global arena.

> The real issue is … to create institutions solid enough to stand the tensions that will necessarily trigger the simultaneous performance of somewhat contradictory functions. The ability to manage such contradictions, while emphasising the role of universities in the generation of knowledge and the training of labour in the context of the new requirements of the development process, will condition to a large extent the capacity of new countries and regions to become part of the dynamic system of the new world economy. (p212)

REFERENCE

Castells, M. (2001). Universities as Dynamic Systems of Contradictory Functions. In J. Muller, N. Cloete & S. Badat (eds), *Challenges of Globalisation: South African Debates with Manuel Castells*. Cape Town: Maskew Miller Longman.

CHAPTER 6

TRISH GIBBON & JANE KABAKI

STAFF

1. APARTHEID LABOUR POLICY AND HIGHER EDUCATION

Prior to the transition to democratic rule in South Africa, employment practices in higher education institutions reflected the dominant characteristics of the apartheid-defined labour market. One of apartheid's most notorious policies, job reservation, ensured that access to almost all professional, high level and high paying jobs in the economy was restricted to whites. The National Commission on Higher Education (NCHE) of 1996 gave the following description of the racial and gender hierarchy that still prevailed in higher education institutions in 1990:

> The higher education sector in South Africa is highly stratified in terms of race and gender. The trend is that the greater the prestige, status and influence particular positions have, the greater the extent to which they are dominated by whites and men. Positions which on the other hand have a lower status and prestige, and which wield little influence, tend to be filled primarily by blacks and women. Most African staff are concentrated at the bottom of the employment ladder. Most are employed as service staff, whereas most whites are employed as academic staff or in senior administrative posts. These disparities in the overall employment structure of universities and technikons increase with rank. (1996:38)

But the collusion (in some instances, unwilling) of higher education in apartheid labour policies and practices was not restricted to employment patterns. With its racially and ethnically defined institutions and its racial distribution of students across particular fields and levels of study, the higher education system itself served to construct and maintain the social, political and economic features of the apartheid order. More importantly, for the purposes of this argument, it contributed to the systematic under-qualification of the majority black population. As Badat et al. (1995) put it, the historically white universities:

> … produced the white human resources to occupy high-level positions in the 'modern' occupational structure in both the economy and the political system; the scientific knowledge required by the advanced capitalist economy and to meet the social, medical and other consumer needs of the white population.

> By contrast, the HBUs [historically black universities] were generally shaped to serve another side of the apartheid development project, namely, development linked to the bantustan scheme and to the separate futures envisaged for the Coloured and Indian communities. That is to say, 'development' programmes which were extremely limited and low level and which thereby gave rise to demands for the production of a very limited range of human resources and at a relatively low level of skill. (p26)

N. Cloete et al. (eds.), Transformation in Higher Education. 123-152.
© 2007 Springer.

The higher education system provided racially differentiated access to opportunities for acquiring the education, training, skills and qualifications that are a prerequisite for participation in the higher levels of the labour market. In other words, the system was not only discriminatory in its employment practices, but also set a ceiling on black academic aspirations and achievements. The consequences are still felt in the existence of a relatively small pool of highly qualified black South Africans for whose services employers in all sectors engage in intense competition. In succeeding arguments, this becomes part of the explanation for the slow pace of change in the racial composition of staff at higher education institutions since 1994.

Race and gender bias, however, were not the only problems. A concentration of students in the humanities and the social sciences, particularly in the black universities (see Chapter 5 on students), led to a disproportionate number of academic staff being employed in those fields. A further skewing of distribution occurred in the homelands, where black institutions employed large numbers of people in the service and administrative sectors to alleviate high levels of local unemployment. For example, in 1990, the University of Fort Hare had 236 academics, 320 administrative staff and 1.128 unskilled workers on its payroll.

1.1. Impact of the academic boycott

Higher education institutions in this period also suffered the political consequences of being part of the apartheid order in their isolation from the mainstream of international academic developments. A 'selective' academic boycott was instituted in the 1980s, driven internally by a coalition of anti-apartheid organisations such as the Union of Democratic University Staff Associations (Udusa) and the United Democratic Front (UDF), and externally by the African National Congress (ANC) in exile and international anti-apartheid organisations. One effect of this boycott was to produce a one-way curtain of isolation that still allowed South African academics to maintain contact with their discipline communities in other parts of the world. Those who were perceived to be politically 'correct', could still attend conferences, and most academics (mistakenly, as it turned out) continued to believe that they were part of contemporary developments in higher education internationally. Conversely, during the late 1980s and early 1990s the academic traffic into South Africa came to a virtual halt. The much publicised Connor Cruise O'Brien affair (1987) was a clear signal to international visitors coming to South Africa that academia, like sports, was an arena dominated by politics. An earlier trickle of foreign academics who came to work in South Africa, dried up completely, further intensifying the insularity of the institutions. Increasingly, institutions appointed their own honours and masters graduates to tenured staff positions in a closed, self-referential circuit.

The second major effect of international isolation was that South African higher education institutions were effectively screened from the changes associated with globalisation which confronted institutions in other parts of the world – competition from foreign institutions and the demands for greater efficiency and accountability.

Thus, on the one hand, the boycott adversely affected international access and participation, while on the other hand, it protected the higher education labour force from trends that were already in full force in developed countries.

Within the South African education system, higher education was growing at around 4% per annum (Bunting, 1994). Staff enjoyed remarkable job security and, within each sector, fairly similar conditions of service and salary packages. There was little pressure to recruit students or raise research funds and consultancy money, and minimal competition amongst faculties and between institutions.

2. POLICIES AND PRESSURES SHAPING THE NEW DEMOCRATIC ORDER

The transition to an open democracy heralded by the elections of 1994, necessitated the construction of a new legislative framework within which major social institutions could be reconfigured in line with the values of a non-racial, non-sexist, non-discriminatory social order. Staff at higher education institutions were affected primarily by two sets of new policy directions emanating from the Department of Education and the Department of Labour. While absorbing the impact of this new policy, the opening up of the country and its institutions to the pressures of a rapidly globalising world economy simultaneously exposed the higher education system to market influences on an unprecedented and unexpected scale.

2.1. Higher education policy after 1994

The first and most dramatic change in the higher education system occurred before the formulation of new policy. The dropping of racial barriers to access in all institutions is so obvious that it often goes without remark. There was no formal policy or legal change to mark this transition, but a weakened apartheid state, already negotiating with the major political parties in exile, no longer had the political will to enforce its racially exclusive regulations. From the late 1980s, black students, in increasing numbers, started enrolling at institutions previously designated white, and African student enrolments increased at the institutions previously restricted to Indian and coloured students. While the demographics of the student populations at the historically black institutions, excluding the Universities of Durban-Westville and Western Cape, hardly underwent any change at all, the student population at other institutions changed substantially between 1990 and 2000 (see Chapter 5 on students).

Policy formulation after 1994 confirmed this freedom of access and further articulated the key principles of equity and redress, democratic participation in a new system of co-operative governance, diversity, development, quality, effectiveness and efficiency, academic freedom and autonomy, and public accountability. The major challenge confronting policy-makers was how to construct something rational and coherent that would undo the entrenched inequities of the apartheid-inspired higher education landscape, correct its skewed distribution of physical and human resources and capacity, and overcome its wasteful and costly duplication of provision. In particular, the system had to become far more effective in producing skilled graduates to power the new economy and far more responsive to the social and economic needs of a developing and modernising society in its provision of appropriate programmes.

Many of the recommendations of the 1996 Report of the National Commission on Higher Education were adopted in the Department of Education's White Paper on higher education transformation (1997), while the Higher Education Act of 1997 gave these principles legal authority. Individual redress in the form of financial aid to academically able but economically disadvantaged students was designed to broaden participation, and it further enabled students to exercise greater freedom in their choice of institutions and programmes. Emphasis, however, was on the planning and co-ordination processes necessary to steer the system towards the goals articulated in the White Paper. As was described in Chapter 4, the first element of this process would be the production of a national plan within the parameters of which institutions would draw up three-year rolling plans that would specify key strategic targets in a number of areas and against which their actual performance could be assessed. Other instruments were specified such as a goal-oriented, public-performance funding framework, with funds explicitly earmarked for redress projects. While the institutions were required to produce two sets of rolling plans, neither the national plan nor the promised funding framework were put in place, and so these policy recommendations operated merely at the level of rhetorical pressure. Nonetheless, many institutions responded to the intentions of the new policy environment in ways that indicated an expectation that implementation would take place, and some of these responses had a direct impact on staff.

2.1.1. Implications for higher education staff – actual and intended
2.1.1.1. Access and redress

The mobility afforded to students by the dropping of racial barriers and the setting up of a student financial aid scheme confronted many of the historically advantaged institutions, for the first time, with a significant number of first-entry students who were ill-prepared for tertiary studies by the poor schooling they had received. Inadequate proficiency in English and poor numerical and conceptual skills translated into an immediate demand on staff for bridging courses, academic development programmes and student support. In this new situation it rapidly became clear that it was not simply a matter of student 'problems' and inadequacies. A culturally, linguistically and educationally diverse student population challenged many of the fundamental assumptions and attitudes of academic staff, and in some instances led to the establishment of staff development programmes that provoked a reassessment of curricula and pedagogical practices.

2.1.1.2. Equity

The intention behind the policy demand for equity in employment practices was to bring staff profiles in closer alignment with student and national demographics. It led to some changes in recruitment and promotion strategies, and challenged institutions to develop more strategic human resource policies and practices. In reality, these have not succeeded in producing significant changes in the staff profile of higher education institutions as the following section demonstrates.

2.1.1.3. Co-operative governance

The statutory requirements of the Higher Education Act (1997) led to the reconstitution of the existing governance structures of council and senate by deepening and extending stakeholder participation, and to the establishment of a new governance structure, the institutional forum, as an advisory body to council. While these measures have afforded greater participation in decision-making to some sectors of staff (and students), the effects on the traditional structure of senates have not been unambiguous. Where professors previously had automatic membership of senate, the highest academic authority of the institution, this has been replaced in some institutions by a representative presence, alongside the representatives of other constituencies, and has produced a considerable undermining of traditional academic authority.

2.1.1.4. Responsiveness and quality

The demand for high-quality academic programmes, that were responsive to both social reconstruction and economic development needs, was reinforced by the establishment of a National Qualifications Framework that governed the provision of all educational and training programmes. Responsiveness and quality became part of the criteria for accreditation of programmes and qualifications. From 1996, academic staff at many institutions gave an enormous amount of time and energy to re-examining and reconstructing academic curricula under circumstances made complex by a number of other factors (see Chapter 8 on curriculum and later arguments in this chapter).

2.1.1.5. Institutional autonomy and public accountability

While policy affirmed institutional autonomy, it did so within the context of a new emphasis on public accountability that made institutions, and the staff within them, accountable for the ways in which public monies were used. The use of national resources was to be assessed against the goals established in government policy and through the mechanisms of statistical returns and three-year rolling plans.

2.2. Labour policies after 1994

In this period, labour legislation sought to build a framework of rights and obligations based on the fundamental provisions of the new Constitution and, in so doing, to move labour relations away from the racially defined, highly exploitative and conflictual relationships of the apartheid past.

The Basic Conditions of Employment Act (No 75 of 1997) set minimum conditions for the most marginalised sectors of the workforce including standardisation of conditions, minimum hours, protection of basic rights and regulation of overtime, holiday work, and maternity and other leave. The Labour Relations Act (No 66 of 1995) heralded a new period of regulation and industrial democracy by legitimising industrial action, regulating collective bargaining, protecting employee rights, prohibiting unfair discrimination and setting up the framework and procedures for dispute resolution and mediation. It aimed at enabling more co-operative and consultative relationships, and set out the procedures governing dismissal, retrenchments and outsourcing.

By far the most ambitious and far-reaching of the four labour statutes enacted between 1994 and 1999 is the Employment Equity Act (No 55 of 1998). It was formulated on the basis of Section 9 of the Constitution which prohibits any person from unfairly discriminating against another person on the grounds of race, gender, sex, pregnancy, marital status, ethnic or social origin, colour, sexual orientation, age, disability, religion, conscience, belief, culture, language, or birth. It requires parliament to enact legislation to prevent unfair discrimination and authorises the adoption of 'legislative and other measures designed to protect or advance persons, or categories of persons, disadvantaged by unfair discrimination'. The act outlaws discrimination and provides for the empowerment of designated groups – blacks, women and the disabled – while compelling employers to consult with workers and disclose relevant information that will allow parties to consult effectively in the implementation of employment equity plans.

Further labour-related legislation in the form of the Skills Development Act (No 97 of 1998) and the Skills Development Levies Act (No 9 of 1999) introduced new institutions, programmes and funding policies designed to increase investment in skills development. The objective is to increase skills within the country by aligning training with equity goals to improve productivity and the competitiveness of industry, business, commerce and services.

2.2.1. Implications for staff of new labour policy

This dispensation incorporated academic staff, for the first time, into the domain of industrial relations by regulating the terms and conditions of their employment in the same way as all other employees. Whereas previously they were organised in loose staff associations that had no legal rights, they were now entitled to form or join trade unions and collectively bargain for sector-wide rights and conditions of service. The relationship of academics to their work environment was now defined primarily by the employment contract, which in turn was governed by the general provisions of the Labour Relations Act (No 66 of 1995).

The second major implication of the new labour legislation for staff was that the Employment Equity Act required institutions to draw up employment equity plans and set equity targets against which their future employment profiles would be measured. Threatening to some and advantageous to others, retrenchments, in order to effect equity gains, were now legally sanctioned, though not without due consultation with affected employees. Generally, however, dismissals, retrenchments and outsourcing were governed by a common set of legal provisions for all employees.

Under the new labour policy, employers were also required to draw up skills development plans for all sectors of employees.

2.3. Market pressures

What pushed higher education institutions into a greater alignment with the market, or subjected them to greater market pressures, was only in part the direct influence of the market itself; more importantly, it was the consequence of the uneven implementation of state policy. The implementation of macro-economic policy measures set limits on public spending and imposed fiscal constraints on higher education institutions. At the same time, the proposed goal-oriented funding framework for higher education was not implemented. In this implementation vacuum, the old funding formula, linked to student enrolments and throughput, continued as the basis for the allocation of state subsidies to institutions. As student enrolments declined, so did subsidies, and this exposed the institutions to market forces in ways that hitherto were almost unthinkable. Previously operating from secure financial platforms, public institutions under these conditions were forced into intense competition for students, both amongst themselves and with a new array of private providers who focused on offering short-duration, low-cost, high-demand programmes.

The National Plan for Higher Education (2001) acknowledges much of this:

> The most important aspect of the absence of a national plan has been the development of a competitive climate between public higher education institutions. This competitive climate has, furthermore, been fuelled by the emergence of a market in higher education as a result of a growing private higher education sector. The increased competition between higher education institutions has further fragmented and exacerbated the inequalities within the higher education system. (p8)

It goes on to say that this increased competition 'also highlights the limits of linking funding narrowly to student enrolments. This is inherently competitive, except when enrolments are growing, and/or unless mitigated by other policy and planning mechanisms linked to national goals.' (p9).

2.3.1. Implications for higher education staff

Fiscal constraint translates into a demand for efficiency – to do the same or more with fewer resources – and to compensate by diversifying income sources. Institutions responded to this demand in two ways:

- With internal budgetary policies and practices that focus on cost-cutting, rationalisation of administrative and academic structures, academic offerings and services, and, in some instances, the closing down of 'unprofitable' academic departments or units, and service sectors.
- With an array of strategies that signal an intense marketisation of higher education and its products.

Some institutions combined both strategies while others, depending on their institutional context, capacity and geographical location, concentrated on one or the other.

Many academics found it extremely difficult to accommodate the new dominance of the terminology, discourse and practices of corporate business in a teaching, learning and research environment. Both discursively, and in the practices it entrenches, corporate culture conflicts sharply with the value system that underpins much academic work, a value system captured broadly in a commitment to the disinterested pursuit of knowledge and truth, and its open dissemination. Within the new market discourse, students become clients or customers and teachers are service providers. Courses must be packaged with attendant services and facilities as attractive commodities to draw buyers from within the student market. While institutions compete with one another for students through extensive and expensive advertising campaigns, so too do faculties and schools within institutions. Within this new environment, however, staff also responded creatively to the need to capture new markets, and developed innovative, trans-disciplinary programmes, as well as multi-mode delivery programmes for non-traditional students such as working adults, or students at a considerable distance from the home campus.

New management practices, often referred to as 'managerialism', produced the contradictory effect of both a decentralised, devolved authority (down to new 'executive' deans with budgetary discretion) and sharper divisions that mark off senior executives and managers from the rest of the staff. At the same time, the drive for efficiency through the achievement of cost savings rendered staff in both the academic and service sectors vulnerable to retrenchment and outsourcing.

Finally, institutions competed not only for students, but also, critically, for staff. Highly qualified black and women staff were and continue to be in demand and may be attracted to institutions by higher salaries, better research opportunities, access to funding for research, and lighter administrative and teaching commitments.

In the period since 1994 the triad of higher education policy, labour policy and market influences intersected and interacted in the complex field of institutional relationships within which staff fulfil their duties, pursue their careers and ambitions, and earn their livelihood. The most significant aspects of these complex interactions will be explored in the following sections by focussing on:

- Equity profiles, staff movement and institutional capacity.
- Governance, new management practices and institutional restructuring.
- Changes in the nature of academic work.

3. EQUITY PROFILES, STAFF MOVEMENT
AND INSTITUTIONAL CAPACITY

3.1. The size and shape of the public higher education workforce[1]

While a 'revolution' occurred in the composition of the student body in South African higher education institutions, the transformation of the staff body was never going to be that easily achieved. Obstacles included a context of resistance to change, severe shortages of blacks and women with appropriate postgraduate qualifications, and affirmative action competition for highly skilled blacks from government departments and business.

In 1994 the South African higher education workforce comprised around 45.000 staff. This figure remained fairly constant, dropping only by about 1.000 between 1994 and 1999. Some reshaping of the higher education labour force is evident, however, with regard to the various personnel categories and to their race and gender composition in certain institutional types (Subotzky, 2001).

In relation to the size of the sector, the overall number of staff in higher education peaked in 1997 and then fell off. Surprisingly though, the number of academic staff did not decline along with reduced student numbers. In relation to the shape of the higher education staff, a growth occurred in the category of professional staff in the universities (reflecting the growing professionalisation of management and administration) and in non-professional staff at the technikons, particularly in administrative staff (probably the result of the redressing of previous inadequacies in resource allocations in these relatively new institutions). The overall numbers of university staff, however, declined by about 3.000 between 1994 and 1999, while technikon staff totals increased by about 2.000 (Subotzky, 2001).

There was an overall decline in service staff, especially at the historically advantaged institutions, as a result of the outsourcing of non-core service and technical functions, an issue to which we shall return later.

Figure 1. *Total permanent[2] higher education workforce by personnel category: 1994–1999*

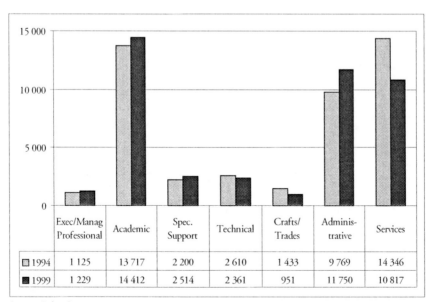

	Exec/Manag Professional	Academic	Spec. Support	Technical	Crafts/ Trades	Adminis- trative	Services
☐ 1994	1 125	13 717	2 200	2 610	1 433	9 769	14 346
■ 1999	1 229	14 412	2 514	2 361	951	11 750	10 817

Source: Subotzky, 2001

3.2. Changes in the racial and gender composition of staff

The racial composition of the workforce changed over the decade from 1988 to 1998, but not dramatically, with the percentage of Africans rising (from 30% to 38%) and that of whites dropping (from 55% to 47%). Similarly, the percentage of women in the sector rose from 37% to 45% over this period.

More pronounced was the wide variation in the racial distribution of staff within the professional and non-professional categories.

Table 1. Proportion of professional and non-professional permanent staff by race and gender: 1994–1999

		African	Coloured	Indian	White	Total		% Women
Professional	1994	12%	4%	4%	80%	17.042	100%	34%
	1999	18%	4%	6%	72%	18.155	100%	38%
Non-professional	1994	52%	14%	6%	30%	28.158	100%	47%
	1999	52%	13%	6%	29%	25.879	100%	51%

Note: 299 staff categorised as 'other' are not shown but are included in the total.
Source: Subotzky, 2001

Taken overall, the racial composition of the academic staff in universities changed the least, with the percentage of white academic staff in permanent positions declining slightly from 87% to 80% between 1993 and 1998, while the percentage of black academic staff increased from 13% to 20%. In technikons the change was more marked, with the percentage of white academic staff declining from 88% to 71% and the percentage of black staff increasing from 12% to 29% (Subotzky, 2001). Sharper distinctions appear, however, when these figures are disaggregated into the categories of historically black and white universities and technikons (see Figure 2).

There are two points to be made here. One is that black academics remained concentrated at the historically black institutions, and the second is that these institutions were the only ones to show a significant increase in the number of black academics employed on the full-time staff.

Similarly, there was a highly uneven distribution of blacks in executive management and senior administrative positions. At historically white institutions, blacks still had a minimal presence in management positions, although there was a substantial difference between the English- and Afrikaans-medium institutions. It is only at the historically black institutions that blacks dominated positions in executive management (Figure 3).

By contrast, women significantly increased their share of full-time academic staff positions across all institutions, with the biggest increases occurring at the historically black technikons (17%), historically white English-medium universities (14%) and the historically black universities (13%) (Figure 4).

Figure 2. Percentage of blacks in full-time permanent academic staff: 1993–1999

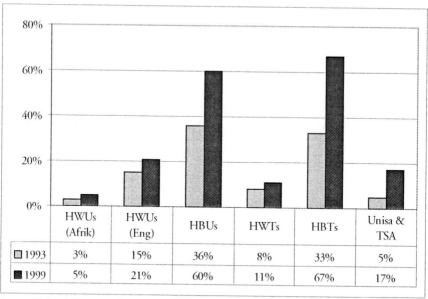

	HWUs (Afrik)	HWUs (Eng)	HBUs	HWTs	HBTs	Unisa & TSA
□ 1993	3%	15%	36%	8%	33%	5%
■ 1999	5%	21%	60%	11%	67%	17%

Source: National Plan on Higher Education, 2001

Figure 3. Proportion of blacks in full-time permanent academic and executive management or senior administrative positions: 1999

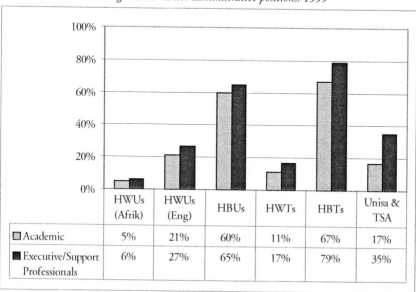

	HWUs (Afrik)	HWUs (Eng)	HBUs	HWTs	HBTs	Unisa & TSA
□ Academic	5%	21%	60%	11%	67%	17%
■ Executive/Support Professionals	6%	27%	65%	17%	79%	35%

Source: National Plan on Higher Education, 2001

Figure 4. Percentage of women in permanent academic staff totals: 1993–1999

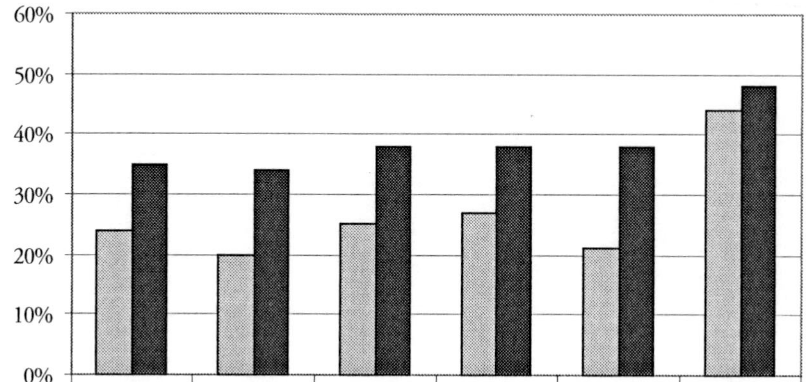

	HWUs (Afrik)	HWUs (Eng)	HBUs	HWTs	HBTs	Unisa & TSA
1993	24%	20%	25%	27%	21%	44%
1999	35%	34%	38%	38%	38%	48%

Source: Subotzky, 2001

Figure 5. Permanent academic staff by rank and gender: 1994–1999

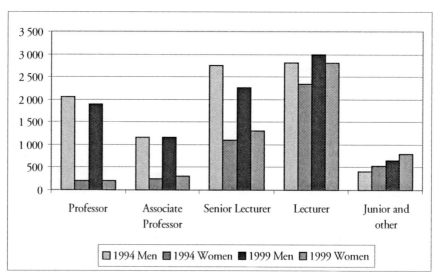

1994 Men   1994 Women   1999 Men   1999 Women

Source: Subotzky, 2001

The picture is not as encouraging, however, when viewed in relation to rank (see Figure 5).

In common with worldwide trends, women were markedly under-represented in the higher academic ranks, and only approached parity at the lecturer level. The severity of gender inequality among academic staff in the academy is reflected in the fact that 90% of professors, 78% of associate professors and 67% of senior lecturers were men.

But this is not the case in non-academic positions. Women made notable incursions into the realms of executive management and senior administrative posts, especially at the historically white English-medium universities, which suggests that women had a greater say in institutional management than in the past (Figure 6).

3.3. Summarising the statistics

The higher education workforce was partially right-sized in terms of the ratio between academics and workers. The number of executive managers did not increase as dramatically as suggestions of 'rampant managerialism' would seem to imply, but the increase in administrative staff numbers is surprising. The overall decline in student numbers has not directly translated into concomitant decreases in academic staff numbers and, in fact, academic staff increased at the African historically disadvantaged universities (by 7%) although these were the hardest hit by diminishing student

Figure 6. *Proportion of women in full-time permanent academic and executive management or senior administrative positions: 1999*

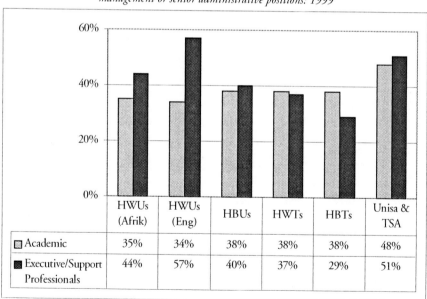

	HWUs (Afrik)	HWUs (Eng)	HBUs	HWTs	HBTs	Unisa & TSA
▦ Academic	35%	34%	38%	38%	38%	48%
▪ Executive/Support Professionals	44%	57%	40%	37%	29%	51%

Source: Subotzky, 2001

numbers. This suggests a decline in efficiency at these institutions, while the historically Afrikaans institutions achieved efficiency gains in increasing their student numbers (largely through enrolling students in distance programmes) without increasing academic staff numbers.

There has been limited transformation of the staff body in terms of race at the historically white institutions, resulting in a situation where the black institutions have become more black and the historically white institutions have remained predominantly white. In terms of equity, women seem to have made the most progress in increasing their numbers generally and in gaining access to senior management positions, but the senior professoriate still remains a male domain. The progress that women have made could be interpreted as a major equity gain, but it is also possible that women are filling positions vacated by men who have left higher education for more lucrative positions in government and business.

The statistics, in other words, reflect a fairly static picture. Any conclusions drawn from this, however, should be modified by taking into consideration movements of staff and different patterns of employment at institutions that cannot easily be captured in this statistical overview. They are the subject of the next section.

3.4. Staff movement and institutional capacity

Explanations for the relatively slow pace of change in the composition of the staff of the higher education sector must be found in a number of factors, including the fact that generally positions become vacant only when senior staff retire and very few new positions are created in a context of general decline in student enrolment. Postgraduate throughput rates are also very slow which means that the pool from which young staff could be recruited is small, and there is intense competition for well-qualified blacks from the government, from the private sector and amongst institutions.

These views are confirmed in a study by four institutions, one historically white and three black, called 'The Next Generation of Academics' (The Pilot Project Consortium, 2001), which found that most of the teaching and research staff were relatively young (between the ages of 35 and 44). Government was less of a recruitment threat than first thought, and although business was a major competitor, most staff losses were to other higher education institutions.

Examining the percentage of blacks and women in the totals of new staff appointed (as an indicator of commitment to employment equity) reveals differences between institutions that are not reflected (and cannot be detected) in the overall equity profiles of institutions.

What becomes clear from Tables 2 and 3 is that there is a much greater discrepancy between institutions in relation to the *race* of new employees than in relation to their *gender*. As a percentage of new academic staff, women captured between 38% and 56% of appointments, indicating a range of only 18% across these ten institutions. The percentage of new black academic appointments, however, ranges from a high of 77% at Medunsa to a low of 17% at the University of Stellenbosch and Pretoria Technikon. In

Table 2. New appointments to full-time permanent and temporary academic staff: 1997–1999

| | Black staff as % of full-time staff employed | | Black staff as % of new staff appointments during period 1997–1999 | Female staff as % of full-time staff employed | | Female staff as % of new staff appointments during period 1997–1999 |
	1997	1999		1997	1999	
Universities						
Western Cape	55%	56%	49%	42%	41%	44%
Medunsa	52%	58%	77%	33%	33%	42%
Wits	13%	18%	32%	35%	38%	40%
UCT	12%	17%	52%	28%	30%	39%
Stellenbosch	3%	6%	17%	28%	30%	44%
Pretoria	3%	4%	19%	34%	36%	38%s
RAU	4%	6%	22%	40%	42%	56%
Technikons						
Pretoria	4%	6%	17%	36%	38%	43%
Cape	4%	7%	30%	29%	32%	47%
Peninsula	70%	70%	75%	33%	33%	41%

Source: Department of Education, 2000

Table 3. New appointments to full-time permanent and temporary professional administrative staff: 1997–1999

| | Black staff as % of full-time staff employed | | Black staff as % of new staff appointments during period 1997–1999 | Female staff as % of full-time staff employed | | Female staff as % of new staff appointments during period 1997–1999 |
	1997	1999		1997	1999	
Universities						
Western Cape	72%	73%	60%	42%	31%	43%
Medunsa	51%	60%	92%	47%	47%	40%
Wits	23%	28%	51%	67%	67%	55%
UCT	39%	34%	50%	60%	54%	45%
Stellenbosch	2%	2%	12%	34%	31%	53%
Pretoria	6%	5%	24%	50%	51%	61%
RAU	0%	2%	40%	42%	48%	20%
Technikons						
Pretoria	8%	12%	24%	43%	38%	35%
Cape	11%	19%	79%	30%	29%	57%
Peninsula	8%	112%	24%	43%	38%	35%

Source: Department of Education, 2000

the category of professional administrative staff, the variations are even more extreme, with Medunsa appointing blacks to 92% of its new positions, while Stellenbosch only gave 12% of its new posts to blacks.

Tables 2 and 3 also show that even a high proportion of new black and women appointments do not necessarily translate into a significantly improved overall profile. Although more than half (52%) of new academic appointments at the University of Cape Town were black, as compared with the University of Witwatersrand's 32%, the percentage of black staff employed at the two institutions remains almost identical. The percentage of black staff employed in the professional administrative category at Cape Town actually dropped from 1997 to 1999 (from 39% to 34%) despite the fact that 50% of new appointments were black. Part of the explanation may be that many of these appointments are temporary and therefore not reflected in the institutional profiles.

What this also suggests is that black staff are leaving the institutions as fast as others are appointed. Reflecting on the poaching of staff, Professor Brian Figaji, vice-chancellor of the Peninsula Technikon, remarks in an interview (see www.chet.org.za/reflections.asp) that this creates particular difficulties for small institutions that are in the process of trying to create a greater research culture. For them, losing a single individual can mean the collapse of an entire research project, which would not be the case for stronger institutions working from a broader base.

> It seems that unless you move people up the ladder quite fast – and it is virtually impossible for us to do that – they go. Free State Technikon needs some colour in its senior management, looks around, has a research focus and poaches this guy, offers him a director's position. Not only does he go, he takes two students with him. So now we sit with a project, with nobody there. So that is the dilemma, when you don't have the sort of broad base, like a UCT has, where three other people can take that thing on. … But when you have helped these guys get to a certain point, you have almost got to nurture and mollycoddle them, otherwise they are out because there are opportunities out there. And the blacker they are the quicker they are out. … So the black institutions are bleeding. (Figaji, 2001)

If this anecdote reflects a general trend, then market competition for staff may well be further strengthening the historically advantaged institutions at the expense of the disadvantaged. Staff are likely to be attracted to and retained by well-resourced institutions that can offer high-quality facilities, research opportunities, efficient administrative systems, relatively light teaching and administrative duties and differential remuneration packages. Nonetheless, the figures for the University of Cape Town reveal that even the strong institutions may have difficulty in retaining highly qualified black staff.

A review of institutional three-year plans (Bunting, 2001) reveals that all institutions have drawn up or are in the process of implementing equity plans as well as developing a number of other strategies to improve equity profiles. Within the category of historically white institutions, the Afrikaans-medium institutions that have shown the least movement and the poorest equity profiles are introducing a range of policies including staff development and bursaries for postgraduate students from designated groups in an attempt to 'grow their own timber'. But by far the most aggressive strategies have been those adopted in some of the historically white English-medium institutions and this is reflected in their recent employment patterns. On the other hand, many of the black and historically white English-medium institutions have contributed staff to the new ANC-led government and its administration, while business, industry and other higher education institutions have recruited others. This has been described as a 'revolving door' phenomenon where black staff are no sooner trained, qualified and employed at institutions than they are poached by other actors in the labour market. It is this phenomenon that explains the contradictory result that although some institutions have aggressively pursued affirmative action employment practices, this has had little or no effect on their overall staff equity profile.

Movements into and out of the sector, and between institutions, have had significant effects on institutional capacity. During the last days of apartheid, many white men in government and parastatal positions realised that they had only a limited future in the public service and looked for other positions. Their flight from the public service was often to the benefit of the historically white Afrikaans-medium institutions. The University of Pretoria, for example, acquired a new vice-chancellor from the Development Bank of South Africa, with extensive World Bank and international connections. It also acquired the services of a deputy president of the Human Sciences Research Council and a chief director of planning from the higher education division of the Department of Education. All three, with established academic credentials and extensive experience in and outside education, brought new perspectives and skills into the leadership of the institution. In subsequent years the university has appointed as special advisor to the vice-chancellor the person who was the education department's first black director-general, and a former senior black member of the Public Service Commission as dean.

While experience of this kind is difficult to quantify, qualifications provide another guide to institutional capacity. The following tables show the distribution of qualifications across the traditional historical categories of institutions:

Table 4. *Permanent academic staff by highest formal qualification: universities in 2000*

University sector	Highest formal qualification							
	Doctorate		Masters		Other		Total	
Historically white (Afrikaans)	1.741	45%	1.098	29%	999	26%	3.838	100%
Historically white (English)	1.330	47%	856	31%	617	22%	2.803	100%
Historically black	880	28%	1.113	35%	1.193	37%	3.186	100%
Unisa	499	28%	327	31%	222	21%	1.048	100%
University Total	4.450	41%	3.394	31%	3.031	28%	10.875	100%

Source: Department of Education, 2000

Table 5. *Permanent academic staff by highest formal qualification: technikons in 2000*

Technikon sector	Highest formal qualification							
	Doctorate		Masters		Other		Total	
Historically white	140	6%	580	26%	1.509	68%	2.229	100%
Historically black	36	3%	234	19%	994	79%	1.264	100%
Tech SA	26	11%	64	28%	139	61%	229	100%
Technikon Total	202	5%	878	24%	2.642	71%	3.722	100%

Source: Department of Education, 2000

The historically white universities and the distance education university (Unisa) show a significant advantage over the historically black universities with 17% to 20% more staff with doctorates, and a considerably lower percentage of permanent staff with less than a masters degree. A similar differentiation occurs in the technikon sector, but here the paucity of staff with doctorates and the generally lower level of qualifications make the differences less extreme.

Disaggregated figures reveal a more complex pattern. Taking the number of permanent staff with doctoral degrees as an indicator of capacity in universities, new groupings of institutions emerge that cut across the traditional historical categories. On the other side of the binary divide, in the technikon sector, a similar picture emerges.

Figure 7. *Numbers of permanent staff with doctoral degrees in each university: 2000*

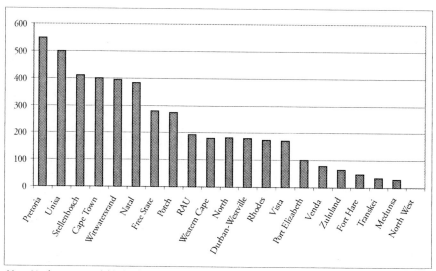

Note: No data was available for the University of the North West
Source: Department of Education, 2000

Figure 8. *Numbers of permanent staff with doctoral and masters degrees in technikons: 2000*

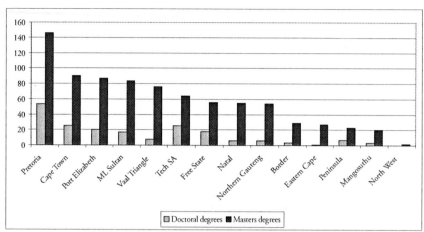

Source: *Department of Education, 2000*

Here, because of their very different genesis, the number of permanent staff with masters degrees is used as the primary indicator of capacity.

In this view, the six high-capacity universities are a mix of historically white English- and Afrikaans-medium institutions, and then there is a middle band of eight universities composed of historically white and black, English- and Afrikaans-medium institutions. A low capacity group includes all the rural, historically black universities, with the historically white University of Port Elizabeth hovering at its upper limit. Capacity in technikons similarly cuts across the traditional categories. The historically black ML Sultan Technikon, for example, shows considerably higher qualification levels amongst its staff than its historically white sister institution, Technikon Natal.

The two urban historically black universities (University of the Western Cape and University of Durban-Westville) are also much closer to the historically white universities in their qualifications profile than to the rural historically black universities. Location is clearly a key factor in the ability of institutions to attract and retain highly qualified staff.

There is another dimension to urban locality that is worth remarking upon. Institutions in reasonably large cities have the option of bringing in significant numbers of highly qualified professionals on part-time contracts to supplement the permanent teaching cadre. The benefit is two-fold in that teaching is enhanced by a rich pool of work experience, and institutions save on their staffing bill because this kind of employment contract excludes the costly benefits (housing allowances, medical aid, pensions) that are part of the package of permanent members of staff.

The degree to which institutions have pursued this strategy provides another line of differentiation. The University of Pretoria is the largest contact university in the country and supports the largest permanent academic staff (approximately 1.500). In numbers, the university that comes closest to it is the University of the Witwatersrand with just under a thousand academics on its permanent staff. By contrast, the Rand Afrikaans University, by no means a small institution, employs a small core of about 350 permanent academic staff, 54% of whom have doctorates, and the institution uses temporary and contract staff to meet the rest of its teaching requirements.

Black rural institutions have no access within their immediate environment to a pool of highly qualified professionals to supplement their academic staff. They have difficulty attracting and retaining highly qualified academics and have no option but to employ almost the full complement of teaching staff in a permanent capacity. For them, the staff profile shows both low capacity and high cost.

4. GOVERNANCE, MANAGERIALISM, AND INSTITUTIONAL RESTRUCTURING

The first phase of the transformation of higher education institutions in South Africa is marked by an intense focus on governance structures and practices. In many institutions this concern predates the 1994 democratic elections and runs in tandem with the broad political pressure for the democratisation of the entire society. In this period, the traditional governance structures of higher education institutions – councils, senates and faculty boards – were extended to give representative status and voice to a much wider range of stakeholder constituencies than had previously been the case. Participation and consultation became the key principles governing institutional life.

The effects on staff were least dramatic in the historically white English-medium universities that had long-established liberal traditions allowing for a fair degree of participation on the part of staff in university affairs. Nor were the effects marked in the Afrikaans universities where a dominant ethos of respect for authority was not seriously challenged (Jansen, 2001). For the most part, the technikons carried into the present an institutional culture that was fairly rigid, and more akin to that of the Afrikaans universities than the English.

In the historically black universities, democratisation in the wake of a history of authoritarian management practices, unleashed powerful forces with contradictory consequences. Groups coalesced around different material and political interests and posed constant challenges to the authority of institutional leaders in the name of democracy, reducing some institutions to a state of permanent crisis. The issues for staff were often complex and ambiguous: democratisation had opened up progressive spaces to promote a transformation agenda and simultaneously allowed a vigorous defence of group interests that were counter to progressive transformation. Nor did political allegiances always manifest themselves with the kind of clarity that had characterised earlier struggles against apartheid. In this situation, almost all groups, no matter what their interests or agenda, harnessed a rhetoric of democratic transformation that, on the discursive terrain, produced a minefield of political ambiguity.

All institutions, in more or less profound ways, experienced the democratisation of governance as a challenge to certain kinds of vested authority. This was, variously, the authority of executive managers to make and implement decisions, the traditional academic authority of the senate vested in professors, and the authority of ruling orthodoxies in pedagogy, knowledge formations, assessment procedures and quality (often understood as an issue of standards). Staff also experienced these challenges in a variety of ways, from exhilaration to feeling threatened and undermined.

The policy documents that emerged from 1996 onwards attempted to address these challenges through promoting the concept of co-operative governance. In the final report of the National Commission on Higher Education (1996) this was articulated as:

- Acknowledgement of the existence of competing and complementary interests, interdependence and common goals.
- Balancing participation with effectiveness.
- Sharing powers, responsibilities and accountability among stakeholders (p199).

The White Paper (1997) proposed a new governance structure, the institutional forum, as a further mechanism to manage the potentially conflictual relationships of newly democratised institutions and these were brought into existence as statutory bodies by the Higher Education Act of 1997.

But policy-makers were acutely aware that the 'democratic phase' currently being experienced by South African institutions had long since been superceded in the developed nations by the 'managerial phase', and they referred to Peter Scott's work that recorded this transition (NCHE, 1996). This led to the telling conclusion in the NCHE Report that: 'there is no space and time to move sequentially from democracy to "managerialism". The co-operative governance model that the Commission is proposing is an attempt to combine, in a particular South African way, more democracy with more modern management'. (p199)

By 1998, the emphasis had decisively shifted from demands for democratisation to demands for efficiency and effectiveness. The policy demand for public accountability and greater efficiency, and the pressure of market competition, thrust South African higher education on to the same terrain as higher education institutions in other parts of the world that are grappling with the effects of globalisation. The first major change (described by Webster and Mosoetsa[3]) is that the vocabulary for managing the employment relationship changed from personnel management to human resource management. The words of a human resource manager illustrate the significance of this shift: 'In 1993 the department decided to change the focus of its work. We no longer wanted to be a paper-pushing department but wanted to be a strategic unit. We had to adapt to running this university like a business unit. We had to comply, like all businesses, with the Labour Relations Act. We had to educate managers about labour legislation. There were problems with academics having to act like managers, having to train and develop staff, recruit new students and do performance appraisals.' (2001:12)

A second change is the relationship of staff to management. In their limited survey of 56 academics from historically advantaged and disadvantaged institutions, Webster and Mosoetsa record that the overwhelming majority of respondents felt that their relationship with management had been reconfigured in a way that now defined them as subordinate employees rather than colleagues. The respondents expressed a surprising degree of antagonism towards management, describing the relationship as one of 'them and us'. In spite of a determined attempt by senior managers on many campuses to inculcate a new set of attitudes through workshops, briefing suggestions and *bosberaads*, respondents felt that these attempts were 'a waste of time'. (p13)

A third change is described as a loss of shared identity and sense of community. In the words of a union representative of academic staff: 'Academics do not feel that fellow academics are running the university. They feel very insecure and feel that they are being monitored. There is no longer that sense of community and trust in the university.' (p15) Some respondents also commented that they increasingly experienced tensions between permanent staff and those on contracts.

The perceptions and experiences described by Webster and Mosoetsa are remarkably similar to those identified by Carnoy (2001) as general workplace changes and by Altbach (2000) for academics internationally. These are the symptoms of what is known as 'managerialism', the kind of response that is produced when higher education institutions begin to function in an increasingly market-like manner. Du Toit (2001) characterises the transition from collegial academic self-rule to academic managerialism as:

- Management by a strategic plan.
- The establishment of senior management teams.
- The shift towards fewer levels of decision-making and flatter administrative structures.
- Decentralised budgeting and devolution to faculty level.

For him, this signifies the demise of collegial faculty practices. He argues that an executive deanship is not compatible with a 'collegial' approach to the conduct of faculty governance in any serious sense, nor is the reluctance of many faculty members to engage actively with the ongoing processes of planning and implementation involved in working through the agenda of university transformation at faculty level.

The gap between senior managers, with 'market-related' packages, and senior teaching and research staff seems to have widened significantly over the past few years (from a ratio of about 2:1 during the late 1980s to a ratio of 4,5:1 in the late 1990s).

Table 6. *Example of salary rations: regulation and deregulation*

Level	Late 1980s Government regulation	2000 Deregulation
Vice-chancellor	2	4.5
Deputy vice-chancellor	1.6	3.5
Professor	1.3	1.3
Senior lecturer	1	1

Note: The SAPSE funding formula uses a senior lecturer as the basis for salary comparisons
Source: SAPSE Return for 2000, University of Cape Town

At one of South Africa's leading institutions, which is not unrepresentative of the South African system, there are now seven salary bands above a professor and more than 30 directors, deans, managers and deputy vice-chancellors above the professorial level. Unlike the situation in the US and other countries, there are no academic super-professors who earn packages equivalent to those of executive deans or deputy vice-chancellors. Some institutions have introduced the category of senior professors who are offered substantially larger packages than those of their colleagues, but they are still not comparable with the salary packages of top managers.

The management at higher education institutions claim that market-related packages are necessary in order to attract and keep senior executives. These packages, in other words, are a consequence of the intense competition for highly qualified executives, particularly those who are black and/or female. But unlike executives in the private sector environment, senior executives in higher education are rarely tied to performance clauses in their contracts. There are two points worth making here. One is that these packages relate to competition at the high end of the labour market but have little to do with the other ways in which institutions have to make themselves market-competitive. Generally speaking, it is the academic staff, particularly the senior academic staff, who attract students, research grants and consultancy contracts. This is the group that is operating in the market, but who are not rewarded in a market-related manner even though it would not be difficult to build a market reward into the packages of entrepreneurial academics.

The second point is that the remuneration packages of senior executives are not necessarily an effect of, or directly connected to, more managerial approaches to higher education administration. In fact, some of the highest paid vice-chancellors in the country do not appear to be pursuing managerial leadership styles at all.

A third problem is that market packages are not enough to prevent prominent vice-chancellors such as Professors Mamphele Ramphele (University of Cape Town), Colin Bundy (University of the Witwatersrand), Johan van Zyl (University of Pretoria) and Brenda Gourley (University of Natal) from leaving higher education for international, or top business positions before completing their tenure (Cultural Capital Flight, www.chet.org.za/issues.asp). The market packages are thus not enough to keep the top group.

It could be argued that this leadership group is market efficient in the sense that some of them have raised millions of rands in donations and contract money during their period as institutional leaders, but this is not true of all of them, and does not prevent the less successful fundraisers from claiming similar high performance packages. A further issue is that the raising of many major research grants is attributed to institutional leaders in the discourse of public affairs promotions, but these grants are actually awarded on the basis of the reputations of academics with international credibility.

Whilst the managerial 'class' did disproportionately well in the new South Africa, the fate of the service workers was less fortunate. The unionisation of workers in the higher education sectors resulted in the ratio between the salary of a senior lecturer and a service worker decreasing from 10.5:1 in 1986 to 8:1 in 2000. The differential between a service worker and a vice-chancellor, however, increased from 20:1 in 1986 to 25:1 in 2000. Service workers whose jobs were outsourced, and who were subsequently hired by the contracting companies, had their packages halved (on average). This means that in the post-apartheid era the differential between the vice-chancellor and certain service workers could be as high as 50:1, in contrast with 20:1 under the apartheid government.

In South Africa, the global pressures for efficiency thus led to the emergence of a sharp divide in decision-making powers, as well as a privilege divide. The likelihood of maintaining collegiality when the remuneration package of the deputy vice-chancellor is 60% more than that of the senior lecturer is far greater than when the former earns 250% more.

In the South African context, managerialism must be understood as a response to two sets of pressures. The first is the external pressure for transformation prescribed by the policy positions adopted by the state and enacted through the implementation of a regime of performance appraisal, and the second is the internal pressure for financial survival in the face of declining student enrolments and diminishing state subsidies. The overwhelming response to these pressures on the part of most institutions was to engage in some form of organisational restructuring.

Internal restructuring on the academic terrain took the form of a reorganisation of faculties, schools and departments, with institutions rationalising smaller units into bigger entities, closing some 'non-viable' departments and withdrawing under-subscribed courses.[4] In some instances this led to the redeployment and retrenchment of academic staff. In terms of numbers, however, many more staff members were affected by the restructuring of service provision in higher education institutions. Historically black universities, particularly those in the homelands, such as Fort Hare, that had been used as sites of employment needed to 'rightsize' the disproportion that existed between service staff and academic staff. Others, like the University of the Witwatersrand, retrenched and outsourced on the basis of a distinction between core and non-core functions of the institution. The rationale here was that the outsourcing of non-core functions allows the institution to concentrate its resources on its core functions of teaching and learning.

These different approaches led to different outcomes. The 'rightsizing' approach led to large-scale retrenchments, while the 'core/non-core' approach led to redeployment, outsourcing and again, significant retrenchments. Retrenchments characterise the restructuring process in general, but are not always accompanied by a process of outsourcing. However, it is estimated that 'up to 20 tertiary education institutions have outsourced at least some support service functions'.[5] Across all the institutions, these were largely the functions of catering, cleaning, gardening services, maintenance, security services and printing. In universities there was a decline of about one third in the number of service staff from approximately 12.000 to 8.500, and of crafts/trades staff from around 1.200 to 700. A smaller drop of about 300 technical staff also occurred (Subotzky, 2001).

In most higher education institutions, academics, administrators and workers developed separate organisational structures to advance their interests.[6] Despite these different organisational bases, however, there was some sense of community among constituencies prior to 1994, and especially during the anti-apartheid struggles. Workers, students and academics attempted to build alliances when taking up issues that confronted them as stakeholders. For example, at various campuses, it was common for students to support workers' struggles for wage increases. By 2000 this had changed dramatically on a number of campuses. An ex-union shop steward at the University of the Western Cape said in an interview: 'At UWC the critical edge is gone. There is no pretence that we are all trying to run a university together here.' The human resource department at the University of the Western Cape echoed a similar sentiment when one of the managers stated that, 'There is no longer a sense of togetherness or belonging. The focus is now on reducing costs, decreasing salaries and so decreasing the number of staff members. Everyone is focused on their careers.'[7]

Outsourcing, as a practice, has had particularly acute consequences for workers. Bernadette Johnson's research shows that outsourced workers came to face two workplace changes: the first is much greater supervision and pressure for performance. Johnson comments that, 'What was striking throughout the interviews with workers was their constant nervousness, nervousness of getting caught not working and chatting, and a fear of exceeding their tea and lunch breaks.' (p7) The second change, much more dramatic, is that in many cases, workers' wages were more than halved – from approximately R3.000 with benefits, to R1.300 without any benefits. Prior to outsourcing, workers were entitled to medical aid and provident fund contributions, and had access to low interest-bearing loans, study bursaries for dependents and housing subsidies. In a hard-hitting critique, Adler et al. (2000) charge that the consequence of this form of outsourcing could be a re-racialisation, as opposed to the de-racialisation, of South African higher education staff.

Workers did not accept outsourcing without opposition: at least three of the major institutions in the country – the Universities of the Witwatersrand, Cape Town and Pretoria – were embroiled in Labour Court disputes with trade unions in the course of 2001.

Johnson concludes her survey with the following observation: 'While unions attempt to come to terms with the meaning and consequences of their experiences within the higher education sector since 1994, the drive towards greater levels of cost reduction and the consequential loss of community, demoralisation and pain, continue to mark the experience of the higher education worker. These experiences illustrate that the stated ideals of democratic labour relations and co-operative governance have not been realised within the higher education sector.' (p10)

For Du Toit, academic retrenchments raise the question of an appropriate conception of academic tenure. 'Tenure' at South African universities has tended to mean a relatively open system, amounting to little more than the default position following probationary appointments. In any serious sense, though, it is a weak system and provides little protection against retrenchments and restructuring (Du Toit, 2001:3–6).

5. CHANGES IN THE NATURE OF ACADEMIC WORK

Du Toit argues that in the context of post-apartheid South Africa no one can be under the illusion that universities can simply assert that they are accountable only to themselves. This does not mean, however, that there are no real and serious tensions between the conditions for disciplinary integrity and necessary levels of institutional autonomy on the one hand, and the demands of social and political accountability on the other (2001:3–6). This tension was brought into sharp focus in the imperative for institutions to respond to the programme accreditation requirements of the Department of Education and the South African Qualifications Authority (SAQA).

For many academics, the process of programme design, or the redrafting of existing programmes in line with the requirements of the accreditation process, constituted an exacting encounter with the contradictory demands of a policy imperative to provide the full spectrum of educational opportunities necessary for social, economic, political and cultural development, and institutional strategies geared to attracting the greatest number of students into cost-effective, self-sustaining courses. Because the processes of academic programme design often ran parallel to processes of institutional restructuring, academic integrity was severely tested in the context of the threat of job losses. Responsiveness in some instances was narrowly interpreted as producing vocationally orientated programmes that were responsive to the labour market, but not necessarily to the wider development needs of South African society.

This was also the process that threw into stark relief the redefined role of the academic profession. What was now demanded was expertise in a whole range of areas such as academic development, quality assurance, assessment, strategic planning, recruitment and marketing, areas that were previously seen to fall outside the domain of academic work. This dramatic increase in the intensity and range of work also involved, amongst other things, having to deal with more students who were not adequately prepared for academic work, greater pressure to publish and fewer support staff. In order to maintain a competitive edge, academics now have to change the quality and nature of their service. Indeed, in some cases, the consistency of 'the product' is monitored through continuous surveys and other forms of assessment. In this context, teaching increasingly requires a standardised display of feelings that is susceptible to measurement. In the process, the identity of professional academics is changed to 'units of resource whose performance and productivity must constantly be audited. … Professionalism is seen as being eroded, and replaced with "the new auditable competitive performer"'. (Webster & Mosoetsa, 2001:14–17)

Staff in the historically white Afrikaans-medium institutions would appear to have accepted this new regime more easily than elsewhere. Without a tradition of democratic resistance to authority, they have accommodated the new managerialism, and thrown themselves into an entrepreneurial approach to the provision of educational services that has significantly increased their market share of students. In other institutions, responses have been mixed, with some academics experiencing high levels of stress, while others have used the spaces opened up by these changes to develop highly innovative, mixed-mode delivery strategies, trans-disciplinary graduate programmes, new research possibilities and linkages to groups outside institutions in communities, business and industry.

6. CONCLUSION

New higher education policy (supported by labour legislation) has two primary focus areas in relation to staff. The first is on changing the composition of staff in the sector to reflect a more equitable distribution of jobs across racial and gender categories (an equity goal), while the second aims to increase the participation of all staff in the significant decision-making processes and governance of institutions (a democratic goal). Further goals relate to capacity-building (a corollary to the achievement of the former goals), efficiency and effectiveness, and a reorientation of academic and research endeavour towards greater social and economic responsiveness.

Equity gains across the entire sector have been minimal, with women marginally better represented than previously. Disaggregation of the information, however, reveals that blacks now occupy significantly more academic, senior administrative and senior executive positions in the historically black institutions than before, that the historically white English-medium institutions are pursuing employment equity with vigour (but that this will only translate into a changed profile if they are able to create the conditions to retain black staff), and that the historically white Afrikaans-medium institutions have been the slowest to implement new employment strategies and, as yet, show the least progress at the level of transformed institutional profiles for staff.

Increased democratic representation and participation has been achieved at a formal level in most institutions. Militating against this, however, is a managerial style (developed in response to demands for efficiency and effectiveness) that represents a shift in power relations away from traditional loci in the formal structures of governance, to new centres of discretionary power associated with flattened management structures and manifest in strategic planning teams and new managerial positions such as executive deans. Reinforced by increasingly differentiated salaries, these developments, in keeping with international trends, have subverted any sense of shared participation in governance and alienated academic and other staff from the new stratum of academic managers.

Labour legislation was intended to protect all staff from unfair practices and secure their general rights. One outcome has been that provisions in relation to equity plans and organisational restructuring have exposed academics and workers alike to retrenchment and outsourcing in pursuit of efficiency. Workers in non-core areas of institutional activity have been the hardest hit by these practices. While there has been some rightsizing of the proportions of administrative/managerial, academic and service workers, there is also an increase in temporary and short-term contractual forms of employment.

The conflation of demands for public accountability, responsiveness, efficiency and effectiveness has transformed the scope, nature, and intensity of academic work. Characterised by a much wider range of activities than before, many of which are associated with the marketisation of higher education, academic work is also subject to new formal performance and quality assessment procedures. While some members of staff have clearly thrived under these conditions, the majority seem to experience them with ambivalence.

NOTES

[1] This section draws on a report prepared for this project by George Subotzky (2001).

[2] Permanent staff are defined as employees on permanent contract who contribute to medical aid and pension schemes. Institutions also employ a significant number of staff on temporary contracts. They are not reflected in these figures.

[3] This section draws heavily on two papers prepared for this project: Webster and Mosoetsa (2001) and Du Toit (2001).

[4] A series of three articles by Gibbon, Habib, Jansen and Parekh (2000, 2001) describe the process of restructuring at one institution, the University of Durban-Westville, and some of the tensions and complexities involved.

[5] Cited in Van der Walt, Negotiating Outsourcing: Project Proposal to Nehawu, unpublished paper, p4.

[6] One exception was the Combined Staff Association at the University of Durban-Westville.

[7] Cited in a report prepared for this project by Johnson (2001).

REFERENCES

Adler, G., Bezuidenhout, H., Buhlungu, S., Kenny, B., Omar, R., Ruiters, G. & Van der Walt, L. (2000). The Wits University Support Services Review: A Critique. Unpublished report. University of Witwatersrand.

Altbach, P. (2000). *The Changing Academic Workplace: Comparative Perspectives*. Boston College: Center for International Education.

Badat, S., Barron, F., Fisher, G., Pillay, P. & Wolpe, H. (1995). Differentiation and Disadvantage: The Historically Black Universities in South Africa. Commissioned report prepared for the Desmond Tutu Educational Trust. Cape Town: Education Policy Unit, University of the Western Cape.

Bunting, I. (1994). *A Legacy of Inequality*. Cape Town: University of Cape Town Press.

Bunting, I. (2001). Institutional Three-year Plans for 2000–2002: Some Comments on Staff Equity Plans and Data. Commissioned paper.

Carnoy, M. (2000). *Sustaining the New Economy: Work, Family and Community in the Information Age*. New York: Russell Sage; Cambridge: Harvard University Press.

Department of Education (1997). Education White Paper 3: A Programme for the Transformation of Higher Education. General Notice 1196 of 1997. Pretoria.

Department of Education (1997). Higher Education Act of the Republic of South Africa, No 101 of 1997. Pretoria.

Department of Education (2000). Research Output 2000. SAPSE Information Systems.

Department of Education (2001). *National Plan for Higher Education*. Pretoria.

Department of Labour (1995). Labour Relations Act, No. 66 of 1995. Pretoria.

Department of Labour (1997). Basic Conditions of Employment Act, No 75 of 1997. Pretoria.

Department of Labour (1998). Skills Development Act, No. 97 of 1998. Pretoria.

Department of Labour (1998). Employment Equity Act, No. 55 of 1998. Pretoria.

Department of Labour (1999). Skills Development Levies Act, No. 9 of 1999. Pretoria.

Department of Provincial and Local Government (1996). *Constitution of the Republic of South Africa*, 108 of 1996. Pretoria.

Du Toit, A. (2001). Revisiting Academic Freedom in Post-Apartheid South Africa: Current Issues and Challenges. Commissioned paper. www.chet.org.za/papers.asp.

Figaji, B. (2001). Interview. www.chet.org.za/reflections.asp.

Gibbon, P., Habib, A., Jansen, J. & Parekh, A. (2000 & 2001). Accounting for Change: the Micropolitics of University Restructuring. *South African Journal of Higher Education*, 14:3; 15:1; 15:3. Pretoria: University of South Africa.

Jansen, J. (2001). Why Tukkies Cannot Develop Intellectuals (and what to do about it). Innovation Lecture, University of Pretoria.

Johnson, B. (2001). The Higher Education Worker. Commissioned paper. www.chet.org.za/papers.asp.

National Commission on Higher Education (1996). A Framework for Transformation. Pretoria: NCHE.

O'Brien, C.C. (1987). Events which Occurred on the Campus on 7 and 8 October 1986. Press release. Cape Town: University of Cape Town.

Subotzky, G. (2001). National Trends: Statistics on Staff Changes. Commissioned paper. www.chet.org.za/papers.asp.

The Pilot Project Consortium (2001). The Next Generation of Academics. Pretoria: CHET.

Webster, E. & Mosoetsa, S. (2001). At the Chalk Face: Managerialism and the Changing Academic Workplace 1995–2001. Commissioned paper. www.chet.org.za/papers.asp.

CHAPTER 7

TEMBILE KULATI & TEBOHO MOJA

LEADERSHIP

This chapter looks at the response of higher education leadership to pressures for transformation emanating from a new co-operative governance policy environment, the marketisation of higher education, and from within institutions themselves. The different pressures set up tensions between equity and efficiency, leading and managing within a democratic context, and maintaining academic autonomy on the one hand, while being responsive to national imperatives on the other. The history, culture, and internal politics of different higher education institutions shaped their responses to the new dispensation post-1994 and had a bearing on the role of leadership in change.

New approaches to leadership emerged, ranging from transformative leadership to managerial leadership, to crisis management. The different approaches are indicative of the fact that no single leadership style would have been appropriate for all institutions. It is quite clear that even though the role of leadership had not been articulated in the new higher education governance policies, the roles played by institutional leaders contributed significantly to changing the apartheid institutional landscape in higher education.

1. A NEW POLICY FRAMEWORK

1.1. The governance debate before 1994

The struggles for the transformation of higher education governance pre-date the promulgation of the higher education legislative framework by a number of years. As outlined in Chapter 3, the genesis of the debate on governance transformation in higher education can be traced to the education struggles of the 1980s that were led by organisations affiliated to the National Education Co-ordinating Committee (NECC) and student organisations in particular. These struggles centred on the demand for the democratisation of existing higher education institution governance structures, particularly the councils, and the establishment of alternative structures of institutional governance, namely the broad transformation forums. For much of this period, the debate on the leadership and management of institutional change was subsumed under broader governance struggles, and there was very little, if any, engagement with issues relating to the management of, and the role of leaders in, the transformation of the apartheid higher education system inherited in 1994.

153

N. Cloete et al. (eds.), Transformation in Higher Education, 153-170.
© 2007 *Springer.*

In their study of institutional governance changes, Mohamed and Cloete (1996) divide the changes into three phases. The first phase focused on the demand for the establishment of alternative democratic governance structures, namely the broad transformation forums, that would challenge the authority of what were considered to be illegitimate and unrepresentative governance structures, in particular the councils and senates. Change was to be achieved through changing the composition of council and senate to ensure that marginalised groups and constituencies were represented in institutional decision-making.

The second phase had as its focus the legitimation of the institutional management structures. This was to be achieved through the replacement of the discredited appointees of the apartheid state in university administrations with progressive institutional leaders, appointed democratically.

The third phase centred on the demand for the processes of governance and decision-making to be more participatory and accountable. At some institutions, mainly historically disadvantaged universities and some English-medium institutions, this process started well before 1994; in others the process started long after the principles and framework for democratic institutional governance had been embodied in the legislation.

To summarise, prior to 1994 the focus of the governance debate was on issues relating to structural reform and, to a lesser extent, on the substantive challenge of participatory decision-making. There was hardly any discussion of how higher education institutions – once transformed at the level of representation in governance structures – ought to be organised and managed, and what role institutional leaders could play in the unfolding transformation processes.

1.2. Legislation and governance transformation

The report of the National Commission on Higher Education (1996) and the White Paper on higher education transformation (Department of Education, 1997) introduced a new governance framework based on the principle of co-operative governance. A brief description of co-operative governance at the national level (the interaction between institutions and the government) is provided in Chapter 3.

Within institutions, co-operative governance starts from the premise that no single stakeholder, be it management, academic staff or students, can take sole responsibility for determining an institution's transformation agenda. The White Paper argued that institutional governance depends on the recognition of the existence of different institutional interests, and the inevitability of contestation among them. The policy stated further that in order for co-operative governance to work, higher education institutions must create structures and conditions that will enable the differences between stakeholders to be negotiated in participatory and transparent ways (Department of Education, 1997).

The new policy framework redefined the relationship between higher education and the state. A complex shift was to be made from parties being conflictual and confrontational to becoming partners within a co-operative model of governance. The legislative framework provided by the Higher Education Act of 1997 gave guidelines for the establishment of the new structures at the levels of both the system and institutions. At the national level the democratisation process entailed setting up a new representative governance structure, the Council on Higher Education (CHE). The locus of power and decision-making was not contested as it was spelled out clearly in the policy documents that the CHE was to be consulted by the Minister of Education for advice. As a political leader, the Minister could follow the advice or disregard it, provided that the public was given reasons for disregarding advice provided by the new governance body.

In terms of the new legislation, the main institutional governance structures are the council, the senate, and the institutional forum. The council is the supreme governing body in public higher education institutions, and is responsible for ensuring the good governance of the institution. The senate is the highest decision-making body in relation to academic matters, and is accountable to council. The broad transformation forums, forged in struggle, had in some institutions seized power from the councils and were to be reconstituted as newly legislated institutional forums.

The institutional forums were to play an advisory role to councils as a way of broadening participation in institutional governance; they were meant to act as 'shock absorbers' in the transformation process by providing the arena in which issues pertaining to the institution's transformation agenda could be debated and discussed. Their advisory role to council encompassed issues pertaining to institutional transformation, the mediation of conflict among campus stakeholders, and oversight of the process of appointing senior managers in the institution.

The primary objective of the legislative framework for governance was to facilitate the establishment of structures that would enable institutions to navigate the various transformation challenges facing them in democratic and transparent ways. By 1998 most institutions had completed the process of changing the composition of the councils, democratised the appointment of the new leadership and established institutional forums. There seems to be general agreement among the key stakeholders that, by and large, the structural dimension of the transformation process had been accomplished by 2001.[1]

With regard to the other objective of co-operative governance, namely ensuring that decision-making is participatory and transparent, the results have been uneven. In many institutions, the new governance structures played a leading role in key institutional processes and decisions, most notably the appointment of vice-chancellors and other senior managers of the institution. Notwithstanding the changes effected in the representation of stakeholders within governance structures, however, there is not much evidence to attest to fundamental change in the way these structures function, particularly in relation to the participation of previously disadvantaged groups. Although more empirical research still needs to be done in this area, it is already apparent that a number of stakeholder representatives do not have a clear idea of their role within governance structures, and consequently have not been able to play a meaningful part in the deliberations of councils or institutional forums. Empowered participation did not automatically follow representation (Harper et al., 2001).

2. THE CHALLENGE OF CHANGE IN
HIGHER EDUCATION ORGANISATIONS

Higher education leaders face particular challenges which stem from and are intertwined with the nature of higher education organisation. In essence, the nature and structure of the higher education organisation and the value framework underpinning its institutional culture, sit uncomfortably alongside the mantra of management. The literature on higher education organisation (Baldridge & Deal, 1983; Becher & Kogan, 1992; Birnbaum, 1988; Clark, 1983) has highlighted some of the organisational characteristics and features that distinguish higher education institutions (especially universities) from other kinds of organisations. These features present a challenge to the exercise of effective leadership in higher education, for three reasons:

- Unlike private sector organisations, higher education institutions have goals and objectives that are not only diverse (teaching, research, and service) and ambiguous, but are also highly contested and even contradictory.
- The fragmented nature of higher education organisation has given rise to a potentially anarchic organisational structure that has led Clark (1983) to remark that '[these] semi-autonomous departments, schools, chairs and faculties act like small sovereign states as they pursue [their] distinctive self-interests and stand over, and against, the authority of the whole'. (p24)
- The decentralised nature of decision-making, organised around the production, preservation and dissemination of an intangible commodity (knowledge), has given rise to a highly fragmented authority structure which is focused on autonomous disciplinary units, in which members' loyalty is split between the organisation – which provides their livelihood – and the disciplinary networks and allegiances that transcend institutional boundaries and are the source of the unit's or individual's (academic) prestige.

There is a growing international literature (Green, 1997; Ramsden, 1998; Reponen, 1999; Smith et al., 1999) that posits a pivotal role for leadership in institutional change. In higher education organisations this role, which is centred in the office of the vice-chancellor, is a function of three distinct and yet related developments:

- The need for higher education institutions to reconfigure their missions and (re)position themselves so that they are more responsive to a rapidly changing external environment.
- Calls for public sector institutions in general to be more accountable in the context of shifting demands and a shrinking public purse.
- The emergence of an 'evaluative state' and the move to monitor and assess the performance of public institutions.

One of the central challenges in the management of change in universities is the resolution of the tension between disciplinary or professional authority that characterise the traditional university, and the managerial and administrative prerogative that is typical of modern organisations (Bargh et al., 1996). Positioned at the fulcrum of this tension is the institutional leader, the vice-chancellor, who has to balance the externally induced pull towards responsiveness, effectiveness and accountability (and establish appropriate mechanisms to achieve these), with the need to maintain the core academic character and values of the institution.

As the higher education institution becomes less of a cloistered, well-financed, inward-looking and disinterested community of scholars, and more of an efficient, relevant and publicly accountable organisation, the need for a different – and perhaps more managerial – approach to leadership becomes more apparent (Green, 1997; Smith et al., 1999). Having said that, the jury is still out as to whether the managerial approach to higher education leadership is the most appropriate in the new context. Scott (2001) states that there is no self-evident, or necessary, connection between the radical and rapid changes in higher education in the last 15 years and the emergence of managerial forms of higher education leadership. Indeed, he argues that at the very time that higher education experienced exponential growth in student numbers, and saw radical changes to the organisation and structure of academic programmes, the governance and management structures in the UK have not only remained remarkably unchanged, but have 'atrophied'.

It is the combination of these features that has given universities their unique and paradoxical characteristic of being the engine of innovative ideas and practices on the one hand, whilst on the other also being extremely resistant to change. So while the ethos of professional autonomy and academic freedom has given rise to a collegial culture that promotes selected participation in decision-making and enriches the process of knowledge production and dissemination, it has also resulted in a lack of institutional cohesion which has made it difficult for those in leadership to drive or steer change in the context of a rapidly changing external environment.

2.1. Institutional leadership and transformation

The new legislative framework in South Africa and the broader challenges of globalisation and market competition put enormous pressure on institutions to devise new ways of managing what have become more diverse and very complex institutions. Within the space of five years, higher education institutions were confronted with many challenges, including the need to:

- Diversify their income streams while doing more, and different, things with increasingly less reliance on the fiscus.
- Reconfigure their institutional missions and the ways in which they traditionally produced, packaged and disseminated their primary product – knowledge – in order to meet the challenges of a diversifying student population, as well as an increasingly technologically-oriented, and globalising, economy.
- Forge new kinds of relationships with other knowledge producers within and outside higher education, especially in industry and the private sector (Kulati, 2000).

The emphasis on institutional effectiveness, efficiency and responsiveness within the new higher education legislative framework positioned the role of leadership – and particularly the role of the vice-chancellor – centre stage in institutional change. In addition, the demand for publicly funded institutions to be more accountable saw many institutional leaders beginning to play a more pivotal role in the governance and management of their institutions. The new policy framework, however, was silent on the role of leadership in the new dispensation. To some extent this had the effect of disempowering higher education leaders, particularly in those institutions where powerful stakeholders competed with executive leadership for power to steer change.

The result was a very high turnover in vice-chancellors, general 'demand overload' (Cloete & Bunting, 2000), and leadership crises at about 25% of the institutions – a phenomenon elaborated upon later in this chapter. In the process, new perceptions about the position of vice-chancellor developed. In the words of a former student leader, 'VCs' positions in South Africa are no longer interesting and prestigious positions. On the contrary, they are just scary jobs' (Mabuza, 2001). But coping with these pressures also made successful South African vice-chancellors 'globally marketable': at least four of them departed during 2000/1 for top positions, one in a South African financial institution, two in top British universities and another in the World Bank (Cultural Capital Flight? www.chet.org.za/issues.asp).

Not unexpectedly, the manner in which institutions have responded to these challenges is a function of a complex interaction between the apartheid legacy that affected them in different ways, individual institutional characteristics and specific leadership styles. The manner in which institutions were governed and managed in the past largely mirrored their role and relationship vis a vis the apartheid state. For example, the historically white Afrikaans-medium universities and the historically black universities were characterised by highly centralised and autocratic management styles and practices. Many of the historically white English-medium universities – which were largely opposed to the government's apartheid policy – were characterised by a stronger collegial tradition where the culture of decision-making was more participatory, at least amongst the professoriate. When interviewed, most of the vice-chancellors acknowledged the importance of the past in shaping their ability to exercise leadership over the change process in their institutions.

Historically white Afrikaans-medium institutions and the historically black institutions shared a common management culture, but their change patterns were starkly different. For example, there is a widely held view that the relatively rapid transformation at many of the historically white Afrikaans-medium institutions can be attributed to their inherited authoritarian institutional culture, which is characteristic of highly administered institutions. Other factors that impacted on their ability to change rapidly included established executive leadership capacity and strong financial resources that were accumulated owing to the unequal distribution of state resources during apartheid, as well as through support received from the private sector. Within these institutions the leadership managed to introduce and drive many changes, as there was very little resistance from within the institutions – either from students or staff – to these transformation initiatives.

In the post-apartheid period, both the historically black institutions and the historically white Afrikaans-medium institutions needed to gain legitimacy: the former needed academic credibility while the latter were desperate to gain political legitimacy. The historically black institutions expected government to provide support for the building of their academic infrastructure. As was shown in Chapter 4, however, this did not occur. Instead, the leadership came under pressure to reshape their academic direction on their own whilst simultaneously having to respond to government demands to implement strict debt collection processes at a time that enrolments were declining. By contrast the historically white Afrikaans-medium institutions managed to attract black students through financial incentives and by offering academic programmes through flexible delivery modes such as distance education and the establishment of satellite campuses.

Historical institutional differences, responses to the new policies and market competition were all factors which resulted in higher education leaders developing a range of approaches to their role in South African institutions. The next section will describe some of the approaches that emerged during the post-1994 period.

3. EMERGING APPROACHES TO LEADERSHIP

In dealing with the challenge of transformation post-1994, higher education leadership had to respond to three sets of pressures. The first was a new governance policy demanding co-operative governance, meaning increased participation and representivity and a strong emphasis on equity. Secondly, a set of market pressures entered the system: these included competition from the emerging private higher education sector, but above all, competition amongst public institutions. The market also introduced a strong efficiency component. Thirdly, institutional culture required that the core values or 'business' of the institution had to be defended, or developed, and this was linked to the academic strength of the institution and its managerial capacity. It is within this crucible of pressures, that different approaches to leadership emerged.

What follows is an attempt to classify the different leadership responses to the challenges of transformation. As is usually the case with classifications, the reality on the ground is much messier than the neat parameters that the categories may seek to convey. Furthermore, the categorisation that is offered below is merely illustrative; some of the overlap across categories has been deliberately de-emphasised in order to accentuate the distinguishing features of the different approaches to leadership. The categorisation is not fixed in the sense that each institution has one type of leadership; rather, it is a shifting continuum.

It is also important to signal that the categorisation of leadership approaches is very much a function of the country's fractured past. Each approach is the product of a complex coalescence of the history and culture of the institution, the institution's internal governance dynamics, and the personality and style of those in leadership. As a result, no attempt has been made to judge which style of leadership is the most appropriate for South African higher education institutions.

3.1. Transformative leadership

Transformative leadership is not a homogeneous category; nor does it imply one single notion of transformation. Rather, it is regarded as transformative in the South African context because it combines elements of leadership which are broadly recognised as being successful, with features of co-operative governance. An in-depth case study (Cloete et al., 2002) of two institutions (University of Port Elizabeth and Peninsula Technikon) revealed the following as some of the key elements of co-operative transformative processes followed by the leadership in those institutions:

- *Critical self reflection* – a process often initiated by the vice-chancellor, where a wide range of members of staff engaged in critical self-reflection on the transformation process. This included more than one attempt to rethink the mission of the institution. In some cases members of the executive leadership wrote regularly about the successes and weaknesses of the processes.
- *Negotiated transformation* – a process where key aspects of the new mission were negotiated through various forums and structures and were accepted by organised constituencies. In this regard the institutional forums were always involved – either actively or as consultative structures.
- *Reconstituted council* – the outcome of a process whereby the council was reconstituted to be more representative of both internal and external constituencies. In many cases the council played an increasingly assertive role in setting and monitoring the direction of the institution.
- *Active forums* – a feature of some institutions where the institutional forum had an active agency role. In other institutions sub-forums or committees dealing with gender or affirmative action issues played an active role in enabling previously excluded voices to be heard.
- *Role differentiation* – the development of an understanding and acceptance of distinctions between governance functions and roles. Considering the lack of clarity in the policy about the role of leadership, a key task was to reach agreement about who has authority over what. This included the acceptance that neither the council nor the institutional forum should try to manage the institution, and that leadership should implement decisions which had been agreed upon in these structures.
- *Expanded leadership core* – the establishment of an expanded management group which in some cases included the president of the student representative council, and the development of a common vision for the institution and a shared discourse of the change process.
- *Trust* – an essential component of the change process which enabled the different constituencies to allow management to implement decisions and to lead.
- *Directive leadership with consultation* – an approach that helped manage the tension between leading and consulting. The manner and sequence of consultation varied according to leadership style and institutional culture.
- *Constructive/critical relationship between the chairperson of council and the vice-chancellor* – central to holding the transformation process together was a supportive

and critical working relationship between the chair of council and the vice-chancellor, based on a clearly understood complementarity of functions and skills.

It must be stressed that putting these processes in place in the two institutions did not depend on a specific leadership style. At the one institution the leader can be described as a philosopher who steered from behind rather than leading from the front: 'Nothing gets done without consultation.' (Kirsten, University of Port Elizabeth) At the other institution a charismatic engineer led from the front, but still within the framework of the elements described above: 'I had to shake the institution out of its complacency at being "the best technikon" and therefore not needing to change much; in other words, to get staff to realise it is not "business as usual"... to get [the] institution to realise that the value framework that it (once) cherished cannot be sustained' (Figaji, Peninsula Technikon). In both institutions, the central characteristic of transformative leadership was the management of the tension between leading and consulting (Cloete et al., 2002).

The features and processes mentioned above are illustrative of managerial and political responses to transformation pressures. It is within this context that two related, but distinct approaches to transformative leadership can be described.

The first approach, referred to as 'reformed collegialism' starts from the premise that at the centre of the transformation of the institution lies the intellectual agenda of higher education, which is non-negotiable. Thus part of the transformation agenda is to reclaim and reassert the centrality of the intellectual traditions of higher education institutions. The starting point of the institutional change strategy is to be sensitive to, and to work within, the confines and limits of the prevailing institutional culture, rather than going to war against it (Birnbaum, 1992). This can be achieved through remoulding the institution so that it is better able to respond and adapt to the new demands that it faces, while holding on to the central tenets of the academic tradition of the university, namely the pursuit of truth, disinterested enquiry, etc. In other words, the leadership challenge is about facilitating academic excellence by supporting, managing, nurturing, and inspiring one's academic colleagues. Collegialists would concur with Ramsden (1998:13) that 'deep at the heart of effective leadership is an understanding of how academics work'.

'Reformed' refers to the fact that even the most devoted collegialists are not totally unaware of the pressures of democracy and global trends on academia, which need to be taken into consideration. By responding to these pressures, however, tensions develop between collegiality and management strategies for change. Du Toit articulates this very well when he argues that currently the greatest threat to academic freedom may not be the state, but a more centralised management approach. For example, he states that 'it is not clear how an executive deanship could be compatible with a "collegial" approach to the conduct of faculty governance in any serious sense' (2001:5).

While acknowledging the importance of the new, participatory governance principles, the other approach, referred to as 'transformative managerialism', is characteristic of leaders who put more emphasis on 'driving' transformation from the centre. In some cases the challenge for the transformative managerialists is to transform the culture of the institution from an authoritarian to a more democratic one. In others it is to manage the academics more efficiently, in line with policy principles or market pressures.

In order to push the transformation agenda through the institution, power is centralised, decentralised and re-centralised. This is done by expanding the 'top' leadership group to include executive deans and certain professionals, such as finance or human resource directors. Key strategic decisions are taken by this group and the deans become the implementers at the faculty level. Traditionally, the deans are supposed to represent and defend faculty interests. Whilst the executive dean and his/her faculty may have an autonomous budget and control over the appointment of new colleagues, the budget parameters and employment equity targets are set centrally.

When taking the faculty decisions back to top management where the decisions could be overturned, the dean is placed in a very complex relationship between management, of which he/she is part, and faculty, which he/she is supposed to represent. This is even further complicated by the fact that in many cases the self-image of the dean is that of a faculty member, and not that of a manager. In a number of institutions, particularly those with strong academic cultures, a few deans have fallen foul of this role schizophrenia which Du Toit describes above as a major threat to faculty governance and academic freedom.

In summary, while transformative leadership grapples with the new demands for participation and responses to the market, major tensions are emerging, accentuated by the academic culture of the institution and the urgency for change. In some instances the institutions may lean more towards collegial power; in others towards central management.

3.2. Managerial leadership

The second broad category of leadership approaches is mainly managerial in style. Within this category, the leadership challenge is to reconfigure the institution to become more competitive and market oriented through the vigorous adaptation of corporate management principles and techniques to the higher education setting.

The change agenda within these institutions is driven by a strong, decisive centre (usually located in the office of the vice-chancellor) that is buttressed by sophisticated management-support systems and structures, that are staffed by a highly competent middle management layer. The leadership style is characterised by a rapid-response management ethos. Where others talk in terms of threats and survival in the face of globalisation and fierce competition from the emerging private higher education sector, the buzz here is about exploiting niches and developing partnerships.

Stumpf (2001) describes the increasing entrepreneurial orientation of some of the historically white institutions as reflected in the way in which many of them established specific structures to package and patent products of intellectual property. One approach to increasing income was to move into flexible modes of educational delivery. Apart from introducing modularised postgraduate programmes on a large scale, these institutions also entered the field of distance education for undergraduate programmes. This they did in partnership with private providers and thus saved themselves massive set-up and logistical costs.

These institutions also established spin-off companies in which staff members who had a direct interest in the development of a particular piece of intellectual property, would have a share-holding along with the institution and private sector shareholders. Others established structures to advance institutional/private sector co-operation in a variety of ways and adjusted their internal allocation mechanisms to reward performance in the field of partnerships with the private sector and in the generation of own income. In addition some of these institutions established separate companies through which they offer short courses in a context relatively free from bureaucracy; these enable the institutions to make use of opportunities of accessing funding in terms of the rules of the National Skills Fund. The larger institutions – especially those in the metropolitan areas – established commercially run student centres where private sector service provision to students was encouraged in an attempt to increase institutional revenue (Stumpf, 2001).

In response to the increasing importance of strategic management, many institutions invested in management training for their senior administrators and established offices of institutional research. Apart from taking care of the formal information requirements of government, these units have usually been responsible for other forms of quantitative (and sometimes even qualitative) planning support to management. In many cases sophisticated systems of performance management were established, based on institutional management information systems. Institutions in which these offices function well are, in general, well poised to respond quickly to new challenges and new opportunities, thereby creating for themselves a competitive edge in the face of increasing competition for students from overseas institutions entering the South African market and the declining pool of available students (Stumpf, 2001).

Two sub-categories can be delineated within the broader classification of managerial leadership, namely 'strategic managerialism' and 'unwavering entrepreneurialism'. These sub-categories follow the distinction that has been made between the 'soft' and 'hard' approaches to managerialism. The 'soft managerialists', although applying management techniques in order to run their institutions more efficiently and effectively, still see higher education institutions as distinct from businesses, governed by their own norms and traditions. This is in contrast with the 'hard' approach to managerialism, where institutional management has 'resolved to reshape and redirect the activities [of their institutions] through funding formulas and other mechanisms of accountability imposed from outside the academic community – management mechanisms created, and largely shaped, for application to large commercial enterprises' (Trow, 1994:12).

The leadership challenge for strategic managerialists is to get the institution to think and act more strategically, and to convince the academics that 'being managed', and working in an institution that is run on sound management principles, does not constitute a threat to the traditional values of the academy, such as academic freedom.

Many of these institutional leaders have a keen sense of the strengths and weaknesses of the institution – having at their disposal access to high-level strategic management skills and management support and information systems – and an ability to formulate strategic responses to a rapidly changing policy and market environment. The change strategy is premised on striking a balance between becoming a top-class, internationally competitive institution and the need to be responsive and relevant to local needs.

According to the strategic managerialists, being a first-rate academic with a good understanding of business principles ought not to be a contradiction in terms. As one South African vice-chancellor put it: 'The vice-chancellor has to be an academic with a business sense. It also depends on what type of institution you're aspiring to be: for a research/comprehensive university, you must have a strong research background; if you don't have it you can't run senate. And if you can't run senate, you're dead.'[2]

For strategic managerialists, globalisation and the market are not viewed as threats, but as opportunities to be exploited in order to make the institution more competitive internationally. Consequently, the managerialists have been more successful in exploiting the fairly loose legislative framework to the advantage of their institutions, having established strong relationships with international funders, developed partnerships with the private sector and parastatal research agencies, recruited top academics from abroad, and built strong links with universities in Africa.

While the strategic managerialist tries to 'run the university as a big business' (Van Zyl, *Sunday Times*, 16 September 2001), the centrality of the academics is at least acknowledged, even if not given much substance in practice. Further along the continuum of the corporatisation of higher education institutions are the *'unwavering entrepreneurs'*. For this group the higher education institution is seen as being a business, as opposed to being run like a business. Institutions are thus in the business of providing their clients – the students – with goods and services that are sold at a competitive price. The institutions have, or try to develop, strong links with industry, and generally lack a collegial tradition.

For them, the transformation project is about developing useful products for the market, in other words producing employable graduates. The challenge is to gear up the institution so that it is responsive to rapidly changing customer needs and expectations. The approach is characterised by an unquestioning application of private sector management procedures and techniques. The executive management, whose central concern is to ensure that the institution is run efficiently, believes in leading from the front, being in the driving seat of institutional change. The institutional strategy for change is underpinned by a very instrumentalist view of education, the primary function of which is seen as preparing young people for the world of work. In the words of one of the vice-chancellors who is a main proponent of this view: 'I think that the days are past where we see ourselves as educational institutions only. We must see ourselves as major players in stimulating the economy of South Africa, and that's our main purpose. We are not an educational institution first of all. We are an institution to serve the country and get the economy going, and it's only high-level manpower that can really do this' (Kulati interviews).

The 'unwavering entrepreneurs' regard the government's regulatory framework as an inconvenience; it is seen as failing to appreciate the demands and challenges facing modern higher education institutions. Government is viewed as not being generally supportive of institutional leadership, and policies such as co-operative governance are regarded as necessary, but a nuisance.

For the managerialists the tension is whether academic excellence remains the core business that needs to be managed more like a business, or whether the core business is about making a profit. While these two approaches seem to be aspects of the same continuum, they actually denote two very different models of a higher education institution, and very different approaches to the role of leadership.

3.3. Crisis leadership

Crisis leadership is more of an institutional condition than an approach to leadership. In the post-1994 period crisis leadership featured mostly, but not exclusively, at the historically black universities where the new leadership operated in an environment marked by continuous challenges to authority. Crisis leadership manifests itself when various factors such as historical legacy, inexperienced new leadership, and new demands and structural problems emanating from the implementation of new policies combine in different ways. On the one hand, leaders at these institutions were expecting government support for institutional redress in order to implement some of their plans for renewal and review of their mission – support that did not materialise. On the other hand, they experienced a decline in student numbers, due only in part to the drop in the number of students qualifying for university entrance. The decline in enrolment at the black and rural universities since 1998 has been particularly dramatic and requires further explanation.

For the first time these universities had to compete for students with the historically white universities, with historically black universities in urban areas (such as the University of the Western Cape and the University of Durban-Westville), with technikons, with the rapidly growing distance education operations of the historically white Afrikaans-medium universities, and with the burgeoning private higher education sector. Perceptions of greater stability, a better reputation, and higher quality education, the prospect of immediate employment, and greater possibility of financial aid, saw black students 'voting with their feet' in favour of historically white universities (particularly the Afrikaans-medium universities) or other categories of institutions. Thus in a relatively short period of time (1994–1999), historically black universities, particularly those located in rural areas, were thrown into a severe crisis that threatened their very survival (Gibbon & Parekh, 2001).

By far the most debilitating dimension of this crisis was the complete breakdown in governance structures and processes, the manifestation of a lack of confidence in, and support for, the management and leadership, and poor financial systems and controls. These weaknesses accentuated internal fissures and brought these institutions to the verge of collapse. Their daily operations were characterised by managerial incoherence and strife, divisive managerial style, the absence of a strategic vision on the part of leadership, a history of long-term 'acting' appointments particularly in senior and middle-level management positions, a breakdown in governance procedures, the complete collapse of key university structures and committees such as the council and senate, the complete disintegration of administrative controls and systems, and gross financial mismanagement (Steele, 2000). The point is underscored in the introduction to a report by one of the independent assessors appointed by the Minister of Education to investigate conditions at one of the institutions:

Conspiracy theories abound at UNIN. Relationships between groups and individuals are characterised by deep suspicion and at times outright hostility. Scepticism about people's motives runs deep: the belief is that everybody has an agenda which he or she will try in all circumstances to advance. The idea of anybody acting from pure motives or to promote the general good is laughingly dismissed as a delusion. It seems to matter little that some allegations might sound preposterous to the impartial ear: one can invariably tell from the passion of the accuser that the belief is strongly held. (Nhlapo, 2000:3)

The leadership approach at these institutions was characterised by crisis management and decision-avoidance; the lack of institutional cohesion made it difficult for leaders to steer, let alone drive, change. Institutional leaders in this situation had less substantive authority than those in institutions in which transformative or managerial leadership could operate. The institutions in crisis were characterised by a very weak, ineffective, second-tier management layer, and there was also a lack of trust between the key stakeholder groups and institutional management. Consequently, the decision-making processes within these institutions were protracted and highly politicised, and outcomes were frequently not conclusive. Even after agreements had been reached, the commitment by stakeholders to decisions made could not be guaranteed.

In many of the institutions characterised by crisis leadership, the new governance structures – that is, the institutional forum and the council – played a leading role in many of the key institutional processes and decisions, most notably the appointment of the vice-chancellor and other senior managers of the institution. There was, however, confusion with regard to the scope of responsibility of governance structures, with students often challenging the role of councils as the primary governance body, and seeking instead to establish institutional forums as alternative structures of governance authority to management. In these institutions, students were pushing for forums not merely to serve an advisory function, but to become alternative policy-making structures. This has been particularly acute in institutions where councils have tended not to assert their role in institutional governance.

In some extreme cases there was very little distinction between the decision-making role of council and the implementation role of management: the council would either be completely ineffectual, or it would micro-manage the institution. For example, in one case the relationship between the chair of council and the vice-chancellor all but collapsed, or at best was non-existent. The senate also did not play a significant role in formulating the transformation agenda of the institution, and tended to be preoccupied with fairly narrow academic issues.[3]

The crises faced by many of the historically black universities cannot be understood in isolation from the roles played by the management and leaders of the institutions. In a study of the causal factors that gave rise to the crisis at Unitra, Habib (2001) cites a range of dysfunctional management/governance behaviours and practices which, along with Unitra's structural location in the context of bantustan development, served to undermine the viability and sustainability of the institution completely.

Gibbon and Parekh (2001) conclude that: 'It would be easy to dismiss weak management and leadership as simply a result of "unsuitable" appointments although in some cases this would be accurate. But perhaps the answer lies in understanding the role that historically black universities played during the apartheid years and the implications that this may have had for the future governance and leadership of such institutions.' In the words of a former vice-chancellor at a historically black university that was under crisis for an extended period: 'In our case, the forces that were at work were overwhelming. We had fragile management structures and then absolutely no resources. It was very difficult to manoeuvre' (Balintulo, 2001).

4. CONCLUSION

The role that leadership was to play in South African higher education was downplayed by the higher education policies that were formulated post-1994. The expectation was that there would be shared direction provided by transformed governance structures. It seems clear that the reliance on governance transformation structures and on the political dividend of stakeholder participation as the main drivers of institutional transformation, proved to be ineffective. Instead, the scale of changes that were expected required skilled leadership capacity at both the level of the system and at the institutional level. An analysis of the situation in South Africa leads us to believe that institutional leaders played an important part in ensuring stability and creating an enabling environment for innovation in some institutions, and in contributing to crisis situations in others.

Using the analytic triangle as a guide, it appears that, contrary to the situation in the pre-1994 period, the main axis of tension in the post-1994 period was not between the institution and the state, but more about the institution in the new market situation. The main challenge facing leadership emanated from tensions within institutions, namely the interaction between leadership, institutional culture, capacity and resources.

In terms of the relationship between the government and institutional leadership, the first term of democratic government (1994–1999) was characterised by a great deal of co-operation, participation and consultation about policy formulation. During the post-1999 phase, however, the legislative framework has been amended to strengthen the role and powers of the state. The establishment in 2001 of the National Working Group, appointed to make recommendations about mergers and institutional missions, signals a more interventionist approach from the Minister. New directions have been charted without much debate on frameworks and implementation procedures. The frustration over a changing culture, and the disappointed expectations about what co-operative governance means, have also been expressed by student leadership (Mabuza, 2001). By 2000 the practice of stakeholder participation and the climate of vigorous debate which had characterised the post-1994 policy formulation period had been shed by government in favour of practices in which stakeholders were limited to responding to government proposals. This shift is reflected in an observation made by a prominent vice-chancellor, namely that the Committee of Technikon Principals (CTP) and the South African Universities Vice-Chancellors Association (SAUVCA) did not know how to respond effectively to the Minister's policy proposals:

New bureaucrats who came into these positions realised that they had some authority and were making statements like, 'we have been elected to govern and we should govern'. And therefore the notion of drawing other people in to help with the capacity issue was anathema to them … the Minister also has the notion that he was elected to govern and this means he should make decisions. While this is correct, the question is: 'How do you arrive at the decisions?' The Minister also wants to correct as much as possible within higher education before his term ends. The latest developments such as the National Plan, the Amendments to the Higher Education Act and the funding formula all seem to have elicited a very mild response from the CTP and SAUVCA. I think these organisations do not know how to respond effectively to this Minister. (Figaji, 2001)

It is not difficult to anticipate that as political pressure on the Minister to restructure higher education mounts, the relationship between the higher education leadership and the government may become a prominent issue for vice-chancellors, as was the case in the pre-1994 period.

Despite considerable hype about the threat of private higher education, the real competition for resources, particularly in terms of students, was amongst public higher education institutions. The strategic responses of leadership to this threat were clearly framed by institutional culture and capacity. Clarke (1983) points out that the strength, or weakness, of the academic 'oligarchy' influences the speed and the types of changes which leadership can effect.

The South African experience shows that management capacity, coupled with disciplinary strength and the history of institutional governance, is the crucial issue. Leadership vision and direction require layers of management with implementation capacity. This problem was most starkly demonstrated in the crisis-ridden institutions: leadership plans were simply not implemented, either due to a lack of skills or because of a contestation of authority. Perhaps the most salient lesson is that institutional change requires institutional strength – both leadership and management skills within an accepted governance framework.

The post-1994 period showed that the wide institutional diversity and history of higher education in South Africa made it impossible to develop an ideal approach to leadership. This is eloquently illustrated by Njabulo Ndebele (2001) who was reflecting on being the vice-chancellor at one of the historically most disadvantaged universities, and is currently leading one of the most advantaged historically white universities:

When I was at Turfloop (University of the North) I was confronted with universal need – wherever you turned, there was a need. I came to UCT with this experience and immediately found being here quite disorientating. From my perspective, everything is here: the labs are functioning, there are A-rated scientists, students have access to computers, everyone has an electronic identity, and the administrative systems are working. So one of my traumas was the need to find an existential, not political, answer to the question: 'What am I doing here? What am I supposed to be doing?' So I had to get acclimatised to the fact that here, at an historically white institution, one is likely to find that the fundamentals are in place, and that one now has to work at a different conceptual and existential level. There is a new level of complexity.

NOTES

[1] This observation is made on the basis of interviews that were undertaken with stakeholders on various campuses in the course of compiling this chapter (Kulati, 2001).

[2] Tembile Kulati conducted a number of interviews with vice-chancellors during the course of 2000 as part of the primary research for this chapter.

[3] As the events at the University of South Africa show, at the time of writing, this 'condition' occurred at historically white universities as well.

REFERENCES

Baldridge, V.J. & Deal, T. (eds) (1983). *The Dynamics of Organisational Change in Education.* Berkeley: McCutchon Publishing Corporation.

Balintulo, M. (2001). Interview. www.chet.org.za/reflections.asp.

Bargh, C., Scott, P. & Smith, D. (1996). *Governing Universities: Changing the Culture?* Buckingham: SRHE/OU.

Becher, T. & Kogan, M. (1992). *Process and Structure in Higher Education.* London: Routledge.

Birnbaum, R. (1988). *How Colleges Work. The Cybernetics of Academic Organisation and Leadership.* San Francisco: Jossey Bass.

Birnbaum, R. (1992). *How Academic Leadership Works: Understanding Success and Failure in the College Presidency.* San Francisco: Jossey Bass.

Clark, B. (1983). *The Higher Education System: Academic Organisation in Cross-National Perspective.* Berkeley: UCLA Press.

Clark, B. (1998). *Creating Entrepreneurial Universities: Organizational Pathways of Transformation.* Oxford: Pergamon.

Cloete, N. & Bunting, I. (2000). *Higher Education Transformation: Assessing Performance in South Africa.* Pretoria: CHET.

Cloete, N. & Bunting, I. (2002). Transformation Indicators: Case Studies of the University of Port Elizabeth and Peninsula Technikon. Pretoria: CHET.

Department of Education (1997). Education White Paper 3: A Programme for the Transformation of Higher Education. General Notice 1196 of 1997. Pretoria.

Department of Education (1997). Higher Education Act of the Republic of South Africa, No 101 of 1997. Pretoria.

Du Toit, A. (2001). Revisiting Academic Freedom in Post-apartheid South Africa: current issues and challenges. Commissioned paper. www.chet.org.za/papers.asp.

Figaji, B. (2001). Interview. www.chet.org.za/reflections.asp.

Gibbon, T. & Parekh, A. (2001). Historically Black Universities. Unpublished paper.

Green, M. (1997). Institutional Leadership in the Change Process. In: M. Green (ed.), *Transforming Higher Education: Views from Leaders Around the World.* Washington DC: American Council on Education.

Habib, A. (2001). Structural Disadvantage, Leadership Ineptitude and Stakeholder Complicity: A Study of the Institutional Crisis of the University of the Transkei. Commissioned Paper. www.chet.org.za/papers.asp.

Harper, A., Olivier, N., Thobakgale, S. & Tshwete, Z. (2000). Institutional Forums in Higher Education. A Study of their Establishment and Functioning at South African Public Higher Education Institutions. Effective Governance Project Report. Pretoria: CHET.

Kulati, T. (2000). Governance, Leadership and Institutional Change in South African Higher Education: Grappling with Instability. *Tertiary Education and Management,* 6(3), 177–192.

Mabuza, M. (2001). Interview. www.chet.org.za/reflections.asp.

Mohamed, N. & Cloete, N. (1996). Transformation Forums as Revolutionary Councils, Midwives to Democracy or Forums for Reconstruction and Innovation. Unpublished research report.

Moja, T. & Hayward, M.F. (2000). *Higher Education Policy Development in Contemporary South Africa.* Higher Education Policy, 13, 335–359.

National Commission on Higher Education (1996). *A Framework for Transformation*. Pretoria: NCHE.

Ndebele, N. (2001). Interview. www.chet.org.za/reflections.asp.

Nhlapo, T. (2000). *Investigation into the Affairs of the University of the North by the Independent Assessor Appointed by The Minister of Education*. Pretoria: Department of Education.

Ramsden, P. (1998). *Learning to Lead in Higher Education*. London: Routledge.

Reponen, T. (1999). Is leadership possible at loosely coupled organisations such as universities? *Higher Education Policy*, 12, 237–244.

Sayed, Y. (2000). The Governance of the South African Higher Education System: Balancing State Control and State Supervision in Co-operative Governance? *International Journal of Educational Development*, 20, 475–489.

Scott, P. (2001). Leadership and Management – Some Thoughts from the UK. Commissioned paper. www.chet.org.za/papers.asp.

Smith, D., Scott, P., Bocock, P. & Bargh, C. (1999). Vice-Chancellors and Executive Leadership in UK Universities: New Roles and Relationships? In: M. Henkel & B. Little (eds), *Changing Relationships between Higher Education and the State*. London: Jessica Kingsley Publishers.

Steele, J. (2000). Findings of the Audits of Five Public Universities. Effective Governance Project. Pretoria: CHET.

Stumpf, R. (2001). Higher Education: Funding in the Period 1994–2001. Commissioned paper. www.chet.org.za/papers.asp.

Trow, M. (1994). Managerialism and the Academic Profession: The Case of England. *Higher Educational Policy*, 7(2), 11–18.

Van Zyl (2001). *Sunday Times*. September 2001.

PART 2

STAFF AND LEADERSHIP

CONCLUSION

Chapters 6 and 7 show that in South Africa, higher education institutions are expected to be, at one and the same time, models of democratic reform, socially responsible and responsive to labour and economic development needs, competitive within the higher education marketplace while maintaining world-class academic standards, and far more efficient and effective in the production of highly skilled graduates. All this in a context of fiscal constraint.

This is a critical theme addressed in Chapter 1, where Maassen and Cloete suggest that one of the global trends is for nation states to demand more efficiency and public accountability from higher education institutions. Coupled with market pressures for institutions to become more competitive, these developments result in a tendency towards greater centralisation of management. The two chapters show that the movement towards centralised management is in full swing in South African higher education institutions and that, just as is the case globally, this increasingly separates management from academics and from workers.

The new hierarchy has set up dynamics that threaten the full achievement of a significant local reform goal – co-operative governance. Although institutional governance structures are now modelled on more egalitarian principles and encourage widespread participation by a variety of stakeholders, centres of power and control have, in many instances, shifted away from these structures. Like policy goals in relation to governance, reforms to labour legislation are also aimed at achieving more consensual, co-operative relationships, but their application has produced contradictory effects. Forms of contractual employment foreground the rights and obligations of employers and employees, but in so doing, undermine the basis for collegiality. On the one hand the opportunity is offered for greater participation, protection against unfair treatment, and the right to negotiate; on the other hand, academics and other workers may be retrenched on the basis of equity considerations or institutional restructuring in the pursuit of efficiency gains. Under these conditions, labour relations have the potential to become more adversarial than co-operative.

Equity is the other major item on the local reform agenda – in relation to staff demographics and employment practices – but Chapter 6 (Staff) shows that the record is fairly disappointing. Policy reforms in the fields of higher education and labour relations – and their concomitant translation into legal statute – have provided both the goals and the legal basis to achieve employment equity in the institutions of the higher education system. The fact that gains have been minimal, provokes the obvious explanation that this is because of lingering racism and protection of white interests and privilege. But this

171

N. Cloete et al. (eds.), Transformation in Higher Education, 171-173.
© 2007 Springer.

explanation is inadequate (even though these dynamics may still operate within the sector) when failure to achieve equity occurs even where there are high levels of commitment and adequate institutional resources to pursue it (Jansen, 2001). The chapter suggests, instead, that the pool of highly qualified black and women graduates from which to recruit staff is still too small, that movement is rapid, and competition for staff, both within the sector and outside, is intense.

But why should this be so? Has the higher education system been so inefficient over the last decade that it has been unable to ameliorate this situation? The chapter on students indicates that part of the explanation lies in the fact that the drop-out rates are high and through-put rates low. Much of this is acknowledged in the most recent policy document to emerge from the Department of Education, the National Plan for Higher Education (2001).

Jansen (2001) argues, however, that the strategies advanced in the National Plan to address this issue, fall woefully short of the mark in failing to acknowledge some of the other fundamental realities. According to Jansen, the suggestion that more postgraduate scholarships should be made available to black and women students is 'remarkable' (p7), considering that the sector is already awash with funding for postgraduate studies. At this level, it is not money that is in short supply, but students. Jansen suggests that this connects directly with declining rates of participation in higher education – a function of inadequate levels of financial aid, the fact that many undergraduates struggle despite having access to financial aid, and a steady decline in the absolute numbers of students graduating from the schooling system with the qualifications necessary for access to higher education.

The issue of staff equity, therefore, is merely the tip of a problem of iceberg proportions. At an analytical level this suggests that there is a skewed relationship between policy goals and the reality they seek to address. While the goals themselves are exemplary, it becomes increasingly clear that the possibility of realising them is dependent on having in place a prior set of conditions. Where those conditions do not exist, goals become unrealistic, and accusations of implementation failure abound. This is not a society with high levels of general education. But widespread general education is probably one of the fundamental conditions for achieving the stated goals of current policy positions. In this context, policy, shaped by the ideals of social democracy and the demand for a world-class system, sets itself impossible tasks. The setting of more modest, realistic goals and corresponding strategies, however, carries little political glamour, and requires, at a minimum, a clear-eyed analysis of the full and complex array of conditions within which the higher education system must operate. And this would include an uncompromisingly honest confrontation with realities of the HIV/Aids pandemic.

The realisation of equity goals in higher education, in other words, would seem to be dependent on the achievement of much greater efficiency and effectiveness within the system as a whole. The two chapters reveal that the capacity of higher education institutions to respond successfully to these demands, under market conditions, depends on a complex interplay of intellectual and organisational capacity, resources and environmental opportunity, and leadership strategies that foster innovative responses. Where that enabling complex of factors is lacking, institutional stagnation, decline and decay are the order of the day.

These changes, registered very unevenly across South Africa's higher education institutions, represent attempts to adapt to the new demands of the age of globalisation and to reconcile being responsive to those demands with performing the traditional functions of teaching and learning, training and research, under new conditions and on new platforms. Institutional and human capacity are clearly central to successful adaptation and may now be the strongest differentiators amongst institutions. How that capacity is used, however, is a critical question for leadership. Speaking of universities, Peter Scott (2000) represents the tightrope that has to be walked in this way:

> If they are not flexible enough, they may become redundant – relegated to the sidelines by new kinds of edu-tainment organisations, or merely as primary producers of academic materials that are processed, packaged, disseminated by global corporations. But if they are too flexible, they may cease to be universities, at any rate in a recognisable form. If they abandon their commitment to liberal learning, to critical knowledge, to disinterested scholarship and science – in other words if they sacrifice their core, their fundamental, values on the altar of novelty – universities may not be worth defending. (p8)

REFERENCES

Jansen, J.D. (2001). Does the national plan effectively address the critical issues facing higher education? Guest editorial. *South African Journal of Higher Education*, 15, 3. Pretoria: University of South Africa.

Scott, P. (2000). Globalisation and the University: Challenges for the Twenty-first Century. Paper presented at the ACE/CHET Seminar on Globalisation. San Lameer, August 2000.

CURRICULUM AND RESEARCH

INTRODUCTION

Higher education institutions produce only two kinds of product: new knowledge, via *research*, by which society economically and culturally rejuvenates itself; and smart skills in the forms of knowledgeable graduates who both replenish the attrition in the workforce and who, through smarter skills, re-define it. The premier medium for producing them is the *curriculum*, an instrument for reproducing both labour market related skills and research skills.

When the curriculum fails to produce smart skills – a relatively rare occurrence, the periodic 'skills shortage' refrain from the side of business to the contrary (see Muller, 1987) – or, more worryingly, when the curriculum fails to produce successive new cohorts of innovative researchers – as the trend in the country suggests is presently the case, and as the research chapter that follows will suggest – then the nature of the curriculum and its reform becomes once again a matter for public concern and debate. This is rarely welcomed by the higher education institutions that have, through their many incarnations, jealously guarded the right to control what they may teach and research. No wonder that, in the domain of national curriculum reform, states have found that reform across the system is frustratingly difficult to achieve (Van Vught, 1991).

The critical reform concept at stake here is 'responsiveness', a term coined in the policy positions adopted by the state to assess whether higher education institutions are displaying accountability to society. Against policy demands for responsiveness the traditional discourse of academic freedom is invoked defensively, but even within the terms of this discourse, there is some contestation. Perhaps it is not accidental that the classical liberal discourse of academic freedom, solemnly unitary throughout the apartheid era, has now split into two: one stream has a modicum of sympathy for state attempts to reform the institutions (see Du Toit, 2000); the other defends the traditional line of maximum autonomy not only against the state, but against all kinds of attempts to make the universities more 'responsive' to the outside world (Higgins, 2000). According to this latter position, responsiveness is viewed almost wholly negatively as emanating from an instrumentalist view of higher education and/or as a code word for a neo-liberal global ideology.

Such disputes, however, look at the relationship between higher education institutions and the state from the *inside out*, that is to say, from the point of view of the institutions themselves. It is not the mode adopted in this volume. Rather, in the two chapters that follow, the issue is examined from the *outside in*: the two chapters in this section concentrate on the sober imperatives of state policy, and the variable ways in which this policy is adopted. Yet in these two most intimate workings of higher education

N. Cloete et al. (eds.). Transformation in Higher Education. 175-177.
© 2007 *Springer.*

institutions – the taught and the produced, the reproduced and the innovative – the institutions have been less than uniformly compliant. Nor is resistance uniform – as the discourse of 'academic freedom' might sometimes persuade us to believe. Rather, it is a variable, but predictable, expression of a complicated mix of history (sedimented resources) and capacity. Higher education institutions, antediluvian and recalcitrant though they are, are not blank slates. They do not simply follow orders. They respond to signals, sometimes scanned from policy, sometimes from their redoubtable global connections, and, depending on differing kinds of capacity, they strive to position themselves in the most propitious current.

When it comes to curriculum and research, then, *institutions* matter. This conclusion is hard to avoid, as the chapters make clear. Nevertheless, institutions are not the whole of the story. The outside world impinges upon, and deeply affects, the way that institutions respond, and this can be far from obvious or predictable.

Where South Africa differs from the mainstream, though not from the bulk of the developing world, is in having some institutions that have so little inherited capacity that they can neither properly respond to the outside world, nor properly respond to policy. How does policy deal with such institutions? A decade of little more than rhetorical redress as far as institutions are concerned has had negligible discernible effect. The shocking disparities between those institutions that operate efficiently and those that don't, can no longer be easily read off the apartheid script. In a decade where the ideological policy was one of a *unified* system – a policy that can be clearly read across the procession of policy documents from Nepi through the NCHE and the various Green and White Papers – the single most significant fact of higher education in South Africa has been *internal differentiation from within*. While this has followed the apartheid faultlines in some instances, in some important respects the institutional landscape has changed considerably since 1994.

The chapters that follow provide a nuanced and empirically documented picture of the variable fortunes of curriculum and research at higher education institutions over the last decade. Where institutions have felt threatened by policy (as with programmatisation, for example), it is striking how many institutions have got by with doing the minimum. Equally striking is the way that South African researchers have responded to imperatives to be 'relevant' and 'useful'. It is of course far too early to judge with any degree of reliability, but the local trends suggest that local researchers, like their colleagues elsewhere, adapt in terms of their capacity, as well as in terms of their view of traditional research practice. When it comes to research and curriculum, the old adage comes to mind: the more things change, the more they stay the same. The chapters that follow document the changes, the lack of change, and the terrain between them by shining a powerful spotlight on the processes and products of higher education institutions.

REFERENCES

Du Toit, A. (2000). From autonomy to accountability: academic freedom under threat in South Africa? *Social Dynamics*, 26(1), 76–133.

Higgins, J. (2000). Academic freedom in the new South Africa. *Boundary 2*, 27, 97–119.

Muller, J. (1987). Much ado: 'manpower shortages' and educational policy reform in South Africa. *Journal of Education Policy*, 2(2), 83–97.

Van Vught, F. (1991). *Autonomy and Accountability in Government/University Relationships*. Washington: World Bank.

CHAPTER 8

PAULA ENSOR

CURRICULUM

Governance, institutional efficiency and accountability, the size and shape of the higher education sector, student access and graduation rates, redress and responsiveness are some of the issues which have vexed planners and policy-makers in higher education in South Africa since the early 1990s. In the shadow of these debates and enjoying far less prominence, have been issues of knowledge production through research, and knowledge reproduction through curriculum and pedagogy.[1] Indeed, it was not until the report of the National Commission on Higher Education (NCHE) in 1996 that the issue of higher education curriculum restructuring was placed explicitly in the foreground and, even then, only in the broadest of brush strokes. To grasp the influences that have shaped thinking about higher education curricula, both pre- and post-NCHE, we need to turn back to the early 1990s, to the educational landscape that was being configured at that time via a number of policy initiatives. These addressed themselves to educational aims and processes in general, rather than specifically to the higher education sector.

This chapter has two aims. In the first instance it provides an analysis of policy documents pertaining to higher education curricula from the early 1990s, and in the second instance it discusses the implementation of this policy in university faculties of science and humanities. The focus on science and humanities was chosen because it is these faculties in particular that have been required to make the most significant change to academic (or curriculum) business-as-usual. Academic restructuring within professional and vocational faculties at both universities and technikons has been excluded from specific discussion here, as their core activities were not fundamentally shaken in the curriculum restructuring processes that were inaugurated from the mid-1990s. While there has undoubtedly been reflection on, and in some cases quite radical reframing of, academic provision in this sector, there was no significant challenge to its core business of producing skilled graduates for employment in the workplace. If anything, government policy on curriculum has strongly affirmed this mission.[2]

1. HIGHER EDUCATION CURRICULUM POLICY
IN THE EARLY 1990s

In policy deliberations on higher education from the early to mid-1990s little has been written specifically on higher education curricula. The earliest large-scale engagement with educational policy development, the National Education Policy Investigation

179

N. Cloete et al. (eds.), Transformation in Higher Education, 179-193.
© 2007 Springer.

(Nepi, 1992a, 1992b, and 1992c), said virtually nothing on the subject. In order to discern the influences on higher education curricula at the time the NCHE began its deliberations and subsequently, we need to turn to the broad systemic policy formulations that emerged from the early 1990s and read from these the implications for higher education curriculum policy. Significant amongst these policy initiatives are:[3]

- The Nepi reports, especially that on Human Resource Development (Nepi, 1992c), which drew significantly on ANC/Cosatu policy at that time.
- The ANC discussion document 'A Policy Framework for Education and Training' (ANC, 1994).
- Policy emerging from the National Training Board's National Training Strategy Initiative (NTSI) in 1994 (see Kraak, 1999 and Jansen & Christie, 1999).
- The government White Paper on Education and Training (Department of Education, February 1995) followed by the South African Qualifications Act, No 58 of October 1995.

Running through all of these documents was a desire to steer South Africa along a 'high skills, high growth' path of economic development which would lay the foundation of a new democratic society. The key mechanism to achieve this was a National Qualifications Framework (NQF), which allowed for credit accumulation and transfer. Strongly influenced by developments in Australasia, the NQF was and is intended to bring formal academic education and vocational training into closer alignment. The rationale for this was clear and compelling. Apartheid had denied the majority of South Africans access to education and training, and hundreds of thousands of working people competently performed jobs for which job reservation legislation denied them certification. An antiquated industrial training system limited the portability of qualifications across industries and even geographically within the same industry. Modularisation of curricula and credit accumulation, it was argued, would allow workers in particular to acquire high skills and enable them to achieve greater mobility. The intended impact of this system upon schooling (and higher education) was to produce curricula that were more relevant to the world of work – 'relevance' which was to be achieved by eroding traditional disciplinary boundaries in favour of interdisciplinarity.

A pivotal assumption underpinning the NQF is the notion of equivalence of different knowledge forms, an equivalence to be established through the specification of outcomes. Specific content, so the argument went (and still goes), was to be backgrounded in favour of generic, transferable skills. Disciplinarity was to give way to interdisciplinarity, the basis for re-constituted, relevant curricula.

It was against the backdrop of the newly established NQF (the implications of which were yet to be fully elaborated both for schooling and higher education) and a discourse that stressed the importance of education for economic development, that the NCHE was established. At this stage, two contending discourses came into play over the structuring of higher education curricula: *a disciplinary discourse, and a credit accumulation and transfer discourse*. They continue to do battle today.[4] (See box on discourses shaping the structuring of the curriculum on page 181.)

DISCOURSES SHAPING THE STRUCTURING OF HIGHER EDUCATION CURRICULA

For the sake of completeness, I developed the following schema to contextualise both the credit exchange and disciplinary discourses. The following figure locates four discourses according to two dimensions of variation: discursive orientation and the extent of student discretion over the selection of curriculum.

		DISCURSIVE ORIENTATION	
		Introjective	*Projective*
Degree of student selection over curriculum	*High*	**Therapeutic**	**Exchange**
	Low	**Disciplinary**	**Professional/ Vocational**

The *professional discourse* shares with the disciplinary discourse, vertical pedagogic relations, and an emphasis upon apprenticing students into specific knowledge domains. Its orientation, however, is not inwards upon itself, but rather outwards to the physical, natural and social world. Its orientation is projective: it faces outwards rather than inwards towards its own development and reproduction.

The *therapeutic discourse* shares with the disciplinary discourse an inward orientation, but differs from it in that this orientation is towards the self rather than towards a body of knowledge. It allows for a high degree of student discretion for the selection of content and explicitly eschews vertical relations between adepts and novices. The aim of a therapeutic pedagogy is to reveal inner competencies. This discourse is significant in higher education, but not dominant.

The first, traditional *disciplinary discourse* is enunciated by academics who argue that education should be an apprenticeship into powerful ways of knowing: of modes of analysis, of critique and of knowledge production. Emphasis is placed on mastery of conceptual structures and modes of argument, which form the basis for the production of new knowledge. In large measure, academic productivity derives from an inward focus upon the development of concepts, structures and modes of argument, rather than outwards upon the world. In this sense, disciplinary discourse has an *introjective orientation*.

A further important feature of disciplinary discourse is its underlying assumption that students, the 'to-be-apprenticed', enter the university with sets of experiences which are other than the knowledge forms into which they are to be inducted. In this respect, the disciplinary discourse rests upon explicit, vertical pedagogic relations between adepts and novices, with the rules of selection of curriculum content and of evaluation residing in the hands of academics. Associated with these vertical pedagogic relations is a foregrounding of disciplinary content and the backgrounding, relatively speaking, of individual student needs and experiences. Disciplinary discourse, then, in the discussion that follows, refers to a discourse about curriculum which emphasises the apprenticeship of students into largely self-referential domains which we call disciplines.

The *credit accumulation and transfer* (CAT) or *credit exchange discourse* is articulated by those who advocate the speediest integration of South Africa into a globalising world economy, to be achieved, *inter alia*, by a university sector that orients its activities towards producing highly skilled graduates for the workplace. A key characteristic of this discourse is modularisation of the curriculum and description of modules in terms of outcomes that can then be matched and exchanged as part of a process of accumulating credit towards academic qualifications (certificates, diplomas and degrees). Modularisation of the curriculum has the function of disaggregating traditional extended university courses; the specification of outcomes allows modules to be evaluated against each other for the purposes of equivalence. For advocates of the credit accumulation and transfer approach, the NQF is to function as a 'clearing house', allowing modules to be matched and exchanged. This point is important to emphasise: the specification of outcomes in the credit exchange discourse is not in the first instance an effort to address issues of quality. It is an attempt to provide a mechanism to facilitate the circulation of knowledge in an organised framework.

The credit accumulation and transfer discourse was evident in the deliberations of the Nepi Human Resource group and the Education and Training White Paper. By the time the NCHE started its work in 1995, this discourse had become more detailed, more robust and more differentiated from the disciplinary discourse, having gained sponsors amongst intellectuals in South African universities who were able to recruit arguments emerging from the academy internationally, most particularly those put forward by Gibbons et al. (1994) and Scott (1995). For the latter, credit accumulation and transfer remains the appropriate response of higher education to globalisation (Kraak, 2000).

According to sponsors of the credit accumulation and transfer approach, globalisation and democratisation impact in particular ways on higher education curriculum and pedagogy, and on research. Higher education curricula, the argument goes, should reflect a shift from *courses* to *credits*, from year-long courses to modules. Kraak (2000), following Scott, comments on courses in such a way as to clearly differentiate the CAT discourse from the preoccupations of the disciplinary discourse: 'these qualifications [based on disciplinary engagement] are associated with powerful canonical assumptions about the need for structured and sequential learning and the need to socialise students into the rules and rituals of particular disciplines and professional cultures' (Kraak, 2000:9). In place of this, he suggests, we should promote a shift to modular degrees, credit accumulation and transfer. 'These new mechanisms offer points of entry and exit without slavish regard to the academic symmetry of the whole ... connections between academic topics and levels are pragmatically derived rather than cognitively prescribed' (Kraak, 2000:9–10).

Along with modularisation, credit accumulation and transfer, comes a shift from *departments to programmes*, looser frameworks that allow the new credit currency to operate, and from *subject-based teaching to student-based learning*. In this scheme of things, an academic as teacher is to act as a 'facilitator rather than expert', one who should place emphasis on competence or skills rather than knowledge or content. In other words, the vertical pedagogic relations associated with academic apprenticeship into domain-specific knowledge favoured by a disciplinary discourse are to be eroded.

This shift in higher education curricula, it is argued, is accompanied by shifts in knowledge production. Research is no longer the preserve of universities, so the 'mode one – mode two' argument goes (see Gibbons et al., 1994; Kraak, 2000; Muller, 2000a). Rather, knowledge is increasingly produced by experts located across a range of different sites, placed within different collaborative networks. Research effort has increasingly become interdisciplinary in its quest to address complex technological, cultural and social problems.

The impact of globalisation on knowledge production has been discussed and debated elsewhere and will not be pursued here. Of interest for the current discussion, however, is the association made between a shift from mode one to mode two at the level of research, to a shift from discipline-based undergraduate curricula to an interdisciplinary form of *curriculum organisation*. It is assumed that because research (knowledge production) increasingly requires the engagement of specialists across a range of disciplines, it necessarily follows that the shaping of the undergraduate university curriculum (knowledge reproduction) should also become interdisciplinary.[5] However, Muller (2000a) has taken issue with this, arguing that over-zealous support for mode two can, in the South African context, weaken mode one knowledge production (and teaching) to the extent of promoting its collapse.

In practice the disciplinary and exchange discourses foreground different aims for university undergraduate curricula. The disciplinary discourse favours formative education at both school and university level, with the apprenticeship of students into specialised domains of knowledge. The credit exchange discourse (as promoted in South Africa, at any rate) favours modularisation of the curriculum, a focus on generic skills, and selection from these modules by students to create curriculum packages to meet their own requirements. This discourse also favours interdisciplinarity and portability. Inter-disciplinarity is facilitated by allowing students to select from a range of modules within different disciplines, and portability is facilitated by the statement of learning outcomes that allows the matching and exchange of credits to take place across various learning sites.

2. THE NCHE REPORT AND THE WHITE PAPER

The NCHE was appointed in 1994 to recommend to government ways in which the racially divided, exclusive, differentiated higher education system could be re-invigorated, modernised and made more responsive. In setting about its task, the NCHE confronted two potentially contradictory pressures: on the one hand, the pressure to prepare South Africa for participation in a sophisticated global economy; on the other hand, to render higher education more responsive to the needs and challenges of a country pulling itself away from its apartheid past, in the context of very real resource constraints. That South Africa's higher education sector should respond appropriately to the imperatives of globalisation and democratisation was uncontroversial; what constituted an appropriate response, however, was a more controversial matter. Nowhere is this more evident than in the NCHE's deliberations on curriculum. The commission was criticised at the time of its report, and subsequently, for remaining silent on the issue of the curriculum. Yet this is not strictly true. The NCHE spoke eloquently on the issue of the curriculum, but not consistently. It spoke in such a way as to incorporate both credit exchange and disciplinary discourses. By doing this, it gave rise to ambiguity and confusion, and to widely divergent readings of its policy texts.

The new unified higher education system was, the NCHE asserted, to address South Africa's need for reconstruction and development, to rebuild civic society on more equitable lines and provide the basis for participation in the global economy. It was to improve access to higher education by South Africa's poor and previously disadvantaged, and provide for lifelong learning. The vehicle for achieving this was the academic programme:

> As has been suggested earlier, a 'mass' or 'massified' higher education system, in the technical sense of the word, denotes more than just the size of the system. Apart from the growth in numbers, mass higher education brings with it a restructuring of the system itself. This includes changes in the types and mixes of institutions as well as changes in assumptions about how the offering of higher education programmes should be structured and organised.
>
> *The traditional currency of courses and qualifications, based on long-standing academic presuppositions about the need for sequential learning within defined disciplines, is for instance giving way to more flexible approaches to the higher education curriculum.*
>
> Stimulated by worldwide changes in the production and dissemination of knowledge, *the traditional model is being augmented in many 'mass' systems by an approach based on modular programmes and the accumulation of credits.* This offers multiple entry and exit points, while progression is based on *pragmatic connections between topics and levels, without, however, abandoning the norms of cognitive coherence.* It also provides greater flexibility for learners and allows for a more seamless interface between work and study. (1996:77, emphasis added)

The italicised sections here illustrate the two discourses at work. The credit exchange system is crisply set out in the references to modular programmes, the accumulation of credits, and the criticism of 'long-standing academic presuppositions about the need for sequential learning within defined disciplines'. At the same time this is softened by such qualifiers recruited from the disciplinary discourse, as 'giving way to more flexible approaches', with the traditional model being 'augmented' by modules and accumulation of credits, which will not lead to the 'abandoning of the norms of cognitive coherence'. The implication here is that these two systems should co-exist: credit accumulation and transfer, and cognitive coherence (i.e. learner development).

Both discourses are evident later in the report where the Commission comments that disciplinary knowledge will co-exist with credit exchange:

> Higher education institutions will increasingly be offering a greater mix of programmes, *some based strictly on disciplinary knowledge and canonical norms, others emphasising in a more flexible way the development of vocationally focused competencies and the skills of interdisciplinary co-operation needed in the workplace.* (p79, emphasis added)

Later in the document, the disciplinary discourse is more strongly apparent:

> Traditionally qualifications rather than the mere completion and accumulation of discrete units of education are visible features of the higher education continuum. They allow for rigour, concentration and coherence to be built into the phases of learning, and ensure that integration as well as the advancement of learner's knowledge takes place. (p84)

In its formal proposal on programmes, the NCHE recommended that 'higher education programmes should consist of a coherent, planned and integrated sequence of learning activities, successful completion of which leads to the award of a formal qualification at certificate, diploma or degree level' (p89). In its glossary, the report defines a programme in higher education as 'the contents and offering of a distinct and well-defined configuration of knowledge, the successful study of which leads to standard qualifications' (p272).

From the above formulations, it would appear that while both discourses influenced the formulation of the final NCHE report, the disciplinary discourse won the day. Yet the White Paper on higher education transformation (Department of Education, 1997) commented that a programme approach allowed learning to take place across 'a multiplicity of institutions and sites for learning' (p17) and encourages

> *an open and flexible system based on credit accumulation and multiple entry and exit points for learners.* This will remove obstacles which unnecessarily limit learners' access to programmes and enable proper academic recognition to be given for prior learning achieved, thus permitting greater horizontal and vertical mobility by learners in the higher education system. *It would also break the grip of the traditional pattern of qualification based on sequential, year-long courses in single disciplines.* (Department of Education, 1997:18, emphasis added)

The credit exchange discourse is asserted strongly here, but because of powerful opposition to this discourse from the higher education sector prior to the publication of the White Paper, the latter went on to note:

> The incorporation of academic qualifications within a national framework is not a straightforward matter and, quite properly, it has been the subject of intense debate. *SAQA has determined that both unit standards and whole qualifications may be presented for registration on the NQF.* This should meet the serious concern among many academic staff that unit standard methodology, and the construction of qualifications from multiple units of learning, are inappropriate foundations for certain academic programmes. (Department of Education, 1997:28 emphasis added)

In this way, the White Paper acknowledged explicitly the operation of both discourses within the system. The South African Qualifications Authority (SAQA) Act (No 58 of 1995) and Higher Education Act (No 101 of 1997) did not take up the issue of curriculum specifically, although SAQA was authorised by the legislation to issue proclamations that would affect curriculum design. While it can be argued that the NCHE report and the subsequent White Paper embodied elements of both credit exchange and disciplinary discourses, SAQA operates very explicitly in terms of the former. This sets the scene for potential conflict between SAQA and the higher education sector, most especially the universities which by and large subscribe to the disciplinary discourse in practice, even while organising their academic offerings as 'programmes'. As indicated above, the NCHE's notion of a programme was marked by two contradictory discourses that have consequently rendered its meaning ambiguous, able to be recruited by advocates of both credit exchange and disciplinary discourses to promote their course of action. Since the time the legislation was enacted, however, the discourse of credit exchange, which underpins the NQF, has become more dominant, and universities have attempted to circumvent it rather than confront it directly. The registration of whole qualifications rather than unit standards (see Department of Education, 1997:28) was a significant step in creating the space for them to do this.

3. ACADEMIC PROGRAMMES IN PRACTICE

Taken together, the NCHE report, the subsequent White Paper and the Higher Education Act are ambiguous about what constitutes an academic programme. The Act, for example, simply used the definition of a programme as a device to distinguish higher education from other levels of education. The NCHE report and the White Paper contained elements of both credit exchange and disciplinary discourses. What entered higher education as a definition of a programme came to be associated with a number of key features: portability, relevance (or 'responsiveness'), coherence and interdisciplinarity (which was offered as the vehicle to achieve relevance). But even nailing down the definition of a programme to a number of key features did not remove the ambiguity, and different institutions invested these features with very different meanings.

Universities responded to the NCHE call for programmes (and in one case at least, pre-empted it) in a context quite different from that envisaged by the NCHE. Instead of a dramatic increase in student numbers (and therefore a relatively generously resourced environment) anticipated by the NCHE, the reality was a sluggish growth in enrolments that placed many institutions in financial difficulties. Competition for students became inevitable. The perception was that students, and the government via the NCHE's definition of programmes, wanted qualifications that would prepare them for the workplace. Consequently, most universities set out to repackage their curricula in ways that might be seen to do this.

The slow growth in overall student enrolments and the financial circumstances in which universities found themselves, imposed a range of pressures on institutions to 'downsize' and restructure. In many cases faculties were merged and departments either amalgamated or dissolved altogether. In at least two cases, the impact of downsizing on curriculum construction was apparent. In the arts faculty at the University of Port Elizabeth, where student numbers had fallen and long-term viability needed to be addressed, academic programme planning offered itself as a rational means to downsize. Academics who were not able to enter strong programmes risked losing their jobs. At the University of Cape Town, the academic planning framework committee simultaneously announced the need to restructure academic offerings as programmes and the desire to reduce the size of the university establishment by some 10%. In the humanities faculty, there was evidence that some programmes were fashioned in such a way as to protect those departments and faculty members most vulnerable to possible retrenchment because of falling student numbers. The resulting programmes succeeded in protecting members of staff in this way, but in a small number of cases these offerings lacked intellectual coherence.

4. TYPOLOGIES OF CURRICULUM DESIGN

How did university faculties of science and humanities take up the call to organise their curricula as programmes? How did faculties that traditionally organised their curricula around largely self-referential disciplinary majors, fashion interdisciplinary programmes oriented towards the workplace? An attempt was made to address these questions through a case study of three universities in the Eastern Cape and a scan of university calendars for science and humanities faculties. It was found that universities responded to the call to organise curricula as programmes in one of four ways, referred to below as types A, B, C and D, depending on how the programme core was constituted, the degree of coherence in the course elements, and the degree of choice students had in selecting courses.[6]

The core of type A is made up of one or two primary, strongly classified vertical subject sequences, with wide choices available amongst the sequences. This is similar to the traditional single or double-major bachelor's degree. This approach to curricular restructuring is the form most widely found. It describes undergraduate curricula in 13 of 20 university science faculties and 14 of 20 university arts and humanities faculties in South Africa.

The core of type B is made up of one or two primary, strongly classified vertical subject sequences, with restricted choices available amongst the sequences. This approach is adopted in all but one of the remaining science faculties and most of the remaining arts and humanities faculties.

The core of type C is similar to that of type B, but its vertical sequences tend to be 'multiple bundles' rather than single or double majors. An example is the University of Pretoria's specialised BA programmes and their respective streams. Elements of this form of curriculum are also in evidence in the science and humanities faculties at Stellenbosch University.

Type D is a variation of type C, but is differentiated from it because vertical sequencing is less clear. The compulsory programme core comprises a cluster of strongly classified modules drawn from different disciplines such as economics, geography, sociology and politics to make up a development studies core, sometimes with a choice between modules. Research evidence suggests that this form of construction was present in the humanities faculties at the Universities of Cape Town and Port Elizabeth, although in neither institution was this the dominant mode of curriculum organisation (which was in the main type B).

5. INSTITUTIONAL RESPONSES

'Academic programme planning' implementation within institutions provoked different levels of anxiety and turmoil. Predictably, in those institutions where inroads upon disciplinary knowledge and organisation have been small (or almost absent, as in the case of Rhodes University), opposition to programme planning has been least evident. In those institutions where attempts have been made to reorganise the undergraduate curriculum more radically (usually along the lines of type D) antagonism from academics has been strongest, especially where this has been linked to 'institutional downsizing' and retrenchments.[7]

Responses to curriculum restructuring defy any attempt at clustering according to institutional type or location. 'Institutional culture' here proves a slippery notion indeed. The Universities of the Witwatersrand (Wits) and Cape Town, both historically white English-medium universities, responded in different ways. The science and humanities faculties at Wits (and Rhodes University) have responded similarly (around type A), and quite differently from UCT (type B). Both faculties at Natal have achieved a hybrid position based on types A and B. Capacity and institutional culture do not, therefore, appear to present regularity in curriculum outcome. This is complicated by very different responses from faculties at the same university. The science faculty at UPE has more in common in curriculum design with its counterparts at Rhodes and Fort Hare, for example, than its own humanities faculty, which seemed to have more in common with UCT's faculty of humanities. The university regarded by many as leading the field in 'entrepreneurial' orientation, the University of Pretoria, has repackaged its programme offerings 'to achieve market-oriented outcomes' (University of Pretoria, 2001) but remains clearly and discernibly organised around disciplines, not dissimilar from those offered elsewhere. Vista University is clustered with others in type A, but by 1999 had not yet modularised. It is not clear whether this is for reasons of principle or because of problems with capacity.

While it is not possible on the basis of the existing data to cluster responses in terms of institutional culture and capacity across the system, it is possible to make some indicative remarks based on the case study research (Ensor, 2001). Rhodes University, the University of Port Elizabeth and the University of Fort Hare all operate in the same geographic region, with different levels of internal capacity. While Fort Hare staff had a range of interesting ideas for curriculum reform, problems with management had created a leadership vacuum that made forward movement problematic. The institution was beginning to deal with this at the time the case study research took place, and it will be interesting to see what progress has been made in this regard. Rhodes University occupies a privileged niche in the area, drawing students both regionally and nationally. Student numbers have remained robust, and even though some departments have been closed or amalgamated, the academic establishment has retained its size over the past few years. The leadership of the university has held fast to its position that the best way to 'respond to the market' is to continue with the general, formative undergraduate education it has prized itself in providing. This view was shared by the science faculty at the University of Port Elizabeth, but not by its humanities faculty. Here, falling student numbers had become an acute problem. The UPE humanities faculty responded to this through a 'radical programme approach' – modularising, offering credit accumulation over time (within specified qualification structures), closing departments in favour of schools and developing programmes in the place of the old bachelors degrees based around majors. Staff unable to find a place within programmes were retrenched. 'Responsiveness', then, meant very different things to Rhodes, Fort Hare and UPE, and in some cases, to the faculties within them.

The University of Cape Town's humanities faculty also went the 'radical programme' route, but in the absence, initially at least, of the same kind of pressures operating at the University of Port Elizabeth. While the academic planning framework specified the intention of downsizing UCT by 10%, senior university staff involved in the programme planning process were adamant that this was not driven by financial imperatives. Rather, academic programmes were motivated by the need to produce 'relevant' programmes, encapsulating both vertical coherence and interdisciplinarity that would better equip undergraduates for citizenry and for work. But even though financial constraints may not have provided the pinch initially, the fear of retrenchments became palpable within the faculty of humanities within a short space of time. Academic programme planning became a vehicle, in some areas, for rescuing departments (and staff) at risk. As indicated above, in a small number of instances this resulted in programmes in which intellectual coherence cannot easily be discerned. In other cases the administrative complexity and inflexibility of humanities programmes and deep staff dissatisfaction resulted in a review that in the end proposed a hybrid situation of type A (bachelors degrees organised around two majors) and type B (named programmes organised around strong vertical pillars).

6. INTERDISCIPLINARITY, PORTABILITY, COHERENCE AND RESPONSIVENESS

The NCHE proposed academic programmes that promoted interdisciplinarity, portability, coherence and responsiveness (or relevance). The question for us is: has this been achieved? The answer is unequivocally 'no' in respect of portability, but with respect to the others, contingent upon how one defines an academic programme and the descriptors involved.

Regardless of definitions, however, there can be little doubt that there is far less portability in the university system now than before programme planning took place. Portability of qualifications across institutions is easily achieved for degrees organised around the traditional single or double major (type A), as students can move from one university to another with easily recognisable credits. With the formation of programmes around tight compulsory cores (types B, C and D) portability is more difficult. In at least two humanities faculties with programmes organised as types B, C or D, students transferring after the first year need to repeat the first year of the programme in the university to which they move in order to progress further. So while modularisation has occurred in most institutions, seemingly a gesture towards credit accumulation and exchange, and towards greater flexibility and portability, this has been cut across in most cases by restrictions on, rather than expansion of, student choice. The end result is a system far less flexible than existed prior to 1995.

In the main, 'interdisciplinarity' in undergraduate science and humanities programmes has been achieved by linking traditional or contemporary academic disciplines (and for the purposes of this discussion we can include knowledge areas such as media studies or environmental studies) in order to establish pedagogic pathways for students over which they have varying degrees of choice (types A, B and C). There is little evidence of interdisciplinarity as might be envisaged by what Bernstein (1975) refers to as an integrated curriculum. Nevertheless, there certainly has been an attempt to organise curricula around a common theme (such as development studies), drawing on existing disciplines (economics, sociology, etc). In some cases this has emerged with strong vertical sequencing, presenting itself much like a disciplinary major in a type A, B or C arrangement. So whether 'interdisciplinarity' has been achieved or not depends upon whether types A, B, C or D are regarded as interdisciplinary, or some further reorganising of knowledge is expected.

To achieve greater 'responsiveness' or 'relevance', a number of institutions have 'packaged' their undergraduate offerings as programmes, with titles that suggest a relevance to the world of work, such as tourism and heritage studies. This suggests an attempt to re-orient discipline-based curricula in a more outwardly direction. The extent to which this has been achieved in practice requires close scrutiny on the ground. On the basis of the documentary evidence provided by the institutional calendars examined in the case study, however, it seems that undergraduate curricula have achieved this more in terms of rhetoric than in practice, and programmes are still organised largely on a disciplinary basis. Efforts to produce curricula that are more 'relevant' and 'responsive', have resulted in the main in types B, C and D. So while student choice may be restricted, and domains of knowledge linked together more tightly than before, the central organising principle of university undergraduate curricula remains the disciplines. In this sense, contemporary curricula in sciences and humanities look little different from the way they did before academic programme implementation began.

Different players in the higher education environment have put a different spin on the notion of coherence. For advocates of the disciplinary discourse, vertical coherence is prioritised over horizontal articulation. For advocates of the exchange discourse, coherence is established contingently, if at all, on the basis of student selection. It is not possible, from the calendars, to establish the degree of vertical coherence within the programmes. In some cases, judging by the interlinking of courses through pre-requisite rules, this appears to be strong. In a smaller number of cases, this seems to be compromised, especially in the creation of compulsory, interdisciplinary programme cores that bind together strongly classified modules whose articulation is not apparent (type D). This has important implications for pedagogy, in that disadvantaged students for whom coherence is a powerful educational support may be further disadvantaged by the relative incoherence of these programmes.

Just as the credit exchange and disciplinary discourses profoundly marked policy texts on higher education curricula, so have they become imprinted on curriculum in practice. The credit exchange discourse has pressurised faculties of science and humanities to provide a professional or vocational face to their academic provision. It has promoted (although is not necessarily responsible for initiating) the move towards modularisation and the specification of learning outcomes.[8] The disciplinary discourse, however, has reasserted itself through the restriction of student choice, the tying of modules through pre- and co-requisites and the emphasis on induction into vertical knowledge sequences. In some cases, represented by type D above, we appear to have a hybrid of both discourses. Credit accumulation is favoured via modularisation and 'interdisciplinarity', while the disciplinary discourse is favoured by restrictions on student choice, ostensibly to construct a pedagogic pathway. The internal coherence of the resulting curriculum is difficult to establish. Overall, though, it would seem that curricula have been re-packaged and redesigned (as types B and C) but remain recognisable in terms of their disciplinary origins.

7. CONCLUSION

Two dominant discourses have shaped higher education curriculum reconstruction since the early 1990s: credit exchange and traditional disciplinary knowledge. The credit exchange discourse wants to fragment the curriculum into 'bits' (or modules) that students can then fit together. It is assumed that students have the competence to do this, and that, together, the modules should equip the student for active participation in the workplace. The second, the disciplinary discourse, wants to organise the modules or courses in such a way as to achieve an apprenticeship, usually into a discipline. Students are assumed to require guidance in the structuring of their curriculum, and emphasis is placed on vertical progression.

Just as both discourses have appropriated interdisciplinarity and modularisation to their own ends, so have they done with the generation of outcomes statements. For the credit exchange discourse, the statement of outcomes is a crucial mechanism for establishing equivalence and exchange between modules, which can then be accumulated across different sites of practice. The disciplinary discourse, in contrast, has appropriated outcomes statements as a mechanism to achieve quality control.

The three-institution case study and the investigation of university calendars suggest that, in general, curricula in the sciences and humanities have altered in some respects, but remain fundamentally discipline-based. Knowledge has been re-organised and repackaged, but there are no significant shifts towards what Bernstein might call an integrated curriculum. On the other hand, many campus administrators (and academics) claim that the programme planning process has made teachers more aware of what they teach and why they do so, which has improved on what is offered to students. In the case of curriculum cores organised according to a type D arrangement, as I have suggested, this claim requires close scrutiny.

For the moment, the turmoil associated with academic programme planning has subsided. However, in 2001 two initiatives were announced which will push the curriculum debate significantly further. The first, the National Plan for Higher Education (Ministry of Education, 2001), lays its emphasis on graduation success rates and expanding postgraduate offerings; this will press upon universities (and technikons) the need to consider further their provision and support for undergraduate (and postgraduate) students. Secondly, the announcement of a review of SAQA by the Minister of Education opens up the possibility of returning to those founding ideas upon which the NQF was built – articulation, flexibility and lifelong learning for all South Africans – to find educationally sound mechanisms for achieving these.[9]

In South Africa, the credit exchange and disciplinary discourses have emerged and developed in antagonism to each other, and it is now perhaps time to explore possible common ground. Proponents of credit exchange have neglected to foreground sufficiently the need for strong curricula to be developed which offer learners proper induction, whether into skilled performances or principled understandings. The proponents of the disciplinary discourse have not addressed with sufficient energy the need to structure curricula that allow learners to enter and exit a qualification route at different points in their lives. We need to find ways of enabling both; of combining articulation and flexibility with vertical coherence and learning in depth.[10]

ACKNOWLEDGEMENTS

I am grateful to Wieland Gevers, Martin Hall, André Kraak, Joe Muller and members of my reference group for their productive and generous engagement with a previous draft of this chapter. The position taken here has benefited greatly from this dialogue, but is my own and does not necessarily reflect the views of my commentators.

NOTES

[1] The Nepi Post-secondary Education Research Group (Nepi, 1992b), for example, announced at the beginning of its report that the central issue within post-secondary education was 'knowledge'. Having declared this, however, it did not return to 'knowledge' again, either in terms of research or teaching, for the remainder of its report.

[2] In spite of the technikon sector and university faculties other than science and humanities not being included, the scope of this chapter still encompasses a significant number of students. According to Department of Education (1999) figures, enrolments at universities increased from 340.000 in 1993 to 372.000 in June 1999, an increase in real terms (although a decrease from 72% to 66% of total higher education enrolments). University students still constitute the majority of higher education students (measured either in headcounts or full-time equivalent student enrolments). In June 1999, within the university sector, students in the science faculties constituted 21% of the total headcount enrolment, business and commerce 20%, and humanities 59%. This means that although this chapter only focuses on two faculties within the university sector, they cater for a sizeable number of higher education students in South Africa.

[3] For a fuller description of the policy environment, see Jansen and Christe (1999) and for a discussion of higher education curriculum issues, see Breier (2001).

[4] A more thorough examination of this schema is found on the website which supplements this book: www.chet.org.za/papers.asp.

[5] An overview of the literature concerning the impact of globalisation on higher education curriculum reform can be found on the website which supplements this book: www.chet.org.za/papers.asp.

[6] The methodology of the research used to explore these approaches, and the details of the findings, are discussed on the website which supplements this book and in my chapter in Breier (2001). The website may be found at www.chet.org.za/papers.asp.

[7] It seems that the response of university academics to the registration of qualifications with SAQA by June of 2000 was not regarded with great enthusiasm (see Muller & Ogude 1999; Ogude et al., 2002). Universities were required to register programmes in terms of outcomes rather than content, so this data base is of limited usefulness for discussions of the present kind which are interested in features of curriculum design.

[8] The shift towards modularisation is much more marked in the historically white institutions compared with the historically black institutions.

[9] For a discussion of the educational implications of the NQF's logic, see Ensor (1997), Jansen and Christie (1999) and Muller (2000b).

[10] Michael Young (2001) provides an interesting review of qualifications frameworks and contrasts the intrinsic logic of frameworks such as the NQF with institutional logics that develop articulation through local collaboration.

REFERENCES

African National Congress (ANC) (1994). *A Policy Framework for Education and Training*. Braamfontein: ANC.

Bernstein, B. (1975). Class, Codes and Control. Vol. 3. *Towards a Theory of Educational Transmissions*. London: Routledge & Kegan Paul.

Breier, M. (ed.) (2001). *Curriculum Restructuring in Higher Education in Post-Apartheid South Africa*. Pretoria: CSD.

Department of Education (1995). White Paper on Education and Training. Pretoria.

Department of Education (1997). Education White Paper 3: A Programme for the Transformation of Higher Education. Pretoria.

Department of Education (2001). *National Plan for Higher Education*. Pretoria.

Ensor, P. (1997). School Mathematics, Everyday Life and the NQF: A Case of Non-equivalence? Pythagoras, 41 (April), 36–44.

Ensor, P. (2001). Academic Programme Planning in South African Higher Education: Three Institutional Case Studies. In: M. Breier (ed.), *Curriculum Restructuring in Higher Education in Post-Apartheid South Africa*. Pretoria: CSD.

Gibbons, M., Limoges, C., Nowotny, H., Schwartsman, S., Scott, P. & Trow, M. (1994). *The New Production of Knowledge: The Dynamics of Science and Research in Contemporary Societies*. California: Sage Publications.

Jansen, J. & Christie, P. (eds) (1999). *Changing Curriculum: Studies on Outcomes-based Education in South Africa*. Cape Town: Juta.

Kraak, A. (1999). Competing Education and Training Policy Discourses: A 'Systematic' Versus 'Unit Standards' Framework. In: J. Jansen & P. Christie (eds), *Changing Curriculum: Studies on Outcomes-based Education in South Africa*. Cape Town: Juta.

Kraak, A. (2000). Changing Modes: A Brief Overview of the 'Mode 2' Knowledge Debate and its Impact on South African Policy Formulation. In: A. Kraak (ed.), *Changing Modes: New Knowledge Production and its Implications for Higher Education in South Africa*. Pretoria: HSRC.

Muller, J. & Ogude, N. (1999). Curriculum Reform in Higher Education in South Africa: How Academics Respond. Paper presented to the Third Tri-National Seminar. Tarrytown, New York. October.

Muller, J. (2000a). What Knowledge is of Most Worth for the Millennial Citizen? In: J. Muller, *Reclaiming Knowledge: Social Theory, Curriculum and Education Policy*. London: Routledge/Falmer.

Muller, J. (2000b). The Well-tempered Learner. In: J. Muller, *Reclaiming Knowledge: Social Theory, Curriculum and Education Policy*. London: Routledge/Falmer.

National Commission on Higher Education (1996). *A Framework for Transformation*. Pretoria: NCHE.

National Education Policy Investigation (Nepi) (1992a). *Curriculum*. Cape Town: Oxford University Press/ NECC.

National Education Policy Investigation (Nepi) (1992b). *Post-secondary Education*. Cape Town: Oxford University Press/NECC.

National Education Policy Investigation (Nepi) (1992c). *Human Resources Development*. Cape Town: Oxford University Press/NECC.

Ogude, N.A., Netswera, F.G. & Mavundla, T.A. (2002). Critical Analysis of the Status and Evolution of Research Activities within South African Technikons. www.chet.org.za/papers.asp.

Scott, P. (1995). *The Meanings of Mass Higher Education*. Buckingham: SRHE and Open University Press.

University of Pretoria (2001). Regulations and Syllabi, Faculty of Humanities.

Young, M. (2001). Qualifications Frameworks and Lifelong Learning: The Road to a High Skill Future? Paper presented at the conference Globalisation and Higher Education: Views from the South. Cape Town, March.

CHAPTER 9

AHMED BAWA & JOHANN MOUTON

RESEARCH

South Africa's bold steps into a new democracy depended fundamentally on a national, broad-based intellectual culture which combined vibrant, intense discussion and debate with high levels of mature social and political tolerance. Over the years this intellectual culture has permeated the various social formations that constitute South African society. It was sharpened in the cauldron of the struggle for democracy, in the international isolation of South Africa during the deep, dark apartheid years and in the challenge of finding new strategies for development.

The impact of the higher education institutions on the development of this intellectual base is difficult to measure – largely because of the often ambivalent and inconsistent relationship between the institutions and the leadership of social and political organisations. Nevertheless, there can be no question about their role in producing intellectuals of different kinds who were central to the broad projects of national development – with, it must be said, both positive and negative results. The ability of a nation to claim as its own a substantial body of natural, human and social scientists helps enormously to build the confidence of that nation state. The creation and development and maintenance of this intellectual culture depends fundamentally on the research culture of its higher education institutions.

This chapter describes the new policy framework for a national research system which was put in place after 1994. It provides a statistical overview of research expenditure and outputs, looks at the new role players, sketches out the emergence of a new research landscape and assesses some of the changes that have occurred since 1994.

1. SOUTH AFRICAN SCIENCE BEFORE 1994

When compared with the research systems of other nations in Africa and indeed those of other nations in the developing world, South Africa's is a substantial and varied one. It is expected to act as a seed for a new generation system, one which is defined in the context of the social, political, and economic transformations that have characterised the first seven years of post-apartheid South Africa.

South African science[1] has a long and proud tradition. Born in the mid-eighteenth century from the works of amateur natural historians and astronomers who travelled to what was then the Cape Colony to satisfy their intellectual curiosity, it developed into the major science base on the African continent. The initial excursions of amateur scientists

N. Cloete et al. (eds.), Transformation in Higher Education, 195-218.
© 2007 *Springer.*

soon gave way to more formalised and institutionalised modes of knowledge production in the nineteenth century. With the discovery of gold and diamonds and the subsequent industrialisation of the Witwatersrand, came a new demand for mining engineers and geologists, and for social scientists of various kinds. This was soon followed – because of major natural disasters (animal epidemics and the proliferation of various plant diseases) – by the establishment of major research centres (most notably Onderstepoort Veterinary Institute) around the turn of the twentieth century.

It was under the ambitious gaze and guidance of former Prime Minister Jan Smuts that South African science came into being as an entity that was recognisable as a system. With its heart in the universities, this became a science system that worked vigorously to make South Africa a global player whilst simultaneously serving South Africa's needs, particularly in the areas of mining and agriculture. It was a system that was to produce the 'nation's' political leadership, provide its creative energy and become the repository for its cultures and traditions.

As was the case elsewhere in the world, the Second World War proved to be a major stimulus for the South African science system – of which the higher education research system was an important element. It gave rise to the establishment of the Council for Scientific and Industrial Research (CSIR), the biggest science laboratory in the country outside of university centres. From its establishment in 1946, the CSIR played a major role in promoting scientific research and through its influence ultimately gave rise to a wider appreciation of the role of research within the country. Directly and indirectly it also gave rise to the establishment of many of the other science councils which were formed between the 1950s and 1970s, including the Human Sciences Research Council (HSRC) which was intended to be the human sciences laboratory of the state.

When the Nationalist Government came to power in 1948, its apartheid policies had major implications for the way in which post-war science in South Africa would develop over the next 40 years. There was a growing emphasis on strategic research within the science councils in order to serve the national security goals of the government. For example, this eventually led to the development of an indigenous nuclear research industry that was able to build atom bombs. Billions of rands were spent on military and defence R&D. It was during this period that the development of a fragmented higher education system occurred, differentiating between the historically white Afrikaans- and English-medium universities and introducing 'ethnic-based' universities.

At the national level the higher education research system was indeed shaped by the needs of the dominant strata of the society in which these institutions functioned. Major influences on the system can be identified quite easily. For instance, in response to the arms embargo, the atom bomb project and the needs of the military-industrial complex more generally, were built on the base of (and fed into) substantial research capacity in the nuclear and materials sciences. These developments were a major force in shaping the national science agenda, and the research systems within that agenda. It is therefore not surprising that such a substantial and outstanding nuclear sciences enterprise emerged in South African universities. Another example is the academic boycott which affected the social sciences much more than it did the natural sciences. This helped to shape a social science research system that was insular and marginalised in the global context. Similarly, the mining and agriculture industries, also central to the survival of the apartheid regime, were deeply influential.

In 1992 the ANC commissioned a study, sponsored by the International Development Research Centre (IDRC), to review the state of science in South Africa. When the first democratic government came to power in 1994, it took these and other findings of the commission as a point of departure in the unfolding policy development process. As the findings of analytical studies of South Africa's science system in the post-1994 period began to emerge, it became clear that the country's substantial research system was hopelessly disarticulated from the needs of the majority of South Africans. For instance, research capacity and excellence in the areas of infectious diseases or community-based medicine was hopelessly lacking at the very time that Chris Barnard performed the world's first human heart transplantation operation.

A second finding was that the South African national science system – of which the universities are an important part – was deeply fragmented and unco-ordinated. A third finding was that the system was both inefficient and ineffective. It was thus not surprising that the social responsibility of South African science and scientists came under political scrutiny during the early 1990s.

2. THE NEW POLICIES

2.1. The national science system

In the Green Paper on Science and Technology and the subsequent White Paper (1996), the government committed itself, among other things, to:

- The creation of a new policy framework for public science.
- Conducting a system-wide review of the national system of innovation in order to establish its strengths and weaknesses and future priorities.
- Creating new structures to develop, implement and monitor the new policy framework.

This policy process vigorously sought to revisit the system in its entirety – the performing science councils, the funding agency science councils, the state corporations such as Eskom, the government laboratories, the higher education system and the private sector laboratories. The major emphasis rested on attempting to understand how to make the science system more responsive to the challenges of South Africa's reconstruction and development needs. As the policy process unfolded, this was captured in the notion of the National System of Innovation (NSI). The core idea was that the NSI would provide a framework within which the different elements of the system could fit to meet this challenge.

The central issues were to overcome fragmentation, promote innovation and to develop a research framework in line with national priorities. The strategy that was adopted to build a coherent system out of the fragmented one depended on three substantial developments, each of which has been partially or fully realised.

The first outcome was a set of structural developments: the establishment of the National Research Foundation (NRF) and the National Advisory Council on Innovation (NACI). The former brings together the funding agency functions for the human and natural sciences. The legislation that guides its activities requires that it fund university research on the basis of the broad socio-economic and political agendas of the state. The National Advisory Council on Innovation serves to advise cabinet on science and innovation matters as well as issues related to the global competitiveness of South Africa's industry and its ability to meet the needs of the majority of South Africans.

The second set of outcomes relates to the establishment of funding drivers for the transformation of the system – the use of significant fractions of the national science vote from parliament to bring about the kinds of changes that are captured in the new policy regime. It may be said that while certain large national strategic projects were identified during the apartheid period – projects (amongst them the atom bomb project) that were funded by the state almost without limit – in the post-apartheid period none have yet been identified. However, the creation of the Innovation Fund, which grew from R30-million in 1999 to R125-million in 2001, provides the means to build the national capacity in sharply defined areas which are likely to be drawn from the national priorities identified by the cabinet.

The third outcome that emerged from this policy process has also been completed viz. the National Research and Technology Audit (NRTA) conducted in 1997/1998, a system-wide review of the science councils and the national facilities undertaken in 1998/1999, and the National Research and Technology Foresight Exercise (1998/2000) which was to plan for South Africa's long-term research and technology needs and opportunities.

For a short time after the first democratic elections in 1994, the Reconstruction and Development Programme (RDP) provided a substantial and highly textured backdrop for the policy development process. Much of the policy discourse during this period was shaped by the reconstruction agenda which provided a set of priorities to which researchers could respond. The adoption of the Growth, Equity and Redistribution (Gear) macro-economic framework in 1996 altered the nature of this discourse substantially and forced into the centre of the debate the need for a science system that was driven by the competitiveness of South Africa's industrial products and hence its innovation system. An issue for future study would be how the advent of Gear altered the 'balance of forces' between the needs of reconstruction on the one hand and industrial innovation on the other.

By 2001 a very impressive canopy of science policies had been put into place to establish a national science system and, although it may be too early assess their full impact, the following sections will shed some light on some of the effects of these developments.

2.2. Higher education research policies

The higher education research system is very much a part of the national science system. This sector, however, underwent its own policy process and attempts were made to ensure that the different processes articulated with each other – largely through the individuals who were involved in both. The post-1994 higher education policy process, beginning with the National Commission on Higher Education (NCHE), was influenced heavily by the relatively unconstrained discussions that characterised the policy debates that occurred under the aegis of the National Education Policy Investigation (Nepi) and the Union of Democratic University Staff Associations (Udusa). Many of these ideas were carried into the later processes.

The White Paper on higher education transformation (Department of Education, 1997) drew heavily on the Report of the National Commission on Higher Education (1996) and attempted to extend the substance of the proposals for research. The White Paper announced that: 'The production, advancement and dissemination of knowledge and the development of high level human resources are core functions of the higher education system.' It went on to reaffirm that research plays a key role in these two functions and identified the key capacity difficulties: the fragmented national system, the lack of research capacity in the higher education sector, the 'stark race and gender imbalances', and the skewed distribution of the capacity between the historically black institutions and the historically white ones. The White Paper picked up the mode one/mode two knowledge generation debate and made a strong argument for a shift towards the mode two research type – research defined in the context of applications rather than in the framework of academic imperatives. More specifically, the document supported the following:

- The development of a national research plan, which was meant to be an outcome of the Research and Technology Foresight exercise carried out by the Department of Arts, Culture, Science and Technology.
- The development of a framework to facilitate greater articulation between the higher education research system and the rest of the science system. The development of the National System of Innovation, described above, provides such a framework. Furthermore, the creation of various funding drivers, such as the Innovation Fund, fuelled this specific transformation strategy.
- The establishment of mechanisms to increase both public and private funding of research. The expansion of the higher education research base was seen as a crucial policy proposition and the White Paper indicated that it saw earmarked funding as a mechanism to achieve this. While state spending on the national science system did increase, this did not impact directly on research in the higher education system for two reasons. First, the 'blind' component 'earmarked' for research within the Higher Education Vote requires no direct accountability on the part of universities and technikons. There are as yet no mechanisms in place to establish whether the amount that has theoretically been allocated for research, does in fact get allocated for research activities at the higher education institutions. Until such time as such mechanisms are put in place, it will in fact remain a 'blind' allocation. Secondly, most of the increases in research funding within the science system occurred in the areas of directed, strategic funding. Two funds benefited from these increases: the Technology and Human Resources for Industry Project (Thrip) and the National

Innovation Fund (NIF). Although the increases were substantial in both cases, both funds are open for application to institutions outside the higher education sector, including, for example, the science councils. Substantial funding from the National Innovation Fund was awarded to the science councils, rather than to universities and technikons.

- The allocation of earmarked funds to build capacity and to develop potential centres of excellence in research and postgraduate training at the historically black universities. Access of black and women students to masters, doctoral and post-doctoral programmes was to be made a priority.

In 1996/7 the National Commission on Higher Education and the White Paper on higher education transformation made scant reference to globalisation. By 2001, however, it was well documented that participating effectively in the global environment depends on the way that four things interact: information technology, knowledge production, human resources and institutions (Castells, 2001). Knowledge and 'informationalism' have become central to globalisation and to development. The sources of productivity and competitiveness are increasingly dependent on knowledge and information being applied to productivity.

The increased generation of knowledge and access to knowledge has led to what is often referred to as the 'knowledge society' (Castells, 1991). It was thus expected that new higher education policies would pay particular attention to these developments. Responding to this expectation, the National Plan for Higher Education identified human resource development, high-level skill development and the production, acquisition and application of new knowledge as the key challenges facing higher education. It then stated: 'These challenges have to be understood in the context of the impact on higher education systems worldwide of the changes associated with the phenomenon of globalisation ... Higher education has a critical and central role to play in contributing to the development of an information society in South Africa both in terms of skills development and research' (Department of Education, 2001:5–6).

However, the National Plan for Higher Education made no reference to information technology and its importance to research and teaching, beyond a cursory statement in the introduction. Apart from not mentioning a national approach to or policy for the use of information technology in higher education, the National Plan did not insist that individual institutions should develop their own policies about how to utilise and develop information technology strategies for teaching, learning, and research.

The National Plan put forward two strategies to improve the research endeavour. The first deals with a new approach to funding. Research funding is to be a separate component, based on research outputs and postgraduate students. Earmarked funding will also be made available for research capacity-building and for inter-institutional collaboration. The measurement of research output would be improved, and postgraduate enrolments will receive considerably greater funding. The second strategy deals with improving postgraduate quality and quantity, through the activities of the Higher Education Quality Committee, and by improving postgraduate enrolments through planning, increased funding and the recruitment of foreign students.

The proposed new funding formula released by the Department of Education in 2001 indicated that earmarked research funding would depend on submissions to the Ministry; no criteria were provided at that stage. In terms of encouraging postgraduate enrolments, the formula proposed to increase substantially the subsidy for postgraduate students.

In summary, the new policy regime aimed at the national level to reorganise science and to enable government to make science more responsive to the needs of the majority. The main policy aims of the Department of Education were to expand and strengthen the research base, develop a national research plan and make access to knowledge production more equitable, both at an individual and an institutional level. There were also significant silences in the policy framework, however, such as how to respond competitively to globalisation. As will be shown in subsequent sections, at the time of writing none of the implementation mechanisms necessary to put the polices into operation had as yet been put in place by the Department of Education.

3. AN OVERVIEW OF CHANGE IN
THE HIGHER EDUCATION RESEARCH SECTOR

This section examines four issues: it looks, firstly, at what has happened to expenditure and secondly, to research output. It then describes changes in the types of research undertaken, and lastly, addresses the issue of improving equity in the higher education research sector.

3.1. Research expenditure

As was outlined above, after 1994 the government moved very actively at the national science level to set into place a new funding regime that would support its commitments to national priorities. At least three different, but related, funding strategies were implemented:

- The establishment of the National Innovation Fund to support strategic, collaborative research and development.
- The consolidation of the existing funding agencies into one national funding agency (the National Research Foundation) and the introduction of a new policy of theme-orientated funding.
- Significant increases in funding via two strategic funds: Thrip (Technology and Human Resources for Industry Project) and SPII (Support Programme for Industrial Innovation), both of which encourage closer links between academia and industry.

How has expenditure on R&D been affected by the policy changes? Surprisingly enough, there is no clear answer to this question yet, the reason being that national statistics on R&D are extremely unreliable at this stage. Although major initiatives and positive changes occurred in the National System of Innovation between 1996 and 2001, one area that was seriously neglected was the gathering and storing of reliable data and information on science and technology indicators.

In order to get an impression of the relative size of the research spend that each sector made to the national system of innovation, we begin this section with Figure 1. The most recent figures apply to the financial year 1997/98. The total R&D expenditure on public science (excluding the private sector) is estimated at R2.91-billion. This is made up of the following estimated contributions:

- Higher education system: R850-million.[2]
- Science councils: R1.1-billion.[3]
- National facilities: R60-million.
- Government departments: R450-million.[4]
- State corporations such as NECSA (Nuclear Energy Corporation of South Africa Ltd): R350-million.[5]

Figure 1 shows that, after the science councils, higher education receives the second highest allocation for research from the state.

If one tracks R&D expenditure within higher education over the past 15 years, an interesting picture emerges, namely that despite huge variations in estimated amounts amongst different researchers, there are a lot more funds in the research system in 2001 than in 1994.

Figure 1. *R&D expenditure: 1997/1998*

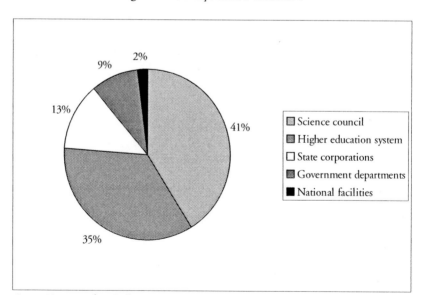

Source: Mouton, J. & Boshoff, S.C., 2000

Figure 2. R&D expenditure within the higher education system (rands thousands): 1983–1997

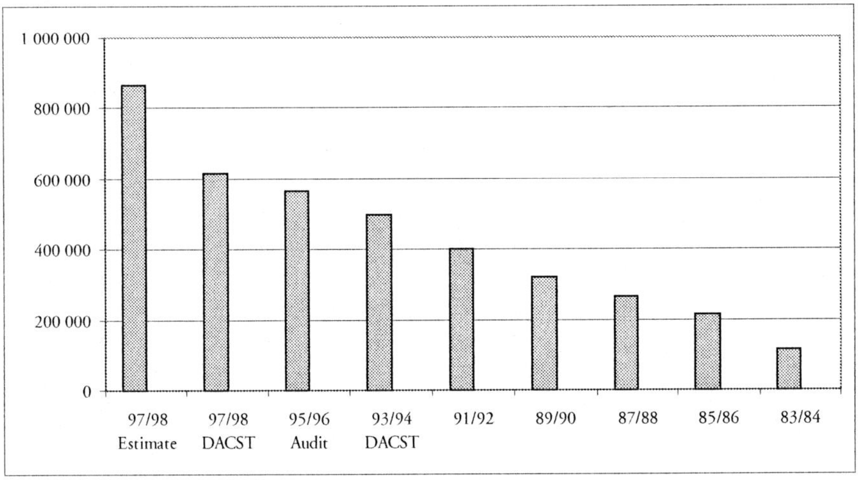

Sources: *South African Science and Technology Indicators, 1996, FRD; National Research and Technology Audit, 1998; DACST website (www.dacst.gov.za)*

The figures for the period 1983/84 to 91/92 are based on biennial R&D surveys conducted by the former Foundation for Research Development (FRD) and the Centre for Social Development (CSD). The 1993/4 and 1997/8 (DACST) figures are based on surveys conducted by a private consultant for the government and which utilised a very different methodology. The 1995/96 figures refer to the National Research and Technology Audit data. The 1997/98 (estimate) represents the data of Mouton and Boshoff (2000).

One reason why we believe that the latest official data (R496-million) is a serious underestimate of R&D expenditure is because of the results of a survey that one of the authors conducted at the top five universities in the country in 1999. Based on information provided by the universities of Cape Town, Stellenbosch, the Witwatersrand, Natal and Pretoria, it was calculated that the combined R&D expenditure of these five institutions alone amounted to approximately R400-million in 1997/98. Taken together, the previous R&D survey results (and the audit) and the five universities reported on here, account for 60%, on average, of all R&D expenditure. If this calculation is applied here, it means that actual expenditure is in the vicinity of R600-million. This amount does not include the technikons and, even more importantly, also does not reflect labour costs – staff time spent on R&D! If all of these factors are taken into consideration we believe that our estimate of R850-million for 1997/98 is itself a rather conservative estimate.

Two points of caution are necessary:

- The increase in Thrip funding and the National Innovation Fund funding (both of which are categories of strategic research funding) that occurred mainly from

1996/1997 onwards, is not yet reflected in these trends. These two categories of funding represent an estimated boost of about 20%–25% of additional funding into the higher education sector. This impact will only be evident in a next round of R&D surveying.

- As mentioned above, there is every indication that the top universities and technikons are increasingly successful in obtaining significant contract funding. We also know that in many cases the amounts of contract funding are under-reported.

Figure 2 shows an increase from about R650-million in 1995/6 to at least R850-million in 1998/9, an increase of approximately 30%, which is about 5% higher than the estimated inflation figure over the period. Direct government research funding may not have increased substantially over the period, but it has kept pace with inflation. Once the funding from Thrip, the National Innovation Fund and substantial increases in private contracts are all taken into account, it can be asserted that by 1999 there was considerably more research money in the higher education system than in 1994.

3.2. Research outputs

What do the latest data show about trends in scientific production in South Africa? The most comprehensive bibliometric analyses of South African science have been undertaken by Pouris (1996). Although the most recent of these (Pouris, 1996) only covers trends up to 1994, it does point to a number of interesting patterns.

In his 1996 study of South African scientific output, Pouris identifies a steady decline in comparative output. He shows how the number of publications by South African authors in ISI (Institute for Scientific Information) journals (*Science Citation Index*, *Social Sciences Citation Index* and the *Arts and Humanities Index*) has been relatively stable (approximately 3.300 a year) between 1987 and 1994. When compared with other countries and calculated as a proportion of world output, however, these figures reveal a steady decline. One indicator of such a decline is the fact that countries that were below or at the same level as South Africa in 1987 have subsequently surpassed her. These countries are Norway, South Korea, Brazil, Taiwan and the People's Republic of China. Pouris' analyses clearly show how South African scientific output experienced a gradual growth between 1980 and 1987 (increasing from 2.200 publications in 1980 to 3.400 in 1987). Over that period, South Africa's output as a proportion of world output increased from 0.4% to nearly 0.7%. However, after peaking in 1987, overall output has remained pretty much the same at an average of 3.300 publications per year until 1994. This in effect has meant a drop in proportion of world share from 0.7% in 1987 to 0.4% in 1994. In 1994, South Africa had about 0.5% of the world's scientists.

These studies currently represent the only bibliometric analyses using ISI data. In terms of scientific productivity, South African scientists seem to have peaked around 1987 and subsequently maintained production at an average of 3.300 publications per year. Whether this implies that a type of 'steady state' has been reached, or not, requires further reflection.

The data on which these analyses are based constitute only a partial perspective on South African science. Given the very small representation of South African journals in the ISI indices (only 31 South African journals out of a total of 205 accredited journals are indexed by the ISI), this analysis needs to be augmented and corrected with one that takes into account the South African journals which are not represented in the ISI set.

In 1985 the Department of National Education, which was responsible for the national education system under apartheid, introduced a new funding formula for universities that incorporated a number of incentives to stimulate research output. Known as the South African Post-Secondary Education (SAPSE) formula (see Chapter 4 for a fuller description of this formula), the new funding formula made explicit provision not only for teaching outputs, but also for the contribution made by research. Research outputs were subsequently subsidised on the basis of the number of scientific articles published. Only articles published in refereed journals accredited by the Department of National Education qualified for subsidy purposes. At a later stage books (but not textbooks) as well as chapters in refereed anthologies were also included for subsidy purposes.

Some black and English-speaking social science and humanities academics refused on principle to publish in SAPSE-accredited journals during the apartheid era. This is one of the constraints which affect the accuracy of the SAPSE data. Other constraints are more technical in nature and would include the time-lag between publication in an unlisted journal and the accreditation of that journal (at least two years). Nevertheless, the SAPSE data does provide a useful additional perspective on scientific production in South Africa.

Figure 3. *Total output (science articles/books) according to SAPSE figures: 1986–2000*[6]

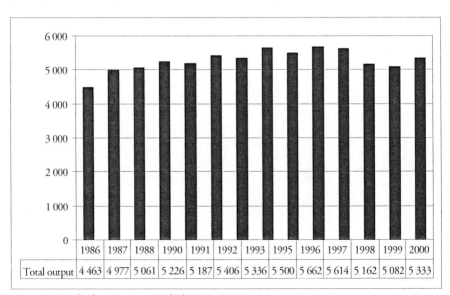

	1986	1987	1988	1990	1991	1992	1993	1995	1996	1997	1998	1999	2000
Total output	4 463	4 977	5 061	5 226	5 187	5 406	5 336	5 500	5 662	5 614	5 162	5 082	5 333

Source: SAPSE database, Department of Education, 2000

Figure 3 summarises the main trends in the output of scientific articles and books as represented in the SAPSE database. It shows that, as in the results derived from the ISI data, the system remained fairly stable during the 1990s, but with a worrying downward trend after 1996.

Unfortunately the current SAPSE database does not allow any further disaggregation of the data. For this and other reasons in 1997 the Centre for Interdisciplinary Studies at the University of Stellenbosch embarked on a long-term project to build a comprehensive database of South African science. This project, called 'SAKnowledgebase', aims to produce a comprehensive, accurate and effective database on South African scientific production.[7] The database currently contains complete information on 57.226 articles produced by South African authors between 1990 and 1998. These articles were drawn from 11.000 journals, including 205 South African journals. It includes all the ISI indices, and especially the expanded version of the Science Citation Index. Figure 4 summarises the trends in output between 1990 and 1998 as compiled by SAKnowledgebase.

In summary then, the overall annual trend for the period 1990 to 1999 – as is evidenced by all three sets of figures (ISI-only, SAPSE and SAKnowledgebase) – suggests that output has not increased since 1990, and displays a slight downward trend during the latter part of the post-1994 period.

How can the apparent decrease in output be explained? The simplest explanation, offered by some vice-chancellors, is that the Department of Education has not added new journals to the official list since 1998 and that the output statistic is simply a bureaucratic under-count. It would be reassuring if the downward trend could be explained as merely poor counting. Another explanation, also of a bureaucratic nature, is offered by Subotzky at the University of the Western Cape's Education Policy Unit. He comments that

Figure 4. *Scientific output: 1990–1998*

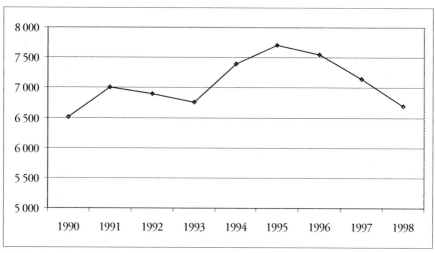

Source: SAKnowledgebase

during interviews conducted with a number of academics, he was informed that they are not completing the forms to report their publications because the effort is simply not worth the small part of the subsidy that comes back to the researcher. In other words, publications could be under-counted due to a lack of incentive. It is not clear, however, whether academics are now more resistant to completing forms than they were before 1995.

A second, and more serious, set of explanations could relate to the loss of top academics, both through emigration and through academics taking up positions in government during the mid-1990s. The decline could also be due to a range of other factors such as staff cuts and rationalisation at universities and technikons, as well as the time taken up with institutional restructuring undertaken by all of the research institutions, activities which have been hugely disruptive. Yet another factor may be that the many and substantial policy initiatives that were introduced were not accompanied by coherent implementation strategies to facilitate the orderly roll-out of transformatory actions. One example of this is the inordinate time commitment demanded of many academics in the chaos that resulted from the establishment of the South African Qualifications Authority. There are other examples. What seems clear is that the human capital base for research may have been severely weakened.

In summary, the higher education sector remains a major player in public knowledge production in the country. Its expenditure on R&D represents approximately 35% of total public R&D expenditure in the country. But in terms of assessing output according to peer-reviewed publications, the research output has not increased since 1994.

3.3. Shifts in types of research

There is little dispute that R&D expenditure and sources of R&D funding have shifted very noticeably over the past five years: the movement has been away from basic and fundamental research towards the support of strategic, applied and product-related research. Compared with earlier R&D surveys, the National Research and Technology Audit of 1995/96 found a significant increase in applied and strategic research being undertaken. The audit classified half of all research in the higher education sector as basic research. This constitutes a substantial decline when compared with 1991 figures where 75% of higher education sector research was classified as basic research.[8]

How substantial this shift has been is also apparent in that half of the research classified as 'basic' is further categorised by scholars to be strategic research and the remaining half as fundamental research in the 1995/6 Audit. According to the classification used during that audit, applied research now makes up 37% and product-related work 13% of all research in universities and technikons. The audit classifies only 23% of all research done in higher education as fundamental or curiosity-driven research. We would suggest that this is one of a number of indicators that signify a clear trend towards more 'application-driven research' (to use Gibbons et al.'s 1994 term) at South African universities and technikons. This research categorisation is difficult to define, is inconsistent over different studies and at this stage these movements should be regarded as trends, rather than definitive indices.

The establishment of the National Innovation Fund and Thrip and the shifts in the way that the National Research Foundation distributes its resources, are clear indications that there is a redistribution of research resources towards the applied and product-related end of the spectrum. This reflects the drive towards responding to local needs and to global changes in knowledge systems, but it is still too early to assess the effectiveness of this shift. It could provide the basis for the theoretical foundations underpinning the philosophical changes in the funding and structures of the national research system.

Directors of research who were contacted at the top research institutions in South Africa all agreed that there has been dramatic increases in contract income over the previous three to five years. Figure 5 reflects the significant increase in this income stream at four institutions between 1995 and 2000.

Figure 5. *Trends in contract income at four institutions (rand millions): 1995–2000*

Institution	1995/6	1998	2000	% increase from 1995 to 2000
Pretoria	27	61	92	480%
Stellenbosch	46	78	119	258%
Natal	46	83	138	300%
Cape Town	102	139	190	186%

Source: Research directors of the institutions contacted

Adjusted for inflation, the increase shown in Figure 5 is still more than 100% over the five-year period. The highest proportional increase occurred at the University of Pretoria, but the University of Cape Town still raises the most money. Currently very few institutions can provide systematic information as to how much of the contract research gets published in reports or in accredited journals, and how much is consultancy rather than research. With such huge increases in contract research it appears that South African academics are working harder, but it is not clear how much of this is counted as published output.

The analysis above shows two 'pulls' towards the strategic/applied end of the research continuum. The one is through a shift in government funds and the other is the significant increase in private research funds becoming available on a contract basis in the 'new democracy' period. In this sense the state and the market are in tandem, pulling academics towards mode two-type knowledge production, and the impact is reflected in academics reporting a decrease in basic research. The question raised in another research project by Mouton (2001) called 'Between Adversaries and Allies' is whether the self-reporting is accurate or whether it is biased towards what academics think the government, the market or their peers want to hear.

Despite the lack of reliable and comprehensive data in the system, a number of interesting points emerge from this analysis:

- The government's policy of increasing support for strategic and relevant research already seems to have an impact on funding sources within the sector. The National Research and Technology Audit which was conducted in 1997 and covered the period 1995/6 picked up this shift, while recent funding initiatives (including Thrip) may have strengthened this trend.
- There is undoubtedly an increase in contract research. The problem is that currently nobody knows the scale of the increase and whether this is seriously affecting published research output.
- The bottom line, however, is that these trends are increasingly putting basic and fundamental research within higher education under severe strain and could seriously constrain the growth of the knowledge base in the sector.

3.4. Equity in the research sector

The Department of Education and the Department of Arts, Culture, Science and Technology White Papers promoted greater access to knowledge production at the institutional level and among individuals. The general output trends reveal some interesting dynamics within the higher education sector. Figure 6 presents the SAPSE output figures disaggregated by 'institutional groupings'. So, for example, it shows that the relative contribution of historically white Afrikaans-medium universities to published research has increased moderately from 37.2% in 1986 to 41.5% in 1999. The proportion of outputs from the historically white English-medium universities declined substantially from 53.5% in 1986 to 37.9% in 1999. Although the contribution of the historically black universities to the overall output is still low, these institutions have more than doubled their contribution from a base of 5.1% in 1986 to 10.7% in 1999. The output from the technikon sector has increased quite substantially from 23.52 units in 1991 (0.4% of the total) to 174 units in 1999 (3.1%). This percentage increase represents more than a seven-fold improvement and suggests that attempts by the sector to raise both awareness of research and research output have been successful.

Although an analysis by these institutional categories is useful, it still masks huge inequalities among the institutions. Within the university sector, five universities continue to dominate scientific production: the University of Cape Town, University of Natal, University of Stellenbosch, University of Pretoria and the University of the Witwatersrand continue to produce approximately 60% of all scientific output within the university sector. Similarly, within the historically black university sector, two universities – the University of Durban-Westville and the University of the Western Cape – continue to produce the bulk of output (22.4% and 21.9% respectively, meaning 44.3%) of all the output of the historically black universities.

As far as the technikon sector is concerned, five technikons (most of them historically advantaged technikons) dominate scientific production: Cape Technikon (19.5%), Pretoria Technikon (16.3%), Port Elizabeth Technikon (13.3%), Natal Technikon (11.1%) and Free State Technikon (9.8%). Together they generate 70% of all articles and books produced by technikons.

Figure 6. *SAPSE output by sector: 1991–1999*[9]

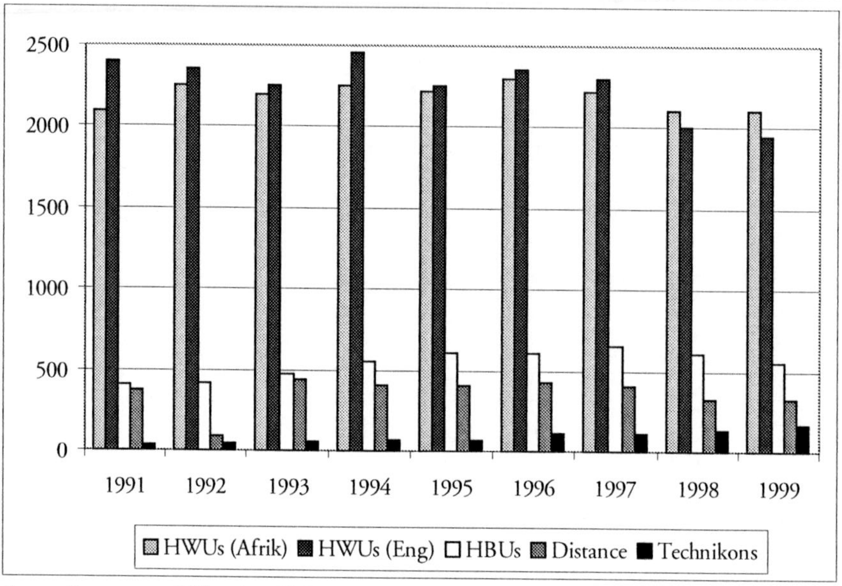

Source: Department of Education, 2000

This evidence suggests a modest increase in research output by two historically disadvantaged institutions, but the overall picture is that in both the university and the technikon sectors, the six institutions that dominated research during the apartheid era are still the dominant forces in knowledge production.

Based on information gathered specifically for this book, it now becomes possible to discern a number of demographic trends related to South African scientific output for the 1990s. Below we present data on race, gender and age trends. These data are important as a measure of the impact of a significant set of redress programmes that have been implemented by the Foundation for Research Development and the Centre for Social Development in the past.

3.4.1. Output by race

As Figure 7 shows, white authors produced by far the largest proportion of scientific articles during the 1990s (93.5%). Indian South African authors produced 3.2% of the total output. And finally, African authors produced 2.1% and so-called coloured authors produced 1% of the total output. However, the data also show that the output by African authors increased from 20 units (1%) in 1990 to 59 units (2%) in 1994 and 63 units (3%) in 1998. For Indian South Africans the number of units decreased from 93 in 1994 to 71 in 1998.

Figure 7. *South African scientific product by race (1990–1998)*

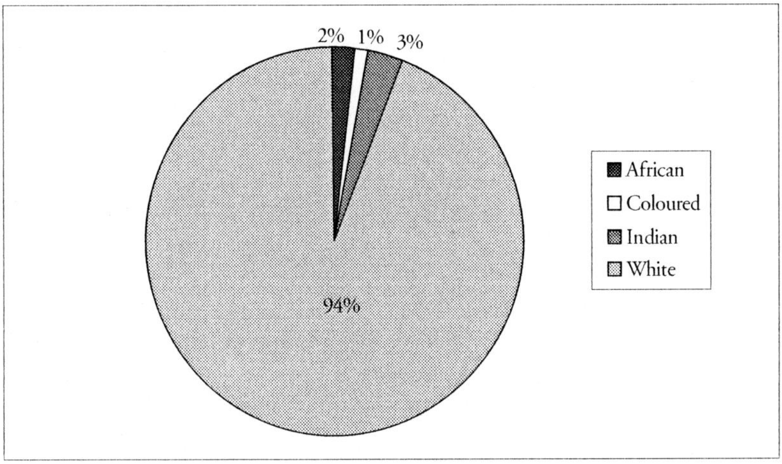

Source: SAKnowledgebase

3.4.2. Output by gender

In terms of gender distribution, male authors produced 83% of total scientific output during the period 1990 to 1998, and women authors produced 17%. Between 1990 and 1998 this output division has been very steady. The more detailed breakdown by year shows that although the number of SAPSE units overall declined from 490 in 1994 to 335 in 1998, women maintained their overall proportion of output at 17%.

In an attempt to deal with the race and gender imbalances referred to above, a significant effort was made to deal with institutional redress and capacity building. The Department of Education, according to the Minister, established a redress fund for capacity development, while the national science councils spearheaded redress in the research activities of the historically disadvantaged institutions – to the tune of R79-million in 2001 (see NPHE). A senior representative from the National Research Foundation says, however, that not all of this is for institutional redress or capacity development. R18-million of this came from the National Research Foundation in 2001 for research and for capacity building in the historically black universities while another R12-million went to all the technikons and R49-million went to bursaries for white and black students at all higher education institutions.

The question of institutional redress remains a central challenge. Various policy initiatives pushed very hard to address the race and gender imbalances that characterise the scientific terrain in South Africa. The data indicates that these represent themselves both at the level of individuals and at the level of institutions. These have been followed by significant implementation strategies, rolled-out in particular by the Foundation for Research Development and the National Research Foundation. These programmes began with the University Development Programme (UDP) in 1989. As the data in the earlier section indicates, however, these processes have not been successful.

3.4.3. Output by age

The production of research papers as a function of the age of the researchers in the system is an extremely important and sensitive diagnostic of the overall state of the research system since it is a first measure of the system's medium- to long-term sustainability. The overall position for the nine-year period is summarised in Figure 8 below. The results show that more than 40% of all articles produced were generated by authors in the 40–49 age bracket. Approximately a quarter of the output was produced by each of the 30–39 and 50–59 age cohorts. This characteristic of the system would have to be benchmarked against other national systems to assess whether or not it is out of line with trends in other countries.

Our overall conclusion with regard to redress is that the production of knowledge within South African higher education continues to be dominated by white male scientists at five historically advantaged institutions. Although there are small shifts towards more gender and race representation in the higher education research sector, these remain insignificant. With the exception of the University of the Western Cape and the University of Durban-Westville, the outputs for the historically black universities have hardly changed during the period under review. The fact that more than 70% of all articles published are by academics over 40 years of age, and the limited increase in the production of PhDs (see Chapter 5 on Students) indicates that a serious problem has arisen with reproducing a next generation of academics.

Figure 8. *Trends in research output by age intervals: 1990–1998*

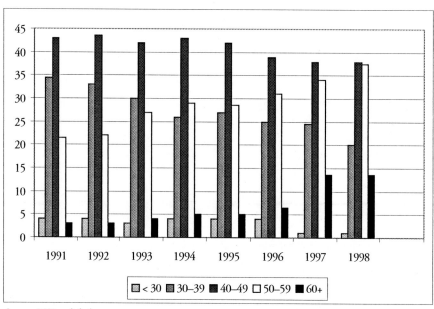

Source: SAKnowledgebase

4. A NEW RESEARCH LANDSCAPE

The analysis undertaken above shows that a new landscape is developing in the research sector – both at the national level and within institutions.

4.1. The national landscape

As the National System of Innovation and the higher education sector within it head towards the end of the first ten-year period after the miracle of 1994, the key questions that must be asked is whether the restructuring processes are meeting the national policy aims identified for the reorganisation of science. The analysis performed in the post-1994 period indicated that in addition to the lack of a coherent strategic direction, the deep fragmentation of the system was a hindrance to reducing the disarticulation which had occurred during apartheid.

The establishment of the Department of Arts, Culture, Science and Technology, the National Research Foundation and the National Advisory Council on Innovation are examples of the structural changes, which, in theory, help to address this fragmentation. Whether the system has the imagination and the political will to achieve what it has set out to achieve, is not fully clear at this point.

An important issue that has yet to be assessed is the effectiveness of the Department of Education in developing policy implementation strategies. Even though we must think of the policy development process as being holistic in nature and influencing various government departments, the policies that have the most potential to impact on the higher education research system are those that were instituted through the Department of Arts, Culture, Science and Technology. The nominal location of the higher education research system within the National System of Innovation presents both advantages and challenges. However, these have not been properly understood and hence there have not been any creative attempts at the development of suitable implementation strategies. The interrogation of these advantages and challenges is crucial since, without this, the higher education research system will simply be drawn into the overall National System of Innovation on the basis of a very economistic approach to the role of science in society. Neither the Department of Education nor the higher education sector has made any attempt to unpack these issues and this is deeply problematic.

The first two sets of institutional three-year plans (1998/99) requested by the Department of Education stressed student numbers and programme mixes and perhaps inadvertently gave the impression that research was not a priority – an impression strengthened by the fact that the National Research Plan promised in the White Paper (1997) has not materialised. In addition, no mechanisms have yet been put in place to give effect to the operational aspects of the White Paper in respect of research; these include steering subsidy funds to build capacity at specific institutions and allocating special funds to identified high-need areas. In the 2001 National Plan for Higher Education the promise of earmarked funding was repeated, but the Minister also said that earmarked funding would be 'onerous' to administer, thus raising questions as to whether the policy intention would be implemented at all.

Currently there is little evidence of greater articulation between the Department of Education and the science councils, the National Research Forum and the other departments such as the Department of Arts, Culture, Science and Technology and the Department of Trade and Industry. Instead, it seems that departments such as the Department of Arts, Culture, Science and Technology and the Department of Trade and Industry are becoming increasingly influential in steering research. The increasing involvement of multiple government departments in shaping research in higher education seems to be a worldwide phenomenon. On the one hand this can perhaps be seen as another indicator of the importance of research in the knowledge society. On the other hand, it signals the decreasing influence of the Department of Education.

There is also evidence of changes taking place in terms of the role of the national research agencies. During the policy discussions of the early 1990s there were heated debates as to whether some of the national research councils such as the Human Sciences Research Council (HSRC) should survive in the new South Africa. While they have all survived, albeit having been scaled down in personnel by up to two-thirds, it seems that these councils are developing divergent roles. The Council for Scientific and Industrial Research (CSIR), for example, entered into an unprecedented partnership with one university, the University of Pretoria. In more recent times the CSIR has also developed partnerships with other universities; for example, with the University of Natal it has developed, amongst others, a Centre for Forestry and Forestry Products Research. The Medical Research Council seems to be continuing to strengthen its symbiotic relationship with medical schools and science laboratories at a number of universities.

The HSRC, on the other hand, seems to be moving back into a situation (similar to that of the late 1980s and early 1990s) where it is competing directly with universities and non-governmental organisations for state tenders and staff. It could be argued that the 'new' HSRC is in exactly the same relationship to the new government as the old HSRC of the 1970s and early 1980s was in relation to the apartheid government! While acknowledging the handmaiden relationship between the 'old' HSRC and the apartheid government, Cloete and Muller (1991) question whether the HSRC actually was useful to the government that sponsored it. The same question can be raised about the 'new' HSRC.

The major response of the new system has been the establishment of funding drivers to develop the desired shift in the system. It would seem that the scale of the drivers – the Innovation Fund, the National Advisory Council on Innovation mechanism for the distribution of the science vote, various changes in the research funding paradigm of the National Research Foundation, the Thrip fund and others – have begun to influence the nature of the research enterprise. However, it is too early to determine whether these are contributing positively to building coherence and whether they are working towards the development of a higher level of articulation with societal needs.

The available indicators show there is a marked increase in strategic and applied research. However, two caveats need to be made: first, the full impact of the funding regime of the state has yet to manifest itself; and second, the indicators from the National Research and Technology Audit are both dated and inadequate. We have no recent information on the substance and content of research programmes, nor on their utilisation by society. Thus it is extremely difficult to assess whether the higher education research system has become more responsive to the challenges of reconstruction and development and, in particular, whether it is responsive to the needs of the majority of South Africans. In a sense this is a question that cannot be answered since the issue of what, precisely, is regarded as the 'needs of the majority' is a contested matter – even within the tripartite alliance between the ANC, Cosatu and the South African Communist Party. This is compounded by the fact that even at the time of the policy development, a thorough study of the nature of the required responsiveness had not been made – except for broad brush strokes based on a very instrumentalist approach to research and development activities.

South African universities are not immune to the vast changes that are occurring in the global higher education system. Perhaps the most important of these is the commercialisation of research since this is a direct challenge to the very essence of 'the university'. Perhaps it is the scale of the activities that is critical to understand here rather than the fact that such activities actually take place. Several institutions are able to raise substantial sums of money for research activities from the various international foundations and from the private sector. Very often this kind of research activity results in research outputs which are measured more acutely for their social or economic impact than by the usual norms for academic research output. Very often they are linked to industrial innovation and this raises a critical question that relates to the public subsidisation of research activities which are profit-driven. In the absence of a national policy in this regard – such as the Bayh-Dole legislation in the United States of America – the institutions are caught by a national policy imperative to enhance partnerships with the private sector and at the same time reconcile themselves to a genuine subsidisation of private sector research by the state. The impact of the commodification of knowledge on higher education is an international phenomenon and it presents the most exciting prospects for the fundamental reconceptualisation of 'the university'. In South Africa, however, because of the small scale of the research system, this may take a form that will have important lasting consequences – consequences that may well be unexpected and severely damaging to the sustainability of the system.

4.2. A new institutional research landscape?

In one sense the marked differentiation of the past remains among the higher education institutions: the same five historically advantaged universities continue to dominate, producing 60% of the output, and six technikons (five of them historically advantaged) produce 70% of accredited articles in that sector. However, certain shifts are beginning to take place. The technikon sector is slowly, and only in certain institutions, beginning to produce more research, while two of the historically black institutions (the University of Durban-Westville and the University of the Western Cape) have increased their output to a level comparable with some of the historically advantaged institutions. The average annual output for the University of the Western Cape for the period 1986 to 1999 is 97 publication units and for the University of Durban-Westville it is 100. This compares favourably with a young historically advantaged institution such as the

University of Port Elizabeth, with an average of 98 publication units, and even with established historically advantaged institutions such as Rhodes University, with an average of 169 units per year, and Potchefstroom University, with an average of 189.

Without further study, it is difficult to explain the increase in the research output of the historically white Afrikaans-medium institutions, compared with the four historically white English-medium institutions. It may be that the incentives provided to individual researchers at the Afrikaans institutions are greater. It is more likely that some of the historically white Afrikaans-medium universities did not prioritise research in the 1960s and 1970s because many of them saw themselves as *volksuniversiteite* that served the cause of Afrikaner nationalism. The advent of the Foundation for Research Development provided them with a framework within which to measure and improve their output – even though they initially resisted the foundation, according to Rein Arndt, its first president. The introduction of the SAPSE research subsidy system gave further impetus to increasing research output. On the other hand, the historically white English-medium universities that had a more fully developed research culture and were already publishing optimally, continued to operate at that level. However, there was indeed a decline in real terms in the publication output of the universities of the Witwatersrand and Cape Town.

Since 1994 there has been a further weakening of the research base at the historically disadvantaged institutions (except for the University of Durban-Westville and the University of the Western Cape) and many of these institutions have suffered substantial administrative difficulties, financial mismanagement, and student and staff strife. There has been an exodus of good academics from these institutions to historically white universities and several of the historically black universities may be financially and academically unsustainable.

This analysis shows that in the case of research it has been more difficult to break down the apartheid legacy than it was in other spheres of higher education (such as student access). Whilst a reshuffling seems to be occurring amongst the high producing institutions, it seems unlikely that any of the previously disadvantaged institutions will join the elite group. Instead, there is evidence that the gap between the 'haves' and the 'have-nots' in knowledge production is widening, not narrowing.

5. CONCLUSION

All in all, the policy development process was an invigorating intellectual enterprise, having drawn in higher education experts, science and technology practitioners, policy experts, government representatives and representatives of the private sector and community-based organisations. It brought into focus the major challenges that face the science and technology system and raised the profile of the tensions that arise in the transformation processes. It also produced interesting approaches to facilitate the management of these tensions. And while significant progress was made in producing policies, which in turn resulted in the promulgation of various key pieces of legislation, what was sadly lacking were coherent and managed implementation strategies. The impact of policy changes on the higher education system are of such enormous significance – whether positive or negative – that a substantial and well-managed implementation strategy should have been a priority. This did not happen and the result was an almost anarchic approach to the implementation of the various policy initiatives, with each institution adopting its own approach to understanding and implementing these policy changes. Where there was some level of national co-ordination this was often inept and variable. Consequently, the impact on higher education, and especially on its research system, was profound. It caused serious erosion of confidence in the system and a sense of despair amongst academics as institutions attempted to understand what was required of them in the new policy context.

The higher education research system needs to be defended and supported on the basis of its contribution to the nurturing and growth of a national intellectual culture. From this flow its numerous contributions to more instrumentalist imaginations that have become the engine for transformation in recent years. As has been argued earlier, the deepening of the nation's democratic ethos and its ability to contribute to the generation of a South African knowledge system, which can be a viable contributing component of the international knowledge system, depends on the enlarged programme of high-level human resource development and the creation of a tradition which sees the production of new knowledge as a national endeavour that must be measured in terms of this nation's vision of itself as a beacon for Africa in the knowledge era.

NOTES

1 This chapter adopts an inclusive definition of science, encompassing the humanities, the social sciences and the natural sciences.

2 The 1997/8 R&D survey released by DACST in August 2000 put this figure at R496-million which we believe is a huge underestimate. The National Research and Technology Audit (NRTA), which was conducted to record information for the years 1995/1996, estimated the higher education system expenditure on R&D at R670-million which was considered conservative. The figure of R850-million constitutes our best estimate based on the Audit figures as well as a survey conducted with the top five research universities in the country.

3 This figure for the science councils reflects the actual amount of funding received from government in 1997/8. Although one could argue that less than this amount was spent on actual R&D, this sector usually attracts around 20% in contract money which is spent on R&D. The 1996/7 Audit figures produced a similar estimate of R1.1-billion devoted to R&D.

4 This figure is based on a reported amount of R150-million spent by government departments in 1996/7 but which excludes the South African Defence Force. Unverified data on the Defence Force estimate R&D expenditure to have been between R300- and R500-million in 1998. We have taken the more conservative figure as our estimate.

5 This figure excludes the spend on R&D made by Eskom, Telkom, Transnet and various other state corporations that do not receive any direct funding from the national science vote.

6 It should be pointed out that the 1999 figure probably does not reflect the late additions which are usually supplied to the Department of Education during a second round. This would make a difference of about 5% in the totals.

7 SAKnowledgebase is a MS Access database that the Centre for Interdisciplinary Studies (CENIS) has compiled over the past five years.

8 The following are the official Frascati definitions: Basic research: Original investigation with the primary aim of developing more complete knowledge or understanding of the subject(s) under study; Fundamental

research: Basic research carried out without working for long-term economic or social benefits other than the advancement of knowledge, and no positive efforts being made to apply the results to practical problems or to transfer the results to sectors responsible for their application. Strategic research: Basic research carried out with the expectation that it will produce a broad base of knowledge likely to form the background to the solution of recognised current or future practical problems. Applied research: Original investigation undertaken in order to acquire new knowledge, and directed primarily towards specific practical aims or objectives such as determining possible uses for findings of basic research or solving already recognised problems. Source: OECD (1992) Proposed standard practice for surveys of research and experimental development. 5th Edition. Paris: Organisation for Economic Co-operation and Development.

REFERENCES

African National Congress (1994). *The Reconstruction and Development Programme. A Policy Framework.* Johannesburg: Umanyano Publications.

Castells, M. (1991). Universities as Dynamic Systems of Contradictory Functions. In: J. Muller, N. Cloete & S. Badat (eds) (2001), *Challenges of Globalisation: South African Debates with Manuel Castells.* Cape Town: Maskew Miller Longman.

Castells, M. (2001). Think Local, Act Global. In: J. Muller, N. Cloete & S. Badat (eds), *Challenges of Globalisation: South African Debates with Manual Castells.* Cape Town: Maskew Miller Longman.

Cloete, N. & Muller, J. (1991). Human Sciences Research Council Incorporated (Pty) Ltd: Social Science Research, Markets and Accountability in South Africa. In: J. Jansen (ed.), *Knowledge and Power in South Africa: Critical Perspectives Across Disciplines.* Johannesburg: Skotaville Publishers.

Department of Arts, Culture, Science and Technology (1996). Science Technology White Paper. www.dacst.gov.za/science_technology.stwp.htm.

Department of Education (1997). Education White Paper 3: A Programme for the Transformation of Higher Education. Pretoria.

Department of Education (2000). Research Output 2000. SAPSE Information Systems.

Department of Education (2001a). *National Plan for Higher Education.* Pretoria.

Department of Education (2001b). Information on the State Budget for Higher Education. Pretoria.

Department of Trade and Industry. Growth, Equity and Redistribution: A Macroeconomic Strategy (GEAR) (1996). Pretoria. www.gov.za/reports/1996/macroeco.htm.

Gibbons, M., Limoges, C., Nowotny, H., Schwartsman, S., Scott, P. & Trow, M. (1994). *The New Production of Knowledge: The Dynamics of Science and Research in Contemporary Societies.* California: Sage Publications.

Mouton, J. (2001). *Between Adversaries and Allies: The Call for Strategic Science in Post-Apartheid South Africa.* Stellenbosch: Centre for Interdisciplinary Studies, University of Stellenbosch.

Mouton, J. & Boshoff, S.C. (2000). South African Science in Transition. A Report by the Centre for Interdisciplinary Studies. Stellenbosch: University of Stellenbosch.

Mouton, J. & Hackman, H. (1998). Survey on Scholarship, Research and Development. Report on the National Research and Technology Audit. Pretoria: Department of Arts, Culture, Science and Technology.

National Advisory Council on Innovation Act (No. 55 of 1997). Government Gazette No.18425, 14 November 1997. Pretoria. www.gov.za/acts/1997/a55-97.pdf.

National Commission on Higher Education (NCHE) (1996). *A Framework for Transformation.* Pretoria: Department of Education.

National Research and Technology Audit (1998). Technology and Knowledge: Synthesis Report of the National Research and Technology Audit. Pretoria: Foundation for Research Development.

Pouris, A. (1996). The Writing on the Wall of South African Science: A Scientometric Assessment. *South African Journal of Science*, 92, 267–271.

SAKnowledgebase. An MSAccess Database compiled by and based at The Centre for Interdisciplinary Studies (CENIS). University of Stellenbosch.

Foundation for Research Development (1996). *SA Science and Technology Indicators.* Pretoria: The Directorate for Science and Technology Policy.

PART 3

CURRICULUM AND RESEARCH

CONCLUSION

Philip Altbach has recently commented that 'a central characteristic of mass higher education systems worldwide is differentiation' (Altbach, 2002:2). He goes on to say that differentiation is a complex and messy business, because it is driven by an increased diversification and specialisation of clienteles, of purposes, of funding, and of accomplishments. Most countries are trying to cope with the challenge of understanding and controlling this 'new academic reality', but few have made much headway with this unruly phenomenon.

South Africa has come at this phenomenon from a particular tangent. Because apartheid had attempted differentiation on an ideological basis, the principal policy goal in the immediate post-apartheid period was unification (a unified system), standardisation (programme equivalence on the National Qualifications Framework), and relevance (a new standard for research), all in the name of equity. It is not too much to say that the early policy impulse was against differentiation in the face of a global environment driving differentiation.

Curriculum and research deal with the production and dissemination of knowledge, and the principal intellectual lynchpin against differentiation in the knowledge domain was, as Ensor points out, the principle of the *equivalence of knowledge forms*. In the area of curriculum, the belief in knowledge equivalence found expression in what Ensor calls the credit accumulation and transfer (CAT) discourse, which in turn led to the policy of programmatisation. In the area of research the discourse of research relevance led to the policy of targeted funding for relevant research.

Both chapters show how this de-differentiating recoil from apartheid found a peculiar resonance with a particular global 'mental frame', to which Maassen and Cloete draw attention in Chapter 1, where 'mode two' knowledge production supercedes 'mode one' (Gibbons et al., 1994). Whatever its original intents and application, in South Africa the 'mode two' story has been understood as buttressing the broad-based generic skills policy approach of the NQF, modularisation and programmes, and relevant ('mode two') research. This is a wonderfully paradoxical instance of policy- borrowing where the intended framework, borrowed to underscore a policy by appealing to 'globalisation', finds itself legitimating a policy that is the antithesis of the global trend.

What then were the outcomes of this paradoxical policy? First of all, we should expect unanticipated and unintended consequences as Maassen and Cloete remind us in the conclusion to Chapter 1. That much should today be a standard policy expectation. We are not disappointed. Ensor shows that the higher education institutions as a bloc resisted the hard modular equivalence of unit standardisation, opting for the softer form of whole

N. Cloete et al. (eds.), Transformation in Higher Education, 219-221.
© 2007 *Springer.*

programme registration on the NQF, thus opening the way for different programme models. At least four different forms of programme emerged, with differences both within institutions and between them. Only one of these forms, type D, resembled the implicit programmatic ideal, and this was only adopted in two faculties at two different universities, one of which then abandoned it. Ensor leaves us with the impression that this non-compliance stems either from academic adherence to a 'disciplinary' discourse rather than to the policy of credit accumulation and transfer, or from a simple lack of responsive capacity. But we may speculate further that highly specialised and hence differentiated knowledge, such as that increasingly purveyed by higher education institutions under globalisation, requires specialised vehicles such as disciplines to carry them, and will resist generic carriers such as the undergraduate programmes envisaged by the policy. This speculation is strengthened by the only really unanticipated outcome of the programme exercise, namely that programme modules, far from standardising qualification units, made them *less* rather than *more comparable*, and made programme qualifications *less* rather than *more portable* as a consequence, hence confuting the principal aim of the policy.

In the area of research, the discourse of relevance led to state targeted funding, as Bawa and Mouton show. What they do not show, but which we can confidently infer, is that private funding followed public funding in supporting the relevance discourse. The result cannot be a surprise: if funding is diverted from basic research, then basic research can be expected to decrease, as the publication count shows it has. In terms of knowledge equivalence discourse, this amounts to a natural adjustment, and is therefore a desirable consequence of the policy. In terms of disciplinary discourse, however, applied research competence rests upon prior basic research competence. If basic research is thus not encouraged, it leads to a general decline in the entire research and development system. Indeed, there is an overall decline in total research output, though the authors wisely point out that it is too early to say whether this is a trend or merely a periodic dip. More worrying though is the completely unexpected finding that the researcher population is ageing. This could mean at least two things. The first is that the higher education institutions are failing to reproduce themselves; that is, they are not producing the next generation of knowledge producers. It could also mean that the bulk of targeted research funding is going not to the previously disadvantaged researchers and the younger researchers, but is going instead to the established researchers. This means that targeted funding is not acting as an incentive for neophyte and disadvantaged researchers. Why not? Disciplinary discourse would say that proficiency in basic research is a condition for proficiency in applied work. This would explain why the bulk of funding still goes to the previously advantaged institutions: by far the bulk of Thrip funding goes to the University of Stellenbosch, and by far the bulk of National Research Foundation funding goes to UCT (News@NRF, 2001). In the realm of research, it seems, there are no incentivised shortcuts to proficiency.

What can be concluded about equity? It seems that there have been moderate gains in research output for historically white Afrikaans-medium institutions and for two historically black universities, and a modest increase in output from the technikons in real terms. Yet we have to ask, what is the role of policy measures of convergence in a system that is, as we can see, willy-nilly differentiating? We are wont to judge indications of output inequity in terms of politics, i.e. lack of political will, or in terms of lack of capacity. Because of different clienteles and missions, these institutions may simply be aiming for something else. The fact of differentiation will doubtless compel a review of how we usually regard and assess the performance of higher education institutions in the future.

REFERENCES

Altbach, P. (2002). Differentiation requires definition: the need for classification in complex academic systems. *International Higher Education*, 26, 2–3.

Gibbons, M., Limoges, C., Nowotny, H., Schwartsman, S., Scott, P. & Trow, M. (1994). *The New Production of Knowledge: The Dynamics of Science and Research in Contemporary Societies.* California: Sage Publications.

Muller, J. (1987). Much ado: 'manpower shortages' and educational policy reform in South Africa. *Journal of Education Policy*, 2(2), 83–97.

News@NRF 2001. Newsletter of the National Research Foundation. 1 (4) November.

PART 4

THE NEW TERRAIN

INTRODUCTION

In the next two chapters, the new terrain of South African higher education, that emerged after 1994, is examined through the lenses of several different sets of theories about higher education transformation that were explicit in the conceptual framework on which new policies were based.

Policy-making is a form of hypothesis testing, according to some policy analysts. And the period after 1994 in South Africa was a time for testing. But the critical question is: exactly what theories about higher education transformation were being put to the test? As seen in Section 1, the goals of higher education reform included increased access, responsiveness to the political, social and economic needs of a post-apartheid country, and a single, co-ordinated system that would be more efficiently and effectively run.

The prevailing theories of higher education reform in the early 1990s suggested that systems seeking these goals would need policies that promoted:

- Diversification of the types of institutions operating within the system (that is, increasing the range of types of institutions).
- Diversification in the structures of these institutions.
- Diversification in the types of research and teaching they carried out (that is, within any given type of institution, having that institution develop a greater range of specialised programmes in which it is engaged).

Goedegebuure (1996) summarised the case for diversity:

> Diversity is seen as a good because it supposedly increases the range of choices for students, it opens higher education up to all of society, it matches education to the needs and abilities of individual students, it enables and protects specialisation within the system, and it meets the demands of an increasingly complex social order. (p9)

Consequently, in many countries policy initiatives have been advanced that seek to increase institutional diversity either by promoting the development of new types of institutions, such as the emergence of private universities and specialised institutes in Latin America, Asia, Africa and Eastern Europe in the later decades of the 20th century, or by the evolution of existing institutions through increasing differentiation of the types of programmes they offer and the modalities through which they are made available to new types of students, such as working adults.

The following chapters trace the contours of a differentiating dynamic within the programmes and institutions, both public and private, of the South African higher education system. They account for this in part by reference to Clark's (1996)

N. Cloete et al. (eds.), Transformation in Higher Education, 223-225.
© 2007 *Springer.*

explanation that this is an inevitable (and desirable) consequence of the development of high levels of specialisation in knowledge fields in the post-war years, but also as a response to particular policy conditions (de-regulation) and market opportunities (widening access to non-traditional students; students at a distance; career-related short courses, etc.).

As Neave (1996), Meek (1996) and Van Vught (1996) point out, however, there are often factors that work against the growth of diversification and differentiation. These factors include the professionalisation of education and training and the rise of national accreditation structures. In some geographic regions, such as Western Europe, the growth of supranational structures tends to promote structural homogeneity in order to facilitate intra-regional co-ordination and collaboration among institutions and within economies of increasingly mobile workers and professionals. Professionalism and accreditation, because of their need for standardisation through quality assurance and other accountability procedures, tend to reduce curricular diversity (Goedegebuure et al., 1996).

So, while one set of theories offers reasons for expecting dynamic growth within institutions and systems, another set offers reasons why it may not happen. The result of pressures driving higher education systems and their constituent institutions to be more like each other is referred to as isomorphism, and it may result from mimicry (that is, institutions having similar programmes), or coercion. Mimetic isomorphism is the result of institutions mimicking the behaviour of each other in order to minimise risk in highly competitive environments. When institutions are highly dependent upon a narrow range of resource providers, such as an education ministry or a very homogeneous population, they will tend to have similar programmes, structures and operating norms. This is apparently what has happened in Australia, according to Meek (1996; 2001) and in Holland, according to Maassen and Potman (1990).

Coercive isomorphism is the result of pressures from the environment, principally government policies, that force institutions to become more similar, thus reducing diversity in a higher education system. Governments might act in this way in order to promote efficiency, on the assumption that too much diversity is inefficient. Another source of coercive or normative isomorphism is from academic cultures intent on preserving long-standing values and norms.

Either way, as Meek (1996; 2001) indicates, this tendency often results in less diversity and differentiation.

One way to gauge whether the terrain is changing is to classify institutions according to differentiating characteristics and observe whether there are shifts in the number of institutions in particular categories, or whether the number of categories change. Policies frequently will have the intention of causing certain shifts. But sometimes the shifts may be the result of other factors. In recent years, globalisation has been cited as a cause for shifts in the typology of higher education institutions in many countries. For example, the rapid rise in private higher education institutions in some countries, and in particular the growth of corporate universities, have been attributed to the pressures of growing international economic competition – pressures with which slow-changing public institutions have not been able to keep up.

Another source of institutional shifts across the categories of a typology have been changes in institutional leadership and institutional culture. The rise of the 'entrepreneurial university' in recent years is an example of a 'type' change in the terrain of higher education.

The next two chapters examine how the terrain of South African higher education has changed, and whether the changes were the result of new policies or globalisation or shifts in institutional culture.

In Chapter 10, Fehnel provides an assessment of the rapidly changing private higher education sector – a type of institution that was resurrected from extinction in South Africa by a combination of factors, the most important of which was new legislation that permitted private, degree and diploma granting institutions to be re-established after almost a century.

In Chapter 11, Cloete and Fehnel examine the dynamics behind shifts in the terrain and suggest a new, emergent typology of institutions. While this clearly differs from the apartheid typology, they question whether the new terrain appropriately meets the needs of South Africa, and suggest that while government policy has more influence with certain types of institutions, with other types of institutions, other factors may be more critical in bringing about desired shifts between categories.

REFERENCES

Clark, B. (1996). Diversification of Higher Education: Viability and Change. In: V.L. Meek, L. Goedegebuure, O. Kivinen & R. Rinne (eds) (1996), *The Mockers and Mocked: Comparative Perspectives on Diversity, Differentiation and Convergence in Higher Education*. Oxford: Pergamon.

Goedegebuure, L. et al. (1996). On Diversity, Differentiation and Convergence. In: V.L. Meek, L. Goedegebuure, O. Kivinen & R. Rinne (eds), *The Mockers and the Mocked: Comparative perspectives on Differentiation, Convergence and Diversity in Higher Education*. Oxford: Pergamon.

Maassen, P. & Potman, H.P. (1990). Strategic Decision Making in Higher Education: An Analysis of the New Planning System in Dutch Higher Education. *Higher Education in Europe*, 20.

Meek, V.L., Goedegebuure, L., Kivinen, O. & Rinne, R. (eds) (1996). *The Mockers and the Mocked: Comparative Perspectives on Diversity, Differentiation and Convergence in Higher Education*. Oxford: Pergamon.

Meek, L. (2001). Reflections on Australian Higher Education: 1994–1999. Commissioned paper. www.chet.org.za/papers.asp.

Neave, G. (1996). Homogenization, Integration and Convergence: The Cheshire Cats of Higher Education Analysis. In: Meek et al., op cit.

Van Vught, F. (1996). Isomorphism in Higher Education? In: Meek et al., op cit.

CHAPTER 10

RICHARD FEHNEL

PRIVATE HIGHER EDUCATION

This chapter provides an overview of the shifting higher education landscape in South Africa. While the primary focus is on the period between 1994 and 2000, the chapter traces the historical relationships among public and private higher education providers, the role of government policies, and pressures from the political and economic environments. The interaction among these forces indicates that the conditions permitting the re-emergence of the private provision of post-secondary education and training in South Africa in the late 1990s were not new to the country. The chapter also takes into account what was happening among public higher education providers during the period after 1994 and the mercurial role of the government after 1998. It compares the development of private providers in South Africa with international trends and concludes by suggesting that revisiting policies and procedures concerning the regulation of the private providers may be in the country's interest.

1. COLONIALISM, APARTHEID AND HIGHER EDUCATION: THE ROAD TO CHANGE

Conventional wisdom suggests that the rise in private higher education in South Africa is a recent phenomenon. However, a closer look at South African history indicates otherwise. The first private provider of higher education was the South African College, founded in Cape Town in 1829 by influential citizens who sought better quality of education for their children. Almost a century later (1918) this institution was granted university status and became what is now known as the University of Cape Town. Later in the 19th century a second private provider of higher education, the Kimberley School of Mines, was created to serve the needs of the rapidly expanding mining industry. The school moved to Johannesburg after the turn of the century and split into two entities in 1908. Both of these eventually became public institutions: one the University of the Witwatersrand (1921) and the other the University of Pretoria (1930) (Mabizela, 2000).

   A third initiative to provide higher education had its roots in religious affairs, as colonial life became more deeply entrenched. Both the Anglican and Dutch Reformed Churches started colleges in several South African locations during the 19th century. Cape Town, Grahamstown, Stellenbosch and Burgersdorp were sites of private church-supported colleges, all of which evolved into public institutions in the 20th century. The early 20th century also saw the beginnings of racially segregated and privately supported

227

N. Cloete et al. (eds.), Transformation in Higher Education, 227-243.
© 2007 *Springer.*

higher education. The South African Native College was founded in 1916; it eventually became the University of Fort Hare. In 1929 a private initiative led to the creation of a technical college for Indian workers in the Durban. This later became ML Sultan Technikon, a public institution (Mabizela, 2000).

The evolution of higher education from private initiatives into public institutions, and into divergent racial groupings was underscored by the passage of the Extension of University Act of 1959, which created separate universities for the 'non-white' population. Not surprisingly, given the framework of 'grand apartheid', racial separation also featured in the legislation in 1967 that created the Colleges of Advanced Technical Education. These colleges were upgraded to technikons in 1979. By 1980 the landscape of higher education in South Africa had stabilised into racially divided sets of universities and technikons the roots of which had long been forgotten.

During the post-war industrial boom of the 1950s and 1960s another set of dynamics in the provision of education and training emerged that would lay the bases for significant changes later in the century. The dual demand for professional training and alternative routes to matriculation fuelled the growth of private providers of professional, technical and vocational education and training programmes. By 1974 there were 32 registered professional institutes, the majority of which were privately run. Some of these private providers also responded to the demand for alternative routes to matriculation – a demand that had led to the creation in 1906 of Intec College, Lyceum College in 1928 and Damelin College in 1945. By the 1950s, all offered certificates and qualifications as well as alternative matriculation programmes (Mabizela, 2000). One can speculate about the linkages between Afrikaner capital in the creation of these private, skills-focused providers and efforts to develop an education and skills base for the Afrikaner population which had been marginalised by British governmental, economic and social powers in the Cape colonies. When the Nationalist Party took control of the country in 1948, it was able to shape education and training policies in a way that reflected its racial values.

As global attention focused on the apartheid policies of South Africa in the late 1960s and 1970s, international donors and South African non-governmental organisations (NGOs) began partnerships addressing some of the deficiencies in education and training opportunities for black South Africans. By the 1980s a number of initiatives of this nature were well established, including the well-respected South African Committee for Higher Education (Sached). It had started in the 1960s as a provider of higher education for black students through a linkage with the University of London. Later, it offered programmes in adult basic education and secondary education, and contact sessions for black students enrolled in the correspondence courses of the University of South Africa (Unisa), the mammoth distance education university that was essentially the only 'non-racial' provider of higher education in the country at the time.

A significant focus of many NGOs was the need to improve the competence of black teachers in South Africa's primary and secondary schools. Research in the late 1980s and early 1990s indicated that more than 80% of these teachers were not adequately prepared for the courses they were teaching, in terms of educational qualifications. Many had little more than high school education; some even lacked that. All had been trained in the philosophy and pedagogy of Christian National Education, the value framework promulgated by the apartheid government. In response, partnerships involving NGOs, foreign universities and sympathetic departments or faculties of education in a few South African universities began creative programmes to upgrade teachers' competencies and qualifications and to offer an alternative to apartheid educational values. For example, the Teacher Opportunity Programme (Tops), a partnership involving the University of South Carolina in the United States and the Universities of Durban-Westville and Western Cape, reached over 10.000 teachers and school administrators through its two-track programme of courses in the 1980s and early 1990s. The supply of these NGO programmes found a ready demand among teachers who were able to earn salary increases by adding to their education qualifications, irrespective of the relationship between their teaching responsibilities and the courses they pursued.

The apparent success of NGOs in attracting international support and the widespread publicity being focused on the shortcomings of teacher education did not pass unnoticed among the private providers of education and training programmes, nor by an increasing number of universities previously not involved in such programmes.[1] This is a significant point, because the growing awareness of the 'black teachers market' was instrumental in motivating a shift in the landscape of higher education a few years later through the rapid growth of distance education programmes offered primarily by three historically white Afrikaans-medium universities in partnership with private providers. This is discussed further at a later point in this chapter, and by Bunting in Chapter 5 (Students) and Cloete and Fehnel in Chapter 11 (The Emergent Landscape).

About the same time that NGOs were launching education and training programmes to address shortcomings in the schooling sector, the private economic sector in South Africa was also pressing for changes in order to meet the growing economic pressures of real or projected shortages of skilled workers, especially in technology-related fields. These concerns reflected fears that a post-apartheid economy would not be able to create jobs fast enough to offset rising social demands and fears of white emigration in high skilled professions. The result was an unusual degree of co-operation among unions, corporate management and education and training leaders both in government and in anti-apartheid education organisations aimed at creating a National Qualifications Framework (NQF) similar to recent initiatives in Commonwealth countries. The proposed NQF was seen as a structure through which educationally disadvantaged groups might be fast-tracked to education and training qualifications that were deserved but denied by apartheid. By embracing the idea that lifelong learning, with appropriate recognition for prior learning, would become a way of life through which South Africa could catch the global economic express, the proposed NQF found widespread support except in the higher education sector where it was initially contested.

2. THE EMERGENCE OF PRIVATE HIGHER EDUCATION UNDER A NEW POLICY FRAMEWORK

The call for a National Qualifications Framework was just one of a growing number of outcomes emerging from policy debates in the late 1980s and early 1990s. These debates drew attention to South Africa's higher education system and the need for it to undertake major changes if the economic, social and political demands generated by 40 years of repression were to be successfully managed. As Sehoole (2001) indicates in his review of higher education policy, these debates led to the adoption of several major policy initiatives by the ANC-led government after its election in 1994. In addition to the adoption of a new Constitution, the key actions included the 1995 creation of the National Commission on Higher Education with the task of developing a vision for a new higher education system, the adoption of the National Qualifications Framework (1995), the adoption of the Technikon Act of 1995 that permitted technikons to award degrees in addition to diplomas, and the adoption of the Higher Education White Paper and the Higher Education Act of 1997.

This suite of policy and legislative actions ushered in a new era for South African higher education. The new Constitution and the Higher Education Act of 1997 made it possible for private providers to offer degrees and diplomas, a right previously reserved for public universities and technikons. Consequently, private providers began to operate differently. In addition to acting as partners to public institutions, some of the private providers began aggressive marketing of their own programmes. As one marketing person stated, in reference to the advertising done by a private provider, 'They basically owned the "Tonight" section of *The Star* [one of the largest daily newspapers in South Africa] for November and January' (Bezuidenhout, 2001).

What caused this sudden interest? At least three probable causes can be suggested: a belief that the government was going to invest heavily in education and training programmes; the absence of a comprehensive regulatory framework, coupled with a belief that government lacked the will or capacity to regulate aggressively; and, a conviction that there were significant profits to be made by providing the skills needed for national economic development. The South African government had taken a position that the country was going to become a part of the global economy, and this required a shift to a more highly skilled workforce than had been the case in earlier decades.

Although many of those professing interest in registering as private providers of higher education were small operators, a few were huge corporations for which the entry into the field of higher education fuelled a boom in the value of their shares in 1998. Notable were four firms: Adcorp, Advtech, Educor and Privest. Three of the four moved to acquire or launch operations that spanned education and training sectors from pre-tertiary through postgraduate levels, while Privest maintained a focus on skill-based training primarily spanning the further and higher education levels. But in addition to these four there were many other smaller, private providers seeking to find a niche in what appeared to be a wide-open playing field. According to a study conducted by the Education Policy Unit of the University of the Western Cape, in 1998 there were 120 private providers with enrolments of less than 1.000 students, and within this group ninety providers had less than 250 enrolments (Mabizela et al., 2000).

There was a rapid growth of private, high profile MBA programmes that attracted media coverage and accentuated public interest in private higher education. According to one source, in 1990 there were five MBA programmes in South Africa (all offered by public providers) serving roughly 1.000 students. Within a decade those numbers had grown to approximately 40 providers, including at least nine foreign and several other locally owned private providers, serving roughly 15.000 students at any one time. What was significant was not just the growth, but also the diversity of delivery modalities and curricular options. Credit was given to the emergence of the private providers for promoting the needed diversity.

> The private providers are very innovative ... they put pressure on the public providers to open up their programmes. (Bezuidenhout, 2001)

Having the world's fastest growing market for MBAs was seen as an asset for a nation trying, with remarkable success despite its limitations, to join the global economy (*Financial Mail*, 21 July, 2000).

By 1991 two private for-profit providers, Midrand Campus and Damelin College had also begun offering contact instruction to students enrolled in Unisa. These two organisations saw a market opportunity with relatively little competition and began building their capacity to respond. Midrand Campus began by providing instruction to a specialised market – white, middle-class, mostly Jewish students who, because of poor matric results, were not able to gain admission to one of the historically white English-medium universities. Damelin, on the other hand, pursued a market of middle-class black students who also had problems gaining access to the better universities or who wanted the benefit of face-to-face contact. Damelin had been very successful as a provider of correspondence and contact education and training at the schooling and further education levels, but saw an opportunity to develop its markets vertically by moving into higher education. By the time legislation changed in 1997, both Damelin and Midrand Campus had broadened their markets and had become part of the Educor stable of private higher education providers. The enrolment of Midrand Campus had grown in less than a decade from 250 students to over 3.500 students (Cairns, 2001).

3. DEVELOPMENT OF PARTNERSHIPS

Paralleling these moves by private providers was rapid growth in partnerships between public and private institutions during the middle of the 1990s. A study of the emerging public-private partnerships commissioned by the Department of Education and the Council on Higher Education indicated that at least 251 such partnership agreements were in existence by the middle of 2000 (Gutto, 2000). According to the EPU study cited earlier, these partnerships involved over 30.000 fulltime equivalent students (Mabizela et al., 2000). Contrary to conventional wisdom that three public universities – Rand Afrikaans, Pretoria and Port Elizabeth – were the most active in implementing such partnerships, these studies suggest otherwise. Nine public universities accounted for 162 partnerships with private providers, and four technikons accounted for 89, with one technikon reporting 82 partnership agreements. Unisa and the universities of Pretoria and Potchefstroom accounted for 134 of the 162 partnerships reported by public universities. Two historically white English-medium universities (Natal and Rhodes) reported having 18 partnerships (Gutto, 2000).

Two factors are noteworthy about the findings reported in these two studies: first, the extent to which such partnerships exist, and second, the fact that only one historically black institution (Peninsula Technikon) reported having partnership agreements. What do these factors suggest about institutional willingness or capacity to engage in this type of activity? Bunting in chapters 4 and 5 indicates that three historically white Afrikaans-medium universities made extensive use of such partnerships to provide education and training programmes for black teachers. These partnerships could be seen as either complementing or competing with the programming provided by Unisa, the distance-education university, and Vista University. The latter is a multi-campus university created in the late 1980s to address the needs of the urban black population of South Africa. Its largest programmes were in the field of teacher education. But the reality is that all the historically black universities had education faculties and were physically located closer to this market. Why didn't they develop such partnerships? Cloete and Fehnel (Chapter 11) indicate that in the early 1990s these institutions had little interest in starting continuing education programmes and by the time they may have seen the need and opportunity to do so at the end of the decade, it may have been too late.

The partnerships involving private providers and public universities reflected creative responses to opportunities implied by drafts of new policy initiatives, as well as a growing awareness of the need for new skill development among employers. Previously, the public universities and technikons providing residential, contact instruction had not been permitted to provide off-campus instruction in either contact or distance mode. The National Commission on Higher Education (1996) challenged that prohibition and it became apparent that the Department of Education was sympathetic to the development of dual-mode capability by institutions. Such a move seemed appropriate in order to meet the calls for increased access to higher education and responsiveness to growing demands from the economic sectors of the country (including government departments) for more skilled human resources to carry out programmes of national development.

Taken together, the role of NGOs as providers of access to parallel forms of higher education in the 1980s, the expansion of the private provider sector from secondary and further education into higher education, and the emergence of partnerships between public universities and technikons and private providers (including NGOs, for-profit providers, and foreign public and private universities) created a climate of expectation among providers regarding the provision of higher education. This resulted in more than 600 organisations enquiring about the registration procedures announced in 1998 – a number far greater than the wildest speculation of anyone knowledgeable about the sector.

4. EXPANDING HIGHER EDUCATION PROVISION:
HOPE, CONTRADICTION AND TURMOIL

As Bunting indicated in Chapter 5, enrolments in public higher education began to grow rapidly in the early 1990s, bringing hope to many for whom degrees and diplomas had seemed beyond reach. Expansion of the system was a response to the calls for equity and development, but it also ushered in a period of confusion and contradictions. The rapid growth in enrolments in public institutions included many students who were unable to pay their fees, or who withheld payment in the belief that payment could be avoided as a form of political dividend in the administratively weak institutions. These were, without exception, the historically black institutions. Between 1995 and 1997 more than half of the public universities and technikons began facing severe problems caused by financial pressures on students for the payment of fees. Their non-payment led to actions by institutions to exclude them from further enrolment, and also created financial problems for the institutions that were dependent on the student fees to supplement the falling level of subsidy support from government. There were violent student demonstrations that sometimes resulted in senior campus administrators being held hostage. Media coverage was dramatic and persistent. The climate of optimism that blossomed in public higher education in 1994 and 1995 gave way to a period of gloom by 1997.

The enrolment landscape in the public higher education sector began experiencing significant and unexpected shifts. As indicated earlier, several of the historically white Afrikaans-medium universities had already begun major outreach programmes, in effect becoming dual-medium institutions offering residential and distance education programmes. At the same time, there was a sharp increase in enrolments across the technikon sector, in both historically white and black institutions. And, simultaneously, all the historically black universities experienced sharp declines in enrolment – as much as a 50% decline in two years in several institutions. For these institutions the threat of financial crisis caused by the sudden loss of students was very real. The financial problems were compounded by serious unresolved crises of governance and management in most of these institutions. At the same time the private higher education sector appeared on the scene, with unconfirmed speculation about rapid gains in enrolments.

In effect, a great student trek was underway, with no one at the time having a clue as to what its dynamics were. About 15.000 fewer white students were enrolled in 1999, as compared with 1997. Had they gone to the new private institutions? Had they emigrated? No one knew. Compounding this situation was the surprising realisation that the secondary school system was producing fewer graduates qualified to enter tertiary institutions. The genuine financial despair experienced by many of the public institutions led to speculation about probable causes, and the private providers of higher education were suspected of having contributed to the problems.

Suspicion grew during the period in 1998, when private providers were engaged in a complex dual process of registration with the Department of Education and seeking accreditation from the South African Qualification Authority (SAQA). This process suffered from frequently changing requirements, and uncertainty about procedures, causing conflicts and tension between private providers and government officials. In the midst of this, a sharp shift emerged in the attitude and policies of government officials towards private providers. As one senior person formerly in a private institution said (on condition of remaining anonymous):

> What I experienced was sharp hostility from government people, and from activists who are now in academia whom I thought had open minds about a lot of these issues. I was extremely shocked about it.

The following sequence gives a powerful illustration of this shift: in early 1998 the Department of Education issued guidelines for private providers on registration procedures. In these guidelines the Department recommended that private institutions form partnerships with public institutions in order to facilitate registration. Less than a year later the Minister of Education proclaimed a moratorium on public-private partnerships.

The moratorium was just one act in a number of actions signalling a significant change in policy towards private providers. Other actions included the passage of the Higher Education Amendment Act of 1999, which gave the Minster of Education much greater powers to regulate private providers of higher education. From government's side, the shift seemed to be justified by growing concerns about the quality of many programmes offered by private providers, as well as fear that the growth of the private higher education sector may be threatening the viability of some public institutions. These positions were held by both the Minister of Education and Director-General of Education (Xako, 2000), and reiterated recently by a Special Advisor to the Minister of Education (Taylor, 2001). Many of the new providers were inexperienced and could not provide necessary registration information to the Department of Education, or appropriate course materials for quality assurance purposes to the South African Qualification Authority. In a number of cases, organisations seeking to register had questionable programmes. The same insider from a private provider reported:

> I was shocked to find that in fact the level of the course material had not been upgraded for up to ten years. In the human resource programmes, for instance, a course on labour relations would not have had the latest legislation on labour law in this country!

And, with few exceptions, many providers were not forthcoming with data about enrolments, which only fuelled speculation about their operations. There was speculation that the historically white Afrikaans-medium universities were being entrepreneurial in using the newly created partnerships in distance education programmes to admit black students, and it was suspected that they structured the mode of delivery so as not have the black students on their campuses.

Response to the shift in attitude and policy from the providers' side ranged from anger to incredulity (Marcus, 2001; Gordon, 2001a, and one unpublished interview). The Alliance of Private Providers of Education, Training and Development, representing about 250 organisations, took the position that amendments proposed in 1999 to the Higher Education Act 'would introduce substantial uncertainty and risk and would seriously prejudice both existing private education providers and those wishing to enter that industry' (Bisseker, 2000). That concern seemed to materialise as many organisations seeking registration withdrew from the process and the share prices of publicly traded firms in the education and training business fell sharply, causing one of the large firms to take the drastic step of delisting, and a second to consider this action.

Despite justifications, the actions taken by education department officials have had serious consequences. The moratorium on public-private partnerships stopped a number of innovative projects that were about to be launched. A similar embargo in early 2000 on new distance education programmes by residential public institutions stopped a project between a leading distance education NGO and a public university to offer an 'open learning option' in science and mathematics aimed at the critical issue of bringing more black students into the science programmes of universities. On the international front, several foreign public universities dropped their plans to register and work with South African organisations. As noted earlier, it has been recognised by South African public institutions that the curricula of foreign universities added value to what was on offer in South Africa and stimulated local institutions to improve their programming. And, the actions by education officials caused investors to withdraw support from the higher education sector at a time when additional support was needed to upgrade programmes and reach new markets of students and workers seeking access to better qualifications.

5. THE EMERGING LANDSCAPE OF PRIVATE HIGHER EDUCATION

What the 20th century demonstrated in South African higher education is that governments, for good or bad, seek to shape the responses of institutions in ways that reflect governmental values and priorities; that institutions, for good or bad, seek to maximise opportunities to assure their future, whether by becoming public institutions (as all the original private institutions did in the early part of the century) or by becoming entrepreneurial and responding to the marketplace (as some, public and private, did in the final years of the century); and that 'the market' is constantly changing, requiring new responses from both government and institutions, often more quickly than policy and structural mechanisms permit. When that happens, pressures for a shift in the landscape of institutions emerge and, depending on the prevailing 'rules of the game', a new landscape may evolve.

What happened in private higher education in South Africa at the end of the 1990s reflects fairly accurately the results of the interaction among policy, the marketplace and institutional initiative. As market opportunities became clearer following the political settlement of 1993/94, the landscape of higher education providers began to reflect responses to new opportunities. One emergent category of providers consisted of the large corporations that moved into the field of higher education in one of three ways: as an extension of existing education and training at the further education level; as partners with public institutions in extending access to new markets for the public institutions; or as part of corporate strategies to provide recruitment, academic qualifications and job placement – a sort of comprehensive career-service agency.

Another category of providers that emerged consisted of small, independent providers which focused on limited knowledge and skill areas and attempted to create a sustainable niche. While loosely falling in the area of management and commerce, they responded to needs across a wide range of economic sectors – from the many facets of the tourism industry to health care delivery and other niches of personal service. A third category that emerged involved the transnational providers which sought to create an educational beachhead in South Africa, either on their own or in partnership with local providers.

And most recently, a fourth category that emerged was the 'corporate university' with several distinguishable variations, including partnerships with public institutions (South African and foreign).

The study referred to earlier by the Education Policy Unit (EPU) of the University of the Western Cape helps to provide a clearer picture of this emerging typology of private providers, and what they offer and to whom (Mabizela et al., 2000). The EPU study analyses data supplied by private providers during the registration process initiated in 1998. It indicates that the provision of higher education by private providers had been meeting some of the goals established by the higher education White Paper and Higher Education Act of 1997. According to the data from 145 providers during the two-year period of 1998 to 2000, 108.700 persons were enrolled in private higher education programmes of whom 39% were Africans and 16% were white. Over 15.000 persons were enrolled in first-degree programmes, but the overwhelming majority (78%) was enrolled in certificate or diploma programmes. This trend reflected a response to the need to right-size post-secondary education and training, where for many years enrolments in university degree programmes were far greater than enrolments in technical and related areas. Since certificate and diploma programmes were not part of the main activities of the historically black universities that were suffering student losses, the data raises questions about whether private providers constituted a threat to these public institutions.

The data from the EPU study also indicates that enrolments in 1998 were concentrated in two areas of study – business/commerce and management studies (48%) and education (24%). Nine per cent were enrolled in physical, mathematical, computer and life sciences. Fifty-six per cent of the providers were located in, or had their head offices in Gauteng, 14% in KwaZulu-Natal and 11% in the Western Cape, the three most heavily populated and economically important provinces.

One of the many riddles the study did not solve was the question of the impact and appropriateness of the many partnerships between some of the private and public providers that had emerged between 1995 and 1999. Other interesting partnerships, such as the one between the University of Pretoria and Damelin to provide computer instruction to residential students on the University of Pretoria campus, were beginning to emerge when the Minister of Education put a moratorium on joint ventures of this nature in 2000. As the EPU study reported, such partnerships reflected strategic initiatives to expand enrolments and increase access. They also served to promote programmatic and institutional diversity, goals of higher education policy increasingly being advocated throughout the world (Salmi, 1994; World Development Report, 1999; World Bank, 2000). As one key person with top roles in both public and private institutions put it:

> You know, if you go into the Commonwealth, there is a very strong move which says it is no longer 'publish or perish', it is 'partnership or perish'. Unfortunately, our friend Minister Asmal is saying 'You can't have it in education'. I think that is incredibly short-sighted and completely contrary to the major South African government moves regarding public-private partnerships. (Marcus, 2001)

This raises the question: are South Africa's current policies towards private higher education providers moving the education sector and the economy in a direction that is in the best long-term interests of the country? One approach to seeking an answer to this question is to consider how government policies have influenced the landscape of private higher education.

6. LANDSCAPE CHANGES: 1995–2000

As we have seen, during the period 1995 to 2000 there was considerable activity among private providers. The 'necessary' condition for this spurt of activity was the change in policy that permitted private providers to offer degrees and diplomas. Without this condition, it is highly unlikely that the magnitude of change would have been as substantial as it was. But other conditions amplified the activities of private providers. These 'sufficient conditions' included at least four key factors: firstly, anticipated governmental economic policy that would provide financial incentives for education and training providers; secondly, available capital for investment in the development or acquisition of delivery capacity; thirdly, a wide pool of entrepreneurial capacity and initiative, some of which was created by the Department of Education through its policy of teacher retrenchment with generous severance packages which many retrenched teachers used to start training programmes; and fourthly, the availability of public institutions as partners, giving the private providers immediate access to 'product' (course materials) and legitimacy in the eyes of the marketplace.

This combination of necessary and sufficient conditions made dynamic growth within the private sector possible. Although little information is currently available to document the details of this growth, anecdotal evidence suggests that more research would be needed to develop a typology that describes and analyses institutional behaviour.[2]

On the basis of available information, however, it is possible to start making some preliminary distinctions. During this period of landscape shift, 1995–2000, one group of private providers could be characterised as the *'empire builders'*. They moved aggressively to acquire smaller, family owned training companies and invested heavily in marketing their 'brands'. They sought to develop 'cradle to grave' human resource strategies by coupling their training divisions with recruitment and placement divisions.

Another group of private providers, the *'niche builders'*, moved differently. Rather than spreading their resources across a broad range of markets (both geographically and programmatically) they focused on creating delivery capability that matched their existing competence and financial capability. This group tended to be the smaller, family operated training programmes that were local or regional in scope.

Within each of these two groups, two different strategic patterns of development seem to have been followed: one in the first phase (1995–1999) which perhaps created the basis for how the organisations responded to the changes in policy in 1999 and 2000, which initiated a second period of landscape shift (1999–2002). The two strategic patterns are differentiated by whether the providers took a long-term or short-term view of their operational mission. Within both the 'empire builders' and 'niche builders', the organisations with a short-term view focused on activities that maximised economic returns. This meant that investment in course materials or academic staff tended to be minimal. In contrast, organisations with long-term strategies, regardless of whether they were 'niche' or 'empire' builders, were more prepared to invest in material, physical and human resources. For example, Monash University's operation in South Africa – 'Monash/South Africa' – invested heavily in building a campus, hiring full-time academic staff and developing research capacity in curricular areas in which it offers degrees. This is in sharp contrast with the University of Wales, which carried out its South African operations through technikons by means of partnership agreements with the Committee of Technikon Principals. Wales provided the 'courseware' but little else, and when the conditions changed in 2000, they quickly abandoned their operation in South Africa.

Just as the policy changes introduced by the Ministry of Education 1997 led to significant changes, the policy changes of 1999 and 2000 also led to significant changes in the landscape of private higher education providers. The main outcome was fewer providers than there were previously. This may not necessarily be bad, if those which left the playing field were not committed to providing quality education in areas needed, nor providing it more efficiently than other alternatives. Perhaps the biggest change, in terms of institutional behaviour, however, was the shift to a shorter-term strategy by the larger providers as a result of the loss of value in share price, and their reluctance to invest in the development of materials and human resources.

Another significant change was the retreat by transnational providers. Although it may be argued that those which left were not the best, that fact that they withdrew sent a message of discouragement to others, perhaps of higher calibre, which were considering partnerships that would have benefited South Africa. The perception of hostility towards transnational providers may come back to haunt South African institutions, public and private, as they start developing more international education programmes and begin to market them in other countries. Finally, it appears from the Department of Education Registry that some of the providers that entered the field of higher education from the further education and training sector have since withdrawn from the higher education sector. Some observers, fearing a watering down of higher education by having too close an association with further education providers, applaud these withdrawals. However, many others, especially employers anxious to improve workers' skills and qualifications, see the division between further and higher education as being too artificial and regret these withdrawals, fearing that employees will have fewer opportunities to earn higher qualifications.

7. POST-2000: BACK TO THE DRAWING BOARD?

The cornerstones of higher education policy formulated in the mid-1990s in South Africa were equity, efficiency, responsiveness and co-operative governance. By the end of the decade the landscape of public institutions had changed remarkably in terms of these policy goals. As Cloete demonstrates in Chapter 12, public sector institutions were developing a very mixed record of successes and shortcomings. The historically black universities were, in general, performing poorly while the historically white Afrikaans-medium universities were performing best in terms of market orientation and income diversification. In the private higher education sector, similar mixed results seem to be evident, though the data is much harder to find on which to base solid analyses. But trends are emerging. The private providers were responding to a broad cross-section of niche markets. Their presence was addressing questions of horizontal and vertical mobility more readily than public institutions. Consequently, the private providers could be seen as providing complementarity to the public sector – a move that could improve the efficiency of the entire higher education sector.

Between 1995 and 2000, enrolment in the private higher education sector grew primarily through black student participation, in fields of study that had most promise of employment and at a credential level that was most easily attainable. Approximately 7% of enrolments were at the masters and doctorate levels, a level not dissimilar to that in public institutions. While one would like to be able to analyse the efficiency of the private providers more closely, the lack of available data does not permit this. Whether these institutions can compete with public institutions in terms of efficiency is a critical issue. As suggested in Chapter 12, many of the public institutions have ample room for improvement in throughput and retention rates, two standard measures of efficiency. Most public institutions in South Africa are well below international standards. One recent report indicated that South Africa spends more than US$160-million per year on students who drop out of the system – as many as one in four (Rossouw, 2001).

A major source of inefficiency in many higher education systems is the disconnection between education and training system components. This is precisely what the National Qualifications Framework was designed to address. A number of the large private providers have the potential to achieve much higher levels of efficiency by creating clusters of programmatically linked networks of credentials within their different corporate divisions. This should encourage students to complete one qualification and move into the next with a minimum of effort around issues of application, admission and transfer of credits. However, this type of vertical market integration has not occurred in South Africa. In large part this may be due to two fundamental reasons.

The first is the reported poor management within some private education corporations. Interviews with 'insiders' revealed how some corporate 'profit centres' failed to develop a long-term strategy based on market co-operation even within the same corporate structures, making it difficult for students to network across different educational programmes. One former insider revealed:

> There were a lot of egos around the board room table, people worth R60-million, R70-million, saying 'this is my business, you don't touch it'; so, you know, there wasn't co-operation. They could actually have created a very interesting thing sharing intellectual property, a common intellectual property chassis, where they could put their different brands on top. But there were too many vested interests in it. And there was a lot of greed, and it was a very 'in for the quick buck' scenario.

On the other hand, experiences in other countries with large, corporate providers of higher education demonstrate that economies of scale and co-operation are manifest when profit centres can share costs and students (Kelly, 2001). These experiences are beginning to influence the way public and not-for-profit universities interact with each other – moving them towards a mode of 'collaborative competition' (Manganyi, 2001).

The second reason that vertical market integration has not occurred may be due to the concerns held by government education officials about the separate classification of students who fall under different governmental funding policies and administrative structures – namely the distinction between further education and higher education – even though more fluidity between these levels may be what is needed to raise throughput rates and improve efficiency. It is felt among many employers and providers in South Africa that the Labour Department's approach to human resource development is much more flexible and consistent with the vision of the NQF than that of the Department of Education. However, the position held by education officials is primarily due to the Constitutional 'division of labour' between national and provincial education departments, and because the funding formula in higher education has different conditions for different categories of students (Sayed, 2000).

The literature on the worldwide growth of private higher education addresses another policy factor that South African policy-makers and implementers have not heeded sufficiently. This concerns the strategic importance, in terms of national human resource development, of managing the growth of a robust private higher education sector to complement public institutions (Altbach, 1998). The existence of a diversity of institutional and programmatic options has important social and economic benefits that, in the aggregate, address goals of equity, efficiency and responsiveness. In a modest way, the limited South African experience seemed to be affirming international trends up until the change in government policy towards private higher education in 1999–2000. The small private sector was addressing niche markets and through its innovations in partnering with public providers it was creating additional access to higher education. In some cases it was also introducing diverse curricular options and a standard of service delivery not previously experienced by learners (Cairns, 2001; Marcus, 2001). These practices had the effect of inducing public institutions to begin imitating some of the private providers (Bezuidenhout, 2001). These are desired outcomes that effective polices in other emerging markets have experienced (Hopper, 1998; Lee, 1998).

As Altbach points out, governments need to assess carefully what policies will strengthen the entire productive capacity of the higher education sector, and move to implement such policies even when this may mean providing financial subsidies to private providers, as is the case in a growing number of countries. It may be far less expensive, in terms of unit costs and aggregate sector budgets, to pay private providers to provide quality education in fields where there are critical shortages of strategically important human resources, than to invest heavily in public institutions by building new facilities and staffing them (Altbach, 1998; Lee, 1999; Yonezawa, 1999).

8. CONCLUSION

The period since 1994 has revealed that in South Africa both public and private sectors of higher education have institutions that are poorly managed and have programmes (and institutions) that need to be closed down to protect the public. It also demonstrated that both public and private institutions could be innovative, well managed and deeply concerned about quality and the welfare of staff and students. And, it showed that public and private institutions could work together, in partnerships, to design and deliver programmes that opened up access to needy and deserving students, and that showed promise of addressing critical skill gaps.

What may be needed now is a review of the goals and objectives of the higher education sector, its role in meeting the growing human resources needs in areas that are critical to national development, and the possibilities that exist to have public and private institutions work in a complementary manner to achieve these ends. This also suggests that it may be possible to imagine the emergence of a differentiated policy structure reflecting the variety of needs, missions and operating cultures of the wide range of public and private institutions that make up a growing and effective national system, rather than a 'one size fits all' policy (Gordon, 2001b).

There are positive signs that such a debate could begin: the South African Universities Vice-Chancellors Association, a key stakeholder organisation representing the public sector institutions, has acknowledged that it is essential that a framework be developed to ensure complementarity between public and private providers of higher education (Kotecha, 2001). The Executive Director of the Council on Higher Education, the statutory body responsible for advising the Minister of Education on higher education policy and on assuring the quality of higher education, has also signalled the necessity of taking a long-term view on the development of policy to support the creation of a strong, high quality private provider sector that complements the role of public institutions (Badat, 2001). The panic over student enrolments in the private sector has subsided as more evidence surfaces to support the understanding that the private providers do not constitute a serious threat to public institutions – that the biggest competitors of public institutions are other public institutions, and that the private institutions are, in fact, beginning to address the kinds of access and equity issues called for in earlier policy documents.

What also seems clear is that new debates about higher education policies need to be shaped by expectations of future demands on the higher education system. The government of South Africa has committed itself to playing a major role in the economic and political recovery of the African continent, through the New Partnerships for Africa's Development (Nepad, 2001). To carry out this role successfully may require a long-term strategy of human resource development that is shaped by the needs of many African nations, not just its own citizens (Fehnel, 2000; 2001). This will require the intellectual, financial and infrastructure resources of a comprehensive, co-ordinated higher education system that embraces public and private institutions, working in close partnership with the private sector and a broad range of government agencies at home and throughout the continent.

NOTES

[1] For insights into this seminal shift, see the reflection interviews with professors T.R. Botha and D. van Rensburg on www.chet.org.za/reflections.asp.

[2] At the time of writing a study of the private sector was being carried out by a team of researchers under the auspices of the Human Sciences Research Council. The study aimed to provide a detailed description and analysis of operational characteristics from a sample of providers within four categories: transnational institutions, 'franchising' colleges, vocational education and training colleges, and corporate 'classrooms'.

REFERENCES

Altbach, P.G. (1998). Private Higher Education: Themes and Variations in Comparative Perspective. *International Higher Education*, (10), Winter.

Badat, S. (2001). Remarks made on a Panel on Private Higher Education, Conference on Globalisation and Higher Education. Hosted by the Society for Research into Higher Education and the Educational Policy Unit of the University of the Western Cape, and held in Cape Town, South Africa, 27–29 March, 2001.

Balintulo, M. (2001). Interview. www.chet.org.za/reflections.asp.

Bezuidenhout, P. (2001). Interview. www.chet.org.za/reflections.asp.

Bisseker, C. (2000). Curbing the Growth of Private and Foreign Colleges. *Financial Mail*, 1 September.

Botha, T.R. (2001). Interview. www.chet.org.za/reflections.asp.

Cairns, M. (2001). Interview. www.chet.org.za/reflections.asp.

Department of Education (1997). Higher Education Act of the Republic of South Africa, No. 101 of 1997. Pretoria.

Department of Education (1999). Higher Education Amendment Act No. 55 of 1999. Pretoria.

Department of Foreign Affairs (2001). The New Partnerships for Africa's Development (NEPAD). www.africanrecovery.org.

Fehnel, R.A. (2000). Forecasting the Future of South African Higher Education. In: J. Hofmeyr & H. Perold (eds), *Delivering Africa's Education Renaissance in South Africa*. Education Africa Forum Fourth Edition. Johannesburg: Education Africa.

Fehnel, R.A. (2001). African Higher Education: Massification and Future Trends. In: P. Altbach & D. Teferra (eds), *Handbook of African Education*. Boston College.

Gordon, E. (2001a). A Smoking Gun ... *Mail and Guardian*, May 18–24.

Gordon, E. (2001b). Are We Regulating Away the Future of Higher Education? *Mail and Guardian*, January 22–29.

Gutto, S. (2000). Constitutional and Legal Aspects of the Recommended Considerations for the Development of a Regulatory Framework for Private Higher Education Institutions. Final report. Pretoria: Department of Education and the Council on Higher Education.

Hopper, R. (1998). Emerging Private Universities in Bangladesh. *International Higher Education*, 10 (Winter).

Kelly, K.F. (2001). *Meeting Needs and Making Profits: The Rise of For-Profit Degree-Granting Institutions*. Washington: Education Commission of the States.

Kotecha, P. (2001). Remarks made on a Panel on Private Higher Education, Conference on Globalisation and Higher Education. Hosted by the Society for Research into Higher Education and the Educational Policy Unit of the University of the Western Cape.

Lee, M.N.N. (1998). Corporatization and Privatization of Malaysian Higher Education. *International Higher Education*, 10 (Winter).

Lee, S.H. (1999). Korean Private Higher Education Faces Economic Crisis. *International Higher Education*, 13 (Fall).

Mabizela, M. (2000). Towards a Typology of Structural Patterns of Private-Public Higher Education in South Africa: A Contextual Analysis. Draft M.Ed thesis. Cape Town: Faculty of Education, University of the Western Cape.

Mabizela, M., Subotsky, G. & Thayer, B. (2000). The Emergence of Private Higher Education in South Africa: Key Issues and Challenges. A Discussion Document prepared for the Council on Higher Education Annual Consultative Conference. Cape Town: Education Policy Unit, University of the Western Cape.

Mangan, K.S. (2001). Top Business Schools Try Collaboration over Competition. The Chronicle of Higher Education. *Daily News*. July 6.

Marcus, R. (2001). Interview. www.chet.org.za/reflections.asp.

Rossouw, H. (2001). South Africa Spends $163-Million a Year on Students Who Drop Out. The Chronicle of Higher Education. *Daily News*. May 17.

Salmi, J. (1994). *Higher Education: The Lessons of Experience*. Washington: The World Bank.

Sayed, Y. (2001). The Growth of Private Higher Education Sector in South Africa: Governance and Regulation Challenges. Paper presented at the Conference on Globalisation and Higher Education: Views from the South. Hosted by the Society for Research into Higher Education and the Educational Policy Unit of the University of the Western Cape, Cape Town.

Sehoole, T. (2001). Higher Education Policy Documents in South Africa: 1990--2000. Commissioned paper. www.chet.org.za/papers.asp.

Taylor, A. (2001). The View from the Ministry. *Mail and Guardian*. May 18–24.

Technikons Amendment Act No.27 of 1995. Government Gazette No. 1059.

Van Rensburg, D.J.J. (2001). Interview. www.chet.org.za/reflections.asp.

World Bank (2000). *African Development Indicators 2000*. Washington: The World Bank.

World Development Report (1999). *Knowledge for Development*. Oxford University Press.

Xako, S. (2000). Bill Seeks Power for Education Registrar. *Business Day*. August 16.

Yonezawa, A. (1999). Further Privatization in Japanese Higher Education? *International Higher Education*, 13 (Fall).

CHAPTER 11

NICO CLOETE & RICHARD FEHNEL

THE EMERGENT LANDSCAPE

Ever since the South African Council on Higher Education (CHE) issued its report 'Towards a New Higher Education Landscape' in June 2000, the higher education community has been occupied with debates about reshaping the terrain. Although there was some debate about it, the CHE proposal was not the scenery envisaged by the National Commission on Higher Education (NCHE) and the White Paper on higher education transformation (Department of Education,1997), which stated that: 'The Ministry of Education favours an integrated and co-ordinated system of higher education, but not a uniform system. An important task in planning and managing a single national co-ordinated system is to ensure diversity in its organisational form and in the institutional landscape, and offset pressures for homogenisation. ... The risk the Ministry wishes to avoid is a laissez-faire proliferation of higher education programmes by an increasing range of providers, without the benefit of a planning framework and without adequate safeguards to ensure the quality of provision. This would almost certainly result in the unplanned blurring of institutional roles and functions ...' (2.37; 2.38).

Drawing on preceding chapters in Section 2, the analysis in this chapter shows that a proliferation of programmes by an increasing range of providers did indeed occur outside a planning framework. It also shows how institutions responded to the changing policy environment and the market, and describes the emergence of a new landscape that is beginning to break the apartheid mould. Appendix 4 provides a statistical overview of the 36 public institutions in the South African higher education system at the end of 2000. Figures are provided for each institution by student headcount, broken down by mode of delivery (contact/distance), black and female student enrolment, as well as enrolment by major fields of study.

1. HARD BOUNDARIES, REAL DRIFT

Prior to 1994, government policy made a clear distinction between academic and career/vocational programmes and the institutions within which these were offered – universities and technikons, respectively. A further boundary existed between institutions dedicated to providing 'contact' or 'distance' programmes. These hard boundaries between academic versus vocational, and contact versus distance started blurring in the post-1994 period.

N. Cloete et al. (eds.). Transformation in Higher Education. 245-260.
© 2007 *Springer.*

1.1. Programme differentiation

As was discussed in Chapter 8 on curriculum, a number of institutions embarked on considerable curricular reforms, informed by the NCHE policy proposals and the new National Qualifications Framework (NQF). The net results of these efforts seem to have been both increased differentiation of curricula in the more enterprising institutions, including the development of many more interdisciplinary courses, and the beginning of 'programme drift': some universities started offering more vocationally oriented programmes in order to attract new students, and some of the technikons began offering B Tech and postgraduate degrees such as MBAs and other postgraduate courses that were previously offered only by universities. Modes of delivery became more flexible as some residential institutions began offering distance education programmes, and some institutions started mixing distance and contact delivery modes, thus breaking down the old rigid distinction between the two. In short, at the programme level in public institutions there was suddenly more differentiation in curricula and a much greater variety of programme options for educational consumers to consider. For the institutions, however, including the private providers, the price was increased uncertainty about their mission.

Clark (1996) and others argue that programme differentiation is not only inevitable; it is desirable because it has the effect of increasing access, responsiveness, and fiscal diversity – all generally regarded as 'virtues' of education policy. Where previously there had been a narrow range of programmes, there quickly emerged a wide range of course options and delivery options, particularly in the urban areas. By 2001 students had a range of programme and institutional choices unprecedented in the history of South African higher education.

Clark (1996) provides a useful conceptual guide to understanding the dominant trend towards higher levels of programme differentiation within institutions. This trend started in relation to the increasing specialisation of knowledge in the post-war years of the mid-twentieth century. Specialisation and the resulting processes of differentiation taking place at the level of academic disciplines have had the effect of making some institutions of higher education more capable of responding to increasingly diverse demands than others in a context where economic, political and cultural systems within nations have grown and become more elaborate in recent decades.

Chapter 8 suggests that it was not cognitive changes in the disciplines that provided a strong stimulus for the introduction of certain types of programmes, but market pressures to attract students and notions of what employers require, particularly within a context of globalisation. In some institutions this coincided with a certain reading, or misreading, of what new government policy prescribed regarding the introduction of flexible, modular programmes. The chapter also suggests that in the South African context, capacity is a crucial factor: institutions with effective leaders and well functioning management systems could choose to embark on curriculum reform, or choose not to, regardless of government policy or market pressures.

As the chapters on funding, students and curriculum show, however, these processes of differentiation and diversification have not been an unproblematic good. Institutions have been slow to put quality regulation measures in place; irrational and inefficient duplication abounds in both the public and private sectors; and pedagogically it is not clear that many of these 'relevant' programmes are appropriate to the learning needs of disadvantaged students.

1.2. Institutional drift

The period post-1994 saw higher education institutions engaging in a range of actions and activities to position themselves in the new terrain: the scramble by some public institutions for programmes that attract fee-paying students and the paralysis of others which were sliding towards possible closure or merger; the 'de-listing' of corporate education providers that only months earlier had been the toast of the Johannesburg Stock Exchange; the decision by most trans-national institutions to abandon their South African dreams – all these behaviours beg description and analysis that will shed light on the interplay among the forces of policy, globalisation and institutional culture.

Considerable drift occurred across the binary divide. According to the National Plan for Higher Education, 'the programme distinction between technikons and universities has been eroded in line with the White Paper's suggestion of a "loosening of boundaries" between institutional types ... [which] has resulted in a slow, but sure, move towards uniformity ...' (Department of Education, 2001: 56–57). Presumably the 'uniformity' refers to the fact that with the closing down of the Advisory Committee for Universities and Technikons (AUT) which previously regulated the introduction of new programmes, universities increasingly started offering career orientated programmes such as tourism and development studies, while the technikons were supposed to be offering mainly technological degrees, but in fact many of them were offering social science and humanities programmes.

To restrict the drift across the binary divide, the National Plan for Higher Education (Department of Education, 2001) declared that for the next five years at least, the boundaries would not be loosened, but would be maintained by the Ministry. Quite contradictorily, the National Plan also stated that a merger would take place (one of the first of its kind in the system) across this binary divide, that is between two universities and a technikon: the Universities of Vista and South Africa, and Technikon SA. The three institutions have in common their predominantly distance mode of delivery, and the merger would create one of the largest higher education institutions in the world (about 200.000 students) with the intention, presumably, of achieving a certain economy of scale. At the same time the merger of two universities with a technikon immediately collapses the binary divide. The question raised by this is whether the vocational/academic divide will be maintained in different institutional types (universities and technikons) or within a single comprehensive institution that offers both types of programmes. It is not difficult to predict that such an arrangement will, in the first instance, help to reduce the 'stigma' attached to vocation or career orientated programmes and secondly, lead to a drift, or a blurring between academic and vocational programmes.

Currently, there is still more coherence in the technikon sector than in the university sector; this is due both to the shared mission and the strong influence of the Committee of Technikon Principals. On the one hand the historically black technikons could be regarded as a fairly focused sector that has done significantly better than the black university sector. On the other hand this group is differentiating into a sub-group of five small technikons in peri-urban areas where they are becoming increasingly unsustainable as independent institutions, and a sub-group of three, soon to be two, urban technikons which are doing well. Technikon ML Sultan, an historically disadvantaged institution, is merging with the previously white Natal Technikon into what could be among the biggest higher education institutions in the country. The third institution, Peninsula Technikon, has been described as 'arguably the most successful historically black institution in South Africa' (Cloete & Bunting, 2002). This has been achieved through a combination of stable leadership, building a campus community, and focusing on, and strengthening a core mission. An historically white technikon, Technikon Witwatersrand in Johannesburg, has become predominantly black, which means that there is now a group of strong, predominantly black technikons emerging in three urban centres.

The diversity of the landscape was reduced through the incorporation of the teacher training college sector into higher education. In 1994 there were 105 state colleges of education, of which 93 provided initial teacher training to about 70.000 students. By 1997 the number of contact colleges had been whittled down to 78, and by 1999 to a mere 50, with a student enrolment of 15.000. The provincial process of identifying colleges for incorporation intensified in 2000 and by the end 27 colleges (25 contact colleges and two distance education colleges) had been earmarked for incorporation into 17 higher education institutions. Those institutions earmarked had served approximately 10.000 contact students and 5.000 distance education students (Pratt, 2001). The incorporation brought to an end a well-established, but poorly functioning provincial system, with a few notable exceptions, that trained teachers for the public school sector.

According to Pratt (2001) this development forms part of the broader transformation process currently underway in the higher education system, and is intended also to address the weaknesses identified in the college sector. It is not without precedent in other parts of the world, but in South Africa the demise of the teacher college sector is regarded by many educators as an inestimable loss in terms of infrastructural and human resource capital. This is felt to be especially acute at a time when the country still faces daunting developmental challenges, and where colleges, unique in character and style of operation, were well-positioned to play a significant niche role alongside other providers of tertiary education.

Another line of argument is that while there was indeed some 'infrastructural and resource capital' in a small number of colleges, as a sector, the teacher colleges were the most expensive and inefficient of all the higher education institutions. In the end, the incorporation of the colleges into other institutions was driven by economics.

The most important contribution to diversity came from the re-emergence of the private higher education sector in the mid-1990s after more than a half-century of being dormant. Its place in the landscape was initially seen as benign and the growth of private higher education was facilitated by important policy changes. Basically, four types of private providers emerged: large, publicly traded firms with different types of operations; small, independent niche providers; trans-national universities operating alone or in partnership with South African institutions and businesses; and lastly, a hybrid form of corporate universities, also operating in partnership with South African public institutions and businesses.

The rapid expansion of private providers, however, ran into an even more rapid policy about-turn by the Ministry that had two concerns: protecting the general public from programmes of dubious quality, on the one hand and, on the other, protecting some public institutions which attributed their diminished student enrolment to competition from the private institutions. These policy changes contributed to a decline in the number of private organisations seeking registration and accreditation. Perhaps most significant was the embargo on partnerships between public and private institutions. This policy development stopped a number of innovative undertakings that were planned and which could have addressed some of the priority areas in higher education, such as increasing enrolments in science, mathematics and technology courses.

In summary, differences in institutional behaviour, lingering advantages and disadvantages from the past, and a greatly deregulated environment resulted in a process of differentiation that, whilst still infused by the legacy of the past, also enabled the institutional landscape to start breaking out of the earlier mould. The next section will attempt to categorise these changes in a new typology that is not entirely overlaid with race and ethnicity.

2. LANDSCAPE CHANGES: A NEW TYPOLOGY

The typology developed below combines the notion of domains with the strategies that institutions have followed to enhance, defend or consolidate themselves in a context of change. *Webster's Dictionary* (1977) defines a domain as a territory over which rule or control is exercised (p338). In the typology which follows, two factors are considered: knowledge as the core territory of higher education, and students as the sphere of operation. The categorisation includes four 'types':

- Domain-consolidation: stable student growth.
- Domain-enterprise: expanding student and income base.
- Domain-seeking: fluctuating student body.
- Domain-crisis: declining student base.

The conceptual types are both analytical and empirical in nature. The analytical aspect is informed by the literature on higher education, particularly Clarke (1996) and Meek (1996); the empirical is provided by the data and insights presented in Chapters 4 to 10. The categories for the new typology are exploratory and there are no hard boundaries. Some institutions may fit mostly into a particular category, while others may overlap categories. More importantly, this categorisation is dynamic in the sense that an institution in one category may be moving towards another category.

2.1. Domain-consolidation: stable student growth

This group of institutions can be described as domain-strong, characterised by strategies designed to strengthen their core business. Strategies included, for example, the strengthening professional training (law, medicine, engineering) at the Universities of Cape Town or Stellenbosch, or focusing on general formative undergraduate education at Rhodes University or career education at Peninsula Technikon.

The core business of higher education includes research, and these institutions developed strong research orientations with focussed and well-directed research portfolios and strong research management. Chapter 9 on research shows that institutions in this category were able to increase research and contract funding dramatically and in this sense they adopted strongly entrepreneurial approaches to change. Institutions such as the Universities of Cape Town, Natal and Stellenbosch attracted substantially more research and contract funding than their 'domain- enterprising' counterparts. The research contract funding of some of these top institutions exceeded the entire government subsidy of about 30% of the institutions in the system.

Research is linked to staff qualifications which are, in effect, the academic capital of the institutions. Chapter 6 on staff shows that these were generally high-capacity institutions with well over 40% of their staff being in possession of a doctorate and 80% at the masters level or higher. Undoubtedly, having a better qualified staff gave these institutions a competitive advantage in terms of teaching and research.

With regard to programmes, the strong faculties in this group of institutions tended to maintain their disciplinary identities while there was programme experimentation in some of the weaker faculties such as the humanities and the social sciences. Institutions such as the Universities of Cape Town, Witwatersrand and Natal responded to the competition for undergraduate students in the humanities and social sciences by introducing more relevant programmes although, as Chapter 8 on curriculum shows, this was not always successful. The most successful programmes were in the professions and the sciences, and the institutions have used these to attract students – a strategy which differs markedly from that of seeking students, as will be shown later.

In the conclusion to Part 1: Funding and Students, this category of institutions is described as adopting an *'internal-consolidation-first'* strategy because they believed that they were not likely to be affected in any major way, either positively or negatively, by the adoption of a new funding framework. They became involved in internal consolidation and adaptation activities, designed primarily (a) to change and/or strengthen institutional missions in line with the requirements of the 1997 White Paper, and (b) to improve internal efficiencies. All of them became aware of costs, and most instituted cost-saving measures such as outsourcing, staff reduction, etc. However, a major difference from the domain-enterprise institutions is that the emphasis in this category was on cost saving, rather than new income generation. Financially these institutions did not grow as much as the enterprise group: they increased their government appropriation by R450-million (36%) over the five years. By 2000 they were all financially sound with three, including an historically black institution, being given a 'blue ribbon' rating (private communication, consultant to the Department of Education, 2001).

According to Bunting, this group consisted primarily of the historically white English-medium universities, one historically white Afrikaans-medium university (Free State)[1] and a few historically white and black technikons. During the years after 1997, this group of institutions had stable, low-growth student enrolments.

In general these institutions demonstrated strong leadership and management cores, but as Chapter 7 on leadership shows, no single style was prevalent. The most common leadership approaches in this category were *'reforming collegialism'* and *'transformative managerialism'*. In these institutions the senior academics, with power based on their disciplines and/or departments still have an important say in the matters of the institution but, as Chapter 6 on staff shows, there are increasing tensions between a collegial and a more managerial approach.

Movement within this category was between remaining 'traditional-collegial' and becoming more enterprising and more managerial. It could be argued that the managerial impulse was driven both by a response to global reform trends, and by government policy demands.

To a large extent institutions in this category defined their core business around the traditional academic mission, and managed student enrolment within a planned range. They experimented with some new activities, but it could be argued that for these institutions, prestige was, and still is, the basis from which students and money follow. Their market strategy was to do better what higher education institutions are traditionally supposed to do – which is not only a market strategy, but foregrounds a traditional conception of higher education.

Overall these institutions had a fairly clear, albeit not uncontested, notion of their core activities and they attained a surprising degree of stability in one of the most rapidly changing societies in the world. This stability, however, laid them open to the charge that they had not transformed sufficiently.

2.2. Domain-enterprise: expanding student and income base

Burton Clarke caused a stir in higher education with the publication of his book *The Entrepreneurial University* (1999) in which he identified five entrepreneurial universities. These institutions were innovative examples that combined academic excellence with successful responses to the market. Part of the stir was that all five were in Europe, and none in the US, but the five criteria identified also provoked much debate, and subsequent imitation. The characteristics are: a strengthened leadership steering core, an enhanced development periphery, a discretionary funding base, a stimulated academic heartland and a pervasive belief in entrepreneurialism.

In South Africa a number of institutions, predominantly the historically white Afrikaans-medium universities, adopted an entrepreneurial approach. In the words of a prominent vice-chancellor from an Afrikaans university: 'The interesting point is that the universities that have been mostly criticised for having nurtured apartheid for many years, were the universities that moved the fastest and are more entrepreneurial. Maybe a factor is that many of these universities are still younger universities, and as a consequence could move faster' (Coetzee, 2001). As will be shown below, it is highly debatable whether South African institutions satisfy Clarke's criteria for entrepreneurialism and therefore the term 'enterprising' seems more appropriate in this context.

What is indisputable is that in the post-1994 period a group of institutions responded to a combination of government policy and the introduction of a higher education market by deciding that it would not be 'business-as-usual'. They diversified curricula, introduced market-orientated courses, increased access through modularisation, provided a range of flexible delivery modes, established 'satellite' campuses to deliver courses to clients in the rural and semi-rural areas and formed partnerships with private colleges for course delivery. In some institutions, such as the Universities of Pretoria and Stellenbosch, a mixed model developed in which certain discipline areas were strengthened and others were commercialised. While the University of Stellenbosch, like the University of Natal, leaned more towards domain-enterprise, both seemed to try and strike a balance between domain-consolidation and domain-enterprise, albeit not always successfully.

Regarding research, these institutions increased contract research, strongly promoted partnerships with industry and supported joint profit-making ventures. Chapter 9 on research describes the orientation as 'entrepreneurial' with an aggressive pursuit of research partnerships and contracts. While there were pockets where basic research was still being conducted, the dominant orientation was towards applications research and strategic research. Chapter 9 shows that an institution such as the University of Pretoria increased its contract research from R19-million to R93-million and that the University of Potchefstroom became the third most successful institution in bidding for Thrip money. Government-steered applications-orientated research funding is still flowing freely to some of the historically white Afrikaans-medium institutions in the new South Africa. It must be remembered that the applications orientation is not new to the Afrikaans universities; many of them had been deeply involved in the apartheid 'military-industrial-research complex' prior to 1994 (see Chapter 9).

The majority of the domain-enterprise universities, like the domain-consolidation group, are located in the high capacity category in terms of staff qualifications. In both types the high capacity was uneven across faculties (see Chapter 6 on staff). In the enterprise group, however, the focus was outward rather than inward, and the strategy was geared towards marketing the institutions' academic capital.

By combining staff capacity with managerial capacity and an outward orientation, these institutions were able to increase their student enrolments dramatically. Since the old SAPSE funding formula was still in place, in the post-1997 period this group of institutions generated considerable increases in their government subsidies. Their combined government appropriation total increased over the five-year period by R820-million (or 69%).

However, the figures also show that this strategy was not an unqualified success. By 2000 those institutions that had invested in delivery mechanisms such as satellite campuses were experiencing severe liquidity problems while those that followed the private college partnership franchising model could be regarded as having achieved a 'blue ribbon' financial status (private communication, consultant to the Department of Education, 2001).

The conclusion to Part 1: Funding and Students describes a subset of five of the six historically white Afrikaans-medium universities and one of the historically white technikons as adopting adaptive strategies that could be called 'window-of-opportunity' and 'increase-the-product-range'. The domain-expansion strategy adopted by these institutions was a simple one: they retained their traditional white student enrolments, modestly increased their black student enrolments on their main campuses, formed partnerships with private providers to enrol large numbers of African students in distance education programmes, and set up satellite campuses in areas where the majority of students enrolling could be expected to be African. In other words, the strategy of these institutions was largely domain expansion in student markets in which they were able to operate unchallenged by government regulators or by competitors.

The dominant leadership style (Chapter 7) in this category ranges from 'strategic managerialism' to 'unwavering entrepreneurship'. The leadership task was seen as reconfiguring the institution to become more competitive and market-oriented through the vigorous adaptation of corporate management principles and techniques to the higher education setting. The change agenda within these institutions was driven by a strong, decisive, centre (usually located in the office of the vice-chancellor) that was buttressed by sophisticated management-support systems and structures which were staffed by a highly competent middle management layer (Stumpf, 2001). Considerable resources were put into fundraising and the marketing of the institution (image-making). The whole institution was 'costed' with identified loss and profit-making 'business units' and non-core activities were outsourced as far as possible. While the 'strategic managerialists' tried to straddle the academic/enterprise divide, and often oscillated between the two, the 'unwavering entrepreneurs' drove a much harder commercialisation strategy.

In this category there is a constant tension between moving towards consolidation, the domain-defence approach, and pursuing more markets. It could be argued that the achieved balance depends on the strength of the academic core and the tension between those academics who see research as their market versus those who see the student market as being more lucrative. The massive expansion in student numbers at these institutions demonstrates the effectiveness of combining reputation with strategies for flexible access.

Among the private higher education institutions in South Africa, were institutions such as Monash and the University of Wales that are traditional mid-level institutions in their home countries. These institutions, behaving like any aspiring local business that wanted to become an international corporation, decided that the local market was saturated, or too competitive, and expanded overseas. The knowledge domain was not expanded since they did not offer different types of courses in the new context; the strategy was merely one of market expansion, derived from a local domain-enterprise strategy. Bond University from Australia, DeMontford and Oxford Brooks in the UK were somewhat different examples in the same category. From the start these institutions were established in South Africa as part of an enterprising strategy to develop a different kind of higher education, and not as conventional institutions that became enterprising in order to survive.

As was shown above, not all the higher education enterprises have been unqualified successes. Financially, those institutions that invested intensively in infrastructure for student expansion found themselves on shaky ground. Some of the public/private partnerships designed to increase student numbers attracted widespread criticism (Kulati, 2000) with the Minister putting a moratorium on all partnerships. At this stage very few academics, let alone entrepreneurs, would bet their pension funds on the future of the international institutions such as Monash and Bond in South Africa.

In terms of the analytical triangle, the domain-enterprise institutions responded to, even exploited, the government policy framework, but their main orientation was towards the market where they utilised their strong links, particularly with the Afrikaner business community and other networks. Particularly striking in the domain-enterprise institutions was the level of awareness of costs and the business approach – an awareness and strategy very different from any institutional behaviour in higher education in the pre-1994 period.

2.3. Domain-seeking: fluctuating student body

Removing restrictions on student movement, programme regulation and the marketisation of higher education undermined the mission certainty of a whole range of institutions. This group of institutions, which included a number of historically white universities (such as the University of Port Elizabeth), black universities (such as the University of the Western Cape) and technikons (such as Witwatersrand, Border, and Northern Gauteng), responded to opportunities in the environment and at the same time perceived these as threats. It was amongst this group that the binary divide was the most permeable with some technikons trying to become 'universities of technology' and some universities offering career-related diplomas and degrees. Many of the technikons, and even a few universities, introduced new, directly market-orientated courses such as degrees and diplomas in tourism. In this category the seeking of a domain was directed outwards – rather than seeking an academic domain, the institutions sought markets.

An interesting feature of this group was that their student numbers generally grew, albeit sometimes with rather dramatic swings. These institutions were not able to manage their student enrolments in as planned a fashion as the domain-defence group, and for this group student numbers were the main source of additional income, not industry partnerships or research grants. They tried to gain market share through a variety of 'innovations', but had most success with increasing student numbers.

This category had a strong pull towards the market, but was also the most threatened by the market. A good example is the University of Port Elizabeth which had a partnership with a private provider for undergraduate students, introduced inter-disciplinary career-orientated programmes in the social sciences, started offering flexible postgraduate programmes in a variety of settings and with different delivery modes and, in its most recent venture, sought to attract students from Israel and Turkey (Cloete & Bunting, 2002). On the one hand this could be regarded as responsiveness; on the other hand it could also be a symptom of an institution with a weak disciplinary base in search of a niche in the new South Africa. For this group, research was almost entirely applications driven, but from the limited data it seems that these institutions were not as successful in increasing contract research as the institutions with established reputations (see Chapter 9).

In terms of staff capacity, a number of the universities in this category fell in the 'middle band' (see Chapter 6 on staff) and the technikons in the middle to upper band. Not only did they have significantly lower numbers of staff with doctorates, but they also had larger numbers of staff who did not yet have masters degrees.

The lack of implementation of a new funding framework, and the abolition of the Advisory Council for Universities and Technikons created opportunities for these institutions to increase their range of programmes, be more flexible about their modes of delivery, and accumulate funds through government subsidy, tuition fees and partnerships. Some increased their proportion of government allocations fairly dramatically, with at least one attaining a 'blue ribbon' rating (private communication, consultant to the Department of Education, 2001). However, for the majority of institutions in this category their proportion of government appropriations increased less than that of institutions in the 'domain-consolidation' and the 'domain-enterprise' categories. A number of these institutions were classified as being financially 'at-risk' (see Chapter 4).

These institutions seemed to be displaying what Dill (2001) calls 'reputation-seeking' behaviour through leadership styles that could be described as either *transformative managerialism* or *unwavering entrepreneurship*. The former group attempted to obtain more political and academic legitimacy, while the latter attempted to become more enterprising. A key issue is whether these institutions had the administrative skills to implement their strategies and, more importantly, whether they had the necessary academic expertise to compete in the market.

Many of the institutions in this category were uncertain as to what their domain of expertise was in the new South Africa and seemed to oscillate between the strategies of strengthening the academic domain and seeking student markets. It was clearly very difficult to do both at the same time, especially as the former is a long-term, expensive process not rewarded directly by government. In the domain-consolidation approach, the institution would market its knowledge and expertise and feel confident that if it had 'good' knowledge, it would attract clients. The domain-seekers on the other hand, would identify knowledge needs, and then try to find the knowledge, either by adapting or 'stretching' existing knowledge resources or by trying to buy in expertise. In terms of quality, hiring part-time people with relevant knowledge may be a better strategy than 'stretching' but this was very difficult for institutions in rural areas where one could not attract people on a part-time basis. An institution such as the Rand Afrikaans University, located in a large urban area, seemed to be following this strategy with its high proportion of part-time staff.

It is exactly in searching for a student market that the public and private institutions seemed to enter into direct competition, but this is not entirely accurate. Many public institutions blamed their post-1994 woes either on a lack of redress, or on competition from the private institutions. In fact the real competition came from other public institutions with greater prestige or better reputations. The greatest potential market, which the domain-seeking public institutions shunned, was at the higher end of the further education market. With public institutions having a mimetic eye 'upwards' they missed the market 'below'. This was where Damelin, Boston College and Varsity College entered the picture, and with a double edge: they provided both a bridge between school and higher education, and a bridge to a job opportunity at the same time.

It must be remembered that the private domain-seeking institutions were really market niche seekers. In South Africa they did not have their own knowledge domain because they did not produce knowledge, unlike private institutions in the US. 'Private' higher education institutions in the third world are simply knowledge traders; they neither produce new knowledge nor do they train academics. They buy knowledge from the local or the international public systems and in this sense they live off the public system. Their competitive advantages are in their marketing strategies, their flexible product delivery and packaging, and their ability to identify niche markets.

It could be expected that in the public domain-seeking group there would be constant movement between those institutions which moved closer to the domain-enterprise category and another group that can be described as 'domain static'. As outlined in the conclusion to Part 1: Funding and Students, the financial and student data give the impression that these institutions were static, or 'go-with-the-flow'. The empirical impression of stasis, however, does not capture the constant (sometimes frenetic) activity in these institutions as they sought to respond to new government policies and the market. Even a cursory look at the three-year plans of many of these institutions reveals that they had a plethora of intentions to expand products and student markets. These plans, without actual implementation or 'movement' could be called 'phantom domains', because in reality the institutions may have had neither the academic capital nor the management capacity to put plans into operation. But it is misleading to imply that these institutions were passive in the new South Africa.

Most of the institutions in this category felt considerable anxiety about their fate in relation to the recommendations from the Minister's National Working Group on mergers, as these had the potential to radically alter their already uncertain identities. The mergers proposed by the Minister's group aimed at overcoming apartheid-induced fragmentation and inefficiencies, and meeting the challenges of reconstruction and development in the context of globalisation (Department of Education, 2001). The key principles were equity, sustainability and productivity, informed by a set of performance indicators. These merger proposals could be seen as a form of 'coerced co-operation' that would have serious implications for institutional domains, and by implication, for mission and identity.

In terms of the analytic triangle, the strongest interaction for this group of institutions was between government and the institutions, with the institutions trying to establish more and diverse links with society and the market, but struggling to do so. The main factors that could have been barriers to a more successful penetration of the market were variable academic and management capacity, and a lack of previous experience with the market.

2.4. Domain-crisis: declining student base

This is a fairly large group consisting of two subgroups of institutions: (a) those with stable student enrolments, and (b) those that had declining student enrolments. The group with stable student enrolments included five historically black technikons, and that with declining enrolments included six historically black universities. This group started with a mission to train homeland bureaucrats and then became sites of struggle against the apartheid regime – one of the first great unintended outcomes of higher education policy in South Africa. During the pre-1994 phase these institutions never really managed to develop an academic project (Ndebele, 2001): their core business was politics, either collaboration or opposition. These institutions were never intended, nor equipped, to become strong academic or research institutions. In the post-1994 period, with unprecedented student choice and staff mobility, and with providers competing for students due to the poor school outputs, this group lost both students and staff.

Located in the poor, rural, or peri-urban areas, these institutions were frequently encouraged to develop a rural or agricultural orientation. In the National Plan, the Minister of Education once again implored the historically black institutions to, 'not only develop a clear mission and sense of purpose, but also ... ensure that the necessary administrative, management, governance and academic structures are put in place to support the mission'(1.4:11). While this advice seems eminently sensible and laudable, the contradiction is that this is exactly what the audit reports (Steele, 2000) and some of the independent assessors (Nhlapo, 2001) claimed was absent at the black universities. The lack of human and material resources was at the heart of the problem; the prescribed remedy by the Minister was thus a description of the problem, and not a solution.

But it was not only a matter of human and material resources. A survey of the historically black universities found that many of the vice-chancellors and senior staff interviewed in the study rejected the development of a new dispensation that might lead the universities in the direction of trying to address the education and training needs of the communities in which they were located. Instead, the dominant vision was one that could best be described as 'Rhodes University in the 1950s' – rural, with a traditional and privileged notion of a university (Siwani & Fehnel, 1992).

The problem of domain uncertainty was well illustrated during a national planning seminar in 2001. The planner from one of these institutions said that the request from the Department of Education for a plan that outlined projected growth and possible niche areas would 'start a whole new debate about the role of the university' – despite the fact that the institution had already submitted two three-year rolling plans (1998 and 1999) in which its role had been articulated.

The chapters on curriculum and research (Chapters 8 and 9) show that even when institutions in this category tried to innovate, the managerial capacity required to implement the proposed ideas was absent. The research output of these institutions increased minimally in the post-1994 period and the small-scale capacity development programmes initiated by the Human Sciences Research Council and the National Research Foundation did not significantly improve capacity.

This was mere 'survivalism' with no capacity to compete nationally and an increased dependency on limited Department of Education/National Research Foundation funding. In the words of Bawa and Mouton (Chapter 9), 'there is evidence that the gap between the "haves" and the "have-nots" in knowledge production is widening, not narrowing.'

According to the classification in the staff chapter (Chapter 6) this set of institutions was the low-capacity group. This was due both to the historical disadvantage of this group and the increased post-apartheid mobility that allowed, indeed encouraged, many good academics to leave – either for more prestigious urban institutions or for government and business.

With regard to students, these institutions hoped that regardless of what individual institutions did, the force of student demand predicted by the National Commission on Higher Education (1996) would cause their student enrolments to continue growing, and that government funds for redress would enable them to deal with expanded enrolments and help them become competitive with the historically white universities. This strategy failed in the case of the historically black university group because the institutions did not receive government redress funds and, furthermore, they lost 35.800 students between 1994 and 2000.

The conclusion to Part 1: Funding and Students describes a *'waiting-for-redress'* strategy according to which institutions expected that in addition to institutional redress funds, they would receive funds for individual redress in the form of student financial aid payments that would be paid directly to them rather than to individual students. The strategy was thus one of waiting for government to deliver on the White Paper commitment to institutional and individual redress funds. Instead, the historically white institutions, which had recruited more black students than initially expected, received an increasingly large proportion of the funds from the National Student Financial Aid Scheme (NSFAS).

The government appropriation total for the historically black universities in this group increased by R200-million from 1996 to 2001 – an increase over the period of only 18%. This increase was below that of South Africa's consumer price index, primarily because of declining student enrolments in these institutions. The historically black technikons in this group, in marked contrast, had experienced rapid growth in their student enrolments during the post-1994 period. Their government appropriation total increased by R250-million (or 76% off a very low base) over the same period. Because institutions in both groups experienced problems with the collection of student fees, and due to low private income, none of the institutions in these two groupings had high financial ratings at the end of 2000. Four of the universities and two of the technikons had ratings which placed them in an 'at-risk' category. The other institutions received 'adequate' financial ratings (private communication, consultant to Department of Education, 2001).

The leadership approach at these institutions tended to be characterised by crisis management and decision-avoidance, and the lack of institutional cohesion made it difficult for leaders to steer, let alone drive, change. Kulati and Moja (Chapter 7) describe this as 'more of an institutional condition than an approach to leadership'. Institutional leaders had less substantive authority under these circumstances than in situations where leaders had the option of adopting transformative or managerial leadership styles. These institutions also tended to have very weak, ineffective second-tier management layers, and there was frequently a lack of trust between the key stakeholder groups and institutional management. Consequently, decision-making processes within these institutions were protracted, highly politicised, and were frequently not conclusive. Even after agreements were reached, the commitment by stakeholders to decisions made could never be guaranteed.

In a situation with strong government pressure (push) for change from the top, and a rampant free market (pull), being static ('waiting-for-redress') led to a situation where other institutions moved on. For the institutions in this category, being left behind effectively meant a slide backwards. In this category constant pressure simply produced a movement between stasis (phantom domains) and crisis. For those already in crisis, innovation did not necessarily bring success; in some cases it only restored stasis.

Crises were not only the domain of some public institutions; many private institutions, particularly those operating on a small resource base, also found that the market did not expand as quickly as expected, that there was more competition for a smaller-than-anticipated pool of students, and that set-up and overhead costs escalated. In the process a number of institutions went under, while at others the in-fighting became as vicious as in some of the public institutions. In some of the private institutions crisis became an 'institutional condition', just as in some of the public institutions. What the private institutions did not do was wait for redress. An interesting study would be to examine the different survival strategies these institutions deployed and which were successful.

In the public sector, descriptions such as 'waiting for redress' create the impression that the problems of these institutions were mainly attitudinal, or agency instigated. A study by Habib (2001) on the University of Transkei shows that a set of serious structural socio-economic changes occurred in the former 'homelands' where these institutions were located. They were built within specific rural-ethnic areas as part of the grand apartheid separate development plan, mainly to provide teachers and bureaucrats for their ethnic groups and received line-item funding from the different departments. At the time of writing the post-1994 government simply did not yet have a rural development policy; consequently these institutions were structurally dislocated and were required to compete on equal terms with much stronger institutions in the higher education market.

The disheartening story that emerges relates what happens when institutions without a strong academic domain, with a lack of human and material resources, and a government redress policy that was never implemented, are placed within a competitive market situation – a final confirmation that 'separate' was never 'equal'.

NOTES

[1] By not joining the other Afrikaans universities in raising income through distance education , the University of the Free State ran the risk of receiving sharply diminished levels of income. This led the university principal to remark at one stage that 'by being pedagogically correct, we nearly bankrupted the institution'. Nevertheless the strategy seems to have worked because by 2001 the institution was in sound financial condition (private communication).

REFERENCES

Botha, T.F. (2001). Interview. www.chet.org.za/reflections.asp.

Clark, B. (1996). Diversification of Higher Education: Viability and Change. In: V.L. Meek, L. Goedegebuure, O. Kivinen & R. Rinne (eds), *The Mockers and Mocked: Comparative Perspectives on Diversity, Differentiation and Convergence in Higher Education.* Oxford: Pergamon.

Clark, B. (1998). *Creating Entrepreneurial Universities: Organisational Pathways of Transformation.* Oxford: Pergamon.

Cloete, N. & Bunting, I. (2002). *Transformation Indicators: Case Studies of the University of Port Elizabeth and Peninsula Technikon.* Pretoria: CHET.

Committee of Technikon Principals (2001). Technikons: Towards becoming Universities of Technology: Philosophy and Characteristics. Report of the CTP Task Team. Pretoria.

Coetzee, S. (2001). Interview. www.chet.org.za/reflections.asp.

Council on Higher Education (2000). *Towards a New Higher Education Landscape: Meeting the Equity, Quality and Social Development Imperatives of South Africa in the 21st Century.* Pretoria: CHE.

Council on Higher Education (2001). Founding Document. Higher Education Quality Committee. Pretoria: CHE.

Department of Education (1997). White Paper 3: A Programme for the Transformation of Higher Education. General Notice 1196 of 1997. Pretoria.

Department of Education (2001). National Plan for Higher Education. Pretoria.

Department of Education (2001). The Restructuring of the Higher Education System in South Africa. Report of the National Working Group to the Minister of Education. Pretoria.

Dill, D. (2001). Reflections on US Higher Education: 1994–1999. Case study. www.chet.org.za/papers.asp.

Habib, A. (2001). Structural Disadvantage, Leadership Ineptitude and Stakeholder Complicity: A Study of the Institutional Crisis of the University of the Transkei. Commissioned paper. www.chet.org.za/papers.asp.

Kelly, K.F. (2001). Meeting Needs and Making Profits: The Rise of For-Profit Degree Granting Institutions. Prepared for the Education Commission of the United States.

Kulati, T. (2000). Governance, Leadership and Institutional Change in South African Higher Education: Grappling with Instability. *Tertiary Education and Management,* 6(3),177–192.

Meek, V.L., Goedegebuure, L., Kivinen, O. & Rinne, R. (eds) (1996). *The Mockers and the Mocked: Comparative Perspectives on Diversity, Differentiation and Convergence in Higher Education.* Oxford: Pergamon.

National Commission on Higher Education (1996). *A Framework for Transformation.* Pretoria.

Ndebele, N. (2001). Interview. www.chet.org.za/reflections.asp.

Nhlapo, T. (2000). Investigation into the Affairs of the University of the North by the Independent Assessor Appointed by The Minister of Education. Pretoria: Department of Education.

Pratt, E. (2001). Remodelling Teacher Education: A Perspective on the Cessation of College-Based Teacher Education 1994–2000. Commissioned paper. www.chet.org.za/papers.asp.

Responding to the National Plan for Higher Education: Meeting the Challenges (2001). CHET Conference Report.

Siwani, J. & Fehnel, R.A. (1993). Adult and Continuing Education Programs: An Institutional Analysis Emphasizing Historically Black Universities and Technikons. A Report for USAID. Pretoria: USAID.

Steele, J. (2000). Findings of the Audits of Five Public Universities. Effective Governance Project. Pretoria: CHET.

Stumpf, R. (2001). Higher Education: Funding in the Period 1994–2001. Commissioned paper. www.chet.org.za/papers.asp.

Webster's New Collegiate Dictionary. 1977. Springfield: G and C Merriam Company.

SECTION 2

CONCLUSION

Is the South African higher education system more or less differentiated in 2001 than in 1994? The immediate post-1994 period saw an explosion of new programmes in the public sector and a whole range of new offerings in the private sector. At one of the last meetings of the Advisory Committee for Universities and Technikons, the committee had more than 700 new programme offerings to consider and many of them crossed the binary divide. To assess this vast supermarket was virtually impossible and it may be one of the factors that contributed to the demise of the regulating body.

The changes in South Africa show considerable similarity with the post-liberation phase in Eastern Europe. Vlasceanu and Sadlak (2001) write that most of the systems could be seen as having passed through three stages. The first stage, pre-1990, was one of *imposed homogeneity*, directed by the state. Stage two, from 1990 to 1995, could be described as *disorganised complexity*, with institutions attempting to assert their differences, and the state offering greater autonomy and providing more resources. Stage three, which is still underway, could be called moving towards *organised complexity*, and consists of the challenge of achieving more orderly complexity with a policy-steering role for the state. South Africa certainly went through a 'disorganised complexity' phase in the post-1994 period, and the intention of the National Plan for Higher Education (2001) is towards more organised complexity – but this is not a certainty yet, since some policies may counteract such a trend.

Two centripetal forces towards standardisation are the strong professional training boards that set fairly narrow limits for training in the traditional professions such as medicine, accountants, architects, etc. The national certification council for technikons (SERTEC) prescribes, and assures the quality on national curricula. Institutions can initiate new programmes, but they have to be approved for all the technikons, with individual institutions allowed a local variation of about 30%. Whilst this ensures mobility and a certain level of quality control, it was a powerful pressure for isomorphism in the technikon sector. It remains to be seen if the new Higher Education Quality Committee will exert the same pressure.

Amongst the technikons there is a move towards becoming 'universities of technology' (Committee of Technikon Principals, 2001), which could be interpreted as a form of mimetic isomorphism. However, in the South African context it could also be seen as an 'aspirational isomorphism', because they are aspiring to the status of universities without having the capacity to imitate them, nor do they really want to become exactly like the universities because they want to retain their vocational, career orientation – different but with the same status (which echoes the apartheid landscape ideology described in

261

N. Cloete et al. (eds.), Transformation in Higher Education, 261-264.
© 2007 *Springer.*

Chapter 2). On the universities' side there is only one university, Venda, which is trying to mimic the technikons by calling itself a 'university of technology'. A major problem is that at many of the institutions aspiring to be technology universities, the majority of students are registered in 'vocational' courses in education and business studies.

The weaker institutions operate strongly in terms of mimetic isomorphism in wanting to look like the stronger ones by having a full range of postgraduate programmes. For example one of these institutions has 25 doctoral programmes with only 26 students and not a single PhD graduate (Department of Education, 2000). It also leads to these institutions not addressing the school/higher education interface – which is where there is a considerable student market. Mimetic isomorphism has contributed significantly to some of the inefficiencies that the national government is trying to rationalise.

During 2002 the Minister (Department of Education, 2002) instructed that the number of public institutions be reduced from 36 to 23 and that six 'comprehensive institutions' be established, meaning the merger of former universities and technikons. It was also decided that technikons could be called 'universities of technology'.

In public sector institutions the National Plan and the National Working Group are trying to bring about greater efficiency, mainly through rationalisation and mergers. But as Van Vught (1996) shows, this may lead to coercive isomorphism, meaning that the price paid for greater efficiency may well be a trade-off against diversity, and so, by implication, undermine responsivity. In Australia the Dawkins mergers aimed at creating large institutions that would be able to exploit new student markets and be more diverse. The current evidence is that they have been hugely successful in making higher education almost as big an earner of foreign currency as tourism, and Africa is the next market, but there is strong mimetic isomorphism developing (Meek, 2001).

In the private sector the government moratorium on public-private partnerships and the strict registration drive is mainly informed by concerns about quality; what still has to be demonstrated is whether the moratorium really will promote quality, or whether it does not, instead, end up as a form of coercive isomorphism that severely restricts diversity. In an interview with the Centre for Higher Education Transformation, a manager of a private sector provider described the regulatory attempts of the Minister as not only wanting to regulate the quality of the McDonald's burger, but also wanting to prescribe the size and the shape of the patty, where it can be sold, and how many can be sold.

Van Vught's (1996) suggestion that institutions that are subject to different conditions are more likely to act differently seems true of the 1995–2000 period in the sense that the opening up of a higher education market resulted in certain institutions becoming more enterprising. South Africa experienced unprecedented market growth in terms of student mobility, an explosion of new programmes, more competition, different institutions and less protectionism.

By 2001 the change in government policy, a market correction and an embargo on public/private partnerships contributed to an overall decrease of institutional types and programmes. The merger and co-operation proposals from the Minister's National Working Group will bring about a further, drastic decrease in the number of public institutions.

Another concern about the possible effect of government policy on differentiation is that at a seminar about implications of the NPHE, a consultant to the education department stated that what is clear is that 'institutional adaptation strategies from 2002 will have to be domain strengthening ones' (Responding to the National Plan, 2001:10). Whilst domain strengthening is in itself a laudable goal for the system, if it means strengthening the existing, still-in-the-process-of-differentiating domains, then the effect could be to seriously curb growth and innovation, thus undermining two (expansion and responsiveness) of the three 'pillars' of the White Paper.

The combination of mergers (coercive isomorphism) and technikons becoming 'universities of technology' (mimetic isomorphism) will blur, if not eradicate, the vocational-academic divide with an overall effect of neither strengthening academic programmes nor career orientated vocational education – thus undermining the very intention of the Minister's National Plan for Higher Education (Department of Education, 2002) not to loosen the boundaries for at least the next five years.

It could be argued that current efforts towards government regulation may severely reduce higher education programme diversity, decrease differentiation in the private higher education sector (through coercive isomorphism), and decrease the market-created differentiation of the public sector. This conclusion, however, may obscure the possibility that differentiation in the public sector was as much a polarisation of inequality as a real differentiation of institutional types. What is more certain is that a largely unanticipated combination of market forces and changing government policies contributed to institutional behaviour not seen in South Africa before 1994, and that in 2001 the country still did not have a single, diversified and co-ordinated system. The verdict is still out as to whether the outcome is significant structural differentiation because a plethora of small, weak institutions doing similar things does not amount to differentiation. Likewise, creating a much smaller group of merged institutions may contribute to mimetic isomorphism.

The unexpected interactions between government policy, changing market and societal conditions and a range of institutional adaptive responses resulted in a landscape that was not predicted by government policy, but is nevertheless more diverse and neither as racially nor ethnically determined as in the previous system.

REFERENCES

Committee of Technikon Principals (2001). Technikons: Towards becoming Universities of Technology: Philosophy and Characteristics. Report of the CTP Task Team. Pretoria.

Department of Education (2000). *Higher Education Information System*. Pretoria.

Department of Education (2001). *National Plan for Higher Education*. Pretoria.

Department of Education (2002). *Transformation and Restructuring: A new institutional landscape for higher education*. General Notice 855 of 2002. Pretoria.

Meek. L. (2001). Reflections on Australian Higher Education: 1994–1999. Case study. www.chet.org.za/papers.asp.

Responding to the National Plan for Higher Education: Meeting the Challenges (2001). CHET/UNCF National Workshop.

Van Vught, F. (1996). Isomorphism in Higher Education? In V.L. Meek, L. Goedegebuure, O. Kivinen & R. Rinne (eds), *The Mockers and Mocked: Comparative Perspectives on Differentiation, Convergence and Diversity in Higher Education*. Oxford: Pergamon.

Vlasceanu, L. & Sadlak, J. (2001). Changes in the Higher Education System and Institutions of the Central and Eastern European Countries: 1994–1999. Case Study. www.chet.org.za/papers.asp.

·

SECTION 3

THE DYNAMICS OF CHANGE

SECTION 3

INTRODUCTION

In this final section of the book, the writers undertake the two critical tasks of assessment and explanation. Chapter 12 is devoted primarily to an assessment of the outcomes of change measured against policy expectations. Readers should not look here for a full explanatory account of change, although some account of how outcomes have arisen inevitably forms part of the description. That full account is instead reserved for Chapter 13, where Muller, Maassen and Cloete attempt the more complex task of unravelling the causal threads of the change process. In performing these tasks, the section as a whole returns to the framework initially laid out in the first section of the book.

Chapter 3 described the policy expectations for the transformation of higher education in South Africa and outlined the model that underpinned the approach to change after the new democracy took effect in 1994: it was expected that national policy, informed by a history of progressive policy formulation that started formally with the National Education Policy Investigation (Nepi, 1992), would provide the framework for change while the newly established higher education division in the national Department of Education would give effect to the policies contained in the White Paper (1997) by developing and putting into action appropriate implementation instruments and mechanisms.

The policy agenda was orientated towards the national (local) concerns of equity, democracy and unity. Global reform pressures such as those outlined in Chapter 1 (efficiency, local and international markets and competition), all of which require institutions to develop strong academic and managerial capabilities, received only a cursory reference in the policy agenda, or were ignored.

Using the data and analysis of the preceding chapters that constitute Section 2, Chapter 12 assesses what happened in relation to the key policy expectations of equity, democracy, efficiency, responsiveness and a single co-ordinated system. It shows that when change occurred in line with policy expectations, it may not have been as a result of government policy. In many other instances, outcomes were quite contrary to what government policy had predicted. Thus, while major changes occurred in the system, the change process did not follow the 'grand policy' assumptions of the post-1994 period.

Chapter 13 builds on this assessment and, using the framework of the analytic triangle which was outlined in Chapter 1, provides a more complex understanding of policy and reform. In keeping with the analytic framework, the analysis explores more broadly the interactions between government, society and institutions in South Africa, within the context of globalisation. It looks at different forms of policy, such as symbolic, grand and differentiated policy, and suggests that a different approach to the relationship between policy, implementation and change has become necessary. This approach also argues for a reconceptualisation of the relationship between government, institutions and society.

267

N. Cloete et al. (eds.), Transformation in Higher Education, 267.
© 2007 Springer.

CHAPTER 12

NICO CLOETE

NEW SOUTH AFRICAN REALITIES

> After Thatcher lost power in 1990 one of her most revealing reflections was that she
> 'confessed' that her 'unintended centralisation' had led to many distinguished academics
> thinking that Thatcherism meant a philistine subordination of scholarship to the Treasury.
> Such an outcome was never her intention, but like so many rulers, she was toppled before she
> could rectify the mistake. (Jenkins, 2000)

The country case studies reviewed in Chapter 1 showed that while having widely
divergent systems, all the countries had one thing in common: reforms in higher
education produced unanticipated outcomes. Using the information and analyses of the
preceding chapters, this chapter provides an assessment of what happened in South
Africa with regard to the policies that were intended to foster equity, democracy,
efficiency and responsiveness in higher education and produce a single co-ordinated
higher education system.

1. EQUITY

Equity was the pre-eminent transformation demand during the first policy phase which
lasted from Nepi (1992) to the White Paper (1997). The redress problematic is
succinctly captured by Badat, Barends and Wolpe (1994): 'The demand is for both the
enrolments and staffing of post-secondary education to begin to reflect the social
composition of the broader society; for resources to be made available to historically
disadvantaged social groups; and for increased funding and qualitative development to
support the historically black institutions' (p78).

During the early period of policy-making it was broadly agreed that redress had to
occur at both individual and institutional levels. While individual and institutional
redress are connected in many complex ways, the outcomes will be discussed separately
below.

1.1. Individual redress

It is difficult to disagree with Cooper and Subotzky (2001) that at the individual level,
South Africa experienced a 'revolution' regarding the increase in proportion of black
students in higher education. Chapter 5 on students shows that the proportion of black

N. Cloete et al. (eds.). Transformation in Higher Education. 269-288.

students in the total university enrolment increased from 32% in 1990 to 60% in 2000 while in the technikons it rose from 32% to 72% over the same period. Thus by 2000, there was a majority of black students both in the universities (60%) and technikons (72%). The most important contributing factor to this increase was undoubtedly the dropping of racial barriers to admission at all higher education institutions. For the first time in the history of the country, students were offered the freedom to apply to any institution of their choice, and this resulted in unprecedented student mobility. At some institutions the composition of the student population changed dramatically: for example, the University of Port Elizabeth changed from being 62% white in 1995 to being 87% black in 2000. These demographic changes must be some of the most remarkable in the world during the 1990s.

The change in racial composition of the student body was much faster than anybody could have anticipated in 1994. The freedom of choice for students was also supported by the putting in place of a significant instrument of individual redress, namely the national student bursary scheme. The former Principal of Pretoria Technikon remarked on the dramatic effect this had:

> ... after 1994, the government came and gave TEFSA [Tertiary Education Fund of South Africa] bursaries, set up the whole bursary scheme. Tremendous bursaries, where they would pay for all the students. Now the moment they did that, they made all the black students in South Africa mobile. If you stayed at Turfloop or wherever and you were poor, you could only study at the nearest university. But if you had a bursary, you could study wherever you wished, you see. And that meant that we were inundated by poor students coming out of the rural areas ... (Van Rensburg, 2001)

While this could be claimed as a major policy success, the story is in fact more complicated. First, government did not put in place any rewards for those institutions that started changing, nor did it apply sanctions to those institutions that did not change. Indeed, by 2000 the University of Stellenbosch still had only 6% African students in their contact programmes (and an overall enrolment of 27% black students) (Department of Education, 2001). Secondly, admitting black students could be regarded as institutions responding as much to a social demand as to policy pressure: in other words, they were responding to societal expectations in order to obtain legitimacy from the society at large as well as from the government. Thirdly, there was no anticipation of the effect of this movement on many of the historically black institutions who lost large numbers of students to the historically white institutions. Finally, institutions did not have to apply complicated affirmative action policies to choose black students over white students, because more than 41.000 white students left the public higher education system between 1995 and 2000. For example, in the historically white technikon sector the proportion of white students fell from 89% in 1990 to 26% in 2000; overall, white participation rates dropped from 70% to 47%.

There are many possible explanations for the white flight. The most obvious is to simply attribute this development to racism. In other words, these students expected the public institutions to become majority black and, perhaps unintentionally, facilitated the process by leaving. Where they went is not clear: many went overseas to travel or to gain work experience (Steenkamp, 2000); it is thought that others enrolled in the burgeoning private higher education sector. There is also anecdotal evidence that white youngsters from lower middle class homes could not afford to study at higher education institutions since their parents' income was too high for them to qualify for the National Student Financial Aid Scheme, but too low to afford tuition and residence costs. What is clear is that it was not government policy to lose so many white students from the public system.

The participation of women students increased at a rate three times faster than that of men and, overall, the proportion of women increased from 42% in 1990 to 53% in 2000. Again this remarkable equity improvement was not brought about by policy instruments, but reflects the changing demographics of the population and the school system.

While it is clear that the new South Africa brought a dramatic increase in higher education access for black students and women, the equity improvements are not unambiguous. The reality is that the overall participation rate decreased. This means that although the composition (complexion) of the student body changed, access was still possible only for a small elite: the participation rate for Africans, for example, increased from 9% in 1993 to 13% in 2000. Furthermore, the access of black students did not improve significantly in the high-status and high-skill areas such as the sciences and engineering, or in postgraduate programmes (see Chapter 5 for a more detailed analysis).

Retention rates are another important indicator of redress and, with the exception of the historically white English-medium institutions, the retention rates for the system started declining in the post-1997 period. In other words, students may have gained access to institutions, but were not successful in completing their studies. For example, in 1993, 17% of the students who registered at universities completed their degrees or diplomas, while in 2000 the figure was only 16%. The corresponding figures for technikons were 10% and 9% respectively. Neither the decrease in throughput rate nor the lack of entry by black students into the high-status areas fit with the policy intentions of the 1997 White Paper (see Chapter 5 on students).

In terms of curriculum, a major policy aim of the programme approach was to achieve greater portability, interdisciplinarity and coherence. It was hoped that a more coherent, but also more flexible approach would provide greater access to, and success in higher education. According to Ensor (Chapter 8) there is little doubt that there is now far less portability in the system than there was before programme planning started. While attempts were made to create compulsory interdisciplinary programmes, some of these bind together cores which do not easily articulate, and may in the process further disadvantage under-prepared students for whom coherence and disciplinarity is important. There seems little evidence that the expected advantages of curriculum reform for disadvantaged students materialised in the post-1994 period.

Regarding staff (Chapter 6) the overall proportion of black academic staff employed at universities increased from 13% to 20% between 1993 and 1998, and at the technikons from 12% to 29%. However, the overall effect has been that black institutions have become more black while the historically white institutions have remained predominantly white, particularly in their academic staff component. In relation to equity, women seem to have made the most progress in terms of the numbers of women employed in the higher education sector and in gaining access to senior management positions within institutions. The senior professoriate, however, still remains a white male domain.

While blacks and women have gained considerably more access to senior management positions, particularly at the historically black and the historically white English-medium institutions, progress at the heart of the academic enterprise – research and publications – is rather dismal. For Africans the published research output increased from 1% in 1990 to 3% in 1998, and that must be understood within the context of an overall decrease in output. Similarly, published output for women remained the same in 1998 as in 1991 – 17% in both years (see Chapter 9 on research).

It can thus be concluded that in terms of individual redress, major gains were made in changing the racial and gender composition of the student body. Central government may claim some credit for these developments, particularly in relation to the implementation of the student financial aid scheme. But the gains can also be attributed to unanticipated changes such as white students leaving the system, societal pressure and institutional behaviour. In the areas in which it is most difficult to effect change – such as bringing black students and women into the high status fields of study and in improving graduation rates – the trend did not follow policy. And in the even more complex area of improving staff equity and research output, central government policy seems to have had minimal effect.

Institutional policies might attempt to claim credit for some of these developments, but can do so only to a limited degree. The institutions did not have to apply strict affirmative criteria to select students from the pool of black and white applicants, because a shortage of students coming through the school system meant that the institutions could admit everyone who satisfied the minimum requirements. So in the areas of student throughput rates, changing the composition of staff and improving the research outputs of black staff, institutions also failed to realise policy goals.

1.2. Institutional redress

While there were considerable, though ambiguous, equity gains at the level of individuals, in the case of institutional redress the picture is unambiguous. Contention over the policy both within the Ministry of Education and between the Ministries of Education and Finance (see Coombe, 2001; Bengu, 2001) meant that this policy was never implemented. The combination of this with the increased mobility of students meant that at the historically black universities the number of headcount student enrolments fell by 35.600 between 1995 and 2000 while, in comparison, the historically white Afrikaans-medium institutions gained 54.200 headcount student enrolments over the same period.

Since student numbers are linked to government subsidy, it is no surprise that the financial position of the historically black universities deteriorated significantly. In rand terms, the government appropriation to the historically black universities dropped by R102-million over the 1999–2001 budget cycle while the historically white Afrikaans-medium universities gained more than R230-million (22%) in subsidies. More dramatic is the fact that the long-term investments of the ten historically white Afrikaans- and English-medium institutions increased by R1.930-million between 1993 and 1999; in both 1993 and 1999 their share accounted for 82% of the total long-term investments of institutions. Only two historically black technikons managed to increase their long-term investments over the six year period (Chapter 4, Funding).

The historically black universities did not manage to attract white students (at the time of writing they were still more than 99% black) and retention rates as well as graduation rates at these institutions declined. The research output of the historically black universities as a group decreased from 11% in 1995 to 10.2% in 2000.

By contrast, the historically black technikons did considerably better than the historically black universities. They increased their student numbers by 12.800 between 1995 and 2000, but this must be seen in relation to the historically white technikons where enrolments increased by 26.600 over the same period. As far as research is concerned, the historically black technikons did not substantially increase their research outputs, nor did they attract significant amounts of research contract funding. The total research output for all the historically black technikons in 2000 was 25 units; for the historically black universities it was 558; and the combined output of the two top historically white institutions was 1.598 (Department of Education, 2000).

By 2000 the historically black institutions were managed by black South Africans, but they also experienced a disproportional loss of black staff to historically white institutions, to government and to business. The new black leadership of these institutions had to deal with problems unimaginable in most parts of the world and many left, voluntarily or involuntarily, long before their contracts expired. In a number of cases this led to very reputable academics leaving these leadership positions with their reputation in tatters. In his review of the audit reports carried out on five of these institutions Steele stated that: 'The perceived lack of skills and experience at all levels of the institutions are common to all reports with the anticipated consequences of a general lack of commitment and low morale' (2000:3).

In summary, the equity objective in the post-1994 period was not met. Instead changes resulted in a more elite public higher education system: while the student population became dramatically more black, this was against an overall decrease in participation rates. Effectively this meant that while the complexion of the elite had changed, the gap between 'those with' and 'those without' higher education had not decreased. It could be argued that this outcome confirms Castells' assessment of one of the effects of globalisation, namely that 'inequality has increased in almost every country, in both the developed and the developing world' (2001:16).

Furthermore, these students were not significantly more successful in higher education than their predecessors, nor did they populate the high-skill, high-status fields of study in the numbers anticipated by the equity policies. This implies that the difficult business of remedying historical disadvantage has not been as successful as had been expected.

For historically black universities the new South Africa was a disaster. The policy intentions of institutional redress and an increase in capacity did not materialise and, instead, student choice meant that many of these institutions bled their traditional students to the historically advantaged institutions. The consequence was that the gap between the historically black universities and the historically advantaged institutions widened. Viewed from a statistical and funding perspective, it would appear that the new South Africa benefited not the black institutions, but the historically Afrikaans-medium institutions – a supreme irony for South Africa's first black majority government but entirely explicable from the perspective of students who, rejecting the 'second-best' institutions set up for them by apartheid, embraced the 'privileged' institutions from which they had previously been excluded.

Decreasing inequality is not a global trend, and global reforms in higher education have seldom set equity as a priority. In countries where affirmative action had been put on the change agenda, such as in the US, it was based on individual advancement and there has since been a significant retreat from this policy. In South Africa the same trend emerged, bringing about a dramatic improvement in individual access to historically advantaged higher education institutions, but doing little to redress the systemic imbalances between historically disadvantaged and historically advantaged institutions.

2. DEMOCRACY

2.1. National level

The adoption of co-operative governance as the central principle underpinning the relationship between government and institutions, as well as relationships within institutions, raised high hopes for increased consultation, participation and transparency. It is well summarised in the White Paper of 1997: 'Co-operative governance assumes a proactive, guiding and constructive role for government. It also assumes a co-operative relationship between the state and higher education institutions. One implication of this is, for example, that institutional autonomy is to be exercised in tandem with public accountability' (53.7). The new government took this intention very seriously and, from the appointment of the NCHE up to the approval of the White Paper, South Africa exemplified one of the most participatory and transparent higher education policy processes anywhere in the world.

At the national level the NCHE proposed two intermediary bodies: a higher education council, which would have policy, advisory and allocatory functions, and a higher education forum that would provide space for debate, consensus-building and lobbying. The intention was that these two bodies would, on the one hand, draw implementation capacity from the wider system and, on the other, continue the consultative forum tradition that had developed during the anti-apartheid struggle.

The Minster of Education did not accept these proposals. Instead he opted for a Council on Higher Education (CHE) that combined, or collapsed, expertise and institutional interests into one body. The CHE (1998/99) was not given a policy framework, nor an allocatory function. Instead its two main duties were to advise the Minister and to establish a quality assurance committee. The higher education branch of the Department of Education thus became virtually the sole implementation agency of the formidable array of new policies prescribed in the White Paper. The earlier chapters on students, funding and research show that many of the key implementation instruments such as an inter-linked planning and funding system, redress funding, a capacity-building plan and a research plan, had not been implemented by 2001.

As certain structural problems in the system persisted, the implementation process was increasingly perceived to be one that required more direct government steering with the corollary of less consultation. The formulation of a report on the 'size and shape' of the system by the CHE (2000) was less consultative than previous processes had been, and while the National Plan for Higher Education (2001) was presented to institutions at a public meeting, it was made clear that it was not a document open to negotiation. The National Working Group (2002) was appointed by the Minister to investigate not 'whether the number of institutions can or should be reduced, but how they can be reduced and the form that the restructured institutions should take' (p89). It was also stressed that the working group was 'appointed by, and reporting to, the Minister' (p90). The Minister gave no indication that once he received the recommendations, that he would consult either the statutory advisory body, the CHE, or the various representative bodies.

In reviewing the governance relationship at the national level, Olivier points out that the 1999 and 2000 amendments to the Higher Education Act (1997) strengthened the Minister's role and powers. The new powers allowed government to determine the scope and range of public and private institutions and to appoint an administrator to manage institutions with serious financial problems. Ministerial approval is required for taking loans and the construction of immovable infrastructure, and all institutions are required to submit an annual report on governance and financial administration (Olivier, 2001:14,15).

For Olivier this approach is more in line with the underlying philosophy of the Green Paper of 1997, which proposed a strong directive role for government, but which was substantially modified in the White Paper after consultation. The post-1999 approach is characterised by:

- 'The incorporation of additional aspects of a strong steering model, resulting in an increase in the role and powers of the Minister in the governance and management of the system as a whole as well as of individual higher education institutions.'
- 'The strengthening of the Minister's interventionist powers, especially with respect to individual institutions, but also to the higher education system (in terms of the Higher Education Plan as issued by the Minister).' (Olivier, 2001:15–16)

This legislative framework was captured in the proposed funding formula announced during 2001. According to one of the authors of the new system, the Ministry's proposed new funding formula breaks away from this (previous) subsidy framework. While the previous system worked in a bottom-up (student numbers at institutions) and then a top-down (adjusted formula) way, the new model will be a top-down one. ... The government will determine what total public funds should be spent in a given year and what the key policy goals should be for that year (Department of Education, 2001b).

It seems that the consultative and participatory process of policy formulation and the first cycles of the three-year planning dialogue gave way to a much stronger state-steering approach, driven by government's frustration at the lack of progress made towards achieving transformation goals. Both the CHE and the NPHE identified continued inefficiency problems, not equity or democracy, as the central transformation problematic. The need for more direct intervention was considerably strengthened by the Minister's advisory body, the CHE, when it said that it 'is convinced that the problems and weaknesses of the higher education system will not disappear on their own or be overcome by institutions on their own ... it will require multiple co-ordinated interventions and initiatives. It will require political will ...' (CHE, 2000:2).

By 2001 it became apparent that at the national level, serious strains were manifesting themselves in the open, co-operative relationship that had characterised the 1994–1999 period.

2.2. Institutional level

The governance challenge at institutional level is well captured in the White Paper: '... For the first time in their history, our higher education institutions have the opportunity to achieve their full potential, but they will not do so until their system of governance reflects and strengthens the values and practices of our new democracy' (1997:3.1).

The first task was structural change, and as the chapter on leadership (Chapter 8) shows, enormous progress was made with the governing councils and the leadership becoming more representative, and with the establishment of institutional forums. Considering the international experience which shows how difficult it is to change higher education governing structures, this re-composition is quite remarkable.

Whether these democratic structures are more effective is debatable. In many of the institutions that experienced financial or administrative crises post-1994, it is quite clear that the new councils were either ineffective or, in some cases, part of the problem. However, in other institutions the recomposed councils have played a significant role in the institutional transformation agenda (Harper at al., 2002). There is also little doubt that the institutional forums played a role in the appointment of institutional leaders, but the evidence is not conclusive as to whether this resulted in better leadership. The forums were something of a mixed success: in some institutions they became an integral part of the formal institutional governance processes; in other institutions the forums were still trying to clarify their functions and, more importantly, their powers (Harper et al., 2002).

The second demand in the democratisation of higher education was for greater participation. A survey carried out in 35 institutions revealed fairly widespread complaints amongst students, workers and other constituencies that gaining access to governance structures had not led to empowerment, nor to effective participation. For example, a number of representatives said that: 'we are moving very laboriously; it is like pulling teeth ... the Institutional Forum is boring' (Harper et al., 2002). The study reports a 'general level of apathy, low morale, and demoralisation on campus, an impasse and hiatus in higher education' (Harper et al., 2002). Legislation such as the Labour Relations Act, designed to improve workplace relations, seems to have undermined a shared, collegial approach to decision-making and resulted in many academics feeling more alienated than in the past. As for the workers in higher education, not only has participation not been strengthened, but their material position seems to have worsened considerably. This is shown by the fact that the differential between the package of a principal and the earnings of a higher education service worker who has been retrenched and now undertakes work on an outsourced basis, deteriorated from 20:1 in the 1980s to 50:1 in 2000. Global trends such as increasing differentiation amongst staff seem to be in full swing in South African higher education.

Co-operative governance assumed that change would be the result of a participatory, negotiated process amongst all constituencies, and that ultimately complementary interests would overcome competing interests. However, the policy remained conspicuously silent about who would initiate, direct and manage change. The chapter on leadership (Chapter 7) shows a wide range of leadership and management styles at work in higher education – transformative leadership, managerial and crisis leadership – each with a range of sub-types. The range of institutional cultures and capacities are reflected in some of the different leadership styles, which implies that there is not one effective or dominant leadership style operating in the present higher education environment. These different approaches, partially shaped by the parameters of institutional contexts and partially by the power of individual agents, contributed to an increasingly differentiating institutional landscape (see Chapter 7 on leadership).

Both transformative and managerial approaches have been used by institutional leaders trying to deal with the tension between direction from the top and bottom-up participation/consultation. As is shown in a study conducted in two very different institutions (Cloete & Bunting, 2002), there is no 'correct' approach to transformative leadership: at one institution the leader was very up-front and charismatic while at the other a 'reluctant' leadership style prevailed. In both cases, however, the tension between leading and consulting was well managed. Whilst the jury is still out on whether leaning towards a consultative/participatory style or towards a top-down managerialist style is more successful, and how one measures that success, what is indisputable is that the demand for more democracy in higher education has contributed to the dynamic and diverse array of responses by institutional leadership.

In summary, the democratisation of higher education has proved to be as difficult to achieve in South Africa, as it has in the rest of the world, and the results thus far are very mixed. As in the case of the equity policy goal, the greatest success has been achieved with changing the composition of the governing structures. Providing staff and students with greater representation on governing structures has not necessarily translated into their having an effective voice; on the contrary, in many institutions greater representation seems to have been accompanied by a sense among some of these stakeholders that they still do not participate meaningfully in institutional decision-making.

A thread that runs through both national and institutional governance is the problem of an increasing tension between efficiency and participation. While a range of responses have developed to manage this tension at the institutional level, at the national level it seems that the approach emerging is the well-known tendency of governments to resort to top-down intervention when frustrated with the slow pace of change. This comes after unprecedented co-operative governance between the national government and higher education institutions in the 1994–1999 period.

3. EFFICIENCY

The National Commission on Higher Education report (1996) and the 1997 White Paper both started with equity as the first transformation principle. The Council on Higher Education report of 2000 started with effectiveness and efficiency challenges before mentioning equity. Most recently, the National Plan for Higher Education (Department of Education 2001:1.1) starts its discussion on the challenges facing higher education with human resource development. These shifts in emphasis in the policy documents are but one indication of the shift towards efficiency after the formulation of the state's macro-economic Gear policy in late 1996.

Simply put, efficiency refers to cost-effectiveness – doing the same with fewer resources or doing more with the same resources.

3.1. Graduation, throughput and retention rates

The CHE (2000) listed the following four areas in which it found the system to be inefficient:

- If reasonable throughput rates of 20% had been achieved, 25.000 more graduates would have been produced in 1998.
- There has been a trend for 25% of new undergraduate intakes to drop out by the end of the first year and at least 100.000 students, out of a population of 600.000, drop out every year.
- While the overall retention rate is low, the system retains unacceptably large numbers of failing students.
- There are widely varying costs per student, often caused by small student to staff ratios in courses. This occurs because institutions were not co-operating to overcome duplication and inefficiency (CHE, 2000:18).

Throughput and graduation rates have also not improved. The CHE (2000) report shows that if the same retention rate had been attained in 1999 as in 1997, there would have been 60.000 more students in the system. In terms of graduation rate, the average for the system increased from 15% in 1993 to only 16% in 1999.

The explanation for low retention rates is very complex. The National Plan implies that it is a problem caused by poor school preparation and that one of the remedies is academic development, which it offers to fund in future (although the proposed new funding formula does not make provision for it). Another explanation which has come to the fore is that many students drop out because they do not have the financial resources to continue their studies.

In two small surveys conducted at the University of the Western Cape (UWC survey, 1999) and the Port Elizabeth Technikon (private communication from Professor du Preez, Port Elizabeth Technikon, 2001) among students who were in good academic standing, but had dropped out of the university, a significant number of students claimed to have dropped out for financial reasons. This raises the question whether the cause of this inefficiency is at the institutional level, or whether the National Student Financial Aid Scheme (NSFAS) is severely under-funded by the national government. It may be that the effect of financial constraints on the drop-out rate is vastly underestimated, particularly in the context of persistent high unemployment, regular increases in tuition fees, and stricter application of financial exclusions and debt collection. The poor retention rates may thus be a combination of the national government not putting enough money into the NSFAS, the institutions not doing adequate enrolment management, and not providing sufficient academic support, and a deteriorating socio-economic climate. The assumption in the National Plan that poor retention rates can be addressed through academic support alone may be underestimating the complexity of the problem, and the role that government could play by increasing contributions to the NSFAS.

3.2. Income

Chapter 4 on funding shows that government subsidy remained constant in real terms and that the number of students enrolled did not increase significantly (total headcounts increased from 571.000 in 1995 to 602.000 in 2000). Higher education as a whole thus cannot claim that in terms of students and funding it is doing more with the same.

One area of significant improvement, however, is in respect of income diversification. Chapter 4 shows that although government block grants to higher education have not decreased, in South Africa less than 60% of the total higher education budget is covered by direct government subsidy. This figure compares favourably with Australia, for example, where more than 60% of the total higher education budget still comes from federal and state government (Meek, 2001). The financial problems of many individual South African institutions can be attributed to their inability to diversify their income to the same degree as other institutions in the system, or to that of institutions in certain developed countries.

3.3. Research

Chapter 9 on research shows that funding for research has certainly not declined. At the same time no increase has occurred in accredited published output since 1990, nor is there a substantial increase in postgraduate outputs (Chapter 5 on students). This could mean that researchers have become less productive, or that they have been distracted by transformation struggles in their institutions. But there is an alternative explanation: the top group of institutions increased their contract research dramatically – in many cases by more than 100%. If the researchers are maintaining the same level of published output, substantially increasing contract research and simultaneously involving themselves in institutional transformation activities, then there is a group of top academics who are working much harder and are being much more productive than before. A research director recently commented that productivity at the top-producing institutions was not equally distributed, and estimated that less than 50% of the academics are productive in publishing and winning contracts.[1] This also implies that at least 50% of the academics at the institutions with the highest output, and the vast majority of academics at the institutions which are not producing research, have not become more productive in the new South Africa.

3.4. Institutional responses

At the institutional level there have been great variations in the attempts to improve efficiency. A study on efficiency commissioned by a national newspaper showed huge discrepancies in the system (CHET, 1998). It showed that cost per graduate at the technikons varied from R43.000 to R193.000 and at the universities, from R38.000 to R91.000. However, in the diverse and complex South African context, such crude comparisons obscure more than they reveal. A more sophisticated regression analysis, controlled for a range of variables, showed that the six universities that performed best in utilising their total income to produce students who pass, were evenly divided between historically white Afrikaans- and English-medium institutions. An analysis of whether institutions managed to reduce the impact of higher tuition fees on student drop-out rates, revealed that two of the six most efficient institutions were from the historically disadvantaged grouping. Similarly, if research output is correlated with academic qualifications, then two of the six best-performing institutions were historically black universities (CHET, 1998).

Stumpf (2001) shows that in order to raise their level of government subsidy, the institutions with capacity, particularly the historically white Afrikaans-medium universities and the technikons, adopted a number of measures such as attracting more students through courses with a greater orientation to business and industry, using more flexible delivery modes, and brokering private/public partnerships. Certain institutions, such as the Universities of Cape Town, Pretoria, Natal and Stellenbosch, which had strong research capacities, dramatically increased their level of external funding through research, consultancy contracts and the establishment of specific structures to package and patent products of intellectual property (see Chapter 9 on research).

Cost-cutting exercises included the outsourcing of non-core activities such as cleaning, gardening, catering and building maintenance. Some institutions invested in management training, focusing mainly on strategic and financial planning; they also strengthened institutional research and managed, for the first time, to determine actual costs per student and to assess the profitability of faculties and departments (Stumpf,

2001). The diversification of income is an illustration that some South African institutions are doing very well in comparison with their international counterparts. The chapter on funding (Chapter 4) also shows that some institutions experienced serious financial difficulties, were not able to control costs, and were ultimately investigated by the Auditor-General's office for the first time ever.

In summary, at a system level it is quite clear that higher education is not more efficient in 2000 than it was in 1994; in fact, there is some evidence that it may be less efficient. At the individual institutional level, however, there are great variations. In general, but not in all cases, those institutions with capacity managed to put in place an array of cost-cutting and funding diversification measures that may be the envy of many first world institutions.

Significantly, the preceding chapters show that there is also a cost to efficiency, or that efficiency is not the same as effectiveness. In some cases the entrepreneurial 'franchising' of undergraduate programmes led to poor quality control with the result that the already disadvantaged students, who required the most pedagogical assistance, received the worst form of distance education. The down-side of outsourcing non-core business was that many black workers lost their jobs or had their remuneration packages halved (see Chapter 6 on staff). Finally, institutions without strong academic programmes and managerial expertise became less efficient, resulting in what Castells (2001) calls 'polarisation' – the gap between the advantaged and the disadvantaged widens because at the same time that the top end strengthens, the bottom end becomes weaker.

While the government certainly embraced the global efficiency agenda, the SAPSE funding instrument did not result in greater research output, nor improved throughputs. Consequently the 1997 White Paper policy aims of greater efficiency were not realised to any significant extent, and the appointment of a National Working group to 'investigate the feasibility of reducing the number of institutions and establishing new institutional and organisation forms' (NPHE, 2001:89) was, amongst others, a drastic measure by the Minister to improve efficiency. The report produced for the Minister by the National Working Group (2001) seems to assume that effecting these proposals will produce long-term efficiency gains, but no hard evidence of this is offered in the report, and many members of the higher education community have yet to be convinced that mergers will in fact lead to efficiency and effectiveness gains for particular institutions, or for the system as a whole.

4. RESPONSIVENESS

According to the 1997 White Paper, higher education was expected to increase its responsiveness to societal interests and needs. This required restructuring the higher education system and its institutions to meet the needs of an increasingly technologically-oriented economy. It also required institutions to deliver the requisite research, the highly trained people and the knowledge to equip a developing society with the capacity to address national needs and to participate in a rapidly changing and competitive global context.

4.1. Skills for socio-economic development

The first and most important requirement of responsiveness is a sufficient supply of high-level skills for socio-economic development. Taking account of the data captured in the preceding chapters, there are a number of indicators which suggest that this requirement has not been met:

- The overall participation rate declined from 17% in 1993 to 16% in 2000.
- The number of enrolled students in 2000 was the same as in 1997, and only marginally (29.000) more than in 1995.
- While there was a modest shift in the proportion of students enrolled in science, technology and commerce, this was not yet being reflected in graduation outputs.
- In a 1999 survey of 273 of South Africa's major employers, 76% reported that they were experiencing a shortage of professional workers. This survey predicted that in the period 1998–2003 the job opportunities at this professional level would grow by between 16% and 18% and that those for unskilled workers would decrease by around 35% (Human Sciences Research Council, 1999).
- In an acknowledgement of these skills shortages, in 2001 the government significantly altered the legislation and procedures for enabling skilled workers to enter the country more easily. This was in addition to special arrangements concluded with countries such as Cuba for the supply of doctors and mathematics teachers.

A key response envisaged by the 1997 White Paper was a change in the shape of the system, away from the predominance of the humanities and education towards science, engineering, technology and business. However, Chapter 5 on students shows that both in terms of enrolments and graduate outputs the system remained dominated by students in the humanities (52%), with only 26% following majors in science, engineering and technology, and 22% majoring in business. Similarly, graduate outputs of the higher education system continued to be dominated by the fields of education and the humanities.

According to the National Plan, responsiveness to 'pressing national needs' (p5) required a focus on human resource development (particularly in the form of lifelong learning), the development of high-level skills (globally equivalent and socially responsible), and the production of new knowledge. The chapter on students shows that the South African system was still primarily a contact/distance education system, and was not yet a lifelong learning system.

The need for globally equivalent skills raises the debate about curriculum relevance. The chapter on curriculum (Chapter 8) shows that the new academic programmes introduced by many institutions were aimed at promoting interdisciplinarity, portability, coherence and relevance. According to Ensor's analysis, portability definitely did not increase. Attempts to achieve interdisciplinarity and relevance led to many institutions 'packaging' their programmes with titles relevant to the workplace, such as tourism, heritage studies, development, etc. In many cases, however, interdisciplinarity was not achieved because the programmes were still organised largely on a disciplinary basis; contemporary curricula in the sciences and the humanities looked little different from the way they did before academic programme implementation began.

There is also a growing concern with regard to interdisciplinarity, particularly at the undergraduate level: without a disciplinary base, a 'little bit of this and of that curriculum dumbs all students down' (Muller, 2001). These inter-disciplinary courses advantage middle-class students with cultural capital and disadvantage those from poor school and home backgrounds. The net result is increased inequality. Muller (2001) also argues that skills for employability require in-depth learning, which is what disciplines provide and what is needed to produce 'self-programmable labour'. As was pointed out in Chapter 6 on staff, Castells (2001) argues that self-programmable labour is labour that has the built-in capacity to generate value through innovation and information, enabling this type of labour to constantly redefine its work and add value. A serious question must be raised as to whether many of the new, loosely configured, career-relevant interdisciplinary programmes can produce self-programmable labour. Nor is it a given that many of the traditional discipline-based courses in South Africa automatically produce innovative, transferable skills.

4.2. Research

With regard to research, the policy goal for an increase in the production of new knowledge (articulated in the National Plan of 2001 and the 1997 White Paper) has not been met. While Chapter 9 shows that there certainly was a big increase in contract research at the most productive institutions, as well as a shift towards relevant research (which in this context means applied, developmental or strategic research), three issues have been raised about this shift:

- Firstly, is the shift due to policy, or to changes propelled from within science, or is basic research simply being 'crowded-out' by market forces and global trends?
- Secondly, can a shift to applied research be maintained if basic research and disciplines are systematically weakened? According to the analysis presented in Chapter 9, Bawa and Mouton clearly do not think so.
- Thirdly, just as it was under apartheid, the pressure is towards strategic, applied research and, just as under apartheid, the question has to be asked whether this is serving the needs of the majority. Currently the evidence is simply not available to provide an empirical answer to this crucial question.

At a more theoretical level, it could be argued that two developments militate against research directly serving the needs of the majority. The first is that while the Reconstruction and Development Plan (1994) provided a framework that identified sets of national needs, Gear (1996) drove an agenda in which the needs of the majority are far less clearly articulated. The second development is this: countries such as South Africa that pursue 'third-way' centre-left political policies and attempt to steer a path between rampant free-market ideology and state collectivism, are likely to have higher education reform strategy statements that 'reflect both the "marketisation" as well as the "equity" strands of the "third-way" political frameworks' (Naidoo, 2000:26). However, 'third way' policies seldom manage this balancing act: instead they often result in widening stratification and exclusion (Naidoo, 2000).

In conclusion, developing the responsiveness of the system to 'pressing national needs' has been a central policy intention and the higher education system is certainly grappling with it in terms of rethinking curricula and research orientations. Minimal gains have been made in terms of increasing the number of graduates with a range of high-level skills, and increasing the production of new knowledge. While the efforts to restructure curricula and change the direction of research show evidence of institutions attempting to become responsive, the value of the outcomes is questionable. For example, while interdisciplinary, vocationally relevant programmes may respond to immediate market needs, they may not produce the 'self-programmable labour' that is required for the new economy. Similarly, more applied research may in the long run undermine the very research base on which it depends, and it is not clear at this stage whose interests this research is serving.

The chapter on research makes a strong case to show that the shift towards applications-driven research has been influenced by initiatives, such as Thrip, which were launched by the Department of Arts, Culture, Science and Technology and the Department of Trade and Industry. The contradiction arises that whilst Bawa and Mouton express some admiration for this positive policy outcome, they also warn against the erosion of basic research. In this case the government, behaving like the market, is reinforcing the pull towards applied research. There are thus two markets operating in higher education research: industry as a market and the government as a market. The implication is that with the market not supporting basic research, and with the government supporting applied, strategic and developmental research, the foundations of applied work – basic research and strong disciplinary training – are being eroded.

From a slightly different angle, Muller (2001) argues that 'it is not that the state becomes market-like, but rather that both state and market threaten *endogenous self-propulsion*, still the mode best suited to the long-term health of the science and innovation system, as the IDRC document has said' (see Chapter 9 on research).

By 2001, the Department of Education, confronted by numerous systemic problems, had not yet been able to develop the research plan prescribed in the 1997 White Paper. It was also having difficulty administering the accredited publications output in a credible manner, and had not managed to build research capacity at the historically disadvantaged institutions. Furthermore, its role in steering research seems to have been increasingly usurped by other departments. Following global trends, the government has tried to steer higher education towards economic development priorities, but in the absence of a clear framework, it might be weakening the research basis in the process – as happened in Australia (Meek, 2001). What is indisputably part of a global trend is the increasing involvement of government departments other than the Department of Education in enticing higher education out of its ivory tower.

5. A SINGLE CO-ORDINATED SYSTEM

The White Paper (1997) stressed that a 'single co-ordinated system' does not mean 'uniform', that diversity must be ensured, and that it would be important to prevent 'a *laissez-faire* proliferation of higher education programmes by an increasing range of providers, without benefit of a planning framework and adequate safeguards to ensure the quality of provision' (Section 2.37).

As was indicated in the chapters on funding, students, curriculum and the emerging landscape, the *laissez-faire* approach that the Minister wanted to avoid, did largely occur, both in the private and public higher education systems. Instead of a planned, regulated environment, the 'system' became a free market characterised by student mobility and public and private institutions competing for 'market share'.

The main market regulator in the public system was the SAPSE funding formula (see Chapter 4 and Stumpf, 2001). This funding system, designed, adapted and implemented by the previous regime was diligently applied during the post-1994 period. In 2001 the proposed new funding formula was still under discussion and would be implemented, at the earliest, in 2003/4. What nobody anticipated was that the new government, with a world-acclaimed new policy framework, would continue for seven years to apply the funding system of the previous regime.

Although the SAPSE funding formula could be mechanically administered, it was not a neutral system because it was driven by student numbers, paid more for students in certain fields of study, and rewarded higher throughput rates and research outputs. According to Bunting (Chapter 4), Stumpf (2001) and Hayward (Pilot Project Consortium, 2001) this formula was not designed for, nor did it favour, the historically black institutions. The formula favoured established, well functioning institutions over smaller, less efficient and rural institutions. The deregulated, market-driven higher education environment meant that institutions would have to rely heavily on their institutional culture and capacity, both of which were intimately connected with the institutions' history and location in the South African apartheid context.

Chapter 11 describes the new landscape that developed under these conditions. It shows that while residues of the apartheid landscape certainly remain, the new higher education landscape comprises a diversity of academic cultures, managerial capacities and leadership strategies, as well as differential institutional access to resources. This has contributed to a new, unco-ordinated, complex, interesting and certainly unanticipated, higher education terrain.

As in the East European system during the early 1990s, the South African system entered a period of 'disorganised complexity' in the post-1994 period. While it is still not clear whether the South African system experienced disorganised differentiation, or a polarisation of inequality (Chapter 11), what is certain is that students had an unprecedented range of institutional and programme choices.

In reflecting on the NCHE and the White Paper's prescriptions for a single co-ordinated system, Njabulo Ndebele makes the following perceptive observation:

> The expression 'a single, co-ordinated system' carried the same declarative and mobilising effect as the expressions about South Africa being 'non-racial, non-sexist' and so on. In

reality, it will be a while before we have such a system. … The idea of a 'single, co-ordinated system' is a desirable policy objective. We don't have such a system now, but we might be working towards it. So, while we might have a policy in place, we have to turn that policy into sustainable sectoral experience. The higher education sector has yet to develop a new sense of itself as a functioning culture. So there are two aspects to this: one, co-ordination at the level of policy; two, co-ordination at the level of building the required human environment. I think the human environment can be a formidable impediment to the desired political outcome and that it may take a while to play itself out. But the strength of the National Plan is that it makes a concerted effort to push us in a particular direction. We will have to adjust to that. (Ndebele, 2001)

6. CONCLUSION

A major achievement of the post-1994 democratic government was to develop, in a participatory, co-operative manner, a comprehensive new policy framework. However, when it came to implementation, there were clearly major problems about developing instruments that could effect the new policy framework. Particularly problematic was the lack of a new integrated funding and planning system that would allow government to steer different aspects of the system.

The three most significant actions were the continued application of the funding system of the previous regime, the establishment of a student financial aid scheme, and the dis-establishment of the system's programme regulatory mechanism. The biases inherent in the funding system, the absence of a regulatory environment and the opening up of the higher education market in post-apartheid South Africa, interacted with huge institutional differences in culture and capacity to accentuate a range of existing inequalities; this provided fertile ground for a new, differentiated, but demonstrably more unequal new landscape. It reaffirmed what is well known: in a market situation with weak government regulation, the strong, with some odd exceptions, will become stronger, and the weak, with some notable exceptions, will remain weak – or spiral into crisis.

In terms of the four main pillars of transformation – equity, democracy, efficiency and responsiveness – the evidence reveals a very complex picture. In each area some progress has been made, but in all cases the gains have been more modest than anticipated by the policy-makers. What is quite clear is that in most cases change can be attributed to institutional responses and the impact of the market, and much less to government policy than one might have predicted from the policy proposals and processes.

As indicated in Chapter 1, all policy initiatives have unintended outcomes. The next chapter will attempt to explain some of the unanticipated outcomes in the South African context and suggest that the critical issue now is not so much the unintended outcomes, but how the system, understood as the complex of relationships between government, institutions and society, requires that policy itself becomes more flexibly responsive to ongoing change.

NOTE

[1] Private communication from the Deputy Vice-chancellor (Research), University of Stellenbosch.

REFERENCES

African National Congress (1994). *The Reconstruction and Development Programme. A Policy Framework.* Johannesburg: Umanyano Publications.

Badat, S., Barends, Z. & Wolpe, H. (1994). The Post Secondary Education System: Towards Policy Formulation for Equality and Development. In: B. Kaplan, *Changing by Degrees. Equity Issues in South African Tertiary Education.* Cape Town: UCT Press.

Bunting, I. (2001). Institutional Three-year Plans for 2000–2002: Some Comments on Staff Equity Plans and Data. Commissioned paper.

Bengu, S. (2001). Interview. www.chet.org.za/reflections.asp.

Castells, M. (2001). Think Local, Act Global. In: J. Muller, N. Cloete & S. Badat (eds), *Challenges of Globalisation: South African debates with Manual Castells.* Cape Town: Maskew Miller Longman.

Cloete, N. & Bunting, I. (2002). *Transformation Indicators: Case Studies of the University of Port Elizabeth and Peninsula Technikon.* Pretoria: CHET.

Coombe, T. (2001). Interview. www.chet.org.za/reflections.asp.

Cooper, D. & Subotzky, G. (2001). *The Skewed Revolution. Trends in South African Higher Education: 1988–1998.* Cape Town: Education Policy Unit, University of Western Cape.

Council on Higher Education 1998/1999. *Annual Report of the Council on Higher Education (South Africa).* Pretoria.

Council on Higher Education (2000). *Towards a New Higher Education Landscape: Meeting the Equity, Quality and Social Development Imperatives of South Africa in the 21st Century.* Pretoria: CHE.

Department of Education (1997). White Paper 3. A Programme for the Transformation of Higher Education. Pretoria.

Department of Education (1997). Higher Education Act of the Republic of South Africa, No. 101 of 1997. Pretoria.

Department of Education (1999–2000). Student Statistics Tables, Higher Education Management Information System. Pretoria.

Department of Education (2000). Research Output 2000. SAPSE Information Systems. Pretoria.

Department of Education (2001). *National Plan for Higher Education.* Pretoria.

Department of Education (2001). The Restructuring of the Higher Education System in South Africa. Report of the National Working Group to the Minister of Education. Pretoria.

Department of Education (2001). Funding of Public Higher Education: A New Framework Discussion Document. Pretoria.

Department of Trade and Industry (1996). Growth, Equity and Redistribution: A Macroeconomic Strategy (GEAR) (1996). Pretoria. www.gov.za/reports/1996/macroeco.htm.

Harper, A., Olivier, N., Thobakgale, S. & Tshwete, Z. (2000). Institutional Forums in Higher Education. A Study of their Establishment and Functioning at South African Public Higher Education Institutions. Effective Governance Project Report. Pretoria: CHET.

Human Sciences Research Council (1999). *South African Graduate Statistics.* Pretoria: HSRC.

Jenkins, S. (2000). A Bewildered Tribe. *Times Higher Education Supplement.* October.

Meek, V.L. (2001). Reflections on Australian Higher Education: 1994–1999. Case study. www.chet.org.za/papers.asp.

Muller, J. (2001). Responsiveness and Innovation in Higher Education. Commissioned paper. www.chet.org.za/papers.asp.

Naidoo, R. (2000). The 'Third Way' to Widening Participation and Maintaining Quality in Higher Education: Lessons from the United Kingdom. *Journal of Educational Inquiry,* 1(2), 24–38.

National Commission on Higher Education (1996). A Framework for Transformation. Pretoria.

National Education Policy Investigation (Nepi) '(1992). *Post-secondary Education*. Cape Town: Oxford University Press/NECC.

Ndebele, N. (2001). Interview. www.chet.org.za/reflections.asp.

Olivier, N. (2001). The Relationship between the State and Higher Education Institutions with Reference to Higher Education Policy Documentation and the Legislative Framework. Commissioned Paper. www.chet.org.za/papers.asp.

Steele, J. (2000). Findings of the Audits of Five Public Universities. Effective Governance Project. Pretoria: CHET.

Steenkamp, J.J.A. (2000). Echea Report: Study and employment intentions of Grade 11 and Grade 12 learners in the Eastern Cape Province of South Africa. Port Elizabeth: Echea.

Stumpf, R. (2001). Higher Education: Funding in the Period 1994–2001. Commissioned paper. www.chet.org.za/papers.asp.

The Best in Higher Education (1998). CHET *Sunday Times* Panel.

The Pilot Project Consortium (2001). The Next Generation of Academics. In: *The Pilot Project Consortium, Implications of the New Higher Education Framework*. Pretoria: CHET.

University of the Western Cape (1999). A Survey of Non-Returning Students. Cape Town.

Van Rensburg, D.J. (2001). Interview. www.chet.org.za/reflections.asp.

CHAPTER 13

JOHAN MULLER, PETER MAASSEN & NICO CLOETE

MODES OF GOVERNANCE
AND THE LIMITS OF POLICY

1. INTRODUCTION

The preceding chapters describe the various efforts, initiatives and policy attempts to realise transformation in the South African higher education system from 1994 up to 2000. Chapter 12 (New South African Realities) is to some extent a summary assessment of the findings and discussions of chapters 4 to 11. As these chapters show, and as we will argue here, transformation in higher education was seen by politicians and laymen, policy specialists and ordinary people as an indissoluble part of moving away from apartheid as a state form to a more open, inclusive, equitable and democratic society. This book describes how the transformation project was launched, with great acclaim, consensus and fanfare – through a series of founding documents such as the National Education Policy Initiative (NEPI, 1993), the ANC Policy Document (Centre for Education Policy Development, 1994), the report of the National Commission on Higher Education (NCHE, 1996), and even the first Higher Education White Paper of 1997 – only to seem to veer off track. A loss of course was detected in at least three areas. First, it seemed as if, after 1997, the policy process gradually became less participatory and democratic, and it even seemed to some that we were returning to something of a top-down style of policy imposition reminiscent of an earlier era. Secondly, it seemed as if the state was forsaking the values of equity and social justice in favour of the values of efficiency, effectiveness and responsiveness. Thirdly, even where policy had been implemented as intended (in the National Student Financial Aid Scheme [NSFAS], for example), it was producing effects different from the ones expected and desired. What was producing these contrary effects? Why had the transformation project in higher education come to be so widely seen as a disappointment?

Two different classes of explanation are usually advanced for the apparent loss of virtuous course.[1] The first, and most common, is a political one that attributes the cause for the surprise outcomes of policy, either in particular instances or in general, to political motives. The most common course change explained in this way is the apparent shift from the Reconstruction and Development Programme (ANC, 1994) to the policy of Growth, Employment and Redistribution (GEAR) (Department of Finance, 1996). There are two variants of the political explanation. The first assumes that government

N. Cloete et al. (eds.), Transformation in Higher Education, 289-310.
© 2007 *Springer.*

once acted in good faith but has since lapsed, for various reasons, into bad faith – the policy 'slippage' argument (Kraak, 2001). The second assumes that government never intended to implement the policy in the first place, and that the virtuous policy was meant to serve the symbolic ends of unity – the 'symbolic' policy argument (Jansen, 2001).

Comparative policy analysts will recognise in this class of explanation a particular version of the rational policy model. The particular form it takes in South Africa – a political and politicised one – is rooted in the political reality of the form of transition from apartheid to democracy, one that places a premium on the efficacy of virtuous political will to effect virtuous transformation (Muller, 2000). The anti-apartheid struggle created the expectation of strong civil society participation in public affairs within a framework of government steering. To put it plainly, if perhaps crudely, the widely held popular assumption and firm expectation was that the achievement of transformation depended principally upon the exertion and application of concerted, collective political will in the form of participatory policy making. This form of the rational policy model is vulnerable to all the vagaries attending it elsewhere. But in this case a particular loading of political hope was added that made its alteration or non-attainment seem less bad luck than political betrayal.

The second class of explanation is a technical one which attributes policy surprise or change of course to one or other implementation or capacity deficit, an explanation resorted to at times by government itself (Department of Education, 2001). This class of explanation locates these deficits at either a national departmental level or at an institutional level. Examples attributed to the former include a lack of progress on finding a new funding formula and the lack of redress funding. An example attributed to the latter is the lack of ability of some institutions to raise external donor funding (Pilot Project Consortium, 2001).

These explanations most definitely explain a part of the reality, as we will go on to argue below. Both sets attempt to depict a greater or lesser derailing of the political project of transformation. On their own, however, they are not only partial but flawed. The principal reason for this is that they are both forms of explanation that rest on a deficit cause; the absence of virtuous political will in the case of the former, the absence of technical capacity in the case of the latter. What makes them misleading is that we are left with the expectation that, were the deficit to be remedied, the policy as expected would have produced the desired results. This is highly unlikely because all deficit explanations leave out of the reckoning at least three sets of social dynamics each of which will produce their own partly independent effects, each setting limits on what could have been achieved under even the most optimal of conditions. These are:

- The effects of facing the necessity of trade-offs on both the process of policy formulation and the ranking of policy priorities.
- The effects of the sociological characteristics of different institutional types on responsiveness.
- The differential possibilities and limits of different governance regimes.

We will examine each of these in turn in the rest of this chapter. What we hope to show with this broader consideration of the policy environment than we have considered up to now in this book is that the vicissitudes of policy, the twists and turns of policies and their effects that this book describes, are to be understood not as some or other kind of policy or political failure, but indeed its opposite. By understanding better the broader context under the three rubrics of policy, governance and institutions, we hope to show that the main failure so far has been a disappointment of expectations.

2. TRADE-OFFS AND THE CONDITIONS FOR POLICY CHOICE

Traditionally, as we have said above, public policy as a driver of change has been viewed as a rational process consisting of causally linked phases: policy formation, policy implementation, policy evaluation, feedback, and policy adaptation. In this view, the effects of a policy are assumed to be 'measurable' in the sense that once a policy is implemented, one can assess how much of the policy intention was realised in practice. Since the seminal work by Pressman and Wildavsky (1973) on the implementation of policy, however, the conviction has grown that a policy process is far more complicated and irrational than is suggested by the linear view. As a consequence, in mature democracies, the focus of public policy analysis has moved from simple implementation analysis to studying the interactive dimension of the policy process as a whole (Gornitzka et al., 2002).

Apartheid was a comprehensive, state driven, 'top-down' system that consisted of policy formulated by government and implemented by the different government departments and state apparatuses. It was a fairly typical 'modern' central planning approach to the changing of society; an approach, if not an intent, shared with apartheid's great ideological foe, communist Eastern Europe. Despite their radically different goals and processes, what the two systems shared was a belief in the 'making' and 'remaking' of society, and that a key instrument in that 'making' would be policy formulated and implemented at the national level. Because both of them pursued an ideologically driven policy agenda, this similarity would have been invisible to both of them, as would a further similarity we have already touched upon – namely, that their best hopes and expectations were bound to be confuted as long as they viewed everything through an exclusively political lens.

Policy formulators preparing for a new democratic state started from the assumption that because apartheid had been such a pervasive, centrally driven state system, its un-doing would likewise require a state driven, planned, policy process, with the key difference being that the goals and processes would be progressive and participatory. Thus, in addition to having different goals, the process would be democratised, but still with a strong, central planning (steering) component. There was widespread agreement that the market could not correct the injustices and imbalances caused by apartheid, and that individual institutional transformation, left to itself, would not result in a co-ordinated, equitable and efficient system.

Along with Gornitzka et al. (2002) and Cerych and Sabatier (1992), we can divide a centralised, policy driven reform process into three distinctive phases:

- *1. Policy formulation.* This involves identifying inadequacies in the existing system, defining or redefining the problem, followed by policy formulation that consists of setting new goals and objectives, targeting groups or institutions, examining one or more means of redressing the situation and suggesting instruments to achieve this. This process culminates in a formal (legal) decision by the cabinet or parliament to establish a new programme, institution or course of action. In South Africa the first (informal) phase started with the National Education Policy Investigation (NEPI, 1993), and the ANC 1994 policy statement (Centre for Education Policy Development, 1994). It begins formally with the appointment of the National Commission on Higher Education in 1995 (NCHE, 1996), the release of the government Green Paper and White Paper in 1997 and the publication of the Higher Education Act No. 101 of 1997. This process did not only involve problem identification and the prescription of certain remedies, but the development of a new framework of values and objectives that tried to embody the key principles of the new government, namely democracy, equity, responsiveness and development.

- *2. Policy implementation.* In higher education, implementation is traditionally regarded as a matter between a national department of education and higher education institutions. This phase usually includes the elaboration of regulations, the creation of new structures necessary to translate government decisions into practice and day-to-day applications, with adjustments of initial decisions and regulations. In the South African context this started with the establishment of the Division of Higher Education within the Ministry of Education, followed by the abolition of the Advisory Committee for Universities and Technikons (AUT), the subsequent formation of the Council on Higher Education (CHE, 1998) and the associated Higher Education Quality Committee, as well as a plethora of implementation activities such as the passing of the National Students Financial Aid Scheme Act of 1999, the establishment of frameworks for accreditation of academic programmes, and the setting of conditions and criteria for the registration of private higher education institutions and programmes.

- *3. Policy evaluation.* This phase is often, but not always, initiated by a new government or a new minister and involves a reformulation stage that revises programme goals, sets new objectives and may change or elaborate implementation instruments. In South Africa the appointment of a new minister after the second democratic election in 1999 led to what could be regarded, on the one hand, as a continuation of the implementation started by the previous minister, but on the other also contained certain elements of a more typical reformulation phase. Continuity of implementation activities consisted of the publication of a National Plan for Higher Education (Department of Education, 2001) that outlined priorities and set certain targets. Two further activities could be regarded as tending towards reformulation. The first of these was the establishment of a National Working Group (Department of Education, 2002) to make recommendations about restructuring the institutional landscape and the subsequent gazetting of a landscape that would reduce the number of institutions from 36 to 23, while simultaneously introducing a new type of institution (the 'comprehensive'). The second consists in a move from a consensus seeking orientation to a more top-down approach, an approach that can be seen in amendments to the Higher Education Act of 1997 that give the minister more powers, and in the manner in which institutional restructuring and the new funding system will be implemented. The first reform (reformulation) dealt with restructuring higher education, and the second with changing government-institutional relations, while both contribute to the ongoing reorganisation of governance relationships. It is this emerging re-alignment that requires explanation.

2.1. Symbolic policy?

The first higher education policy announcement made in South Africa after the transition to democracy in 1994 declared with fanfare that it was necessary for the new government to show that there would be a clean break with the past, a demonstrable break with the higher education system created by and inherited from the apartheid regime. However, this did not imply that such a break would be made through a fundamental, revolutionary process. This is clearly reflected in the following comment made by the first Minister of Education in the new democratic government: '... owing to the sophistication and fragile nature of higher education a radical approach to transformation was not adopted' (Bengu, 2002). What then would constitute such a clean break?

Jansen (2001) has argued that the new policy had to be pre-eminently symbolic. It was more important for the government, in the first instance, to declare its intention of breaking with the past, than it was to develop policies that might have an immediate impact, for example, from a fiscal point of view. However, the fact that a policy is largely symbolic in nature does not mean that it will lack impact. On the one hand, as Scott states, 'symbolism, the mechanism by which meanings are shaped, exerts great social power' (1995:129). The chapters in Section 2 (4 to 11) show, for example, that without the new South African government putting any explicit redress instruments in place with regard to student enrolment, institutions responded to the policy and acted in a variety of ways to change the composition of the student body.

Jansen (2001), on the other hand, questions whether symbolic policy can be positive, arguing that in South Africa the intention was never to implement, but only to signal intent. While this may be true in certain instances, we do not think this was the case in 1994. Rather, the prime intention was to declare a break with the past and to signal a new direction. The need to declare a break with the past implied that the main items on the policy agenda had to reflect political priorities. This implied that the new policy issues with respect to higher education in 1994 were mainly concerned with the need to create more equity and democracy in the sector. But at this time the political imperative towards transformation acted to obscure both the nature of the necessary trade-offs that might have to be made to realise policy intentions, as well as their possible divergent effects. Indeed, we may say that a principal effect of symbolic policy, taken as 'actual' policy, is precisely to disguise this point.

The developments in Central and Eastern Europe after the changes of the late 1980s/early 1990s show a similar pattern (Vlasceanu & Sadlak, 2001). First the new higher education policy signalled a break with the past. This implied an initial emphasis on the 'de-ideologising' of some of the curricula in higher education, as well as an attempt to strengthen institutional autonomy. Because of the difficult fiscal situation faced by the governments in those countries, neither of these two original policy aims improved the position and functioning of the battered public universities. What followed was a succession of symbolic policy attempts, none of which were co-ordinated with overall state policy or with efficient allocation instruments. The result was a constantly changing policy focus described as 'changing the changes' which led to policy fatigue and scepticism, especially among the academic staff.

In this case, as in South Africa, what was missing was an understanding of policy as requiring trade-offs, hence as requiring a supercession of the explicitly political phase of building unity through signalling political consensus. This requires further examination.

2.2. Trade-offs and weak infrastructural power

In order to proceed from policy proposal to policy realisation, priorities have to be decided upon and strategic trade-offs made. In the South African case, GEAR (1996) is an attempt to develop and implement such a strategic framework with respect to macro-economic policy. It is worth noting that when GEAR was announced, the Minister of Finance, to the great surprise of many ANC supporters, declared that it was 'not open to consultation or negotiation'. We will argue below that this move, ostensibly from democratic consensus to state-centred decision making, was determined by a particular feature of the state at the time.

After the divisions of apartheid, unity, even if illusory, was a discursive political priority. After all, the first post-1994 government was called the Government of National Unity (GNU). However, we will argue that, in Gelb's (2001) terms, the state was operating within a context of weak infrastructural power, meaning that, politically, it was not able to construct a framework within which explicit trade-offs could be negotiated and agreed upon across divergent interest communities without alienating potentially crucial allies. This problem did not only occur in higher education; it was observable in many other sectors and could be attributed to a variety of factors. The inestimable prize of the negotiated transition was the avoidance of another bloody civil war in Africa. The price, however, was the continuation of antagonistic interests that symbolic policy could unify only by simultaneously deferring making trade-offs between competing interests.

While the intentions outlined in the White Paper framework had broad support within the higher education community, it soon became clear that within and outside higher education there was no political consensus on the trade-offs that would be necessary to give effect to the policy. It can be argued that there were three types of disagreement.

The first type of disagreement can be described as differences within the higher education community. The Pilot Project Consortium Report claims that: 'some of the historically advantaged institutions were strongly opposed to redress funding. Many argued that it was wasteful to support apartheid institutions, that they should be closed.

Others were concerned that this effort would cut into their own funding. There were also differences of opinion among the historically disadvantaged institutions about how redress funding should be allocated. Some wanted it allocated equally, rather than based on the quality of proposals for funding, demonstrated need, or ability to carry out proposed projects' (Pilot Project Consortium Report, 2001). This report asserts that a combination of opposition to redress and differences about goals and methods undermined the implementation of the policy on institutional redress.

The second type of disagreement was between powerful political actors within the new government. One group had studied at the historically disadvantaged universities and through this experience had been exposed to some of the worst faces of apartheid. As students they had opposed the management of these institutions as well as the apartheid government, but they had also developed strong emotional attachments to these institutions and the educational role they could play in socio-political development. After all, an institution such as the University of Fort Hare pre-dated apartheid and had in the past produced some of Africa's most eminent leaders.

In the new government, however, there was another group of powerful actors who had opposed the establishment of the historically disadvantaged universities, and who still regarded them as creatures of apartheid and 'as a product of the geo-political imagination of apartheid planners' (National Plan on Higher Education, 2001:Foreword). Many of these political actors were profoundly ambivalent about building up the historically black universities, particularly if that implied propping up all of them through state support.

The third, and arguably the most telling factor, was the government's macro-economic policy. When government formulated GEAR (1996) as an action plan intended to give effect to the Reconstruction and Development Programme of 1994 which was an inclusive all-things-to-all-people policy list, the trade-offs necessary for growth were rendered visible. GEAR is a package of mainly macro-economic measures that include faster fiscal deficit reduction, budget reform, consistent monetary policy, stable and co-ordinated policies, and a strong emphasis on efficiency and restraint on government spending (GEAR, 1996). The main aims were to stimulate growth through foreign investment and improved competitiveness. With GEAR, efficiency, effectiveness and responsiveness took precedence over redress.

We hope that the above makes clear that it is only when a strategic decision, or trade-off, is made, that the bouquet of policy values agreed upon in the consensus phase must be ranked and prioritised. Only at this point does it becomes clear what is chosen and what is not. It is hard to over-estimate the disconcerting effect this must have had on the politicians and civil servants involved who had not anticipated this dynamic, as can be seen in the words of two erstwhile officials and the former Minister of Education in the endnotes.[2]

2.3. Towards differentiated policy

As is evident in many of the chapters in this book, comprehensive governmental policy intentions were articulated after 1994 to change the higher education system as a whole, but without the necessary trade-offs having been made to realise these policy intentions.

'Comprehensive policy' refers to a set of broad general principles and benchmarks for a whole sector (such as those in the 1997 White Paper). Both before and after 1994, South Africa traditionally concentrated on 'comprehensive' policy, thereby neglecting the difficult priority decisions and differential levers that have to be designed to implement it. Indeed, we may say that 'comprehensive' policy was the form that 'symbolic' policy took in the immediate post-1994 period. By the same logic, relinquishing comprehensive policy means relinquishing symbolic policy and the discursive facade of unity in the sector. 'Comprehensive' policy-making has to be distinguished from differentiated policy-making, which means identifying and agreeing upon particular institutional targets that prescribe the route each university and technikon is supposed to follow against broad systemic benchmarks, as well as the creation of an environment of pressure and support necessary to facilitate progress along the route.

Policy differentiation is not necessarily aimed at creating institutional differentiation. It can have quite the opposite intention, namely to reduce differentiation. In contrast, a comprehensive policy that is 'the same for all' often has highly differentiating effects, as the application of the funding formula based on the South African Post Secondary Education (SAPSE) information system has demonstrated in the South African case. One of the most important factors hindering the design of specific policy levers since 1994 has been the absence of an up-to-date information system and a common set of informational formats so that benchmarks can be constructed and each institution's performance can be compared – both with the performance of other institutions in the system and with their own performance over time. The National Working Group's greatest contribution to systemic governance may well turn out to be their commissioning of a benchmarking system which is robust and sophisticated enough to serve as the beginning for future systemic development.

A key aspect of differentiating policy is experimentation. Policy is a form of explicit and deliberate governmental intervention. It is very important that policy-makers design a policy in such a way (through experiments) that the effects of the intervention can be assessed; in other words, that knowledge about which measures and instruments work and which do not can be increased. It is risky to make any statements or come to any conclusions concerning interventions and their effects without using experimental or quasi-experimental research methods. Too much is assumed concerning the effects of policies and policy instruments and very little is actually known about these effects. No national system can prosper without continual monitoring and research that creates the kind of information and analysis around which collaboration most usefully occurs. This circulates information and allows all the actors – government, society/market and institutions – to be responsive.

The above discussion points to the fact that unidirectional comprehensive policy has not worked in South Africa in the post-1994 period. Instead, a different notion of higher education transformation, based on a more targeted, differentiated, information-rich policy interaction between government, institutions and society has to be developed.

This is in many respects in line with Olsen's corporate-pluralist state model of state governance (Olsen, 1988) discussed in the first chapter of this book. This network, or corporate-pluralist state is entirely dependent on knowledge – the production of knowledge for purposes of competitiveness as well as the use of knowledge to better fulfil its steering and policy-making roles. It requires, in other words, greater infrastructural power than South Africa possessed at the time of transition to democracy in 1994. The shift from a comprehensive to a differentiated policy model is going to demand a more efficient government, together with a new approach to consultation. It will require that government is more sensitive to the self-regulating capacity of the higher education institutions and the consequences of the complex relations between higher education and society. It is to this area that we now turn.

3. INSTITUTIONAL DYNAMICS

In a wide ranging overview of institutional adaptation to demands for reform, Gumport and Sporn (1999) detect a global increase in the salience of management within higher education institutions. They attribute the expanding role of administration to three inter-dependent dynamics: resource dependency that is primarily motivated by organisational survival, institutional isomorphism that is motivated by legitimacy concerns, and professional authority that is motivated by a struggle for professional identity.

Primarily, management is responsible for maintaining the organisation's exchange relationships. Whether it be as a bridge or a buffer, it must transact in an increasingly complex environment that contains not only government and business agents, but also an escalating range of 'stakeholders' (Maassen, 2000; Neave, 2002). Management becomes more important because it is increasingly responsible for the development of strategies that increase existing sources of income, tap into new income sources and help to reduce existing dependency relationships.

A key resource is legitimacy, and it is increasingly important that institutions be seen to be responding to demands for reform in a business-like manner. By presenting a more unified and business-like front an expanded management core is much better positioned to represent the institution than the often fractious collegium singly and severally. Gumport and Sporn (1999) describe the effects of this as a shift in the authority structure within higher education organisations that entails an expanding domain for the administrators and the leadership, and a narrowing authority domain for the academic faculty.

The above mentioned factors come into play very forcibly, as has been the case in South Africa in the post-1994 period, when institutions are faced with a sudden increase in demands for reform from the government and the society, and an unleashing of market forces, by both the government and a burgeoning local and global private higher education sector. Secondly, through a process of mimetic and normative isomorphism, institutional management's notions of 'successful' institutions have been exchanged, mimicked and adopted through professional networks that are responding, on the one hand to resource and legitimacy demands and on the other to promoting their position (Cloete & Kulati, 2003). Under these circumstances, *capacity to evolve managerially* becomes a crucial resource variable.

Given the rudimentary stage of policy evolution discussed above, it was, in practice, up to the higher education institutions themselves to interpret the policy innovations announced in and after 1994. Institutions were, however, not only attending to national government policy; they were also casting an eye on global developments. This is well illustrated by the former vice-chancellor of the University of Potchefstroom:

> Simultaneous with the change in the new world order, the fall of the Berlin Wall and the totally new international dispensation, occurred also, of course, the change in South Africa itself...So, the university, belonging to the knowledge production part of the world as a university, had to take notice of this totally new dispensation ... (Reinecke, 2001)

A number of institutions transformed rapidly in the direction of a predominantly outward orientation. Others decided to stick to an inward orientation of 'academic business as usual', opting to rely on their traditional academic strengths. A third group was left behind trying desperately to survive without being able to anticipate and respond to the intentions of the announced policy innovations, nor to survive on dwindling government subsidies only. From the viewpoint of resource dependency theory, it could be argued that the historically black institutions simply could not adapt if a change in the environment threatened critical resource relationships. Symbolic government policy generated unrealistic expectations about redress and at the same time, unexpectedly, these institutions faced intensified market competition for students. Most of them were located in impoverished rural areas without strong academic and management capacity, and as a consequence had virtually no resources on which to fall back in order to avoid a crisis.

In addition to management capacity, an especially important key to understanding the different higher educational institutional responses is the factor of *academic capacity*, which determines any institution's particular academic identity or niche. An institution's academic capacity resides not only in academics with reputable qualifications, but also in their ability to restructure programmes, to attract good undergraduate and postgraduate students, to engage with business, local communities and government in research and contract work, to be part of international academic networks, and to have effective relationships with funding agencies (Chapters 7, 8 and 9). Academic capacity thus enables an institution to establish extensive links with the larger society and with the possibility of increasing and diversifying its financial resources whenever necessary. In higher education the basic resources are not only financial and human, but also reputational, with finance following reputation, not necessarily the other way around. Chapter 4 on funding shows that most of the institutions with strong academic capacity and a diverse funding basis did well financially in the post-1994 period. In a much more precarious situation were those institutions with weak academic capacity that had to rely on a single source of income, in most cases government funding.

But strong academic capacity does not necessarily equal institutional homogeneity. Nor does strong leadership and managerial capacity mean uniformity of strategy and style. Management may develop a strong, unitary sense of purpose and use academic capacity to drive an enterprising agenda. More often though high academic capacity fosters diversity. In such a diverse institution the established culture, or the power of the academics with their extensive societal links, may tend to resist the imposition of a unified purpose, making the institution much less centrally governable, and setting up a fluctuating tension between the central leadership and management and the faculties.

Every institution embodies a determinate mix of academic and managerial capacity. Below are three counter-intuitive conclusions about how this mix of capacity may affect institutional orientations with respect to reform:

1. Institutions may be unresponsive to reform or the market from positions of weakness or strength.

- An institution may be unresponsive from a position of strength where domain consolidation can take precedence over active responsiveness to policy or the market.
- An institution may be unresponsive as a consequence of managerial weakness.
- An institution may be unresponsive from both managerial and academic weakness. This is the most vulnerable place to be.

2. Institutions may be responsive to reform from positions of weakness or strength.

- An institution may be responsive in order to consolidate, to be enterprising or domain-seeking from a position of relative strength. In this case strength can be compounded.
- An institution may be responsive from a position of weakness, using either the market or higher education policy to act as a gyroscope for seeking a domain. This is a precarious strategy because here applied research or relevant curricula are sought in advance of consolidated disciplinary capacity. It is a strategy that is not sustainable in the long term.

3. Institutions may be responsive to the state, but unresponsive to the market and vice versa, from positions of weakness or strength.

- For institutions with stronger academic and managerial capacity, the state and the market are both exogenous forces with variable possibilities, and both need to be treated with caution, but both also provide opportunities (Muller, 2001:23–24).
- Among institutions that are weak in academic and managerial capacity, state support in the form of input-based subsidies is a lifeline, whereas the demands of the market are most likely to generate a crisis. When the state moves to output-based subsidies, however, the difference dissolves.

Institutional theory suggests that strong organisations are easier to influence from without when the external signals correspond to their internal criteria of, and learnt capacities for, relevance. When the external signals go against these, the institutions become highly resistant: they are able to 'ignore control signals, to forego incentives, and to absorb sanctions, without changing their ways in the direction desired by government policy makers' (Scharpf, 1987:105). Higher education institutions are an especially good example of this.

This section makes it clear that a realistic assessment of what institutions may do in the face of changing societal conditions or changing policy, or both, requires an understanding of their constituent sets of capacities, simplified above as being of two key kinds, managerial and academic. It also tries to make clear that a determinate mix of capacities might translate into stable dispositional strategies which might be highly labile and adaptable, or which can harden into entrenched habits that are very difficult to change. Institutional case studies, of which there are so far all too few, will show, we predict, that both these dispositional tracks have their advantages and disadvantages.

4. MODES OF GOVERNANCE

One of the central tasks for the post-1994 period was to change the relationship between government and higher education. Democratising the mode of governance was seen as the key process in developing a new value framework for the whole society and for higher education in particular. New policy, and its implementation, was to occur through a process of democratic participation at national and institutional levels. In Chapter 12 it is argued that: 'It seems that the consultative and participatory process of policy formulation and the first cycles of the three-year planning dialogue gave way to a much stronger state-steering approach, driven by government's frustration at the lack of progress made towards achieving transformation goals'. We will also show, however, that, government rhetoric to the contrary, this seeming return to state steering was overlaid by a number of market driven features that yielded in effect a hybrid market/state-steering mode of governance. To many observers, this hybrid seemed both contrary to accepted policy as well as incoherent. The rest of this section will argue that this governance hybrid was not only possible, but probably inevitable, given a series of key structural features of the state form at the time. In what follows, we will briefly review the contemporary literature on governance, developing a conceptual language for discussing the apparent U-turn.

4.1. First reconceptualisations

The first point to note about the concept of 'governance' is that currently renewed academic discussion of governance has to do with the development of alternatives to hierarchical government control, i.e. to the traditional mode of state-dominated co-ordination (Mayntz, 1998; Peters, 2001). Despite variations between countries it can be argued in line with Peters (2001:4–13) that the traditional governance model was based on the following common principles:

- The civil service has to be apolitical, in other words 'neutrally competent' (Kaufman, 1956). In addition, politics and administration have to be seen as separate elements of governance.
- Public management has to be based on hierarchical principles and rule-boundedness.
- The governmental organisations have to be permanent and stable.
- Civil service should be institutionalised and governed as a corporate body.
- The civil service should be strictly controlled and regulated in detail.

- Finally, equality should be an important principle in governance, with respect to outcomes as well as organisation.

The importance and appropriateness of these principles for modern day governance has been questioned at the very least, if not wholly rejected (Kersbergen & Waarden, 2001; Peters, 2001). Many authors have identified possible causes for a decrease in the effectiveness of traditional governance arrangements and hence the rationale for introducing new governance modes. A cause referred to by many authors is the economisation of societies. It is argued that the economic crises of the 1980s and early 1990s have forced governments to adapt their governance arrangements and to put economic considerations at the forefront of their governance approach (Savoie, 1995). However, other authors have suggested that this explanation alone cannot account for the fundamental and far-reaching nature of the shifts in governance. Peters (2001:14–15), for example, points to demographic factors, including the ageing of Western societies and the decreasing social and political homogeneity among individuals and groups in society.

There is a growing 'lack of common ground' with respect to many issues. As a consequence, the traditional pattern of government-led negotiations between various interest groups has become problematic, and arriving at social and political compromises has become more difficult. In addition, traditionally stable governance arrangements and organisations have become destabilised, making it more complicated for government to intervene in society (Cohen & Rogers, 1994). These general developments are observable worldwide, even though many variations can be found at the national level.

With respect to governmental strategies for dealing with the 'governance crisis', higher education offers interesting examples. Amongst other things, the high level of public expenditure on higher education and the growing acceptance of an economically instrumental interpretation of the role of higher education in society (Gumport, 2000) makes the sector an obvious target for governance reform.

Since the late-1980s, a number of higher education scholars have used state or steering models developed by other social scientists to analyse changes in the relationship between the state and higher education. Van Vught (1989), for example, introduced a central planning and a self-regulation model of government steering, later elaborated into state control and state supervision models (Neave & Van Vught, 1991; Maassen & Van Vught, 1994; Maassen, 1996). These models were based on the classic work of social science authors such as Meyerson and Banfield (1955), Ashby (1956), Lindblom (1959, 1965), Steinbrunner (1974), and Beer (1975). The implicit assumption in the state control and state supervision models was that a development from state control to state supervision should be promoted because if the state had a supervisory role it would lead to the better performance of higher education than if it had a controlling role. From this perspective, state steering in the form of state supervision was the preferred alternative to the by now widely discredited, traditional, 'top-down' form of co-ordination. In this period, however, these were not the only models to emerge that proved to be useful for analysing and understanding the relationship between the state and higher education.

During the 1990s a number of European higher education researchers (see, for example, Heffen et al., 1999; Gornitzka & Maassen, 2000) began to work with the four so-called state models introduced by Olsen (1988): the *sovereign* (or unicentric) state, the *institutional* state, the *corporatist* (or segmented) state, and the *market* state. Of these four models the first two, the sovereign state model and the institutional state model, can be regarded as variations of the traditional governance model discussed above. The other two models are alternatives to the traditional governance approach. These four models are not necessarily mutually exclusive, nor are they normative. They represent different ways of organising the relationship between the state and society that correspond more or less to state dominance and control (the unicentric state), state protection of specific social values and norms (the institutional state), the state as one of the involved interest groups (the corporatist state), and the minimal state (the market state, that intervenes minimally and allows the dominance of market forces).

The steering models introduced by Van Vught (1989) and the state models developed by Olsen (1988) reflected the real governance shifts of the 1980s. This was a transition period in which states were experimenting with new governance approaches without the old ones having been rejected completely. Researchers studying the shifts during this period, such as Maassen and Van Vught (1988, 1989), talk about the *Janus-headed* character of state governance with respect to higher education. (See also Amaral & Magelhães, 2001).

Fifteen years down the line, it is clear that the transition period is over and that the traditional governance model in its basic form has been 'left behind' in practice and as a model advanced by governance theory. As a consequence, instead of comparing 'old' and 'new' models it is now assumed that the traditional model is no longer acceptable and that various alternatives have been developed to replace the traditional model in practice.

Peters (2001) makes a distinction between two waves of reform to traditional approaches to governance. The first wave consisted of ideologically driven reforms that were enacted in the 1980s and early 1990s, and the second was a more recent, pragmatic set of reforms that combines further 'repair work' to the traditional model with attempts to deal with some of the flaws of the earlier ideological reforms. In the first wave, four alternative approaches to governance emerged, namely, governance through applying market mechanisms, governance through increased participation, governance through greater flexibility, or governance through deregulation. The ideological nature of the reforms was especially clear in the case of the market approach that was introduced in many countries as an unquestioned improvement to, and advance on, the traditional governance approach.

Even though there is some overlap between various aspects of these models, the four approaches can be distinguished on the basis of their different problem diagnosis with respect to the functioning of the traditional governance model and their ideas about the nature of the reforms necessary to address these problems. In addition, even though in governance reforms one can observe various elements of different approaches implemented at the same time, these combinations are not always compatible in practice. In general one can argue that the market approach appears to be most compatible with the flexible governance approach, just as the participation approach is most compatible with the deregulation approach (Peters, 2001:95).

In the second, current governance reform wave, two basic types of change can be observed. First there is change that is a continuation of the reforms introduced in the first wave, although now it is more pragmatic, less ideological and employs different instruments. The use of the market mechanism in public governance, notably extolled by Margaret Thatcher in the UK, for example, was ideological and fairly controversial in most countries in the 1980s and 1990s. In the meantime it has become more generally accepted and embraced by governments of all political shades, including traditional anti-market parties such as the Labour parties in Germany and the United Kingdom. Secondly, there are changes that are responses to problems created by the first wave of reforms. This concerns, for example, the perception by governments that the first reform wave has led to excessive autonomy of public sector institutions, leading to a loss of governmental control over their functioning. Related to this is the feeling that the reforms resulted in a decrease in public accountability of public sector institutions, leading to the need to set up formal performance evaluating bodies (Peters, 2001:119–121).

A number of publications discuss hybrid modes of governance in considerable detail.[3] Applying insights derived from these to the South African situation we can say that, if one reads solely through the policy documents and avowals of educational politicians, it seems that the Department of Education started off with a participation approach, only to change course half way to a market approach overlaid with deregulation and flexible mode features. That these approaches are indeed radically different can be discerned from examining their five constituent features (Table 1, after Peters, 2001).

Table 1: *Charting the path of discursive shifts in governance reform with respect to South African higher education*

	DoE's first version (NCHE; White Paper) participation mode (1996/97)	DoE's revised version (NPHE) market/hybrid mode (2001)
Diagnosis of what's wrong in the previous model	• Wholly tainted because of association with apartheid • Too centralised ('top-down'); not 'democratic'	• Lack of managerial capacity and 'expertise' • Inadvertent 'destructive competition' (market forces)
Most valued public interest	• Democracy • Equity • Redress	• Efficiency and accountability • Rational allocation and distribution of resources
Structure	Unitary, co-ordinated system (decentralised)	• Rationalised institutional landscape (mergers) • Institutional differentiation
Management	Co-operative governance (team-based democratic decision-making)	Professional management and output-based performance management
Policy making	• Consultation and negotiation • Comprehensive policy, vision-based	• Policy by commissioned expert review • Target-based allocation by the DoE

With these conceptualisations of the governance of higher education, we have a clearer grip on the anatomy of the governance reform process. What remains to be examined is why it took the form it did in South Africa.

4.2. Determinate features of the global and local context

Governance theory tells us that governance-mode change in stable, mature democracies happens incrementally and on the basis of the prior mode. Where a clean break is targeted, albeit only symbolically as we argued above, in the desire to move decisively away from a dual system with two, parallel, racially-crafted versions of the traditional approach, it is never as clean as the aspiration inscribed in the rhetoric would have it. In fact, as this case shows, there was a symbolic shift in much of the comprehensive policy rhetoric, but at the level of policy instruments (for example, the retention of the SAPSE-based funding system) it remained a largely traditional approach, albeit now consolidated from two versions into one. This traditional governance mode, however, proved to be highly unstable as a framework for the state–higher education relationship. This was partly because it not only maintained, but actually amplified the disadvantage of the poorer institutions, a situation visibly at odds with the symbolic rhetoric. But a confluence of other circumstances also contributed to its instability. Some of these, identified by higher education analysts, are reported above. Others, specific to South Africa, will be discussed below. As the decade passed the halfway mark, the governance mode had shifted into a stalled, unstable and ultimately contradictory position: it had created a stalemate between a participation approach advanced in rhetoric and an unstable, comprehensive, traditional approach exercised in practice. The situation was ripe for a stalemate breaker.

The following key pressures are among many contributing to the instability of the comprehensive traditional mode:

- Rapid globalisation of higher education, i.e. global diversification of finance, global competition for students further stimulating international student mobility, research collaborations, policy borrowing and the escalating costs of higher education put a premium on managerial adaptability ('responsiveness'). As we showed earlier in the chapter, this increases pressure on managerialism (see Savoie, 1995; Peters, 2001; Gumport, 2000), especially at the institutional level. However, this is a specific kind of managerialism, in the sense that it pushes towards the flexible governance mode, towards multiple clients, including the market, and away from the traditional mode. As we saw above, however, successfully deploying such a mode at the institutional level depends upon a certain level of academic and managerial capital in the institution, which the disadvantaged institutions, by definition, did not have, and it therefore increased institutional heterogeneity still further.
- Macro-state policy, in the form of GEAR, set the policy template for all other state portfolios. As we stated earlier, this drives a higher education system to both fiscal austerity and towards market types of governance.

- Finally, the state had weak infrastructural power (Gelb, 2001), which meant that policy trade-offs, which would advantage some stakeholders and not others, could not be negotiated but rather had to be imposed and consolidated through symbolic legitimisation. GEAR again is the paradigm case. The added difficulty in higher education was that there were real competing interests, and the ones with least cachet for the sector (i.e. the historically black universities) were also the ones with most political clout, at least as far as national politics was concerned.

These imperatives bearing on higher education were partly contradictory. But together, they all drove against the tenability of a participatory approach. That the stalemate described above retarded this mode from realistically getting going (moving from symbolic to real policy) leads to the conclusion that we never managed to get beyond the rhetorical promotion of a participatory governance mode. In this first phase of governance reform (Peters, 2001; see also Table 1), most South African commentators were led by the rhetoric, i.e. they imagined that consultative agreements would compel both policy and the mode of governance to move in this direction. In practice, structural features of the national and global environment simply superseded the rhetoric of participation. What we had, in effect, was a partial shift from an authoritarian, bureaucratic version of the traditional mode, to a racially reformed version. However, because of the increased reliance on the market mechanism, the intensifying effects of globalisation and the growing requirements for responsiveness, this implied in practice a rapidly expanding managerial power in those institutions that had the capacity to handle it, and continued steering together with some interventions to compensate for the worst depredations of the market for the weak institutions. That the strongest of these weak institutions decided to resist steering, and to fight the centre, only confirms the managerial crisis from which they suffered.

This policy shift, interpreted by some as an aberration, was really only an inevitable move: from a dual traditional governance model to a differentiated, market-driven model with dual versions – a flexible version for the strong institutions and a deregulated, bureaucratically steered version for the weak. This is partially disguised by the symbolic political necessity for the government and bureaucracy (a necessity for national politics, not for the sector) to be seen as treating all institutions in 'the same' way. This implies that some residual remnants of comprehensive rhetoric are likely to remain a part of policy in order to justify public intervention in not only the weak but also the stronger institutions, intervention aimed, for example, at the 'lack of transformation' of their staff racial profile. The decisive factor here though, is the continuation and amplification of an extremely heterogeneous sector. While this heterogeneity could be expected to force the government to develop a differentiated governance mode for the sector, the differentiated governance mode used in practice is unlikely to alter the stratification in the sector along the lines of colour and class. This is because it resembles an arrested market model, with some unconstrained features (e.g. student mobility via NSFAS), and some highly constrained features (e.g. private universities). And the implications of the new subsidy formula remain as yet unclear. Thus, South Africa appears to confirm rather than confute global trends.

5. CONCLUSION: OUR OWN HYBRID JANUS HEAD?

South Africa had the good fortune (in retrospect, a mixed blessing) to initiate and undergo a period of radical reform during what has come to be known globally as the 'Roaring Nineties', roughly bracketed by the fall of the Berlin Wall and 9/11. This was the decade, for nearly all of the developed countries and many of the developing countries, of unprecedented economic growth and new levels of prosperity. This rapid growth, requiring rapid adaptability, fuelled the gathering rejection of the 'iron cage' of the traditional governance approach in the private and public sectors alike. Leading the charge were the apostles of growth, dubbed the 'deficit-reducers' by Joseph Stiglitz, leading to what he has called the 'misguided "ascendancy of finance"' (quoted in the *New York Review of Books*, 15/1/04, 28). What this meant in general terms was that criteria of efficiency and productivity came to trump values of participation, equity and justice, at least in the short term. What this meant in the South African case was that once GEAR, a deficit-reducer par excellence, had been installed as the premier instrument of finance policy in South Africa, it was only a matter of time before its hegemonic effects would be felt in all other domains of policy and governance. Under these circumstances, the Department of Education's participation approach to governance and policy in higher education, the antithesis of GEAR's market-led approach, stood no chance of being implemented. Its sole function, during the middle years of the decade, was to buy symbolic legitimisation and consensus, whatever had been the undoubted good intentions of its proponents.

This chapter has also sought to show, however, that on its own, such a conclusion can all too easily regress to political pessimism, underlain by a naively rationalist conception of policy. The chapter consequently explored three key domains that shed light on, clarify and complicate the picture.

- The weak infrastructural power of the state in the early years of the decade, up to the decision on GEAR, saw to it that the participation approach was frozen in a symbolic phase and never proceeded beyond tokens and good intentions. This was because the trade-offs necessary to implement it could not be successfully negotiated in a sector that was driven by powerful interests and different kinds of political backing. This log jam was only broken when global currents tipped the balance towards the 'ascendancy of finance' and the decision on GEAR, significantly not through any participatory process. Following that super-ordinate decision, taken at the highest level of the state, came the slow process of conforming sectoral policies and approaches, to a greater or lesser extent, to the hegemony of finance. Starting as it did at the opposite end of the ideological spectrum, there should be no surprise that the resultant mode was a hybrid (Cloete et al., 2004).
- Having to conform to national macro-policy pushed higher education into the market, while it partly still clung to remnants of traditional governance steering and at the same time clung ideologically to the rhetoric of participation/equity/social justice. This curious composite mode, with a benign mythical superstructure and a

more destructive, but invisible base, was understandably represented and responded to quite differently by different constituencies, expressing different interests:

° The Minister of Education and his Department expressed themselves in philosophical opposition to the market, while technically implementing market features, or at least features that were to have market effects, like the NSFAS funding scheme, the SAPSE-based formula, etc. In addition they were intervening to control the worst depredations of the market, such as the collapse of some historically disadvantaged universities, or to dampen the damaging effects, for example, of private higher education.

° The policy analysts allied to the ANC, by the same logic but drawing diametrically opposite conclusions, lamented the betrayal of participation, thereby curiously fulfilling the party's necessary ideological role of unity-construction in a time of market-fuelled dispersal of interests.

° The weak institutions complained that it left them dangling in the wind of the market (true), and about the lack of state intervention (not entirely true).

° The strong institutions invoked university autonomy (a questionable proposition under conditions of such exaggerated institutional heterogeneity), and complained of too much state intervention (also not entirely true).

Little wonder then that there was, and remains, such confusion about the real direction of the modes of governance with respect to higher education. In this chapter we have characterised this direction, following Peters (2001), as a market-led governance approach with two distinct subtypes: a flexible/managerial sub-type with minor interventionist features, and a deregulatory/interventionist sub-type with substantial market features that may continue to pose threats to the weaker institutions. It would not be adequate to describe this approach as a political U-turn, nor would it be adequate to attribute it solely or principally to a technical deficit. It comes about as a result of a broader structural set of forces shaping the field.

We can conclude, with some confidence, that South Africa has reached the end of the traditional governance era, and in this respect conforms more nearly to the global trend than is usually conceded. We may also conclude, with reasonable confidence, that Peters' (2001) first phase of ideological tinkering is by and large over, and that, in higher education at least, hard-nosed efforts to stabilise the new governance mode will become increasingly sophisticated and differentiated. A cardinal feature which will continue to have determinate effects on the future direction of policy is the extreme heterogeneity in the system, which has increased, rather than decreased since 1994. The symbolic rhetoric of the now ending first phase may yet linger awhile since it may have some use, but it cannot last long. It is probably fair to say that South African higher education policy is in that Janus-headed phase described by Maassen and Van Vught (1988; 1989) for the Netherlands and Amaral and Magelhães (2001) for Portugal. In all of this, South Africa follows in well-trodden reform footsteps – albeit not with the effects expected from the 1994 'revolution'.

NOTES

[1] This identification of two types of explanation can also be found in Bovens et al. (2002) who have discussed success and failure of public policies by making a distinction between the programmatic and political mode of assessment of policy success or failure. The former is based on a view of policy making as social problem solving, related to questions such as: do governmental policies contribute to the solving of social problems, and do they work in a sensible way? The latter refers to the way in which policies and policy makers 'become represented in the political arena. It is not the social consequences of policies that count, but the political construction of these consequences, which might be driven by considerations of wholly different kinds.' (Bovens et al., 2002:20)

[2] Trevor Coombe, Deputy-Director General in the Department of Education in charge of systems and finance between 1994 and 1999, commented on the tension between the two approaches (Coombe, 2001): 'The Department of Finance had to be convinced that a redress fund or allocation made sense. And there was a counter-argument, namely that the whole country has been screwed up by apartheid. If a redress principle had to be applied consistently – and a budget policy looks for consistency – it would have to be applied across the board. Now what would that actually mean? Would it mean that historic deprivation would have to be compensated for through the budget by special grants to all institutions that have been deprived? Consider the implications at school level, for instance, or in the hospital set-up? It is an intolerable proposition, especially if you are running a tight fiscal ship, if you are attempting to bring down a budget deficit and there are certain limits on your expenditure ceiling. And, of course, that was the prevailing policy. So there was really no encouragement on the part of the Department of Finance for a major fund or allocation under the name of redress and it was a very difficult matter to argue, because we were not in a position to argue a similar case with respect to the school system.'

Chabani Manganyi, Director General of the Department of Education from 1994 to 1999 reflects: '... the most difficult thing was to persuade the new democratic government that you could put something called "redress" into your budget – as strange as it sounds.' (Manganyi, 2001).

The different positions of the actors involved in the institutional redress policy are clearly reflected in the following comments made about the outcomes of the policy process by the democratic government's first Minister of Education (Bengu, 2002): 'I honestly believed in institutional redress. I fought valiantly for the operationalisation of institutional redress and I was fully supported and partly pushed by the historically black institutions. When I left office I was, however, not a winner because my Department was not as committed to redress as I was. The question of institutional redress was also a bone of contention within the Universities' and Technikons' Principals Forums.'

[3] For a more elaborate discussion about hybrid modes of governance, see Gornitzka and Maassen (2000), while Maassen (2003) has discussed the relevance of Peters' governance models for higher education. For a more detailed application of Peters' models to the South African shift in governance in higher education, see Cloete, Maassen and Muller (2004).

REFERENCES

ANC (African National Congress) (1994). *The Reconstruction and Development Programme* (RDP). Johannesburg: Umanyano Publications.

Amaral, A. & Magelhães, A. 'On markets, autonomy and regulation. The Janus Head revisited'. *Higher Education Policy*, 14, 1–14.

Ashby, W.R. (1956). *An introduction to cybernetics.* London: Chapman & Hall.

Beer, St. (1975). *Platform for change.* New York: John Wiley.

Bengu, S. (2002) Interview. www.chet.org.za/reflections/Bengu.

Bleecker, S.E. (1994). 'The Virtual Organization'. *The Futurist*, 28, 9–13.

Bovens, M.,'t Hart, P. & Peters, B.G. (2002). *Success and Failure in Public Governance. A Comparative Analysis.* Cheltenham: Edward Elgar.

Bunting, I. (2003). Memorandum. Pretoria: Department of Education.

Campbell, D.T. (1988). 'The Experimenting Society'. In: C. Campbell (ed.), *Methodology and Epistemology in the Social Sciences: Selected Essays*. Chicago: University of Chicago Press.

Centre for Education Policy Development. (1994). A Policy for Education and Training. Johannesburg.

Cerych, L. & Sabatier, P. (1992). *Great Expectations and Mixed Performance. The Implementation of Higher Education Policies in Europe*. Stoke-on-Trent: Trentham Books.

Cloete, N & Kulati, T. (2003). 'Managerialism within a Framework of Co-operative Governance?' In: A. Amaral, V.L. Meek & O. Larsen (eds), *The Higher Education Managerial Revolution?* Netherlands: Kluwer.

Cloete, N., Maassen, P. & Muller, J. (Forthcoming). Great Expectations, Mixed Governance Approaches and Unintended outcomes: The post-1994 reform of South African higher education. In: Å. Gornitzka, M. Kogan & A. Amaral (eds), *Reform and Change in Higher Education: Policy implementation analysis*. Dordrecht: Kluwer Academic Publishers.

Cloete, N & Bunting, I. (2002). *Transformation Indicators: Case Studies of the University of Port Elizabeth and Peninsula Technikon*. Pretoria: CHET. Available at: www.chet.org.za/transformation.html.

Coombe, T. (2001). Interview. www.chet.org.za/reflections.asp.

CHE (Council on Higher Education) (1988/9). *Annual Report of the Council on Higher Education*. Pretoria: CHE.

CHE (Council on Higher Education) (2000). *Towards a New Higher Education Landscape: Meeting the Equity, Quality and Social Development Imperatives of South Africa in the 21st Century*. Pretoria. CHE.

Cohen, J. & Rogers, J. (1994). 'Solidarity, Democracy, Association'. *Politische Vierteiljahrschrift*, Sonderheft 25, 136–159.

Department of Education (1997a). *Education White Paper 3: A Programme for the Transformation of Higher Education*, Pretoria: Government Gazette.

Department of Education (1997b). Higher Education Act of the Republic of South Africa, No 101 of 1997. Pretoria: Government Gazette.

Department of Education (2001). National Plan for Higher Education. Pretoria: Government Gazette.

Department of Education (2002). Transformation and Restructuring: A New Institutional Landscape for Higher Education. Pretoria: Government Gazette.

Department of Finance (1996). Growth, Employment and Redistribution: A Macroeconomic Strategy. Pretoria.

Gelb, S. (2001). Globalisation, the State and Macroeconomics. In: J. Muller, N. Cloete & S. Badat (eds), *Challenges of Globalisation. South African Debates with Manuel Castells*. Cape Town: Maskew Miller Longman.

Gornitzka, Å. & Maassen, P. (2000). 'Hybrid steering approaches with respect to European higher education'. *Higher Education Policy*, 13, 267–285.

Gornitzka, Å., Kyvik, S. & Stensaker, B. (2002). Implementation Analysis in Higher Education. In: J.C. Smart (ed.), *Higher Education: Handbook of Theory and Research Volume XVII*. New York: Agathon Press. pp381–423.

Gumport, P. (2001). 'Academic Restructuring: Organisational Change and Institutional Imperatives'. *Higher Education*, 39, 67–91.

Gumport, P. & Sporn, B. (1999). Institutional Adaptation: Demands for Management reform and University Administration. In: J. Stuart & W. Tierney (eds), *Handbook of Theory and Research*, Vol. XIV. New York. Agathon Press.

Heffen, O., Van Verhoeven, J. & De Wit, K. (1999). 'Higher education policies and institutional response in Flanders: Instrumental analysis and cultural theory'. In: B. Jongbloed, P. Maassen & G. Neave (eds), *From the Eye of the Storm. Higher Education's Changing Institution*. Dordrecht: Kluwer Academic Publishers. pp263–295.

Jansen, J. (2001). 'Rethinking Education Policy Making in South Africa: Symbols of Change, Signals of Conflict'. In: A. Kraak, & M. Young (eds), *Education in Retrospect: Policy and Implementation Since 1990*. Pretoria & London: Human Sciences Research Council and University of London.

Kaufman, H. (1956). 'Emerging doctrines of public administration'. *American Political Science Review*, 50, 1059–1073.

Kersbergen, K. & Waarden, F. (2001). Shifts in Governance: Problems of Legitimacy and Accountability. Paper on the theme 'Shifts in Governance' as part of the Strategic Plan 2002–2005 of the Netherlands Organization for Scientific Research (NWO). The Hague: Netherlands Organization for Scientific Research.

Kraak, A. (2001). Policy Ambiguity and Slippage: Higher Education under the New State, 1994–2001. http://www.chet.org.za/papers/Kraak.

Lindblom, Ch.E. (1959). 'The Science of muddling through'. *Public Administration*, 19, 79–99.

Lindblom, Ch.E. (1965). *Intelligence of Democracy*. New York: Free Press.

Maassen, P. (1996). *Governmental steering and the academic culture. The intangibility of the human factor in Dutch and German universities*. Utrecht: De Tijdstroom.

Maassen, P. (2000). 'Editorial. Higher Education and the Stakeholder Society'. *European Journal of Education*, 35, 377–385

Maassen, P. & Van Vught, F. (1988). 'An intriguing Janus-head. The two faces of the new governmental strategy for higher education in the Netherlands'. *European Journal of Education*, 23, 65–76.

Maassen, P. & Van Vught, F. (1989). *Dutch higher education in transition*. Culemborg: LEMMA.

Maassen, P. & Van Vught, F. (1994). Alternative models of governmental steering in higher education. An analysis of steering models and policy-instruments in five countries. In: L. Goedegebuure & Van Vught, F. (eds), *Comparative policy studies in higher education*. Utrecht: LEMMA. pp35–65.

Manganyi, I. (2001). Interview. www.chet.org.za/reflections.asp.

Mayntz, R. (1998). 'New Challenges to Governance Theory'. Jean Monnet Chair Paper RSC No. 98/50. Florence: European University Institute.

Meyerson, M. & Banfield, E.C. (1955). *Politics, Planning and the Public Interest*. Glencoe: Free Press.

Moja, T., Muller, J. & Cloete, N. (1996). 'Towards New Forms of Regulation in Higher Education: The Case of South Africa'. *Higher Education*, 32, 129–155.

Muller, J. (2000). 'Reclaiming Knowledge: Social Theory, Curriculum and Education Policy'. London: RoutledgeFalmer.

Muller, J. (2001). Responsiveness and Innovation in Higher Education. http://www.chet.org.za/papers/Muller.

National Commission on Higher Education (1996). *A Framework for Transformation*. Pretoria: July.

Neave, G. (2002) The Stakeholder Perspective Historically Explored. In: J. Enders & O. Fulton (eds), *Higher Education in a Globalising World: International Trends and Mutual Observations*. A Festschrift in Honour of Ulrich Teichler. Dordrecht: Kluwer Academic Publishers, pp17–39.

Neave, G. & Van Vught, F. (1991). *Prometheus bound, the changing relationship between*

NEPI (National Education Policy Investigation) (1993). 'The Framework Report and Final Report Summaries'. Cape Town: Oxford University Press/NECC.

New York Review of Books (2004). L1, 1, 28–31.

Olsen, J.P. (1988). 'Administrative Reform and Theories of Organization'. In: C. Campbell & B.G. Peters (eds), *Organizing Governance, Governing Organizations*. Pittsburgh: University of Pittsburgh Press.

Peters, B.G. (2001). *The Future of Governing*. Second edition, revised. Lawrence, KS: University Press of Kansas.

Pilot Project Consortium (2001). The Next Generation of Academics. In: F. Hayward (ed.), *Implications of the New Higher Education Framework*. Pretoria: CHET.

Pressman, J. & Wildavsky, A. (1971). Implementation. Berkeley: University of California Press.

Reinecke, C. (2001). Interview. www.chet.org.za/reflections.asp.

Savoie, D.J. (1995). 'What is Wrong with the New Public Management?'. *Canadian Public Administration*, 38, 112–121.

Scharpf, F. (1987). The limits of institutional reform. In: T. Ellwein, J. Hesse, R. Mayntz & F. Scharpf (eds), *Yearbook on Government and Public Administration*. Baden-Baden: Namos Verlagsgesellschaft.

Scott, W.R. (1995). *Institutions and Organizations*. Thousand Oaks: Sage Publications.

Steinbrunner, J.D. (1974). *The cybernetic theory of decision: new dimensions of political analysis*. Princeton: Princeton University Press.

Torres, C.A. & Schugurensky, D. (2002). 'The political economy of higher education in the era of neoliberal globalization: Latin America in comparative perspective'. *Higher Education*, 43, 429– 455.

Van Vught, F. (ed.) (1989). *Governmental strategies and innovation in higher education*. London: Jessica Kingsley.

Vlasceanu, L. & Sadlak, J. (2001). Changes in Higher Education Systems and Institutions of the Central and Eastern European Countries: 1994–1999. www.chet.org.za/papers/Europe.

APPENDIX 1

COMMISSIONED PAPERS

These can be found at www.chet.org.za/papers.asp:

Du Toit, A. (2001). Revisiting Academic Freedom in Post-apartheid South Africa: current issues and challenges.

Habib, A. (2001). Structural Disadvantage, Leadership Ineptitude, and Stakeholder Complicity: A Study of the Institutional Crisis of the University of the Transkei.

Johnson, B. (2001). The Higher Education Worker.

Kraak, A. (2001). Policy Ambiguity and Slippage: Higher Education Under the New State, 1994–2001.

Muller, J. (2001). Return to User: Responsivity and Innovation in Higher Education.

Ogude, N.A., Netswera, F.G. & Mavundla, T.A. (2001). Critical Analysis of the Status and Evolution of Research Activities within South African Technikons.

Olivier, N. (2001). The Relationship between the State and Higher Education Institutions with Reference to Higher Education Policy Documentation and the Legislative Framework.

Pratt, E. (2001). Remodelling Teacher Education: A Perspective on the Cessation of College-Based Teacher Education 1994–2000.

Scott, P. (2001). Leadership and Management – Some Thoughts for the UK.

Sehoole, T. (2001). Higher Education Policy Documents in South Africa: 1990–2000.

Strydom, K. (2001). Critical Perspectives on Quality Assurance in Higher Education in South Africa.

Stumpf, R. (2001). Higher Education: Funding in the Period 1994–2001.

Subotzky, G. (2001). National Trends: Statistics on Staff Changes.

Thobakgale, S. (2001). Reflections of a Former Student Leader.

Webster, E. & Mosoetsa, S. (2001). At the Chalk Face: Managerialism and the Changing Academic Workplace 1995–2001.

CASE STUDIES

These can be found at www.chet.org.za/papers.asp:

Amaral, A. (2001). Reflections on Brazilian Higher Education: 1994–1999.

Arimoto, A. (2001). Trends of Higher Education and Academic Reforms from 1994 onwards in Japan.

Dill, D. (2001). Reflections on US Higher Education: 1994–1999.

George, K.K. & Raman, R. (2001). Changes in Indian Higher Education – An Insider's View.

Meek, L. (2001). Reflections on Australian Higher Education: 1994–1999.

Ngwana, TA (2001). The Implementation of the 1993 Higher Education Reforms in Cameroon: Issues and Promises.

Vlasceanu, L. & Sadlak, J. (2001). Changes in the Higher Education System and Institutions of the Central and Eastern European Countries: 1994–1999.

APPENDIX 2

REFLECTIONS

These interviews can be found at www.chet.org.za/reflections.asp:

Balintulo, M. (2001). Vice-Chancellor. Cape Technikon.
Bengu, S. (2001). Minister of Education 1994–1999.
Bezuidenhout, P. (2001). Formerly Millpark Business School: Educor.
Botha, T.R. (2001). Vice-Chancellor and Rector. Rand Afrikaans University.
Cairns, M. (2001). Manager: Administration, Midrand University.
Coetzee, S. (2001). Vice-Chancellor. University of the Free State.
Coombe, T. (2001). Deputy Director-General. Department of Education 1994–1999.
Figaji, B. (2001). Vice-Chancellor. Peninsula Technikon.
Gourley, B. (2001). Vice-Chancellor. University of Natal.
Hayward, F. (2001). Chief Executive Director. Centre for Higher Education Accreditation (CHEA).
Mabuza, M. (2001). (Former) National President – South African Students Congress (Sasco).
Manganyi, (2001). Director-General. Department of Education 1994–1999.
Marcus, R. (2001). Managing Director, Adcorp.
Ndebele, N. (2001). Vice-Chancellor. University of Cape Town.
Reinecke, C. (2001). Vice-Chancellor and Rector. University of Potchefstroom.
Smit, F. (2001). (Former) Vice-Chancellor. University of Pretoria.
Strydom, K. (2001). Chief Director: Strategic Service. University of the Free State.
Van Rensburg, D.J.J. (2001). Vice-Chancellor and Rector. Pretoria Technikon.

APPENDIX 3

REFERENCE GROUP

NAME	INSTITUTION
Monica Bot	Consultant
Mark Bunting	Rhodes University
Neil Butcher	South African Institute for Distance Education
Dave Cooper	University of the Western Cape
André du Toit	University of Cape Town
Brian Figaji	Peninsula Technikon
Stephen Gelb	Formerly Development Bank of South Africa (DBSA)
Trish Gibbon	Consultant
Brenda Gourley	University of Natal – Durban/The Open University – England
John Gultig	University of Natal
Fred Hayward	American Council on Education
Bernadette Johnson	Consultant
Jan Kirsten	University of Port Elizabeth
André Kraak	Human Sciences Research Council
Themba Maseko	Formerly Damelin (Educor)
Joe Muller	University of Cape Town
Zandile Ndlovu	University of Fort Hare
Piet Naude	University of Port Elizabeth
Nthabiseng Ogude	Technikon SA
Nic Olivier	Consultant
Angina Parekh	Department of Education
Pundy Pillay	Consultant
Cheryl-Ann Potgieter	University of Pretoria
Herman Rhode	Consultant
Ari Rip	University of Twente
Aki Sawyerr	Association of African Universities
Yvonne Shapiro	South African Qualifications Authority
Flip Smit	University of Pretoria
Kallie Strydom	University of the Free State
Rolf Stumpf	University of Stellenbosch
George Subotzky	University of the Western Cape
Derrick Swartz	University of Fort Hare
Eddie Webster	University of the Witwatersrand
Michael Young	London School of Education

APPENDIX 4

PROFILES OF PUBLIC INSTITUTIONS IN
THE SOUTH AFRICAN HIGHER EDUCATION SYSTEM

SELECTED STATISTICS FOR 2000

This appendix provides a statistical overview of the 36 public institutions in the South African higher education system at the end of 2000. Figures are provided for each institution by student headcount, broken down by mode of delivery (contact and distance), proportion of black and female student enrolment, as well as enrolment by major fields of study.

NOTES

1 Source of data is the Higher Education Management Information System (the HEMIS system) of the Department of Education.
2 For ease of reading, all student data have been rounded up or down to the nearest 100.
3 Data for the University of the North West have not been included, because this institution has not been able to meet HEMIS requirements. This historically black university had a headcount enrolment total of about 5.000 in 2000.
4 Definitions of terms employed in table:
   - *Headcount enrolment* total treats all students as units, regardless of the course load that they may be carrying.
   - *Contact students* are those following programmes in which the delivery method is primarily traditional on-campus teaching in lectures, seminars etc.
   - *Distance students* are those following programmes in which the delivery method is normally by correspondence or by off-campus electronic means.
   - *A black student* is one who under apartheid would have been classified as African, coloured or Indian.
   - *The major categories* are the broad fields of study into which the academic programmes of students fall. The *SET* category includes all majors in science, engineering and technology (including health sciences), the *business category* includes all majors in business, finance and management, and the *humanities category* all fields such as languages, law, education and the social sciences.

314

Table 1. South African public universities: 2000

	Headcount student enrolments (thousands)			Proportion of black students as a % of headcount total	Proportion of female students as a % of headcount total	Proportion of students in major fields of study as % of headcount total		
	Contact	Distance	Total			SET	Business	Humanities
Historically black universities								
Durban-Westville	8.1	0	8.1	98	57	34	10	56
Fore Hare	4.4	0	4.4	100	66	16	16	68
Medunsa	3.5	0	3.5	96	54	97	0	3
North	8.8	0	8.8	100	54	32	7	61
Transkei	3.9	0	3.9	100	61	25	34	41
Venda	5.2	0	5.2	100	50	20	16	64
Vista	12.8	9.6	22.4	99	63	11	9	80
Western Cape	9.7	0	9.7	94	56	22	13	65
Zululand	5.3	0	5.3	97	60	23	7	70
Total/averages for HBUs	61.7	9.6	71.3	98	59	25	11	64

Table 1. (cont.)

	Headcount student enrolments (thousands)			Proportion of black students as a % of headcount total	Proportion of female students as a % of headcount total	Proportion of students in major fields of study as % of headcount total		
	Contact	Distance	Total			SET	Business	Humanities
Historically white universities (Afrikaans)								
Free State	12.1	0	12.1	45	52	34	7	59
Port Elizabeth	7.0	15.1	22.1	87	62	10	4	86
Potchefstroom	12.9	5.2	18.1	55	60	22	12	66
Pretoria	28.9	30.3	59.2	64	59	24	9	67
Rand Afrikaans	13.7	6.0	19.7	50	59	16	16	68
Stellenbosch	17.6	1.9	19.5	27	52	39	12	49
Total/averages for HWUs (Afrik)	92.2	58.5	150.7	58	58	23	10	67
Historically white universities (English)								
Cape Town	17.5	0	17.5	48	47	41	26	33
Natal	23.0	0	23	79	54	35	21	44
Rhodes	5.8	0	5.8	49	57	28	13	59
Witwatersrand	17.8	0	17.8	57	46	50	18	32
Total/averages for HWUs (English)	64.1	0	64.1	62	50	40	21	39
UNISA	0.1	115.2	115.3	62	55	8	39	53
University totals and averages	218.1	183.3	401.4	67	56	22	20	58

Table 2. South African public technikons: 2000

	Headcount student enrolments (thousands)			Proportion of black students as a % of headcount total	Proportion of female students as a % of headcount total	Proportion of students in major fields of study as % of headcount total		
	Contact	Distance	Total			SET	Business	Humanities
Historically black technikons								
Border	4.7	0	4.7	100	62	22	20	58
Eastern Cape	4.3	0	4.3	100	61	39	48	13
ML Sultan	9.4	0	9.4	99	51	52	26	22
Mangosuthu	5.2	0	5.2	100	50	50	20	30
North West	4.2	0	4.2	100	67	23	52	25
Northern Gauteng	9.4	0	9.4	100	51	40	28	32
Peninsula	8.8	0	8.8	98	55	43	23	34
Total/averages for HBTs	46.0	0	46.0	99	55	41	29	30
Historically white technikons								
Cape	10.3	0	10.3	56	44	52	34	14
Free State	6.0	0	6.0	65	48	27	68	5
Natal	9.7	0	9.7	81	47	50	35	15
Port Elizabeth	8.7	0	8.7	71	44	43	37	20
Pretoria	21.8	11.6	33.4	79	47	30	20	50
Vaal Triangle	14.7	0	14.7	87	48	47	29	24
Witwatersrand	12.5	0	12.5	83	42	53	42	5
Total/averages for HWTs	83.7	11.6	95.3	77	46	41	32	27
Technikon SA	0	60.1	60.1	82	40	30	20	50
Technikon totals and averages	129.7	71.7	201.4	84	46	38	27	35

Table 3. Overview of South African public higher education system: 2000

	Headcount student enrolments (thousands)			Proportion of black students as a % of headcount total	Proportion of female students as a % of headcount total	Proportion of students in major fields of study as % of headcount total		
	Contact	Distance	Total			SET	Business	Humanities
Universities	218.1	183.3	401.4	67	56	22	20	58
Technikons	129.7	71.1	201.4	84	46	38	27	35
Total averages for public systems	347.8	255	602.8	72	53	27	23	50

Source: Department of Education. Information on the State Budget for Higher Education. June 2001